PRESENTED TO

____

FROM

____

May the God before whom Abraham and Isaac walked, the God who has been my shepherd all my life, to this day, and who has redeemed me from all evil—bless you and let His name live on in you and in your children after you, forever. Amen!

(based on Genesis 48:15-16)

____

____

____

OLD TESTAMENT

SALLY MICHAEL

ILLUSTRATED BY FRED APPS

 MORE THAN A STORY 

EXPLORING THE MESSAGE OF THE BIBLE WITH CHILDREN

Truth:78

More Than a Story: Old Testament

by Sally Michael

Illustrated by Fred Apps
Art Direction and Design by Shannon Brown
Cover Design by Shannon Brown

Our vision at Truth78 is that the next generations know, honor, and treasure God, setting their hope in Christ alone, so that they will live as faithful disciples for the glory of God.

Our mission is to inspire and equip the church and the home for the comprehensive discipleship of the next generation.

We equip churches and parents by producing curriculum for Sunday School, Midweek Bible, Intergenerational, Youth, and Backyard Bible Club settings; vision-casting and training resources (many available free on our website) for both the church and the home; materials and training to help parents in their role in discipling children; and the Fighter Verses™ Bible memory program to encourage the lifelong practice and love of Bible memory.

First Printing 2020. Second and Third Printing 2021.
Published in the United States of America by Truth78.

ISBN: 978-1-952783-23-4

Truth:78

Toll-Free: (877) 400-1414
info@Truth78.org
Truth78.org

Project Management: Brian Eaton, Steve Watters
Project Coordinator: Betty Dodge
Editing: Karen Hieb, Jill Nelson
Theological Review: Gary Steward
Proofing: Suzy Plocher and Candice Watters

DEDICATIONS

Dedicated to my husband David, who has been a faithful and zealous partner in striving for the discipleship of the next generation for more than four decades.

May our children, grandchildren, and all our descendants be remembered by the LORD forever, and may your passion for the faith of the next generation be served through this book.

> *He established a testimony in Jacob and appointed a law in Israel, which he commanded our fathers to teach their children, that the next generation might know them, the children yet unborn, and arise and tell them to their children, so that they should set their hope in God and not forget the works of God, but keep his commandments;*
>
> *—Psalm 78:5-7*

Dedicated to John Piper, who taught me the theology in this book. May your God-centered, passionate teaching of the Word extend to generations beyond you through this book.

> *"Blessed are you, O LORD, the God of Israel our father, forever and ever. Yours, O LORD, is the greatness and the power and the glory and the victory and the majesty, for all that is in the heavens and in the earth is yours. Yours is the kingdom, O LORD, and you are exalted as head above all."*
>
> *—1 Chronicles 29:10b-11*

ACKNOWLEDGEMENTS

This book has been in my heart, mind, and prayers for decades. Throughout that span of time, there have been many individuals who have encouraged me to pursue a project like this. But chief among them has been my husband David, who continually encouraged me to pursue my heart-burden to write a Bible story book for children and instilled in me the confidence that "God will help you." A close runner-up is my close friend and co-writer Jill Nelson, who has always given me honest feedback and strong encouragement.

There are so many others who have contributed to make this long-term dream a reality—my daughters who heard so many of these stories in some form or another growing up; my daughter Kristi, who patiently listened to story after story, stopping me when something needed to be reworded or suggesting better wording; my daughter Amy, who together with her children (*my precious grandchildren*) helped "test" these stories; my son-in-law, Gary Steward, who graciously checked for theological accuracy; Karen Hieb, who smooths my wording and corrects my grammar; Brian Eaton, who approved the project and brainstormed illustration ideas; Fred Apps, who came out of retirement to use his remarkable talents in pencil and paint to capture the heart of the text; the whole team at Truth78, who prayed, encouraged, and worked diligently to make computer files into a book; the many friends who have prayed consistently and fervently; and the financial contributors who gave sacrificially to make what was impossible for Truth78 a viable project.

The front cover of this book may have two names on it, but in reality, there are so many more names representing a host of people who have been associated with this book. Without their prayers and support, this book would not have happened. Their names may not be written on the cover, but they are written in my heart . . . and most importantly, they are written in the Lamb's Book of Life. Thank you, brothers and sisters.

TABLE OF CONTENTS

OLD TESTAMENT

PREFACE

There are amazing stories within the pages of the Bible! There is a story of a boy who defeats a giant with a sling and a stone, and a story about a big fish that swallows a prophet and spits him up on the shore. There's one about a city whose walls come tumbling down when people shout, one about a blind man who receives his sight, and one about a troubled sea that is made calm. But these true stories are not isolated incidents. Though amazing in themselves, they tell a bigger story. They tell the story of our Creator who made all things simply by speaking them into being. He placed every planet in its orbit, gathered billions of stars into galaxies, intricately formed every plant and living creature, and fashioned man in His image from the dust of the earth. Throughout all these wonders is our sovereign Creator God who planned every day of every life, every happening in history, and every detail of every moment in this universe.

Though the Bible is full of stories, it is *MORE THAN A STORY.* It is the authoritative Word of God that weaves throughout its pages the majestic character of God, His work in this world, and His plan of redemption for sinful people through His Son, Jesus Christ. As you read this book, you will discover His goodness, His greatness, His holiness, His wisdom, His power, His justice, His mercy, His faithfulness, His self-sufficiency. You will discover that He is a Refuge, a Deliverer, a Rock, and a Strong Tower to those who trust in Him. Every word He speaks is truth. Every promise He makes will be fulfilled.

When you read about the perfect world God created where man could live in perfect fellowship with God, may you yearn for that fellowship with your Creator. May the tragic reality of man's rebellion against God and the darkness of sin, misery, sickness, and death that came into the world, cause you to grieve over your own sin. May God's promise of a Redeemer and its fulfillment through the sacrifice of His own Son on the cross bring you to repentance and faith. And when you read the prophetic vision of the end of history, may you overflow with hope and joy that Jesus will make all things new. He will redeem His people to live with Him forever!

May this book, *More Than a Story: Old Testament,* lead you to THE BOOK, the unchanging, clear, sufficient, necessary, true Word of God.

Forever, O LORD, your word is firmly fixed in the heavens. (Psalm 119:89)

Your promise is well tried, and your servant loves it. (Psalm 119:140)

INTRODUCTION

By Jill Nelson

For the past three decades, I have had the great privilege of teaching the Bible to children. I can honestly say that the longer I teach, the more I am absolutely stunned by the grandeur and power of God's written Word. The answer to every pressing question, every longing of the heart, every struggle of the will, and every hope of all-satisfying joy is found in the Bible. Therefore, there is no more pressing need than for our children to become fully acquainted with the Bible. Parents—and every believer—this is your sacred responsibility and privilege. Timothy's mother and grandmother knew this to be the case. Here is what the Apostle Paul wrote to Timothy:

> *"But as for you, continue in what you have learned and have firmly believed, knowing from whom you learned it and how from childhood you have been acquainted with the sacred writings, which are able to make you wise for salvation through faith in Christ Jesus. All Scripture is breathed out by God and profitable for teaching, for reproof, for correction, and for training in righteousness, that the man of God may be complete, equipped for every good work." (2 Timothy 3:14-17)*

Now more than ever, our children need to know, understand, and embrace the truths of Scripture. Toward that end, they also will benefit from solid Bible resources that not only reveal and explain the grand narrative of Scripture but also clearly help children understand the particular parts. Furthermore, they need Bible resources that serve to guide, challenge, and urgently impress upon them the need to whole-heartedly respond to God's Word with faith in Christ, resulting in love, honor, obedience, and worship of Him. I am delighted to say that *More Than a Story* is such a resource. It stands out as a unique discipleship tool for acquainting children with God's holy Word. Here are some distinguishing features that I deeply appreciate about this resource:

A Reverence for God's Holy Word

More Than a Story treats God's Word in the manner it rightly deserves. The clearest evidence of this is the sizable amount of biblical text included in every chapter and the meticulous care given to explain biblical truths clearly and accurately—nothing fanciful, exaggerated, silly, or speculative. Your child will be continuously reminded of the authority, clarity, necessity, and sufficiency of the Bible. God's Word is truly "more than a story"!

A Comprehensive Introduction to the Breadth and Depth of Scripture

By the time your children finish reading the Old and New Testament volumes of *More Than a Story,* they will have taken a chronological survey of the entire Bible from Genesis to Revelation. They will have discovered the Bible's many books and literary genres, as well as the major events, people, places, and themes. Additionally, your children will be exposed to the disciplines of biblical theology, systematic theology, and moral instruction, all grounded in the gospel.

Child-Appropriate Without Compromising the Text

There is a great tendency when writing for children to take too much creative license in order to make the resource more "child-friendly"—fun and engaging. Sadly, children are often left with a delightful and memorable storyline but one that leaves out or minimizes essential biblical truths. This resource uses child-appropriate language to creatively convey biblical stories and truths, without compromising the nature or intent of the text.

A Clear Presentation of the Key Doctrines of the Christian Faith

Throughout *More Than a Story*, you will find numerous phrases and statements highlighted in bold font. These serve to develop a systematic theology for your children by highlighting key doctrines essential for the Christian life—doctrines concerning God, creation, man, the fall, redemption, providence, the church, and many more.

A Serious and Sober Portrayal of the Problem of Sin

One of the unique features of *More Than a Story* is its depiction of the essence, pervasiveness, and problem of sin. Chapter after chapter your children will be confronted by the utter wretchedness of man's sin against a holy and righteous God. Rather than being distressed by this, consider it a great gift meant to point your children toward utter dependence on Christ. As D. A. Carson has stated:

> *There can be no agreement as to what salvation is unless there is agreement as to that from which salvation rescues us. The problem and the solution hang together: the one explicates the other. It is impossible to gain a deep grasp of what the cross achieves without plunging into a deep grasp of what sin is; conversely, to augment one's understanding of the cross is to augment one's understanding of sin.*
>
> *To put the matter another way, sin establishes the plot line of the Bible.*[1]

Grounded in the Gospel

Every chapter in this book is grounded in the glorious reality of the gospel. Every chapter points Christ-ward. However, in saying this, it is important to note that not every chapter in the Old Testament volume of *More Than a Story* overtly mentions Christ's redeeming work on behalf of sinful man. Rather, the author carefully lets the historical, progressive nature of Scripture unfold. This lays the crucial foundation on which to build true understanding and appreciation for the person and work of Christ. Where warranted, key connections to Christ are emphasized.

Guides Children in How to Study the Bible

Not only do children need to become acquainted with the actual text of Scripture, they also need to be taught how to study the Bible. *More Than a Story* has been written in an

1. D.A. Carson, "Sin's Contemporary Significance," Chapter 1 of *Fallen: A Theology of Sin, edited by Christopher W. Morgan and Robert A. Peterson, (Wheaton, Ill.: Crossway, 2013), as republished on www.monergism.com.*

interactive manner that prompts children to observe and ask specific questions of a text in order to discover the meaning. This type of interaction not only encourages children to be eagerly and actively engaged, but it also develops critical thinking skills that will serve a lifetime of biblical study as they grow and mature.

Addresses the Mind, Heart, and Will

It isn't enough for a child to simply *know* the Bible—although that is the first step in the life of faith. God's Word must also be embraced by the heart and acted upon by the will. *More Than a Story* keeps all three realities in mind. Woven throughout every chapter are questions guiding your children to respond to what they read: How does God want me to respond? What should my heart feel and desire? What does God want me to think, be, and do?

Inspires Worship of God, for the Glory of God

Psalm 86 gives a beautiful summary of what biblical teaching is meant to inspire, fuel, and produce.

> [9]*All the nations you have made shall come*
> *and worship before you, O Lord,*
> *and shall glorify your name.*
>
> [10]*For you are great and do wondrous things;*
> *you alone are God.*
>
> [11]*Teach me your way, O LORD,*
> *that I may walk in your truth;*
> *unite my heart to fear your name.*
>
> [12]*I give thanks to you, O Lord my God, with my whole heart,*
> *and I will glorify your name forever.*

More Than a Story has been written with this glorious, God-centered goal in mind. Every chapter clearly and readily shines forth the incomparable greatness and worth of God, inspiring children to eagerly and whole-heartedly worship Him as their greatest treasure and delight!

In conclusion, *More Than a Story* is a wonderfully engaging discipleship tool for parents, grandparents, teachers, and anyone else who cares for the faith of the next generations. But bear in mind that it is also a serious tool, one conveying weighty truths that require our utmost attention. Will it be worth the added effort? Consider this thought and exhortation from John Piper:

> *The issue of earning a living is not nearly so important as whether the next generation has direct access to the meaning of the Word of God. We need an education that puts the highest premium under God on knowing the meaning of God's Book, and growing in the abilities that will unlock its riches for a lifetime . . . Lord, let us not fail the next generation!*[2]

2. John Piper, "A Compelling Reason for Rigorous Training of the Mind: Thoughts on the Significance of Reading," July 13, 2005. https://www.desiringgod.org/articles/a-compelling-reason-for-rigorous-training-of-the-mind

A NOTE FOR PARENTS ON READING WITH CHILDREN

There is a difference between reading *with* children and reading *to* children. Reading to children is when an adult reads and children listen; but reading with children is experiencing the story, the words, and the ideas together. It is an interactive exchange that takes place as the adult and the children discover meaning, wonder at the marvelous, mourn over the heartaches, ponder the incomprehensible, and rejoice in the beautiful together. Reading with children requires engaging your mind and heart in the text, letting your emotions overflow as you read together. It also takes a little bit of practice, a fair amount of abandonment, and, when reading to engage the heart and soul, a lot of prayer.

There are also some techniques we can employ in our quest to engage not only the minds of our children but also their hearts. Below are some suggestions to involve your children as you interact together to discover who God is, what He has done, and how we are to respond to Him.

- Pray briefly with your children before you begin reading. Ask God to open your minds and hearts and to show you who He is.

- Read with appropriate tone and emotion. The narratives and Scripture portions you will be reading warrant a response of enthusiasm, anger, sadness, joy, wonder—all kinds of emotions. Engage your heart in what you are reading and let your voice express that emotion.

- All the chapters include texts directly taken from the Bible itself. These are God's precious words meant to impart life, convict the soul, strengthen the weak, encourage the heart, inspire worship, warn the rebellious, comfort the fearful; so they should be read with understanding, feeling, and conviction. These are not emotionless scripts, but the words of the living God, which "[revive] the soul . . . [make] wise the simple . . . [and enlighten] the eyes." They should be read as such, for they are "more to be desired than gold . . . sweeter also than honey" (Psalm 19:7-10).

- Encourage your children to read some of the Bible texts so that they become familiar with God's Word.

- Involve your children in discovering the glorious truths in the chapter. Explain concepts or words your children do not understand. Encourage your children to ask questions. Engage your children by interacting with them and asking them to interact with the text. Ask them to read a portion of the text or to read a Bible verse. Stop and ask questions both to capture their wandering minds and to encourage them to think deeply about the truth. Some questions are included in the text itself. Some are rhetorical, but others, *in italics*, are meant to be answered. In some cases, these may be a springboard to further discussion. Don't feel tied to the text but add your own questions as you read.

- After asking a question for your children to answer . . . wait. Children need time to think. Sometimes they are intimidated and don't want to give the "wrong" answer. Encourage your children to be contributors by gently encouraging them and waiting patiently. Respond encouragingly, while still correcting, clarifying, or redirecting when needed.
- Examine the pictures and ask questions about them. Help your children to see the emotion and the realities expressed in the illustrations.
- The goal is not to "get through the chapter" but to encourage your children to discover who God is and ponder the eternal. It may take one sitting to finish a chapter, or it may take many sittings. Take your time and linger over discussions. Stop when your children are ready to stop and pick it up again later.
- Follow up after you finish the chapter or at a later time with some or all of the ideas in the application boxes. It may take several sittings just to follow through on the application box.
- Apply the truths discovered in the chapter to everyday life. Be concrete and practical. How can the truth be lived out in your family, church, and your community? Ask your children how God may want them to act on what they have learned.
- Discuss the verse in the application box. Explain unfamiliar words, talk about the meaning and application of the verse. Check the context when needed.
- Memorize key verses and refer to them in everyday life, include them in your prayers, and encourage others with them.

As your hearts are drawn together through the shared experience of reading this book together, may your hearts be drawn to the One who "is the blessed and only Sovereign, the King of kings and Lord of lords, who alone has immortality, who dwells in unapproachable light, whom no one has ever seen or can see" (1 Timothy 6:15-16a).

BEFORE THE BEGINNING . . .

GOD

CHAPTER 1

BEFORE THE BEGINNING . . . GOD

God's Nature and Character—Genesis 1:1-13

Before the mountains were brought forth, or ever you had formed the earth and the world, from everlasting to everlasting you are God. (Psalm 90:2)

Do you ever marvel that there are billions and billions of stars? Where did they all come from? What holds them up in the sky? Why does the sun come up every morning and go down every night? How is it that the earth is the perfect distance from the sun—close enough to give heat so we don't freeze, yet far enough away that we do not burn up? Some people believe there was something like an explosion a very long time ago . . . and then, just by chance, billions of tiny lifeless specks began to gather together. They formed billions of stars, all the planets, the sun, and even living things. But stop and think. How amazing is it that the sun doesn't crash into the earth! How can there be a regular pattern of day and night? The perfect design of the world couldn't *just* happen! Everything in this world shows that there is a Designer, a Maker, a glorious and powerful Creator who made it all happen and created it perfectly—not through chance but by His own wisdom and power. The glory of nature reveals that there is an all-powerful, astoundingly wise, and incredibly creative being who was before the beginning . . .

Before the mountains were brought forth, or ever you had formed the earth and the world, from everlasting to everlasting you are God. (Psalm 90:2)

Before the beginning . . . there was God. He was before anything in creation. He was even before time itself. This is what it means to say that **God is eternal—He has no beginning or end.** He has always been, and He will be forever! **He is utterly unique**—different from everything and anyone else. He is the magnificent One, the majestic One, full of splendor and glory and power and joy. He is most important and the best and greatest of all!

Splendor and majesty are before him; strength and joy are in his place. (1 Chronicles 16:27)

We really can't fully understand the magnificence of God. There are no words grand enough to describe Him. He is so much greater, better, grander, and more majestic than we could ever imagine. **God and only God is perfect in every way. He alone is the one true God.** No one and nothing is like God!

> *"Before me no god was formed, nor shall there be any after me . . . I am the first and I am the last; besides me there is no god . . . For I am God, and there is no other." (Isaiah 43:10b, 44:6b, 45:22b)*

> *"Who is like you, O LORD, among the gods? Who is like you, majestic in holiness, awesome in glorious deeds, doing wonders?" (Exodus 15:11)*

There are many mysteries in our world. We have figured out some of them, like how our voice can travel long distances on a telephone or how satellites can send pictures to a computer. But no one can fully understand all the mysteries of God. **God is incomprehensible**. This means that God is so much greater than us that He is more than we can fully understand. But this glorious God wants us to know Him! He has given us a book, His precious Word, the

Bible, so that we can know who He is, what He is like, and how we can have a relationship with Him.

In His Word, God has shared what we must know about Him and what is true about the world. He tells us in the Bible that everything in this world began with Him—the almighty, all-wise, all-creative God. Only God knows all things, and only He can tell us what is true about creation. We don't have to wonder or guess about how the world began; we can know for sure because God has told us about it in His Word:

> *In the beginning, God created the heavens and the earth. (Genesis 1:1)*

God created the world and everything in it. He continues to work in sustaining the world or keeping it going—providing oxygen to breathe, creating new life, keeping the sun in its path, and holding the stars in place. How did our glorious, incomprehensible God create the world? He spoke. That's it. He just spoke and His powerful word created the world! On the first day of creation, He simply spoke and said, *"Let there be light,"* and there was light. *What does this tell you about God?*

> *The voice of the LORD is powerful; the voice of the LORD is full of majesty. (Psalm 29:4)*

God's creation shows His incredible power. God spoke, and brilliant light burst forth. *God thunders wondrously with his voice; he does great things that we cannot comprehend.* Then on day two, He spoke and created the enormous, beautiful sky. But God didn't stop creating. He powerfully gathered the waters together and created dry land. God's commanding voice created the vast earth and the mighty, deep seas. But He did even more! He spoke all the plants into creation—tall trees, thick bushes, flowing grasses, colorful flowers, and all kinds of delicious growing plants. *And God saw that it was good. And there was evening and there was morning, the third day.*

Just think of the amazing power and creativity of God. He spoke, and trees appeared, strong and tall; flowers bloomed in dazzling reds, pinks, oranges, yellows, blues, and purples. And not just one kind of flower, but daisies, roses, violets, sunflowers, lilacs, apple blossoms, lilies . . . Oh, the amazing works of God! We can't even begin to imagine the creativity of a God who can create a mighty oak tree and a delicate buttercup.

The Bible tells us very clearly about some of God's creative work. But the Bible only gives us hints about other things, like the creation of the "heavenly hosts" or angels. The Bible tells us that angels are created beings. They were created to worship God—to adore, honor, and to be in awe of Him. We don't know exactly when the angels were created, but it was sometime during creation, and they "shouted for joy" when the earth was formed.[1] *Why do you think they shouted for joy?*

When you see something beautiful and amazing, do you just keep quiet? No, you talk about it. You express your feelings with words like, "Wow! That is amazing!" Sometimes you even shout with excitement and awe, even though nothing you have seen is as marvelous as the powerful and glorious act of God making the world. What must it have been like for the angels to see God's incredible work of creation? *Can you imagine what they might have shouted?*

Everything in creation shows us God's glory—His greatness and worth. We didn't see God create the world. But we can see His amazing creation, which shows us that He is powerful, wise, and good. Such a display of the glory of God should cause us to say,

> *Great is the LORD, and greatly to be praised, and his greatness is unsearchable. (Psalm 145:3)*

How does God's creation show us His greatness? Where do you see God's greatness shown in His world today?

"Ah, Lord GOD! It is you who have made the heavens and the earth by your great power and by your outstretched arm! Nothing is too hard for you." (Jeremiah 32:17)

MAKING YOU WISE FOR SALVATION

What does this chapter tell us about God? Talk about and apply the **biblical truths** in **bold** text.

Salvation Thread: God is the one true God. He was before all things, so all truth comes from God. Why is God worthy of our worship?

Talk About: *Before the mountains were brought forth, or ever you had formed the earth and the world, from everlasting to everlasting you are God. (Psalm 90:2)*

Pray: Praise God for who He is.

Think About: Read Job 38:4-7. God is telling Job that he was not present at creation. What do these verses show you about the difference between God and man? What is true of God that is not true of anyone else? Why does this make God worthy of our praise and worship?

Memorize: Psalm 90:2; Psalm 145:3; or Jeremiah 32:17

1. Job 38:4-7; Colossians 1:16; Nehemiah 9:6; Psalm 148:2-5

C H A P T E R 2

FROM HIM ARE ALL THINGS

Creation of the World—Genesis 1:1-25

For from him and through him and to him are all things.
To him be glory forever. Amen. (Romans 11:36)

W*hy does the Bible say that all things are "from God"?* We know that before the beginning, there was God—that God always was and always will be. He is **eternal**. With His mighty voice, He created the world. *Do you remember what He created on the first three days of creation?* The first day God created brilliant light. The second day He created the vast sky. Then on the third day, He gathered the waters, formed the land, and created plants. All of this came from God the Creator and Owner of all things.

But God wasn't done with His wonderful work of creation. Listen to what the mighty voice of God spoke into creation on the fourth day:

> *. . ."Let there be lights in the expanse of the heavens to separate the day from the night. And let them be for signs and for seasons, and for days and years, and let them be lights in the expanse of the heavens to give light upon the earth". . . (Genesis 1:14-15)*

And then the Bible tells us, *And it was so.* **Every word of God is powerful**. Every word accomplishes His purpose! God spoke and made two great lights—a big one to rule the day and a smaller one to rule the night. *Do you know what they were?* They were the sun and moon. But God made even more lights. He made billions and billions of bright, light-giving stars. How good it was of God to give light to the world and warmth from the sun. *What does this tell you about Him?*

What does the Bible say about each day of creation? It says, *And God saw that it was good. Do you know why God's creation is good?* Because **God is good**, all that came from Him in creation is good. But God didn't just create the world, and

then go away and ignore it. Not only are all things *from Him*, but they are *through Him*, too. This means God keeps the stars in space, the sun in its path, and the moon in the sky. God keeps on "holding up" the world. He is actively taking care of it, every moment of every day.

On the fifth day of creation, by the power of His word, God created all the creatures in the sea and the birds of the air—*"Let the waters swarm with swarms of living creatures, and let birds fly above the earth across the expanse of the heavens." How many sea creatures can you name? What kinds of birds can you name?* God made them all! Not only that, but He told them to multiply so there would be more and more of them.

O LORD, how manifold are your works! In wisdom have you made them all; the earth is full of your creatures. (Psalm 104:24)

Do you know why the Bible tells us that God made the world "in wisdom"? Because all that God made, He made well. God was very wise in the way He made the world. He made fruit trees to bear fruit we could eat. But do you know what was so wise about the way He made fruit trees? He put seeds inside the fruit that would grow more fruit trees. He made some plants like potatoes that grow stems. Those stems could then grow more potatoes underground. God made birds and fish to lay eggs that would give us more birds and fish . . . that would give us more eggs . . . to give us even more birds and fish. He made sure that life could go on and on. **God is wise** in all His ways, and all of creation shows God's wisdom.

God made the light, the sky, the sea and land, trees, bushes, grass, and all kinds of plants . . . and the sun, moon, and stars. He made all the sea creatures like whales, sharks, dolphins, jellyfish, octopuses, and crabs . . . and all the flying creatures like eagles, seagulls, parrots, robins, chickens, turkeys, flamingos, storks, pelicans, ducks, butterflies, bees, and flies . . . but *still* He kept creating! He didn't run out of energy or power. **God is independent**—He doesn't need anything. He never gets tired or runs out of strength.

On the sixth day, God made living creatures—*livestock and creeping things and beasts of the earth according to their kinds. How many of these can you name?* Did you think of a horse, cow, sheep, camel, elephant, hippopotamus, tiger, cheetah, lion, giraffe, bear, deer, moose, beaver, porcupine, skunk, rabbit, mouse, lizard, frog, or snake? That is just the beginning of the countless strange and extraordinary animals God created. Some of them we have only seen in pictures or at the zoo. Some, like dinosaurs, are no longer on earth. In wisdom, God made male and female animals so they could have baby animals, and there would be more and more animals. God thought of everything when He created the world. He made no mistakes. *And God saw that it was good.* God delighted in all that He made!

Everything in creation shows His power and His wisdom. **All creation shows us God's glory—His greatness and worth**. And all of creation was created to praise Him:

> *Praise him, sun and moon, praise him, all you shining stars! Praise him, you highest heavens, and you waters above the heavens! Let them praise the name of the LORD! For he commanded and they were created. (Psalm 148:3-5)*

> *The heavens declare the glory of God, and the sky above proclaims his handiwork. (Psalm 19:1)*

But God still had one more special creation to make. It would be special because it would be able to show God's greatness and worth in a different way from all the rest of creation.

All of creation was created to show God's greatness and worth and to cause us to praise Him. How can you show God's greatness and worth?

For from him and through him and to him are all things.
To him be glory forever. Amen. (Romans 11:36)

MAKING YOU WISE FOR SALVATION

What does this chapter tell us about God? Talk about and apply the **biblical truths** in **bold** text.

Salvation Thread: God is the Creator and Owner of all things. *How does this apply to your life?*

Share with your child how creation should lead us to worship God.

Talk About: *For from him and through him and to him are all things. To him be glory forever. Amen. (Romans 11:36)*

Pray: Read Hebrews 11:3. Pray for faith to believe that God is the Creator, and that He is all-powerful and all-wise.

Think About: Explore God's creation. Study an animal or insect, discover different kinds of plants, learn about the stars, etc. What does creation tell you about God? Some people think that God did not make the world. What did you discover that shows you there has to be a Creator or Maker?

Memorize: Romans 11:36

C H A P T E R 3

LET US MAKE MAN

Creation of Man—Genesis 1:26-2:25

So God created man in his own image, in the image of God he created him; male and female he created them. (Genesis 1:27)

What are some of the millions of things God's mighty voice created? Just think of the power of God's voice. Yet God created His most special creation in a very different way than He created everything else. This is what the Bible tells us:

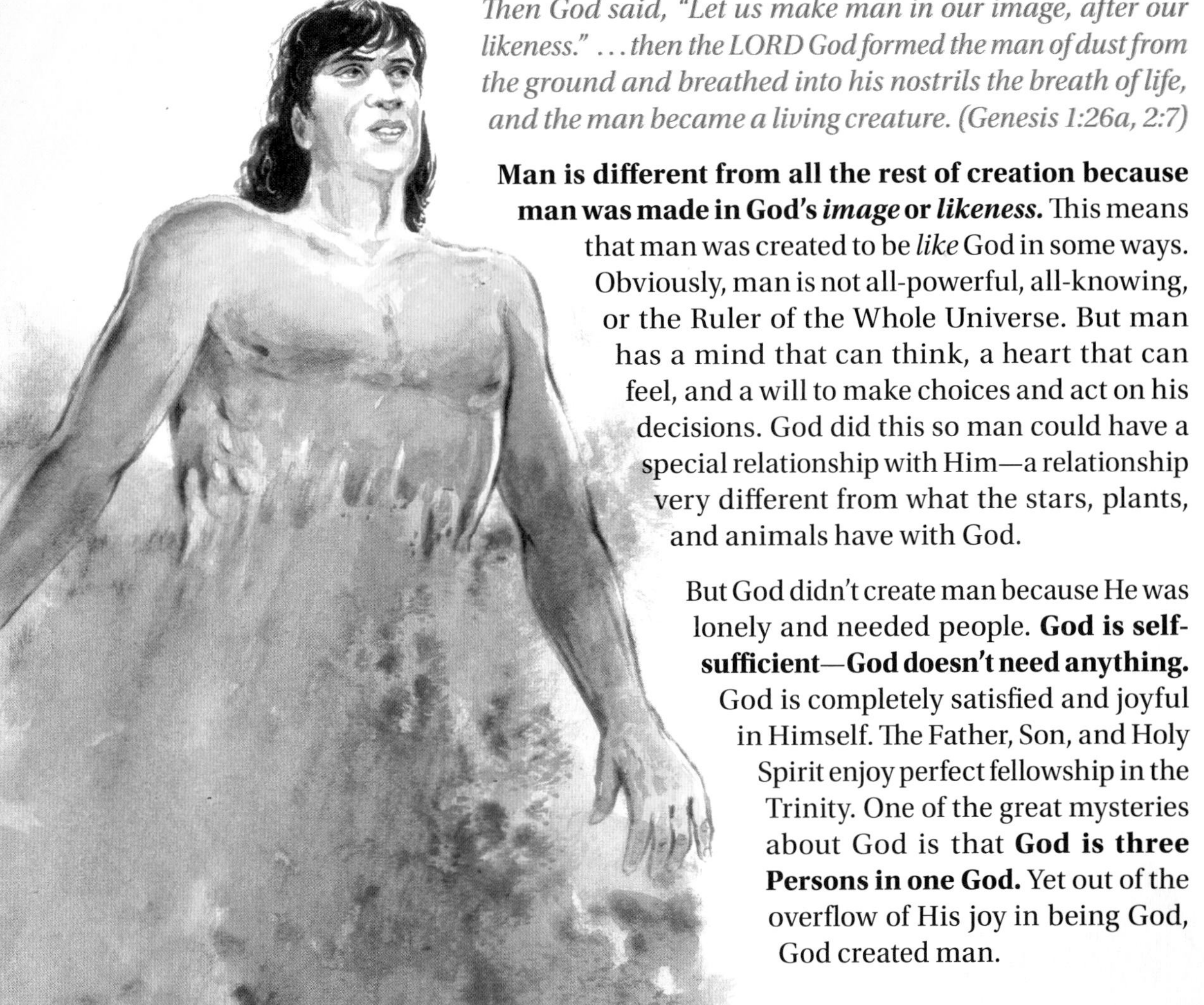

Then God said, "Let us make man in our image, after our likeness." . . . then the LORD God formed the man of dust from the ground and breathed into his nostrils the breath of life, and the man became a living creature. (Genesis 1:26a, 2:7)

Man is different from all the rest of creation because man was made in God's *image* or *likeness*. This means that man was created to be *like* God in some ways. Obviously, man is not all-powerful, all-knowing, or the Ruler of the Whole Universe. But man has a mind that can think, a heart that can feel, and a will to make choices and act on his decisions. God did this so man could have a special relationship with Him—a relationship very different from what the stars, plants, and animals have with God.

But God didn't create man because He was lonely and needed people. **God is self-sufficient—God doesn't need anything.** God is completely satisfied and joyful in Himself. The Father, Son, and Holy Spirit enjoy perfect fellowship in the Trinity. One of the great mysteries about God is that **God is three Persons in one God.** Yet out of the overflow of His joy in being God, God created man.

And the LORD God planted a garden in Eden . . . and there he put the man whom he had formed. And out of the ground the LORD God made to spring up every tree that is pleasant to the sight and good for food. The tree of life was in the midst of the garden, and the tree of the knowledge of good and evil. The garden was a lovely place full of luscious fruit and beautiful plants, with a refreshing river that watered the garden. *What does this tell you about the goodness of God?*

God named the man *Adam* and gave him a very special job. Adam was to take care of the garden, but God also gave man *dominion* over every living thing. That means Adam was in charge; he was to rule over all the creatures. Adam was not the Ruler of the Universe like God. But Adam and all men made in the likeness of God do rule. We see this *likeness* of God today when a man trains a dog, clears land to build a house, or makes decisions for the good of his family.

God gave Adam everything in the garden to take care of and enjoy, except for one thing.

> *The LORD God took the man and put him in the garden of Eden to work it and keep it. And the LORD God commanded the man, saying, "You may surely eat of every tree of the garden, but of the tree of the knowledge of good and evil you shall not eat, for in the day that you eat of it you shall surely die." (Genesis 2:15-17)*

Why did God tell Adam not to eat the fruit of the tree of knowledge of good and evil? God put man to the test. Would man believe that **God knows what is best**? God warned Adam, saying,

"Don't eat from this tree. If you do, you will die. Trust me and obey my command." Only by following God's good commands could man find true joy and happiness.

Then the LORD God said, "It is not good that the man should be alone; I will make him a helper fit for him." (Genesis 2:18)

So, God brought every animal and every bird to Adam to name them. The right to name something means you have *authority* over something—you have the right to make decisions, give commands, and expect obedience. *If you were Adam and saw a big animal with a long trunk, what would you name it?* Whatever name Adam gave the living creature, that was its name. This was showing *dominion* or leadership. Adam was doing what God created him to do.

Through naming the creatures, Adam saw that God's creation had a male and female pattern—male horses and female horses, male rabbits and female rabbits. But there was no female human. Out of all the creatures, there was no helper "fit for Adam." So, God caused Adam to fall into a deep sleep. And, while Adam was sleeping, God took a rib bone from Adam. He lovingly closed up Adam's flesh and, from the rib, He made a woman. Then God brought this perfect helper to Adam. *Do you know what Adam said when he saw the woman?*

..."This at last is bone of my bones and flesh of my flesh; she shall be called Woman, because she was taken out of Man." (Genesis 2:23)

Adam realized that she was the completion of God's design. She was the perfect companion and helper for him! Adam named her *Woman*, and she became Adam's wife. The Bible tells us that a husband and wife become one. They complete each other in a special way, and together they become one. God's work of creation was finished.

And God saw everything that he had made, and behold, it was very good. And there was evening and there was morning, the sixth day. (Genesis 1:31)

On the seventh day, *God rested from all his work that he had done in creation. What does this mean? Was God so tired from His work of creation that He needed a break?* That can't be what the Bible means, because **God is self-sufficient—He doesn't need anything—and God is almighty, all-powerful.** God doesn't need to sleep or take a break; He never gets tired.

Have you not known? Have you not heard? The LORD is the everlasting God, the Creator of the ends of the earth. He does not faint or grow weary; his understanding is unsearchable. (Isaiah 40:28)

"God rested" means that He stopped His work of creation. All that God had created was good and complete. His work of creation was done. All of His creation lived together in peace and joy. The man and woman enjoyed a special relationship with God and with each other. There were no tears or sickness, no sadness or anger. There were no secrets or reasons to hide from each other. The Bible says that man and woman were naked—totally uncovered—but they had no reason to be ashamed or embarrassed. There was nothing that needed to be hidden. Together they completed God's design to show God's perfect work—to show God's goodness, wisdom, greatness, and worth in all that they thought, felt, and did. They enjoyed God's presence in the Garden of Eden—walking with and talking with God in sweet friendship.

We can know what is true about God by reading the Bible. But, like the first man and woman, we can also actually know God personally. We can have a friendship with God, too.

You make known to me the path of life; in your presence there is fullness of joy; at your right hand are pleasures forevermore. (Psalm 16:11)

MAKING YOU WISE FOR SALVATION

What does this chapter tell us about God? Talk about and apply the **biblical truths** in **bold** text.

Salvation Thread: God created all things, including you, for His glory. *How can you show God's greatness and worth?* God created man to have a relationship with Him. *Do you want to have a personal relations*

hip (a friendship) with God?

Talk About: *So God created man in his own image, in the image of God he created him; male and female he created them. (Genesis 1:27)*

How are men and women different? How are they the same? What is the importance of Adam naming the woman? What was Adam's role (job)? What was the woman's job as companion and helper? (Make sure your child understands that men and women have different roles, but both are made in God's image and are equally important.)

Pray: Thank God for making you in His image. Ask Him to make you a good "image-bearer"—a boy or girl who reflects (or imitates) God's thoughts, desires, and actions.

Think About: Read Psalm 8:3-5. What is the writer of this psalm feeling? What is his attitude toward God? What is your attitude toward God?

C H A P T E R 4

SIN AND DARKENED HEARTS

The Fall and Sin—Genesis 3

For although they knew God, they did not honor him as God or give thanks to him, but they became futile in their thinking, and their foolish hearts were darkened. (Romans 1:21)

If you came home from a week of vacation and found a big branch had broken off one of the trees in your yard, would you know when it fell off? You would know that it fell off some time while you were gone, but you wouldn't know *exactly when* it happened. You would only know *that* it happened.

The Bible gives us some hints about something that happened. We don't know exactly when or how it happened. We know that God created many angels and that they were in heaven with God. The Bible also tells us that angels were created to worship God—to show the greatness of God and to obey Him. God is the one true God, who alone is the Most High. Only God is perfect in love, goodness, wisdom, beauty, and power. **Only God deserves to be worshiped**—to be loved and honored above all. There was much joy in heaven worshiping the one true God!

God also created the angels to be His messengers and servants to carry out some of His plans on earth.[1] But there was one angel who was not satisfied to worship and serve God anymore. Though he was created good, he became proud and rebellious. He did not want to worship or serve God; he wanted to *be* God. This angel and some of the other angels rebelled and turned against God.

The rest of the angels loved and worshiped God as they were created to do. A war broke out in heaven between the angels who worshiped God and the angels who turned away from God and fought against

Him. But nothing, not even an angel, can fight against God and win. No one can take God's place or put himself above God. **God is the Most High.** Because God is holy and pure and righteous, no evil can stand in His presence.

> *You who are of purer eyes than to see evil and cannot look at wrong, (Habakkuk 1:13a)*

So this rebellious angel was thrown out of heaven and was called Satan or the devil, the enemy of God.[2] All the angels who followed Satan are called demons, and they were also cast out of heaven.

Like the angels, man and woman were made to worship God. They were made to live in perfect friendship with Him. They were made to trust His goodness and wisdom, and to obey every one of His commands. Adam and his wife walked and talked with God. Their life in the Garden of Eden was joyful and peaceful . . . until one day. Satan, the enemy of God, took the form of a serpent and came to them.

> *He said to the woman, "Did God actually say, 'You shall not eat of any tree in the garden'?" And the woman said to the serpent, "We may eat of the fruit of the trees in the garden, but God said, 'You shall not eat of the fruit of the tree that is in the midst of the garden, neither shall you touch it, lest you die.'" But the serpent said to the woman, "You will not surely die. For God knows that when you eat of it your eyes will be opened, and you will be like God, knowing good and evil." (Genesis 3:1b-5)*

Satan hates God, and he hates it when people worship and obey God. Satan is also very sly, or wickedly clever. He slyly tried to make Eve doubt or question the truthfulness and goodness of God—*"Did God actually say, 'You shall not eat of any tree in the garden'?"* God had graciously given man all the trees except one. He warned him that eating from that tree would mean death. But Satan told the woman that she would *not* die if she ate the fruit from the tree. *"You will not surely die. For God knows that when you eat of it your eyes will be opened, and you will be like God, knowing good and evil."* Satan spoke very convincingly, tempting the woman to doubt that God is truthful and good. Would the woman trust God, or the serpent and her own ideas?

Everything God says is true. But the Bible tells us that **Satan is the father of lies**. Satan told the woman a lie about the fruit and about God. By telling her that God was wrong in what He said, he was saying that God cannot be trusted; he was saying that God's word is not true and that God was keeping something good from her. *What should she have done?*

She didn't run from the serpent. She didn't shout, "God is good, and His words are always true!" And she didn't ask God for help. Instead, she looked at that tree . . .

> *So when the woman saw that the tree was good for food, and that it was a delight to the eyes, and that the tree was to be desired to make one wise, she took of its fruit and ate, and she also gave some to her husband who was with her, and he ate. (Genesis 3:6)*

What happened? The woman saw that the fruit looked good, and she wanted it! *What wrong ideas might she have been thinking?* She may have been thinking, "That fruit looks good, so it won't hurt to eat it. Maybe God is wrong about the fruit. It won't make me die." *What wrong heart attitudes might have tempted the woman?* Maybe pride, distrust, or a desire for power entered her heart—"Why should God get to decide what I should eat? I should be able to decide for myself. Maybe God really isn't good. Can I really trust Him? I could be wise like God. I could be as great as God."

Then she reached out and took the fruit . . . and ate it. The woman was not satisfied with being God's special creation, loving and worshiping Him. She wanted *to be God,* just as Satan had wanted to take God's place. She didn't trust God's word, or His goodness or His wisdom. She rebelled against God. She trusted her own wisdom and thought she could make her own rules about what is true and right.

What about Adam? He was created to lead the woman and protect her. *Is that what he did?* No, he didn't try to stop her. He didn't remind her of God's truth. What would he do about the fruit the woman gave him? Would he trust God's goodness and wisdom? Would he trust that God is the Creator who knows what is best—what is true and right? Would he trust the One who had given him a special friendship, who had generously given him all the other trees in the garden? Tragically, he followed his wife and ate the fruit. He, too, disobeyed God and decided for himself what is true and right instead of trusting God. *Then the eyes of both were opened, and they knew that they were naked. And they sewed fig leaves together and made themselves loincloths.* They wanted to hide their bodies now. Instead of being wise, they were embarrassed and ashamed. Both man and woman sinned. **Sin is disobeying or breaking God's law. It is rebelling against God and rejecting God's law instead of trusting and obeying God.** Sin causes a separation between man and God.

When Adam and his wife heard God walking in the garden, instead of joyfully running toward Him, they hid themselves. *Why would they hide themselves from the God who had created them, loved them, and blessed them with so many good things*? Something had changed. Sin had come into God's perfect creation. Rebellion against God had come into the world. Things would never be the same. Although the man and woman knew God, they dishonored him by not trusting and obeying Him.

> *For although they knew God, they did not honor him as God or give thanks to him, but they became futile in their thinking, and their foolish hearts were darkened. (Romans 1:21)*

How foolish it was for Adam and his wife to think that they could hide from the all-knowing God! God knew where they were hiding, and He knew what they had done. *But the LORD God called to the man and said to him, "Where are you?" And he said, "I heard the sound of you in the garden, and I was afraid, because I was naked, and I hid myself." He said, "Who told you that you were naked? Have you eaten of the tree of which I commanded you not to eat?"*

When God questioned them, what did they do? Adam blamed the woman. Adam even made it sound like it was God's fault. *"The woman whom you gave to be with me, she gave me the fruit of the tree, and I ate."* Then the woman blamed the serpent. What would happen now? What would God do?

Just like the first man and woman, you were created to love, honor, trust, and obey God. You were created to give thanks to Him and to worship Him. Will you ask God to give you a heart to worship Him and to turn away from rebellion?

Create in me a clean heart, O God, and renew a right spirit within me. (Psalm 51:10)

Surely I was sinful at birth, sinful from the time my mother conceived me. (Psalm 51:5, NIV 1984)

MAKING YOU WISE FOR SALVATION

What does this chapter tell us about God? Talk about and apply the **biblical truths** in **bold** text.

Salvation Thread: Sin creates a barrier or separation between God and man. *How does this affect you?*

Talk About: *For although they knew God, they did not honor him as God or give thanks to him, but they became futile in their thinking, and their foolish hearts were darkened. (Romans 1:21)*

How were Adam and Eve "futile in their thinking"—how was their thinking wrong?

Pray: Ask God to give you the desire to thank, trust, obey, and honor Him.

Think About: Adam and Eve believed lies about God and lies about themselves. *What lies am I tempted to believe about God and about myself? What do I know to be true about God?*

1. Wayne Grudem. *Systematic Theology: An Introduction to Biblical Doctrine.* (Grand Rapids, Mich.: Zondervan, 2000), 402-404.
2. 2 Peter 2:4; Jude 6—Note: The rebellion in heaven must have happened after the sixth day of creation. In Genesis 1:31 the Bible tells us, "And God saw everything that he had made, and behold, it was very good."

CHAPTER 5

THE CURSE AND THE PROMISE

Results of the Fall—Genesis 3

For as by the one man's disobedience the many were made sinners, so by the one man's obedience the many will be made righteous. (Romans 5:19)

Instead of honoring God by trusting Him and obeying His command, Adam and his wife rebelled against God. They did not believe that what God said was true and right. Instead, they pridefully thought they could decide for themselves what was right and good. They did not give thanks to God or honor Him as the one true God. Their hearts, which were created good, were now darkened or ruined by sin. What should God do about man's and woman's sin? Should He just treat it as if it doesn't matter and forget about it? Should He destroy Adam and his wife and start over with another man and woman? Should He forget about humans and enjoy the rest of His beautiful and vast creation?

God is holy—He is perfect in every way. He cannot accept or permit sin. **God is righteous and just—God always does what is right.** His good and right command had been broken. He couldn't just pretend it didn't happen.

After man and woman sinned against God by believing Satan and following his lies, God first turned to the serpent and said that it would be punished by having to crawl on its belly and eat dust. But God knew that Satan was speaking through the body of the serpent, so He gave Satan a curse, too:

> *"I will put enmity between you and the woman, and between your offspring and her offspring; he shall bruise your head, and you shall bruise his heel." (Genesis 3:15)*

God's curse is His punishment carried out with His almighty power. Do you remember the power of God's word? God's word created the universe. What He spoke happened. His words accomplish His purposes. Satan would now be the deadly enemy of all humans, of all the "offspring" of woman—everyone born from Eve . . . and her children . . . and their children . . . and especially of one very special child.

God also had a powerful word of punishment for Adam and his wife.

> *To the woman he said, "I will surely multiply your pain in childbearing; in pain you shall bring forth children. Your desire shall be for your husband, and he shall rule over you." (Genesis 3:16)*

The woman would have great pain in giving birth. She would also want to be in charge and try to take Adam's job of being the leader. The man would continue to be in charge, but

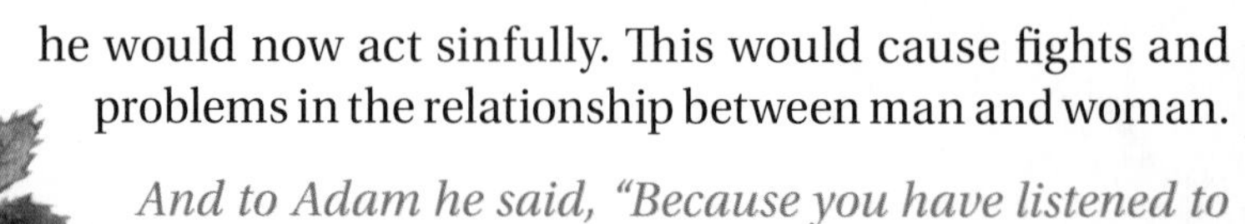

he would now act sinfully. This would cause fights and problems in the relationship between man and woman.

And to Adam he said, "Because you have listened to the voice of your wife and have eaten of the tree of which I commanded you, 'You shall not eat of it,' cursed is the ground because of you; in pain you shall eat of it all the days of your life; thorns and thistles it shall bring forth for you; and you shall eat the plants of the field." (Genesis 3:17-18)

Working in the garden had been pleasant for Adam. There were no weeds or thorns in the beautiful Garden of Eden. The animals were friendly, and the work was easy. But now prickly weeds and thorns would grow on the earth. Because of his sin, work would now be hard for Adam.

But there was still another serious consequence of sin. *Do you remember what God said the consequence of eating the fruit would be?* Man would die. God had decided that **the punishment for sin is death**. God is the Owner and Ruler of the universe, and He has the right to determine the punishment for sin. He had told Adam what would happen if he ate the fruit, and **God's word always proves true**. Adam and his wife would now die:

"By the sweat of your face you shall eat bread, till you return to the ground, for out of it you were taken; for you are dust, and to dust you shall return." (Genesis 3:19)

Adam and his wife deserved to die . . . and they would die. But they would not die right away. Little by little, their bodies would wear out. Sickness and death had come into the world through their sin.

God is just and right to punish sin; but **He is also merciful—God is kind to undeserving sinners**. *Did you read any promises or signs of hope in God's punishment?* God said that the woman would have "offspring" or children. God was not done with man! He did not give up on the human race. He would continue to give life. What a glorious, wonderful, undeserved blessing from God. Adam understood God's wonderful mercy and *called his wife's name Eve, because she was the mother of all living.* New life would come from Adam and Eve! But things had changed. Their sin nature or darkened heart would be passed on to their children and their children's children . . . to every person ever born from Adam and Eve. Just as elephants have baby elephants, sinners have baby sinners.

For as by the one man's disobedience the many were made sinners . . . (Romans 5:19a)

Men and women would still be made in the image of God, but that image was no longer perfect. It was damaged by sin. Evil, hatred, selfishness, and pride would now grow in the hearts of man. Every person would be born a sinner, and every person would die.

> *Therefore, just as sin came into the world through one man, and death through sin, and so death spread to all men because all sinned— (Romans 5:12)*

God showed another amazing mercy to Adam and Eve. The covering for sin that Adam and Eve made from fig leaves was not *sufficient* or acceptable. The right payment for sin is death. But God did not require the death of Adam and Eve. He provided a substitute death—something else to die in their place.

> *And the LORD God made for Adam and for his wife garments of skins and clothed them. (Genesis 3:21)*

God Himself covered their sin with the skin of animals. *What had to happen to the animals for God to use the skins?* The animals' blood was poured out, and their death made a way for Adam and Eve to be covered. Man and woman could once again come near to God through the blood of a sacrifice. But this covering for sin wasn't complete or lasting—a greater sacrifice would have to be made.

There was an amazing promise of this greater sacrifice within God's curse—a most wonderful, glorious promise! *Do you know what it is?* God made the promise when He cursed Satan:

> *I will put enmity between you and the woman, and between your offspring and her offspring; he shall bruise your head, and you shall bruise his heel." (Genesis 3:15)*

This was God's promise that He would send a Savior, born from a woman, who would crush the enemy Satan. He would also bring a lasting solution or cure for man's sin. This would be a complete and final taking away of man's sin. This is the greatest promise God could ever make to man. **A Savior, a sin-bearer, would come to be the perfect, complete, and final substitute to die for man's sin.**

Do you know why a Savior is needed? It is because **sin offends God's holy nature.** Adam and Eve's sin of rebelling against God, not trusting Him, and disobeying God was offensive or unacceptable to a holy God. Their sin had placed a barrier or wall between them and God. Their sin separated them from a holy God.

> *but **your iniquities have made a separation between you and your God**, and your sins have hidden his face from you . . . (Isaiah 59:2a)*

God sent Adam and Eve out of the garden. Then He placed an angel with a flaming sword at the garden entrance to keep them from the Tree of Life. Adam and Eve could not return to the wonderful garden. They could no longer walk and talk with God enjoying His sweet presence.

There is a rhyme to help you remember this story: "In Adam's fall, we sinned all."[1] This means that you, too, have a sin nature, a darkened heart. You were born with it. It was passed on from Adam to every person. But God's great promise is this:

For as by the one man's disobedience the many were made sinners, so by the one man's obedience the many will be made righteous. (Romans 5:19)

For the wages of sin is death, but the free gift of God is eternal life in Christ Jesus our Lord. (Romans 6:23)

MAKING YOU WISE FOR SALVATION

What does this chapter tell us about God? Talk about and apply the **biblical truths** in **bold** text.

Salvation Thread: God promised He would send a Savior. The Savior would destroy Satan and save people. *What do you know about this Savior?*

Why did God have the right to determine the punishment for sin? Explain God's justice and His mercy.

Talk About: *For as by the one man's disobedience the many were made sinners, so by the one man's obedience the many will be made righteous. (Romans 5:19)*

Pray: Thank God for His promise to send a Savior and for keeping His promise. Thank Him that every word of His proves true.

Think About: *Where do I see the consequences of sin in the world? Where do I see sin in my own heart? Why do I need a Savior?*

Apply: *What should I think? Be? Do?*

1. *The New England Primer,* published in 17th-century colonial America.

C H A P T E R 6

RULE SIN, OR IT WILL RULE YOU

Cain and Abel—Genesis 4

"If you do well, will you not be accepted? And if you do not do well, sin is crouching at the door. Its desire is for you, but you must rule over it." (Genesis 4:7)

Something had drastically changed in God's perfect world. Thorn bushes and weeds grew among the good plants and fruit trees. Animals that had been tame and playful now became wild. Some of them were even dangerous. Adam had to work hard "by the sweat of [his] face" to grow food. There were now conflicts or arguments between Adam and Eve. All of creation "groaned." Sin had come into the world and changed everything. *Think about how sin has changed everything. What would this world be like without sin?*

God had been kind to Adam and Eve in covering their sin. But even so, they could not return to God's beautiful, peaceful garden. Life would forever be different. Yet God remained the same. **God is unchanging. He is kind and forgiving.** In His kindness, God gave Adam and Eve a son named Cain. Giving birth was hard work and extremely painful for Eve, just as God had said. But when Cain was born Eve said, *"I have gotten a man with the help of the LORD."* God continued to bless Adam and Eve and gave them another son named Abel.

God had told Adam in the garden to *be fruitful and multiply and fill the earth.* Now Adam and Eve had two sons to help them do what God had commanded. They could please God by trusting Him and doing what is right.

Adam and Eve, and Cain and Abel ate and slept. They took care of sheep, pulled weeds, and made clothes...and they sinned because they had darkened, sinful hearts. Adam and Eve's sin nature had been passed on to their sons, who were also sinners. Their greatest problem, their sin problem, had not gone away. But God had made a way to cover their sin so they could still have a friendship with Him. *Do you remember what God decided to accept as a temporary kind of covering for sin?* Adam and his family could offer to God the death of an animal as a covering for their sin.

Cain was a farmer. But now the job of farming was more difficult. Cain had to pull up weeds and prickly plants that would choke out the good plants. Abel was a shepherd—he watched their sheep and kept them safe. *What kind of danger do you think there could be to the sheep?* The sheep could be scratched by thorn bushes, become sick, or be killed by wild animals. Remember that pain, sickness, and death had come into the world.

Eventually, both Cain and Abel brought offerings to God. Cain, the farmer, brought an "offering of the fruit of the ground." Abel, the shepherd, brought a lamb born from his flock of sheep. He gave the firstborn and the best of his flock. Surely, Abel truly wanted to honor and please God. Abel had to kill the lamb to offer it. He probably understood how awful sin is and what a big price has to be paid to cover sin. *What does this tell you about Abel's heart?*

> *By faith Abel offered to God a more acceptable sacrifice than Cain, through which he was commended as righteous, God commending him by accepting his gifts. And through his faith, though he died, he still speaks. (Hebrews 11:4)*

God was pleased with Abel's faith in Him and accepted Abel's offering of his firstborn lamb. **Faith is trusting in God and in what He says.** Abel's faith in God made him righteous or right before God. **Faith pleases God.**

But God did not accept Cain's offering, and He was *not* pleased with Cain. *What might be some reasons that God did not accept Cain and his offering?* The Bible does not tell us exactly why God was not pleased. Perhaps the fruit was old or bruised, or of very poor quality. Perhaps it was because Cain's offering was not an animal. But what is most important to God is *how* a person comes to Him. Abel came in faith to honor God. But it was not that way with Cain. Cain did not come to honor God through faith. So God did not accept his offering. The Bible tells us that Cain was very angry that God did not accept his offering.

> *The LORD said to Cain, "Why are you angry, and why has your face fallen? If you do well, will you not be accepted? And if you do not do well, sin is crouching at the door. Its desire is for you, but you must rule over it." (Genesis 4:6-7)*

Did Cain have a right to be angry at God? Cain did not "do well." He did not do what is right. If he had come with the right heart to honor and obey God, he would have been accepted. But Cain was not eager to please God. He was not honoring to God. He had his own idea of what was right, rather than trusting and obeying God. Sin was "crouching at the door" of his heart.

What does crouching mean? Have you ever tried to hide, and then jump out and startle someone? Or has someone done that to you? You squat down and quietly wait . . . ready to jump out and pounce on that person . . . who probably then screams in surprise! That squatting down and being ready to jump out and grab the person is called "crouching."

God told Cain that sin is like that. It was crouching down ready to grab him. It was waiting for a good chance to get him in its power. But God told Cain something very important about that crouching sin, *"you must rule over it."* God warned Cain to watch out for sin, to resist it or stand against it. Be in charge of sin, rule it, and tell it, "No!" The only way to rule sin is to be ruled by something greater. That something greater is someONE—God. **To turn away from sin, a person must turn to God.** God was giving Cain a chance to repent—to turn *away* from sin and do what is right by turning *to* God. Abel lived under God's rule. He had faith in God, who is more powerful than any sin. His faith in God made him able to resist sin. But Cain was not ruled by love and respect for God. He did not live under God's rule. Cain ruled himself apart from God. So Cain could not turn from sin. *Do you think that Cain listened to God's good and wise words?*

Sadly, Cain did not listen to God's warning. He did not come to God in repentance and live under God's rule. He was jealous and angry that God accepted Abel and his offering. Later, when Cain and Abel were in the field, and sin was crouching at Cain's heart, Cain did not resist it. He did not submit or give in to God's rule. Instead, he allowed sin to rule his heart. And the horrible result was that Cain killed his brother. What a horrendous, evil thing to do! **Sin is so very, very dangerous**—which is why it is so important to resist it by running to God. God knew what was in Cain's heart, and the wicked, sinful thing Cain did.

> *Then the LORD said to Cain, "Where is Abel your brother?" He said, "I do not know; am I my brother's keeper?" And the LORD said, "What have you done? The voice of your brother's blood is crying to me from the ground. And now you are cursed from the ground, which has opened its mouth to receive your brother's blood from your hand. When you work the ground, it shall no longer yield to you its strength. You shall be a fugitive and a wanderer on the earth." (Genesis 4:9-12)*

Even when God confronted Cain, Cain did not repent. He lied to God and pretended he didn't know about Abel. His heart was full of rebellion and pride. *Can you see how extremely dangerous sin is?* No consequence is too great for sin. But Cain did not admit his serious sin and repent. And he did not rightly accept the consequence for his sin. Instead, Cain complained:

> *. . ."My punishment is greater than I can bear. Behold, you have driven me today away from the ground, and from your face I shall be hidden. I shall be a fugitive and a wanderer on the earth, and whoever finds me will kill me." (Genesis 4:13-14)*

Even though Cain deserved God's fierce anger at sin and just punishment, God is not cruel. His punishments are very fair, and He shows mercy, though it is not deserved. Cain was still punished by being separated from his family and from God. But God put a mark on Cain to protect him from being killed.

Both Cain and Abel were born with a sin nature, which they received through Adam. But Abel believed what God said and trusted God's word. He had faith in God and, with God's help, he fought the sin that was crouching at his heart. His faith in God helped him to turn away from sin and follow God's desires. This is a great story of faith! But Cain did not have faith in God, so he could not rule the sin in his heart. Instead, sin ruled him. This is a very tragic story of unbelief. How very, very sad! **Without faith in God, we cannot rule over the sin in our hearts.**

> *We should not be like Cain, who was of the evil one and murdered his brother. And why did he murder him? Because his own deeds were evil and his brother's righteous. (1 John 3:12)*

Adam and Eve had lost both sons—one was killed, and one was sent away. However, in His kindness, God gave Adam and Eve another son, and they named him Seth.

Abel was a righteous man of faith, but Cain was an evil, unrepentant man. How can you tell that from this story? What warning is there in this story for us?

> By faith Abel offered to God a more acceptable sacrifice than Cain, through which he was commended as righteous, God commending him by accepting his gifts. And through his faith, though he died, he still speaks. (Hebrews 11:4)

MAKING YOU WISE FOR SALVATION

What does this chapter tell us about God? Talk about and apply the **biblical truths** in **bold** text.

Salvation Thread: Abel's faith made him acceptable to God. Cain could not please God because he was trusting in himself. Without faith, we cannot please God. *What does it mean to have faith in God?*

Tell your child about a time when you ruled over the sin in your heart. Tell your child what helped you to resist sin.

Talk About: *If you do well, will you not be accepted? And if you do not do well, sin is crouching at the door. Its desire is for you, but you must rule over it. (Genesis 4:7)*

Pray: Ask God to show you what is in your heart and to give you the faith to trust Him.

Think About: *What sin is crouching at my door? Do I truly trust that God's ways are best?*

Remember: Remember this phrase: "Rule sin, or it will rule you." Without faith, we cannot please God or rule over the sin in our hearts.

CHAPTER 7

GOD'S JUDGMENT AND MERCY

The Flood—Genesis 6-9:1

"When the bow is in the clouds, I will see it and remember the everlasting covenant between God and every living creature of all flesh that is on the earth." (Genesis 9:16)

Do you remember that Adam and Eve had another son? His name was Seth, and he was born when Adam was 130 years old. *How long do you think Adam lived after Seth was born?* He lived 800 more years and died at 930 years old! *How many children do you think he could have had in that time?* He could have had many children. Also, Cain had children. Seth had children. Adam's other children had children. And their children had children. Children were born to those children . . . until there were millions of people in the world. God's command to multiply and fill the earth was being fulfilled.

These were people created in God's image to bring glory to God by imitating or copying His goodness and wisdom. But they were also born with a sin nature passed on from Adam. Sadly, instead of turning to God, they were wicked and violent, and acted very foolishly. Things had gotten worse and worse since the Fall when sin came into the world. In those days, people lived about 800 to 900 years. *How much wickedness could a person do in that many years?* Think how such wickedness in the world grieved or saddened a good, wise, loving, and just God. Man could not be allowed to live so long. *Then the LORD said, "My Spirit shall not abide in man forever, for he is flesh: his days shall be 120 years."* God decided it was time to put an end to so much evil and wickedness.

The LORD saw that the wickedness of man was great in the earth, and that ***every intention of the thoughts of his heart was only evil continually.*** *And the LORD was sorry that he had made man on the earth, and it grieved him to his heart. So the LORD said, "I will blot out man whom I have created from the face of the land, man and animals and creeping things and birds of the heavens, for I am sorry that I have made them." But Noah found favor in the eyes of the LORD. (Genesis 6:5-8)*

One man, Noah, *was a righteous man, blameless in his generation. Noah walked with God.* God was pleased with Noah and chose him to build an ark—a boat shaped like a very large box. God gave Noah clear instructions for building the ark. He told Noah exactly how long, wide, and high to make it.[1] God told Noah to use gopher wood, and to cover the outside of the ark with pitch (a glue-like substance made from tree sap). The ark was to have three decks or floors divided into rooms. God also gave very specific instructions about the roof and the one door. The door was to be placed on the side of the ark. Noah was to bring at least one pair—male and female—of every kind of animal into the ark, along with every sort of food. With such a big boat and so many animals, wouldn't it seem like the ark should have more doors? *Why did the ark have only one entrance—only one door to salvation?*

God was sending a big flood of waters on the earth to rightly punish all the wicked people. But God would make a covenant, a very special agreement, with Noah to save Noah, his wife, and his three sons and their wives. Eight people would be saved. Why would Noah believe God and follow His instructions? Noah had never even seen anything like a flood before. But God gave Noah faith to believe Him, and Noah started to build the ark. It was a huge job. He must have had help. But even so, it took 120 years to build the ark! Cutting wood, sawing it to size, putting it together piece by piece, covering the outside of the enormous ark with pitch . . . *What do you think other people thought of Noah while he was building the ark?*

They didn't believe a flood was coming to cover the earth! They didn't have faith in God's words to Noah. Noah must have warned them of the flood and the consequences of their sin. He must have preached about God's good and right ways and told them to repent, to turn away from their sin. They probably made fun of him and thought he was crazy. But for 120 years, Noah kept building the ark, and he kept preaching to them. We know this because the New Testament calls him a "preacher of righteousness."[2]

The Bible tells us that Noah *did all that God commanded him.* He built the ark exactly as God told him. He trusted God's word, and not his own ideas. It took great faith for Noah to do what God asked. He had *faith* in God's word, even though he had never *seen* a flood. **Faith is trusting God and believing His word.**

Then the LORD said to Noah, "Go into the ark, you and all your household, for I have seen that you are righteous before me in this generation . . . For in seven days I will send rain on the earth forty days and forty nights, and every living thing that I have made I will blot out from the face of the ground." And Noah did all that the LORD had commanded him. (Genesis 7:1, 4-5)

Noah and his family and the animals entered the ark by the one door. *And the LORD shut him in. What do you think the millions of people outside the ark were thinking?* The Bible tells us that they continued eating, drinking, and doing everyday things. They were completely unaware or ignorant that destruction was coming.[3] But it did come . . . *in the second month, on the seventeenth day of the month . . . all the fountains of the great deep burst forth, and the windows of the heavens were opened. And rain fell upon the earth forty days and forty nights . . .* just like God said it would. **Every word of God is true.**

The waters covered the whole earth. They covered the houses, the trees, the hills, and even the mountains. Everything on earth was covered with the waters of **God's judgment—God's right punishment**. In His justice, God had destroyed every living thing on the earth. They were "blotted out," just as God had said. He had given the people many chances to repent. They had seen God's creation that showed His power and goodness. They knew about the punishment of Adam, Eve, and Cain. They had heard Noah's preaching.[4] But their hearts were hardened.

Only Noah and his family were saved, along with the animals. They were safe in the ark. God had saved them from destruction. After the rain stopped, the water covered the earth for a long time. It took 150 days for the water to s l o w l y seep away into the oceans. *But*

God remembered Noah and all the beasts and all the livestock that were with him in the ark. And God made a wind blow over the earth, and the waters subsided (went down). Finally, there was dry ground again. Noah, his family, and the animals could leave the ark. God, in His mercy, had saved mankind and the animals of His creation.

What do you think Noah did after leaving the ark? He made an offering to God. *Do you think he offered plants like Cain did, or an animal like Abel?* Noah, who had perfectly obeyed God's instructions in building the ark, followed God's command about offerings. He brought animals. This pleased God, and God made a wonderful promise to Noah and to all people.

> *"I establish my covenant with you, that never again shall all flesh be cut off by the waters of the flood, and never again shall there be a flood to destroy the earth." (Genesis 9:11)*

Though there may be small floods, there will never again be a worldwide flood—a flood covering the whole world. *Do you know what God did to show that He would keep His promise?* He put a rainbow in the sky. God said the rainbow is a sign of His promise and His everlasting, forever covenant between Him and every living creature. **God is perfect in every way,** and **His word is always true**.

God is a just God who will punish sin. And **God is also a merciful God**, saving eight people and every kind of animal. Noah escaped judgment and was saved because he trusted and obeyed God. The ark provided the only way of salvation from the flood and God's judgment. *The ark is one of the many hints or pictures in the Old Testament that show us the one way of salvation for us. Do you know what is the one way of salvation?*

For the LORD watches over the way of the righteous, but the way of the wicked will perish. (Psalm 1:6, NIV 1984)

MAKING YOU WISE FOR SALVATION

What does this chapter tell us about God? Talk about and apply the **biblical truths** in **bold** text.

Salvation Thread: There was only one way to escape judgment–trusting in God and entering His ark of salvation. *How does this point to Jesus? What salvation truth was God showing by only having one door to the ark?*

Though all but eight people died in the flood, God first showed great mercy before He brought judgment. *How was God merciful to people who rebelled against Him? How has God been merciful to you?*

Talk About: *"When the bow is in the clouds, I will see it and remember the everlasting covenant between God and every living creature of all flesh that is on the earth." (Genesis 9:16)*

Pray: Thank God for being a promise-keeping God. Thank Him that He is just and merciful.

Think About: God has made a way of salvation for us from eternal judgment and punishment. *Do I have faith in God's promise of salvation? Am I trusting in Christ alone?*

1. Measured in feet the ark was 450 feet long, 75 feet wide, and 45 feet high. Modern shipbuilders use approximately the same proportions today as the necessary ratios for stability.
2. 2 Peter 2:5 (NIV 1984)
3. Matthew 24:37-39
4. Because of his 930-year lifespan, Adam would have been alive when Lamech, Noah's father was born. Many generations would have heard the story of the Fall and of the punishment of Cain firsthand. And those in the time of Noah would have heard it secondhand.

C H A P T E R 8

NOW MY EYE SEES YOU

The Testing of Job—Job

"I had heard of you by the hearing of the ear, but now my eye sees you;" (Job 42:5)

Who was Job? We don't know exactly when Job lived, but we can learn much about God and about ourselves from Job's life. Job honored or *feared God and turned away from evil.* This does not mean that Job never sinned, but that he hated evil and sin. He made offerings to the LORD for his sin and the sins of his children. Job had ten children, many flocks and herds of animals, fields, and servants. He was a very important and enormously rich man.

In the book of Job, the Bible gives us a very unusual peek into what was happening in heaven. The angels came before the LORD, and Satan also showed up, even though he did not live in heaven. Satan told God he had been roaming the earth. *And the LORD said to Satan, "Have you considered my servant Job, that there is none like him on the earth, a blameless and upright man, who fears God and turns away from evil?"*

How do you think Satan, God's enemy, felt about what God said? Satan hates it when someone trusts God. His evil nature wanted to prove God wrong! He spitefully told God that Job only trusted and obeyed God because God had been so good to Job. Then Satan dared God, *"But stretch out your hand and touch all that he has, and he will curse you to your face."* God was not afraid of this challenge. **God is confident** or sure **of all He knows and does**. So, God gave Satan permission to take away all that Job had, but Satan was not allowed to hurt Job's body.

After Satan's meeting with God in heaven, four different messengers brought Job awful news. *Imagine what it must have been like for Job to hear terrible news... four times, one messenger after another!* First, his oxen and donkeys were stolen. Enemies had killed his servants in the field, and only one servant escaped. Such awful news. Then, his sheep and the servants guarding them were burned by "fire from heaven" (probably lightning). More awful news for Job. Next, other enemies stole his camels and killed the servants with them. Job had lost all his wealth through terrible tragedies. Still more terrible, awful news. But then came the worst news! A great wind came and a house fell in on his children. Every one of his children died. Such horrible, sad news. How much pain and sorrow this must have caused Job. *What do you think Job did when he got all this terrible news?*

The Bible tells us that Job fell on the ground and worshiped God! *"And he said, "The LORD gave, and the LORD has taken away; blessed be the name of the LORD." In all this Job did not sin or charge God with wrong.* Even in his grief over all his terrible losses, Job understood that he was born with nothing, and all good things were given to him by God. He did not deserve God's good blessings, and when they were taken from him, he still trusted that **God is right in all He does**.

Satan must have been furious with Job's response. His despicable plan had failed miserably! If only he could hurt Job's body. Maybe that would change Job's attitude. But Satan needed God's permission to do this. **Everything is under God's control**. So, Satan went to God again. This time, he said that Job would curse God if he suffered pain and sickness. God knew this was not true. Satan was wrong. So, God gave Satan permission to make Job sick, but Satan was not allowed to kill Job.

Aha! This time Satan determined that he would win! He gave Job terrible, painful sores over his entire body. Now Job's wife was angry. She couldn't understand how Job could still trust God. Job had already suffered so much! She bitterly told Job to curse God and die. But, in faith, Job answered:

> *"Shall we receive good from God, and shall we not receive evil?"* (Job 2:10b)

Satan was actually the one who brought evil on Job. **God is good,** and He cannot do anything evil. God is continually holding back the evil in this broken, fallen world. But sometimes, God allows or even directs man and Satan to carry out their evil deeds to accomplish His good purposes. God does not always hold evil back, but no evil can happen apart from God's control.

Job's three friends came to comfort him. They saw that his suffering was great and tried to understand why Job was suffering. They told him that he must have sinned greatly. But Job said he was innocent of such terrible sin. Job's suffering was so great that he wished he had never been born. At times, he doubted God's goodness as he struggled to trust God. His friends kept trying to convince Job that God was punishing him for some great wrong he had done. But Job was sure that he was innocent. Finally, Job asked God to defend him and to explain why he was suffering so much. He felt angry that God did not stop his suffering. To Job, God seemed far away and unconcerned.

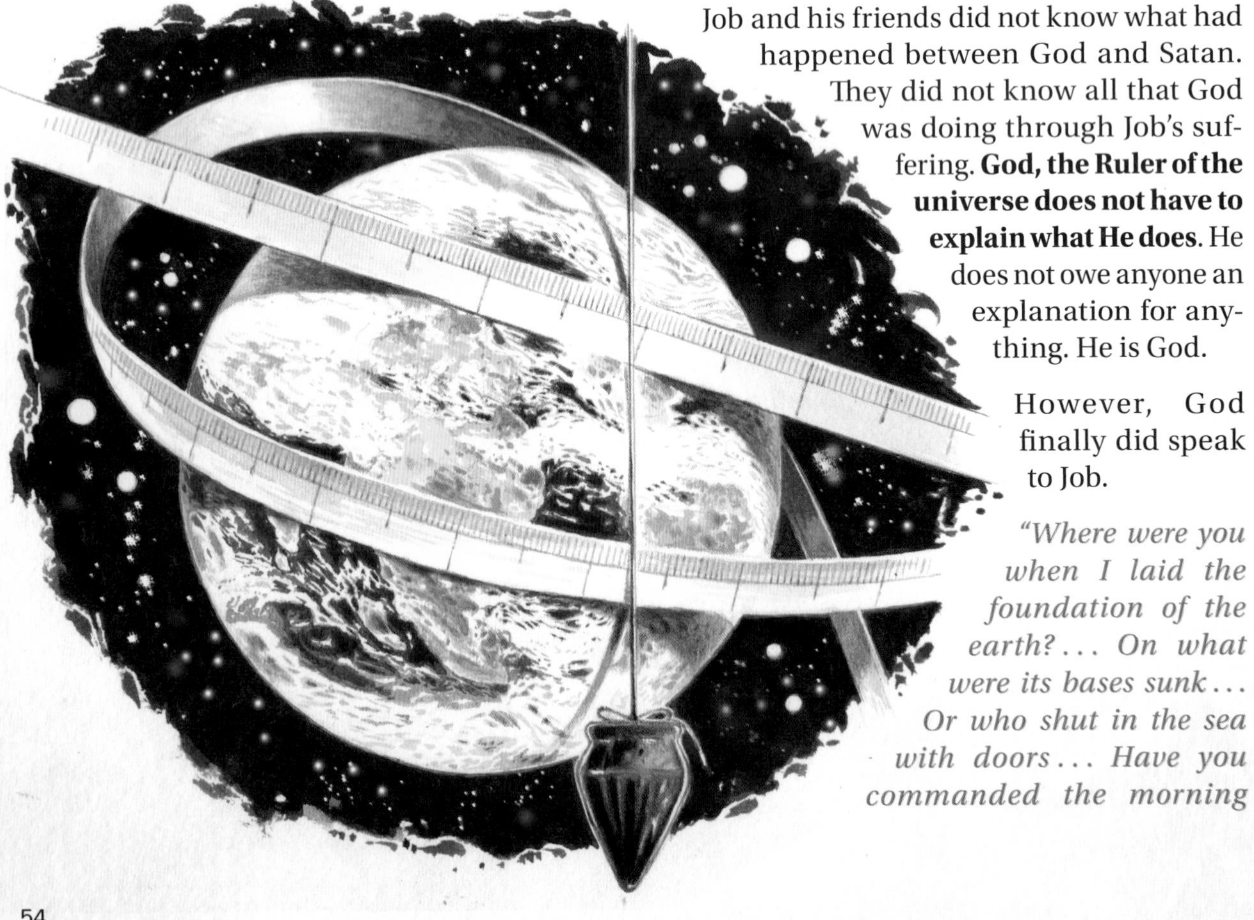

Job and his friends did not know what had happened between God and Satan. They did not know all that God was doing through Job's suffering. **God, the Ruler of the universe does not have to explain what He does.** He does not owe anyone an explanation for anything. He is God.

However, God finally did speak to Job.

> *"Where were you when I laid the foundation of the earth?... On what were its bases sunk... Or who shut in the sea with doors... Have you commanded the morning*

since your days began . . . Where is the way to the dwelling of light, and where is the place of darkness . . . Have you entered the storehouses of the snow, or have you seen the storehouses of the hail . . . Can you send forth lightnings, that they may go and say to you, 'Here we are'? . . . [Who has] given understanding to the mind? Who can number the clouds by wisdom? . . . Do you know when the mountain goats give birth? . . . Do you give the horse his might? Do you clothe his neck with a mane? . . . Is it by your understanding that the hawk soars and spreads his wings toward the south? Is it at your command that the eagle mounts up and makes his nest on high?" (selections from Job 38-39)

God never told Job why he had to suffer. He simply used these questions and many others to show Job there were many things Job did not know or understand. Job didn't know the whole story. He couldn't see what God saw or know what God knows. It is enough to know who God is and that He has greater understanding than we do. **God always has good purposes for what He does.** Job finally understood this and humbly repented of his pride.

God's power, wisdom, and goodness are sure. He is the Creator who has freely given all good things. He has the right to do as He pleases. He made this clear to Job:

"Who has first given to me, that I should repay him? Whatever is under the whole heaven is mine." (Job 41:11)

Though God didn't tell Job why he suffered, God did something better. He showed Job that though His wisdom, power, greatness, and goodness is more than we can understand, we can always trust Him to do what is best. *Then Job answered the LORD and said:*

"I know that you can do all things, and that no purpose of yours can be thwarted. 'Who is this that hides counsel without knowledge?' Therefore I have uttered what I did not understand, things too wonderful for me, which I did not know . . . I had heard of you by the hearing of the ear, but now my eye sees you; therefore I despise myself, and repent in dust and ashes." (Job 42:1-3, 5-6)

Job had known about God, but now he had the personal experience of seeing the greatness and majesty of God. He clearly saw that **God is sovereign—He has the right, wisdom, and power to do all He pleases**. Job said that **God is wise—He causes everything to work out perfectly**. And he said that **God is good in all He is and does.** Job understood that God has the right to govern His world and His people, and all His works are right and good. In the end, Job repented of demanding an explanation, and he prayed for his friends. All that Job learned about God is perfectly true! God is so good that He gave Job twice as much as he had before. *And the LORD blessed the latter days of Job more than his beginning.* God gave Job more wealth than he had before, ten more children, and *in all the land there were no women so beautiful as Job's daughters.* Best of all, Job gained a deeper understanding of God and His great wisdom.

Satan was wrong. Job did not serve God because of the good things God gave him. Job worshiped God because **God is God and is worthy of worship**. Job's friends were wrong, too. Job's sin was not the cause of Job's suffering. God was working out His perfect and wise plan to teach Job—and us—that He is sovereign, wise, and good.

Suffering can't always be explained, but we must trust God's goodness, wisdom, and sovereign power, even when we don't understand what is happening. *Do you recognize that your understanding of what is going on in the world and in your life is very limited? Why is this so? What does this tell you about your need to trust in God?*

MAKING YOU WISE FOR SALVATION

What does this chapter tell us about God? Talk about and apply the **biblical truths** in **bold** text.

Salvation Thread: God uses suffering to bring about His good purposes. In his suffering, Job would not curse God; Job trusted God. One day, God would allow His Son to suffer horrifically to bring about the greatest good to man. His Son would willingly suffer, trusting the wisdom and goodness of His Father.

Tell your child about a time when you suffered. Explain to your child how God brought about something good from the situation. Did you understand it at the time?

Talk About: *"I had heard of you by the hearing of the ear, but now my eye sees you;" (Job 42:5)*

Pray: Thank God that He can be trusted to know what is best for you. Ask God for a humble heart that trusts Him.

Think About: *We can know a lot about God, but we learn to trust Him more through experiences He brings into our lives.*

C H A P T E R 9

GOD SCATTERS THE PEOPLE

Tower of Babel—Genesis 11

It is he who sits above the circle of the earth, and its inhabitants are like grasshoppers; (Isaiah 40:22a)

D*o you remember how many people lived through the flood?* Just eight. That is not very many people to *"multiply and fill the earth"*! But Noah's sons, Shem, Ham, and Japheth, and their wives, had children. Then Noah's sons had more children, who had children. Once again, men and women began to "multiply," but they weren't interested in "filling the earth" as God had commanded. They traveled to a plain (a flat land) in Shinar and decided to stay there. Then they decided to make bricks and build a city and a high tower. They were definitely *not* going to "fill the earth." Instead of doing what God told them to do, they thought they had a better idea. Instead of worshiping or honoring God as the Most High, they wanted to prove their own greatness. Like Adam and Eve, they wanted to *be* God. They

wanted to "make a name" for themselves—to show themselves as great. And they would do this by making a tower so high that its top would be in the heavens. They would also build a great city so they could all stay together. *What do you think of their idea?*

Not only was their idea foolish, but *they* were foolish to think that they could stand against God's plans. They were foolish to think they could make a great name for themselves, rather than show God's greatness and worth. This is what the Bible tells us about God and about man:

> *It is he who sits above the circle of the earth, and its inhabitants are like grasshoppers; (Isaiah 40:22a)*

God is sovereign—He rules over everything. Compared to God, men are like tiny grasshoppers! God saw the tower the people had started to build, and He said, *"Behold, they are one people, and they have all one language, and this is only the beginning of what they will do."* God knew they would find more and more ways to dishonor Him and disobey Him. The people would not help each other do what is right and good.

To show these proud people that they were like grasshoppers, and to stop their rebellious plan, God confused their language—He gave them different languages so they couldn't understand each other. One person might say, "Voíthisé me."[1] Another might say, "Adiuva me."[2] But neither understood that they were asking each other for help. If they couldn't help each other, how could they work together? How could the tall, magnificent tower get built? It couldn't. God had stopped them from building it. **No one can stand against God's purposes. God always wins.**

But God did more than stop the building of the tower and city. He also scattered the people. If you took a handful of sand and threw it into the ocean, or a handful of seeds and threw them across a garden, the sand or seeds would go in all directions. They wouldn't stay together. That is just what happened to the people when God changed their languages. They couldn't understand each other, so they didn't stay together. They moved away in different directions to fill the earth as God had commanded them. They proudly thought they had a better way, but God's way was best... and they could not stand against the almighty God. The place where God confused the language of all the earth was called Babel, which later became Babylon.

Everyone likes to feel most important, but we must remember that compared to God we are like tiny grasshoppers. We can never stand against God's plans and win. **We were created to honor God and show His greatness and worth.** *How do people try to make a name for themselves today? What is the difference between making a name for yourself and showing others that God is great and worthy of our praise?*

So, whether you eat or drink, or whatever you do,
do all to the glory of God. (1 Corinthians 10:31)

MAKING YOU WISE FOR SALVATION

What does this chapter tell us about God? Talk about and apply the **biblical truths** in **bold** text.

Salvation Thread: At Babel, the people wanted to show their greatness and make a name for themselves. But God created man for His glory—to show His greatness and worth. You were created to know, trust, and love God most of all and bring Him glory.

How do people try to show that they are important (that they want "to make a name for themselves)? How can you show that God is great and most important? Give an example. Explain 1 Corinthians 10:31.

Tell your child about a time when you were able to share with someone the greatness and worth of God.

Talk About: *It is he who sits above the circle of the earth, and its inhabitants are like grasshoppers; (Isaiah 40:22a)*

Pray: Praise God for being mighty and sovereign (in control of all things). Confess how you have dishonored or rebelled against Him.

Think About: *Am I more concerned about making God's greatness known, or bringing attention to myself? Do I recognize that God is sovereign—He has the right, wisdom, and power to do all He pleases—and humbly submit to Him?*

Apply: *What should I think? Be? Do?*

1. Greek for "Give me a hand."
2. Latin for "Help me."

C H A P T E R 1 0

GOD'S CALL AND PROMISE

The Call of Abram—Genesis 12-13

..."Abraham believed God, and it was counted to him as righteousness." (Romans 4:3b)

When we read Bible stories, we read about a lot of strange places. Those places still exist today but they have different names. Babel was in the country that is now called Iraq. When people left Babel, they went in all directions—north, south, east, and west. Do you remember that all these people were descendants of Noah and his sons Shem, Ham, and Japheth? *Do you know what a descendant is?* A descendant is someone who comes from a particular family. For example, you "descended" or came from your father. You are his descendant or child. You are also your grandfather's descendant, part of his family. Everyone in your family who comes after you will be your descendants. Descendants are all part of the same family. For example, Shem had sons who had sons who had sons . . . all belonging to the same family. Terah was part of Shem's family. Then Terah had a son who was born into his family. Terah's son or descendant was Abram.[1]

Terah decided to leave his home near Babel to travel to a land called Canaan. Terah brought with him his son Abram, his grandson, Lot—who was Abram's nephew—and Abram's wife, Sarai. However, Terah never got to Canaan. Instead, when he got to Haran, in the country that is now called Turkey, he decided to stay there with his family.

Terah and his family were not worshipers of the one true God. Instead, they worshiped many false gods.[2] But when Abram was seventy-five years old, God Almighty spoke to Abram! God showed amazing grace to Abram and chose him from all the peoples of the earth! He gave Abram a *call* (a special command) and a *promise:*

> *Now the LORD said to Abram, "Go from your country and your kindred and your father's house to the land that I will show you. And I will make of you a great nation, and I will bless you and make your name great, so that you will be a blessing. I will bless those who bless you, and him who dishonors you I will curse, and in you all the families of the earth shall be blessed." (Genesis 12:1-3)*

God *called* Abram to obey Him and leave his home and go to an unknown land—a land Abram had never seen. He also gave Abram some promises. *Can you find the promises in Genesis 12?* They start with God's words, "I will." We will see in the next few stories that God's promises are about a *land*, a *nation*, and a *blessing*.

The Bible says that *Abram believed God, and it was counted to him as righteousness.*[3] This means Abram trusted God; he packed up his family, animals, and servants, and he set off for Canaan,[4] the land God promised him. It was a long journey, but when Abram arrived in Canaan, God repeated His promise, *"To your offspring [descendants] I will give this land."* So Abram built an altar—a place to make sacrifices and to worship God. Abram, who once worshiped false gods, was now a worshiper of the one true God.

But there came a famine in the land, a time when there was not enough food for the people. So, Abram, Sarai, Lot, and their servants packed up again and went to Egypt where there was food. However, there was a problem—Abram's wife, Sarai, was a very beautiful woman. That doesn't sound like a problem, but it was. Abram was afraid that if the Egyptians knew Sarai was his wife, they would kill him to take Sarai for themselves. *Do you know what Abram told Sarai to do?* He told her to tell the Egyptians that she was his *sister.* If the Egyptians didn't know Abram was really Sarai's husband, they would not have to kill Abram to take Sarai as a wife. *Do you think this was a good plan? Why do you think that?*

God had promised to give Abram many descendants and to make them into a great nation. Certainly, God would protect Abram and his descendants because **God always keeps His promises.** Abram was afraid of what the Egyptians might do, but God knew about Abram and the Egyptians, and no problem is too hard for God. Abram did not need to lie; he just needed to trust God.

Can you guess what happened? The Egyptian king, who was called Pharaoh, saw how beautiful Sarai was. He gave gifts to Abram . . . and he took Sarai to be his wife! Now what? The problem just got bigger! But certainly, it was not a problem for God! **God is all-powerful, all-knowing, and faithful. God is also kind**, and He rescued Abram, Sarai . . . and Pharaoh. He sent "great plagues" or sicknesses to Pharaoh and those in his house. Then Pharaoh knew something was wrong. He discovered that Sarai was Abram's wife and gave her back to Abram. He didn't want someone else's wife. He also gave orders to keep them safe in their travels back to Canaan.

It was wrong of Abram to lie instead of trusting God. But God still protected Abram and rescued Sarai because God had promised to make of them a great nation. With perfect wisdom and power, God saved Abram and Sarai and once again showed them that He can be trusted.

Abram, Sarai, and Lot returned to Canaan, the land God promised to give Abram. By now, they had so many flocks of sheep and goats, herds of cows, and servants that they could not live in the same place. Abram let Lot choose which part of the land he wanted. The Jordan Valley had lots of fresh water and green plants for animals to eat. It looked very good to Lot, so he chose this beautiful land and moved close to the city of Sodom.

The LORD said to Abram, after Lot had separated from him, "Lift up your eyes and look from the place where you are, northward and southward and eastward and westward, for all the land that you see I will give to you and to your offspring forever. I will make your offspring as the dust of the earth, so that if one can count the dust of the earth, your offspring also can be counted." (Genesis 13:14-16)

God promised to give Abram land in all directions. God would give this land to Abram and his descendants forever. What an amazing, generous promise! So, Abram took the land that Lot did not choose, put up his tents, and built an altar to the LORD.

Abram showed his faith in the one true God when he obeyed God and left his home. Then Abram saw God's faithfulness in protecting Sarai and him from Pharaoh and bringing them safely back to Canaan. This made Abram's faith in God stronger. Little by little, Abram was learning to trust God more and more. God considered Abram righteous or blameless because of his faith.

You, too, can become righteous through faith, even though you may not be born a descendant of Abraham. *Have you put your faith in the one true God—the God of Abraham? How do you demonstrate this faith? Faith is a gift from God. Have you asked God to give you a growing faith and trust in Him?*

Know then that it is those of faith who are the sons of Abraham. (Galatians 3:7)

MAKING YOU WISE FOR SALVATION

What does this chapter tell us about God? Talk about and apply the **biblical truths** in **bold** text.

Salvation Thread: *Abram believed God, and it was counted to him as righteousness.* A person becomes right before God through faith.

Tell your child about a time when God showed you His faithfulness.

Talk About: *Know then that it is those of faith who are the sons of Abraham. (Galatians 3:7)* (Make sure your child understands that righteousness comes through faith in God, not by being born into the "right family.")

Pray: Thank God for His many promises in His Word. Thank Him that He always keeps His promises. Ask God for the faith to trust Him and believe His Word.

Think About: Abram lied to "solve" his problem instead of trusting God. *How have I tried to solve my problems this week? Is the way I solve problems honoring to God?*

1. There were ten generations from Adam to Noah, and ten generations from Shem to Abram.
2. Joshua 24:2
3. Romans 4:3, Galatians 3:6, and James 2:23
4. Modern-day Israel and parts of the surrounding region.

AN EVERLASTING COVENANT

Abrahamic Covenant—Genesis 15-17

"…I will establish my covenant between me and you and your offspring after you throughout their generations for an everlasting covenant, to be God to you and to your offspring after you." (Genesis 17:7)

Abram was in a strange situation. God had promised that from Abram He would make a great nation with so many people or descendants that they couldn't be counted. But there was a problem. *Do you know what the problem was?* Abram didn't have any children (or "offspring"). How could he be the father of a great nation if he didn't have even one child? Would a servant in his house be his "heir" and inherit or receive all his animals, wealth, and God's blessing when he died? Or would he have a son?

God had a great plan and great promises for Abram. He told Abram that Abram's very own son, not his servant, would be his heir. His own son would be the beginning of the great nation promised by God to Abram. One night, God brought Abram outside and said:

> *… "Look toward heaven, and number the stars, if you are able to number them." Then he said to him, "So shall your offspring be." And he believed the LORD, and he counted it to him as righteousness. (Genesis 15:5-6)*

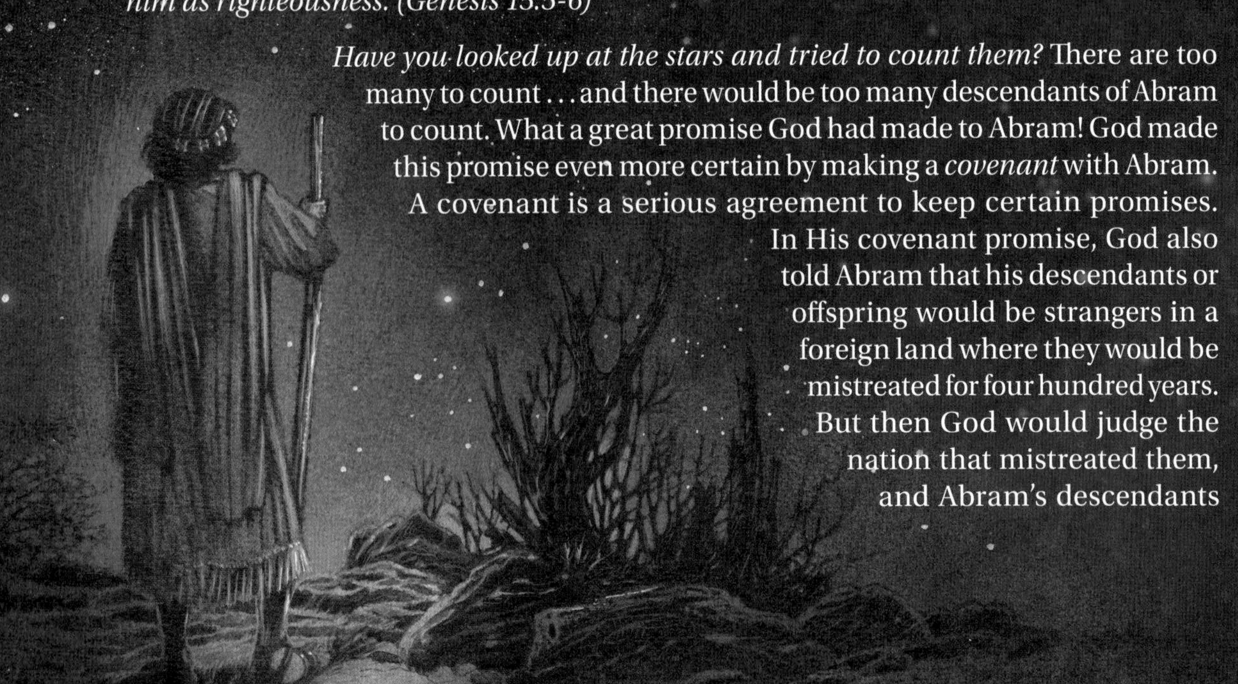

Have you looked up at the stars and tried to count them? There are too many to count…and there would be too many descendants of Abram to count. What a great promise God had made to Abram! God made this promise even more certain by making a *covenant* with Abram. A covenant is a serious agreement to keep certain promises. In His covenant promise, God also told Abram that his descendants or offspring would be strangers in a foreign land where they would be mistreated for four hundred years. But then God would judge the nation that mistreated them, and Abram's descendants would leave with many possessions (animals and wealth). Abram believed God's word; he trusted God, and his faith made him righteous, or acceptable, to God.

Still, Abram had no children, and Sarai was getting impatient. So she decided to do something about it! She gave Abram her Egyptian servant, Hagar, as another wife, so Abram might have a child. This was not right, but she did it anyway. Hagar got pregnant and was proud that she was carrying Abram's child. *Do you think this made Sarai happy?* Not at all! Instead, Sarai was angry and jealous, even though it had been her idea for Abram to take another wife to give him a child. Sarai was so angry that she treated Hagar very harshly, so harshly that Hagar ran away into the wilderness.

What would happen to Hagar and her baby? The God who sees all saw Hagar in the wilderness and sent an angel to her. The angel told her to return to Sarai and obey her. But that wasn't the whole message from God. Hagar would have a son, whom she should name Ishmael or "God hears." God had listened to and understood Hagar's difficulties. *So she called the name of the LORD who spoke to her, "You are a God of seeing," for she said, "Truly here I have seen him who looks after me."* **God is a "God of seeing"—a God who is full of compassion, or kindness.** He watches over everything in this world. Nothing goes unnoticed by Him.

> *For the eyes of the LORD run to and fro throughout the whole earth, to give strong support to those whose heart is blameless toward him. (2 Chronicles 16:9a)*

Hagar obeyed the word of the LORD and returned to Abram and Sarai. She had her baby boy. And just as she had been commanded, she named him Ishmael. Now at eighty-six years old, Abram had a son, a descendant. But this was not God's plan; it was Abram's and Sarai's plan to try to have a son their own way. Ishmael was the son of a slave woman; he was not the son of God's promise to Abram.

When Abram was ninety-nine years old, God appeared to Abram again. Once again, God reminded Abram of His covenant promises.

> *"Behold, my covenant is with you, and you shall be the father of a multitude of nations. No longer shall your name be called Abram, but your name shall be Abraham, for I have made you the father of a multitude of nations. I will make you exceedingly fruitful, and I will make you into nations, and kings shall come from you. And I will establish my covenant between me and you and your offspring after you throughout their generations for an everlasting covenant, to be God to you and to your offspring after you. And I will give to you and to your offspring after you the land of your sojournings, all the land of Canaan, for an everlasting possession, and I will be their God." (Genesis 17:4-8)*

What an amazing promise God pledged to Abraham again! Abraham would inherit or receive the Promised Land of Canaan. He would have many descendants. And, as God promised earlier, he would be a great blessing to all the nations of the world! Best of all, God would be his God. He would be his Helper, his Protector, his Provider, and his Friend—to Abraham and to his offspring. *How long would this covenant last?* It was an everlasting covenant—a forever covenant of promises that God would surely keep.

God also changed Sarai's name to Sarah, and He promised to give Sarah a son. *What do you think Abraham thought about that? Then Abraham fell on his face and laughed and said to himself, "Shall a child be born to a man who is a hundred years old? Shall Sarah, who is ninety years old, bear a child?"* After the flood, people as old as Abraham and Sarah did not have babies! That would be like your grandma and grandpa having a baby . . . or your great grandma and grandpa! This was impossible! Surely, it was a better idea, Abraham thought, for God to make His promise come true through Ishmael. But that was not God's way . . .

> *God said, "No, but Sarah your wife shall bear you a son, and you shall call his name Isaac. I will establish my covenant with him as an everlasting covenant for his offspring after him." (Genesis 17:19)*

God would still bless Ishmael because he was born from Abraham. But he was not the promised child. He was not the chosen one of God. God was very firm about this.

> *". . . I will establish my covenant with Isaac, whom Sarah shall bear to you at this time next year." (Genesis 17:21)*

Sarah laughed when she heard God's promise that she would have a son. She was ninety years old. She was "worn out," and Abraham was "old." How could this possibly happen? Surely, this could not be true!

But it was true. God not only makes promises, but **He fulfills all His promises. God does everything He says He will do**. Sure enough, just as God had said, ninety-year-old Sarah became pregnant! Something impossible and miraculous had happened—something only God could do!

Why is nothing impossible for God? What proof do you have of your answer? What does this tell you about whether God can be trusted?

. . . "What is impossible with man is possible with God." (Luke 18:27)

MAKING YOU WISE FOR SALVATION

What does this chapter tell us about God? Talk about and apply the **biblical truths** in **bold** text.

Salvation Thread: God was calling a people to be in His family through Abraham. God is still calling people to be His children. *Do you have to be a descendant of Abraham to be in God's family? How does a person become a child of Abraham? How does a person become accepted by God as righteous?*

Tell your child about a time when God did something impossible (either from the Bible, in your life, or in the life of someone else.)

Talk About: *". . . I will establish my covenant between me and you and your offspring after you throughout their generations for an everlasting covenant, to be God to you and to your offspring after you." (Genesis 17:7)*

Why do you think God repeated His promise to Abraham? How could this help Abraham to keep believing God's promise? (God made His promise to Abraham four times–Genesis 12, 15, 17, and 22. This repetition shows how important this promise is.)

Pray: Praise God that He always keeps His promises. Ask Him to help you to trust Him even when you have to wait a long time for an answer to prayer or to see His work in a situation.

Think About: *What does it mean to have God as "my God"?*

Memorize: Luke 18:27

CHAPTER 12

GOD IS MERCIFUL AND COMPASSIONATE

Rescue of Lot and Destruction of Sodom and Gomorrah—Genesis 18-19

The LORD is gracious and merciful, slow to anger and abounding in steadfast love. The LORD is good to all, and his mercy is over all that he has made. (Psalm 145:8-9)

D*o you remember what land Lot chose?* He chose the beautiful land of the Jordan Valley and made his home near the city of Sodom. The people of Sodom and the nearby city of Gomorrah were very wicked, doing all sorts of evil things that God hates. They did not follow God's ways or trust in God. God had been very patient with them, but the people had proven that their hearts were hardened. They kept sinning instead of turning away from sin. They were like the people in the days of Noah. **God is good, just, and holy, so He cannot ignore sin.** Because the sin of the people was so great, God decided it was time to send judgment on them.

Judgment was coming! Would God tell Abraham about this? What would happen to Abraham's nephew, Lot?

The LORD said, "Shall I hide from Abraham what I am about to do, seeing that Abraham shall surely become a great and mighty nation, and all the nations of the earth shall be blessed in him? For I have chosen him, that he may command his children and his household after him to

> *keep the way of the LORD by doing righteousness and justice, so that the LORD may bring to Abraham what he has promised him." (Genesis 18:17-19)*

God had chosen Abraham to be the father of many nations and to be a blessing to the whole world. Abraham was to teach his descendants to follow God and to do what is right and just. So, God would not hide from Abraham what He was going to do. He told Abraham that the sin of Sodom and Gomorrah was so great that He must put an end to it.

Abraham knew that **God is just and good**. God would be right to destroy the wicked. But Abraham also knew that **God is merciful**. So, Abraham said to the LORD,

> *"Will you indeed sweep away the righteous with the wicked? Suppose there are fifty righteous within the city. Will you then sweep away the place and not spare it for the fifty righteous who are in it? Far be it from you to do such a thing, to put the righteous to death with the wicked, so that the righteous fare as the wicked! Far be that from you! Shall not the Judge of all the earth do what is just?" (Genesis 18:23-25)*

Abraham was pleading with God to spare the righteous. *What do you think God said?* He could have told Abraham that there would be no mercy. But He didn't. He said that He would spare, or save, the whole city of Sodom if there were only fifty righteous people! **God is patient—He is slow to anger and slow to punish.** He patiently calls people to repent. But God also knows that some people will refuse to repent, and there comes a time when God must punish them.

Maybe there weren't fifty righteous people. What if there were five less? Abraham decided to ask God to spare the city if there were only forty-five instead of fifty. God said He would spare the city if there were only forty-five righteous people . . . or forty . . . or thirty . . . or twenty . . . or even ten! It is amazing that God would save the whole city from being destroyed if there were only ten people who trusted Him and loved what is right! **God is merciful and kind to undeserving sinners.**

But sadly, there were not even ten people in Sodom who turned from sin to love God and do what is right. So, Sodom would be destroyed because of the great wickedness of the people.

What about Abraham's nephew Lot? He lived in Sodom. Would he be destroyed? God is faithful, and He showed His kindness toward Abraham by sending two angels to warn Lot. The angels told Lot to take his family and quickly leave Sodom before it was destroyed. This was serious! They had to get away fast! But the Bible tells us that Lot "lingered." That means that he dawdled, hesitated, or took his time. Maybe he was thinking of the great wealth he would lose when the city was destroyed. Everything he had would be gone. He wasn't leaving quickly . . . and destruction was coming!

> *. . . So the men seized him and his wife and his two daughters by the hand, the LORD being merciful to him, and they brought him out and set him outside the city. And as they brought them out, one said, "Escape for your life. Do not look back or stop anywhere in the valley. Escape to the hills, lest you be swept away." (Genesis 19:16-17)*

> *Then the LORD rained on Sodom and Gomorrah sulfur and fire from the LORD out of heaven. And he overthrew those cities, and all the valley, and all the inhabitants of the cities, and what grew on the ground. (Genesis 19:24-25)*

Everything that God does, He does with just or right judgment. These were very wicked people who refused to turn from their sin. God had been very patient with them, but they continued in their wickedness and unbelief. However, Lot and his family escaped. They were safe as long as they ran to the hills and did not look back. What kindness God had shown them!

> *But Lot's wife, behind him, looked back, and she became a pillar of salt. (Genesis 19:26)*

What a startling judgment on Lot's wife! What would it be like to be turned into salt? Why did Lot's wife disobey God and look back to Sodom? Did she not trust God's warning? Was rebellion in her heart? The Bible doesn't exactly tell us what she was thinking or what was in her heart, but later in the Bible, Jesus warns,

> *"Remember Lot's wife. Whoever seeks to preserve his life will lose it, but whoever loses his life will keep it." (Luke 17:32-33)*

Jesus' warning is about loving earthly things and this life more than loving spiritual things. It seems that Lot's wife was upset about the things she was losing, instead of being grateful for the rescue from destruction. She was looking back to her life in evil Sodom, rather than to the better life God had for her away from wickedness. She desired Sodom, the things she owned, and her old way of life more than she desired God.

Lot's wife is a good warning to us to love God more than anything in this world—to look for the joy of knowing, trusting, loving, and obeying God, to believe that **God is the greatest treasure.**

Do not love the world or the things in the world. If anyone loves the world, the love of the Father is not in him. For all that is in the world—the desires of the flesh and the desires of the eyes and pride in possessions—is not from the Father but is from the world. (1 John 2:15-16)

God is both merciful and just. The people of Sodom and Gomorrah did not turn away from their sin and turn to God. They deserved God's fierce anger and right punishment... and they were destroyed. God was eager to show mercy and would have saved the cities if only ten righteous people lived there. But there weren't even ten righteous people. There were not even ten people who loved and trusted God. There were not even ten people who wanted the things of God more than worldly things.

Lot believed that God would do what He said He would do, and he escaped God's judgment. Abraham had faith in God. He believed that God is who He says He is—that He is wise, good, and powerful; faithful, always keeping His promises; merciful and forgiving; and just and right in all He does. And God, in His love for Abraham, spared Lot and his family.

So it was that, when God destroyed the cities of the valley, God remembered Abraham and sent Lot out of the midst of the overthrow when he overthrew the cities in which Lot had lived. (Genesis 19:29)

What comfort is there in this story? What warning is there? Does this story give you encouragement or fear? Why?

The wicked are overthrown and are no more, but the house of the righteous will stand. (Proverbs 12:7)

MAKING YOU WISE FOR SALVATION

What does this chapter tell us about God? Talk about and apply the **biblical truths** in **bold** text.

Salvation Thread: God is just and will punish unrepentant sinners. He is also merciful and will receive anyone who trusts in Him.

Talk about how God is both merciful and just. *What does this story show you about the judgment of God and the kindness of God?*

Talk About: *"The LORD is gracious and merciful, slow to anger and abounding in steadfast love. The LORD is good to all, and his mercy is over all that he has made." (Psalm 145:8-9)*

Pray: Thank God for being both merciful and just. Ask Him to give you the faith to believe that He is who He says He is, and that He will always keep His Word.

Think About: The destruction of Sodom and Gomorrah is an example to us of what happens to the ungodly (2 Peter 2:6). Why is it good of God to give us this example? Why is it good that God punishes wickedness or evil? Where do you see God's mercy in the world today?

Memorize: Psalm 145:8-9

CHAPTER 13

THE PROMISED SON AND THE SUBSTITUTE SACRIFICE

Birth of Isaac; Abraham's Test and God's Provision —Genesis 21-22

Now faith is the assurance of things hoped for, the conviction of things not seen. (Hebrews 11:1)

Ninety-year-old Sarah was getting bigger and bigger! Abraham's baby was definitely almost ready to be born. Sure enough, at just the time God had said it would happen, Sarah gave birth to a baby boy! God was keeping His promise. From this descendant of Abraham would come a whole nation—a nation that would be a blessing to all peoples. Abraham was one hundred years old and had waited twenty-five years for this son! He named this promised son Isaac or "laughter."[1] What a happy time this was! God had given Abraham a son! **God always keeps His promises.**

God is not man, that he should lie, or a son of man, that he should change his mind. Has he said, and will he not do it? Or has he spoken, and will he not fulfill it? (Numbers 23:19)

The birth of Isaac was a miracle from an all-powerful, promise-keeping God. Think of how much joy and laughter Isaac must have brought to Abraham and Sarah. They must have really loved their miracle baby. God was so good to give them this special son in their old age. Yet one day, when Isaac was older, probably when he was a young man . . .

... God tested Abraham and said to him, "Abraham!" And he said, "Here am I." He said, "Take your son, your only son Isaac, whom you love, and go to the land of Moriah, and offer him there as a burnt offering on one of the mountains of which I shall tell you." (Genesis 22:1-2)

Offer Isaac as a sacrifice? How could Abraham do this? What God was telling Abraham to do did not make sense. God had made an everlasting covenant with Abraham that a great nation would come from this promised son. Through his descendants, all the nations of the world would be blessed. Isaac had to get married and have children. Those children would need to have children ... and more children would have to come from those children ... until they became a great nation. God's plan to make a great nation couldn't happen if Isaac was dead! Was this a mistake?

God never makes mistakes. God was testing Abraham. Would Abraham trust and obey God ... or would he question God, argue with Him, and rebel? Did Abraham love God most of all, or did he love Isaac more? Did Abraham believe God's promise and trust that God has a way when things look impossible? *What do you think Abraham did?*

... Abraham rose early in the morning, saddled his donkey, and took two of his young men with him, and his son Isaac. And he cut the wood for the burnt offering and arose and went to the place of which God had told him. (Genesis 22:3)

They traveled to the land of Moriah and, on the third day of their travels, Abraham and Isaac went alone up the mountain. Isaac carried the wood, and Abraham carried the fire and the knife. But Isaac knew that something was missing. *What was it?*

And Isaac said to his father Abraham ... "Behold, the fire and the wood, but where is the lamb for a burnt offering?" Abraham said, "God will provide for himself the lamb for a burnt offering, my son." (Genesis 22:7-8a)

Do you remember why people in the Old Testament offered sacrifices or offerings? Sacrifices were a temporary covering for sin. They did not take away a person's sin, but the death of an animal sacrifice made a way for sinners to have a relationship with the holy God.

Abraham built an altar (a place to make sacrifices) and laid the wood on it . . . What would he do next? Would he trust God? . . . Then Abraham tied Isaac to the altar on top of the wood. How agonizing this must have been! What must Abraham be feeling? What must Isaac have thought? . . . Then Abraham took the knife to kill his beloved son . . . How could Abraham do this?

> *By faith Abraham, when he was tested, offered up Isaac, and he who had received the promises was in the act of offering up his only son, of whom it was said, "Through Isaac shall your offspring be named." He considered that God was able even to raise him from the dead . . . (Hebrews 11:17-19a)*

Abraham had faith in God. God had proven to be a promise-keeping God. God had shown His faithfulness in protecting them in Egypt. God had shown His power by giving Abraham a child when he and Sarah were too old to have children. God had shown Himself as good, faithful, and right in all He does. Even if it meant that God would raise Isaac from the dead, Abraham had faith that God would keep His promise and fulfill His purposes. So, Abraham raised the knife . . .

> *But the angel of the LORD called to him from heaven and said, "Abraham, Abraham!" And he said, "Here am I." He said, "Do not lay your hand on the boy or do anything to him, for now I know that you fear God, seeing you have not withheld your son, your only son, from me." (Genesis 22:11-12)*

Then Abraham looked up and saw a ram (a male sheep) caught in the bushes. God had provided a *substitute*—something to take Isaac's place! Isaac would live! The ram would be sacrificed instead of Isaac. The blood of the ram would be the offering for sin.

> *. . . And Abraham went and took the ram and offered it up as a burnt offering instead of his son. So Abraham called the name of that place, "The LORD will provide". . . (Genesis 22:13b-14a)*

Abraham had passed the test. God had proven Himself to be a faithful God once again. Once again, God reminded Abraham of the covenant God made with him. Abraham could be sure that God would keep His promise.

> *And the angel of the LORD called to Abraham a second time from heaven and said, "By myself I have sworn, declares the LORD, because you have done this and have not withheld your son, your only son, I will surely bless you, and I will surely multiply your offspring as the stars of heaven and as the sand that is on the seashore. And your offspring shall possess the gate of his enemies, and in your offspring shall all the nations of the earth be blessed, because you have obeyed my voice." (Genesis 22:15-18)*

Little by little, as God showed Himself to be faithful, Abraham's faith and confidence in God grew greater and greater. God is still showing Himself to be a faithful God. *How has God shown Himself to be faithful to you? Do you have a growing faith in God?*

And without faith it is impossible to please him, for whoever would draw near to God must believe that he exists and that he rewards those who seek him. (Hebrews 11:6)

MAKING YOU WISE FOR SALVATION

What does this chapter tell us about God? Talk about and apply the **biblical truths** in **bold** text.

Salvation Thread: Faith is believing that God is who He says He is, and that what He promises He will do. *What do you know about God? Is knowing the same as believing?*

What are some good reasons for God to wait so long to keep His promise to give Abraham a son?[2] How does this story help us to trust that God will keep His promises?

Talk About: *Now faith is the assurance of things hoped for, the conviction of things not seen. (Hebrews 11:1)*

A *sin-bearer* takes the sins of others and carries it away. A *substitute* is someone or something that takes the place of another (like a substitute teacher takes the place of a teacher). Was an animal truly able to be a substitute for sinners? Could an animal truly be a sin-bearer for sinful man?

Pray: Ask God for faith like Abraham—faith to believe that He is God, that His promises are true, and that He will provide all you need.

Think About: *God is faithful. How has He shown Himself to be faithful in my life?*

Memorize: Hebrews 11:6

1. Isaac means "laughter." At first, Sarah laughed at the thought of having a baby in old age. Now she was laughing with joy.
2. Some possible answers: God wanted to increase Abraham's faith—He wanted to teach Abraham to trust Him no matter how the situation appears; God wanted to do the impossible to prove that Isaac was the promised child, not just a normal pregnancy and birth; God wanted to receive glory for His mighty act; etc.

C H A P T E R 1 4

GOD'S STEADFAST LOVE

A Wife for Isaac—Genesis 24

Know therefore that the LORD your God is God, the faithful God who keeps covenant and steadfast love with those who love him and keep his commandments, to a thousand generations, (Deuteronomy 7:9)

Sometimes when a person has died, people share memories about that person at the funeral. Someone might tell a funny story about the person. Someone else might share that the person loved music or baseball. People might talk about what kind of a person he or she was—that the person was kind or generous, or funny. *What would you want people to remember or say about you?*

What do you think Abraham was remembered for? God had shown steadfast—faithful, unwavering—love to Abraham, and Abraham had become a great man of faith. This is what the Bible says about him:

> *In hope he believed against hope, that he should become the father of many nations, as he had been told, "So shall your offspring be." He did not weaken in faith when he considered his own body, which was as good as dead (since he was about a hundred years old), or when he considered the barrenness of Sarah's womb. No unbelief made him waver concerning the promise of God, but he grew strong in his faith as he gave glory to God, fully convinced that God was able to do what he had promised. That is why his faith was "counted to him as righteousness." (Romans 4:18-22)*

God had blessed Abraham "in all things." Now as an old man, Abraham was concerned about a wife for Isaac. *Why was it important for Isaac to have a wife?* God had said, *"Through Isaac shall your descendants be named."* God would fulfill His promise to make a great nation come from Abraham through Isaac. But Isaac needed a wife so he could have children, who could have children, who could have children . . . until there was a great nation.

Even though God had promised to give Abraham and his descendants the land of Canaan, Abraham was certain of two things. Isaac's wife must not be a woman from the unbelieving Canaanites, and Isaac could not leave the land of promise to go back to the country Abraham left. So, Abraham asked his oldest and most trusted servant to go to the land of his family, find a wife for Isaac, and bring her back. However, Abraham's servant was a bit concerned. What woman would want to leave her family and country to go to an unknown country to marry an unknown man? What if she wouldn't leave her family and go with him? But Abraham had great faith in God's steadfast love:

"The LORD, the God of heaven, who took me from my father's house and from the land of my kindred, and who spoke to me and swore to me, 'To your offspring I will give this land,' he will send his angel before you, and you shall take a wife for my son from there." (Genesis 24:7)

So the servant left with ten camels and many gifts, and traveled to the land of Abraham's brother, Nahor. How would he find the wife God had chosen for Isaac? *What should he do?*

Abraham's servant led his camels to the well where the young women would be coming to get water . . . and he prayed.

And he said, "O LORD, God of my master Abraham, please grant me success today and show steadfast love to my master Abraham. Behold, I am standing by the spring of water, and the daughters of the men of the city are coming out to draw water. Let the young woman to whom I shall say, 'Please let down your jar that I may drink,' and who shall say, 'Drink, and I will water your camels'—let her be the one whom you have appointed for your servant Isaac. By this I shall know that you have shown steadfast love to my master." (Genesis 24:12-14)

What special woman would God send to the well? Whom had He chosen for Isaac? Before the servant even finished his prayer, a young woman named Rebekah came to the well carrying her water jar. Could she be the one? After she filled her jar, the servant asked her for a drink. Not only did Rebekah give him a drink, but she also watered his camels, just as Abraham's servant had prayed! The servant wondered who this woman was. Could she be the one God had sent to marry Isaac? Imagine how surprised he was when he found out that Rebekah was the granddaughter of Nahor, Abraham's brother!

The man bowed his head and worshiped the LORD and said, "Blessed be the LORD, the God of my master Abraham, who has not forsaken his steadfast love and his faithfulness toward my master. As for me, the LORD has led me in the way to the house of my master's kinsmen." (Genesis 24:26-27)

Abraham's servant went to Rebekah's home and spoke to her father, Bethuel, and her brother, Laban. He told them the whole story of Abraham's wealth and God's blessing. He told them about Isaac and about Abraham's desire for Isaac's wife to come from his own family. Then he told them about his prayer and God's perfect answer. Rebekah's father and her brother knew that God had done this. They said Abraham's servant could take Rebekah to be Isaac's wife. But what would Rebekah think?

And they called Rebekah and said to her, "Will you go with this man?" She said, "I will go." (Genesis 24:58)

So Rebekah left her home and her family to follow God's call to marry Isaac. God had led the servant to her. God had made her family willing to let her go. And God had given Rebekah the desire and courage to follow Him. Rebekah traveled with the servant all the way to Canaan

where she met Isaac and married him. God had shown His steadfast love to Abraham... and He showed that **He rules over all circumstances**.

God has steadfast love—faithful, never-ending, loyal love—for His children. God blessed Abraham just as He said He would and kept His promises to him. *Can you trust God's Word and His promises? How do you know this?*

Know therefore that the LORD your God is God, the faithful God who keeps covenant and steadfast love with those who love him and keep his commandments, to a thousand generations, (Deuteronomy 7:9)

MAKING YOU WISE FOR SALVATION

What does this chapter tell us about God? Talk about and apply the **biblical truths** in **bold** text.

Salvation Thread: *What promises did God make to Abraham? Did He keep them? What does this tell you about God?* God is faithful. He keeps all His promises. What He says you can trust.

What is "steadfast love"? How did God show steadfast love to Abraham? How has He shown steadfast love to your family?

Talk About: *Know therefore that the LORD your God is God, the faithful God who keeps covenant and steadfast love with those who love him and keep his commandments, to a thousand generations, (Deuteronomy 7:9)*

Where do you see God's rule over all things in this story?

Pray: Praise God for being a faithful God who has steadfast love for His people. Thank Him for the kindnesses He has shown you and your family. Ask Him to give you a love for Him and the desire to keep His commandments.

Think About: *Do I love God and keep His commandments? What evidence of this do I see in my life?*

Memorize: Deuteronomy 7:9

CHAPTER 15

TWO NATIONS AND GOD'S FAVOR

Jacob Is Chosen to Inherit the Birthright and Blessing of God—Genesis 25-27

..."I will have mercy on whom I have mercy, and I will have compassion on whom I have compassion." (Romans 9:15)

Do you remember how long Abraham waited for the promised son? He waited twenty-five long years for Isaac. Now Isaac needed a son, so his descendants could become a great nation that would bless all nations. But a year passed . . . five years passed . . . ten years passed . . . twenty years passed, and Isaac and Rebekah had no children. Would God keep His promise?

Isaac prayed to the LORD for a child. Soon it became clear that Rebekah was pregnant! God had kindly answered Isaac's prayer. But something was strange. There was a lot of movement in Rebekah's womb. What was happening? Only God could answer that, so Rebekah asked the LORD about it.

> *And the LORD said to her, "Two nations are in your womb, and two peoples from within you shall be divided; the one shall be stronger than the other, the older shall serve the younger." (Genesis 25:23)*

What did God mean . . . two nations . . . the older shall serve the younger? When it was time for Rebekah to give birth . . . she did not have one baby, but two! She had twin boys! The first boy to be born had red hair all over his body, and they named him Esau. Then the second baby was born right after him, holding onto his brother's heel. They named him Jacob. The two boys grew up, and Esau became a very good hunter, roaming the fields looking for wild animals. But Jacob was very different from his brother. He was quieter and stayed close to the family tents. He was not a hunter but a shepherd. Esau was Isaac's favorite son, but Jacob was Rebekah's favorite.

In those days, the oldest son would have the "birthright." This meant that he would be given special privileges or rights because he was born first. So when his father died, Esau would receive twice as much of his father's wealth (animals, servants, possessions, and money) as Jacob would. He would be in charge of the family—having more authority or leadership and responsibility. The birthright was very precious.

One day, Esau went hunting in the field. He must have walked for hours because when he got back he was very tired. In fact, he was exhausted. And he was so hungry. He needed rest and a good meal! He found Jacob at home cooking stew. This stew must have smelled delicious to hungry Esau. How good it would taste! So Esau asked Jacob for some stew. But Jacob was very cunning. Instead of just giving his brother the stew, as he should have, Jacob said, *"Sell me your birthright now." Do you think this is a good trade—a bowl of stew for the birthright?* It was a very foolish trade, but Esau said, *"I am about to die; of what use is a birthright to me?" Do you think Esau was actually going to die?*

At that moment, Esau just wanted to fill his growling stomach with food. What did he care about a birthright then? He wanted food, and it was more important to him than his birthright. He was ruled by his desire for food. So he gave Jacob the birthright for some stew and bread. What a foolish choice! He got some very temporary pleasure—eating food that would last a little while—and lost a privilege and inheritance that would last his whole life. He "despised his birthright"—he did not see it as precious, and he didn't guard it.

The younger son, Jacob, got the privileges of the oldest son. Jacob would inherit a lot of wealth with the birthright because Isaac had become a very rich man. But there was still something even more important than Isaac's wealth. Isaac had God's promise of great blessing:

> *"I will multiply your offspring as the stars of heaven and will give to your offspring all these lands. And in your offspring all the nations of the earth shall be blessed," (Genesis 26:4)*

That promise would be passed on to Isaac's son. Esau had sold his birthright, but he would still have the blessing of his father. After all, he was the firstborn, and his father loved him. But Isaac did not have the right to choose who would inherit or receive God's special promise. God can show mercy to whomever He wants. **God is sovereign**—He is in charge of all things. Before Esau and Jacob were even born, God had chosen Jacob ("the older would serve the younger"). **God can be trusted to bring about His purposes** in His time and in the right way.

Eventually Isaac became old and sick. It was time to pass on God's blessing to his son. Isaac asked Esau to go hunting for meat and prepare a delicious meal for him. When Esau returned, Isaac would bless him. However, Rebekah had heard what Isaac said. Because she loved Jacob, she wanted him to receive his father's blessing. So, she decided to do something about it... something deceitful and sinful. Rebekah told Jacob to get two goats from their herds so she could prepare food for Isaac. Jacob would pretend to be Esau and receive his father's blessing. Instead of waiting to see God fulfill His promise that *the older shall serve the younger*, Jacob decided to do things his own way—a cunning and sinful way.

Isaac could no longer see very well, but he could still smell and feel. So Jacob needed to feel and smell like Esau. He put on Esau's clothes to smell like Esau. His mother put goatskin on his hands and neck so he would feel hairy like Esau. Then Jacob brought his father the food and lied to his father, telling him that he was Esau. He smelled like Esau and felt like Esau... and so his father blessed him:

> *"May God give you of the dew of heaven and of the fatness of the earth and plenty of grain and wine. Let peoples serve you, and nations bow down to you. Be lord over your brothers, and may your mother's sons bow down to you. Cursed be everyone who curses you, and blessed be everyone who blesses you!" (Genesis 27:28-29)*

When Esau got back from hunting, he found out what Jacob had done. He "cried out with an exceedingly great and bitter cry." Jacob had taken his birthright and now his blessing! He had cheated Esau two times! Esau hated Jacob! Why was Esau so angry? Esau had shown disrespect for the covenant God made with Abraham by marrying two Canaanite women. He showed no concern for the wishes of his parents or their faith in God. Yet he still wanted his father's blessing. But it was too late. Jacob had been given the blessing.

Esau was so angry that he decided to kill Jacob! But Rebekah found out about Esau's plan and warned Jacob. She told him to go far away to her home country and stay with her brother Laban until Esau was no longer angry. What sad consequences sin had brought!

Jacob wanted the promise of God, but he got it by sinning. God had already chosen Jacob before he was born. Jacob should have waited for God to fulfill His promise. Rebekah was separated from the son she loved, and she died without ever seeing him again. As for Esau, he loved the wrong things and had despised his birthright and lost the blessing.

How sinful and foolish it is to trade the wonderful things that God has for us to get something that doesn't last. *How can you seek spiritual blessings—the promises of God and the joy of trusting and obeying Him?*

Do not love the world or the things in the world. If anyone loves the world, the love of the Father is not in him. For all that is in the world—the desires of the flesh and the desires of the eyes and pride in possessions—is not from the Father but is from the world. (1 John 2:15-16)

MAKING YOU WISE FOR SALVATION

What does this chapter tell us about God? Talk about and apply the **biblical truths** in **bold** text.

Salvation Thread: Jacob received God's favor, even though he didn't deserve it. This is called grace.

Did God have the right to choose Jacob instead of Esau? Why?

Talk About: ... *"I will have mercy on whom I have mercy, and I will have compassion on whom I have compassion." (Romans 9:15)*

Why is it so easy for us to love the things of this world? How can we fight against the "desires of the flesh, the desires of the eyes, and the pride of possessions"?

Pray: Ask God to help you to love Him more than the things of this world.

Think About: *Do I want spiritual blessings? Or do I mostly want earthly things?*

Memorize: Romans 9:15

CHAPTER 16

GOD ALMIGHTY KEEPS HIS PROMISE

God Blesses Jacob—Genesis 28-35

..."I am God Almighty: be fruitful and multiply. A nation and a company of nations shall come from you, and kings shall come from your own body." (Genesis 35:11)

Jacob had gotten what he wanted—the birthright and the blessing. But the way he did it was sinful, and the consequences were painful. His brother hated him, and Jacob had to leave his family and the land promised to Abraham and Isaac. Before Jacob left, Isaac blessed him again. This time, Isaac was not deceived; he gave his blessing freely and by choice. He also told Jacob not to marry a Canaanite woman but one of the daughters of Laban, his mother's brother. So Jacob left alone ... but with his father's prayer that God would bless him with the promise given to Abraham, and make from him a great nation.

Traveling far from home by himself, outside in the dark, Jacob laid down to sleep with his head on a rock. As Jacob slept that night, God gave him a dream, a dream of blessing. He saw a ladder going from earth to heaven with angels on it. The LORD stood at the top and said:

> *..."I am the LORD, the God of Abraham your father and the God of Isaac. The land on which you lie I will give to you and to your offspring. Your offspring shall be like the dust of the earth ... and in you and your offspring shall all the families of the earth be blessed. Behold, I am with you and will keep you wherever you go, and will bring you back to this land. For I will not leave you until I have done what I have promised you." (Genesis 28:13-15)*

God had given His promise of blessing to Abraham, Isaac, and now to Jacob . . . not because Jacob deserved it, but because **God is merciful to undeserving sinners.** God has mercy on those He chooses to bless, and He chose Jacob even before he was born, to inherit the covenant promises of Abraham. Jacob had sinned against God and his family, but God did not take away His promise**. God is faithful and always keeps His promises.**

Jacob got up the next morning and started on his journey again. But now, instead of having no one and nothing, Jacob had God and His promise. He continued the long journey until he came to the country where Rebekah's family lived. There he found a well—a welcome sight to a weary traveler. Shepherds were there watering their sheep. At the well, Jacob met a young woman. He found out that her name was Rachel and she was Laban's daughter! God had led him right to his relatives. His Uncle Laban welcomed him, and Jacob started working for him as a shepherd.

After a month, Laban asked Jacob what he wanted to be paid. Jacob knew immediately what he wanted. *Do you know what payment Jacob wanted?* Jacob loved Rachel and wanted to marry her. Yet he had nothing to offer for her except his hard work. This time though, he would make a fair trade—a trade that would not cheat Laban—and not a trade like the one he made for the birthright. God had changed Jacob's cunning heart. Jacob told Laban that he would give Laban seven years of hard work so that he could marry Rachel.

> *So Jacob served seven years for Rachel, and they seemed to him but a few days because of the love he had for her. (Genesis 29:20)*

But Laban deceived Jacob and cheated him. Laban had a big wedding feast for Jacob and his bride. Because the bride's face was covered with a veil, Jacob did not know until after the wedding that he had not married Rachel, but her older sister, Leah! How shocked and disappointed Jacob must have been! He loved Rachel, but he was married to Leah! How could Laban do this?

Laban made excuses for his sinful actions. Then he made another agreement with Jacob. He would give Rachel to Jacob in a week if Jacob would work for him for another seven years. This was not a fair trade. Instead of working for Laban seven years for Rachel, as they had agreed, Jacob would work fourteen years for Rachel. Jacob now knew what it was like to be cheated. But he loved Rachel and would work seven more years for her.

Now Jacob had two wives—one he loved and one he didn't love. What would life be like for unloved Leah? **God, who sees all things, sees with eyes of compassion.** He saw that Leah was not loved, so he gave her a son whom she named Reuben. Leah thought that now Jacob might love her. But Jacob loved Rachel. God gave Leah three more sons—Simeon, Levi, and Judah. Now Leah had four sons . . . but Rachel had no children. *How do you think Rachel felt about this?*

> *When Rachel saw that she bore Jacob no children, she envied her sister. She said to Jacob, "Give me children, or I shall die!" (Genesis 30:1)*

Rachel was envious of her sister with her four sons. But God is the one who gives children. Instead of trusting God's wisdom and plan, Rachel decided she would give her husband children herself, in her own way. So she gave Jacob her servant, Bilhah, to be his wife, too. Bilhah gave Jacob two sons, Dan and Naphtali. *What do you think Leah thought of this?*

This started a real battle! Leah gave Jacob a fourth wife! She gave him two sons, Gad and Asher. Now Jacob had eight sons! God was fulfilling His promise to make a great nation from Jacob's offspring (descendants). Then God was merciful to Leah and gave her two more sons, Issachar and Zebulun, and a daughter named Dinah.

> *Then God remembered Rachel, and God listened to her and opened her womb. (Genesis 30:22)*

Rachel named her son, Joseph. Jacob loved Joseph more than his other sons, because Joseph was the son of Rachel, the wife he loved. Jacob was rich—rich in wives and children anyway. Although he had worked for Laban for fourteen years, and had made Laban a wealthy man, Jacob didn't own anything. It was time for him to leave Haran and go back home and start building flocks and herds of sheep and goats of his own. But Laban didn't want this. He knew God had blessed him because of Jacob. So he made a deal to pay Jacob with animals for his work.

Laban cheated Jacob and changed Jacob's wages (what he earned) ten times! But God blessed Jacob's flocks and herds, and Jacob earned many sheep, goats, servants, camels, and donkeys. This made Laban and his sons very angry.

Then the LORD said to Jacob, "Return to the land of your fathers and to your kindred, and I will be with you." (Genesis 31:3)

At last, Jacob would be returning home to the land God promised to Abraham, Isaac, and Jacob. Jacob had left home with nothing, but he would return with wives, children, animals, servants, and, best of all, God's favor or kindness upon him. As Jacob was coming home, he heard Esau was coming to meet him. What would Esau do? Did he still want to kill Jacob? When Esau saw Jacob, he ran to him to . . . hug him! God had changed Esau's heart toward Jacob. There would now be peace between them. God, in His mercy, would make Esau into a nation of people, too—but not the chosen nation of God's blessing. God's covenant promise was for Jacob:

> *And God said to him, "Your name is Jacob; no longer shall your name be called Jacob, but Israel shall be your name." So he called his name Israel. And God said to him, "I am God Almighty: be fruitful and multiply. A nation and a company of nations shall come from you, and kings shall come from your own body. The land that I gave to Abraham and Isaac I will give to you, and I will give the land to your offspring after you." (Genesis 35:10-12)*

God is God Almighty. Jacob's sin could not ruin God's plan. God blessed Jacob because **God is faithful to His promises**. Because of His steadfast love and kindness, God changed Jacob, "the deceiver," to be Israel, the chosen one whose descendants would bless all nations.

God is still God Almighty. Nothing can stop His plans for your life. *How have you seen His almighty power, love, faithfulness, and kindness in your life?*

The LORD of hosts has sworn: "As I have planned, so shall it be, and as I have purposed, so shall it stand," (Isaiah 14:24)

MAKING YOU WISE FOR SALVATION

What does this chapter tell us about God? Talk about and apply the **biblical truths** in **bold** text.

Salvation Thread: God will fulfill His covenant promises, and no one can stop Him. His people would come from Abraham, Isaac, and Jacob.

Why was God merciful to Jacob? Did Jacob deserve mercy? What mercies did God show Jacob? How did Laban try to stop God's plan for Jacob? What happened instead?

Talk About: *"I am God Almighty: be fruitful and multiply. A nation and a company of nations shall come from you, and kings shall come from your own body." (Genesis 35:11)*

What changed Jacob? (You may want to read Genesis 28:10-22 and 32:22-32.)

Pray: Thank God for being a merciful God. Ask Him to be merciful to you.

Think About: Jacob could not earn God's favor (kindness). Neither can you. No one receives God's blessing through good works. God's blessing is a free gift. *Why can't salvation be earned?*

CHAPTER 17

A COLLAR OF IRON FOR A DREAMER

Joseph's Dreams and Slavery—Genesis 37-39

The LORD is a stronghold for the oppressed, a stronghold in times of trouble. And those who know your name put their trust in you, for you, O LORD, have not forsaken those who seek you. (Psalm 9:9-10)

W*hen you go away on a long trip how does it feel when you get home again? Can you imagine what it must have felt like for Jacob to come home after being gone for twenty years?* Jacob was back in the land of promise. He was at peace with his brother, Esau. God had appeared to Jacob again reminding Jacob of His promise to bless him. God also gave Jacob a new name—Israel. But there was still more to cause Jacob to rejoice. His beloved wife, Rachel, was about to give birth to another child. Jacob was coming home with great hopes, joy, and blessing.

While they were still traveling, the day came for Rachel to give birth. But it was a difficult birth . . . and Jacob's beloved wife Rachel died. She had given Jacob one last son. There was joy mixed with sorrow. Jacob named the baby Benjamin but had to bury the baby's mother. Jacob continued traveling on to the home of his father Isaac. Again, great joy awaited him as he greeted his aged father. How good God was to keep Isaac alive until Jacob and Isaac could see each other again! Then, at 180 years old, Isaac died.

Now with twelve sons, Jacob (Israel) was starting to see the beginning of the promised nation. But there was trouble in Jacob's house. *Do you know what it was?* Joseph's brothers didn't like him because he was a tattletale and brought bad reports about them to his father. But there was also another reason they didn't like Joseph. Jacob loved Joseph more than his other sons because Joseph was the first son of Jacob's beloved wife Rachel. When Joseph was seventeen years old, Jacob made him a beautiful, colorful robe—a robe of many colors just for Joseph, Jacob's favorite son. *What do you think the brothers thought of this?*

But it got worse. Joseph had dreams that he would rule over his brothers. When he shared his dreams with his brothers, they hated him even more. In one dream, he and his brothers were tying stalks of grain together and the brothers' stalks bowed down to Joseph's stalk.

> *His brothers said to him, "Are you indeed to reign over us? Or are you indeed to rule over us?" So they hated him even more for his dreams and for his words. (Genesis 37:8)*

The second dream was about the sun, moon, and eleven stars bowing down to him. Now, in this dream, not only were his eleven brothers bowing down to him, but his mother and father, too! You would think Joseph would know better than to tell this dream to his family. But he did tell it . . . and even his father scolded him this time. His brothers were even more jealous of Joseph when they heard this dream, but his father knew the dream was important. Perhaps these dreams were from God?

One day, Jacob sent Joseph to check on his brothers who were watching their flock of sheep far away. When his brothers saw Joseph coming, they sneeringly said, *"Here comes this dreamer. Come now let us kill him and throw him into one of the pits."* Reuben, the oldest son, convinced them not to kill Joseph but instead just throw him into a pit in the wilderness. He planned to come back and rescue Joseph later.

The brothers stripped off Joseph's colorful robe and threw him into a big empty pit without water. What would happen to Joseph? Would he die of thirst in the pit? Were his dreams just silly dreams with no meaning?

While Joseph sat helplessly in the pit, his brothers sat down to eat. Just then, a caravan of traders came along on their way to Egypt. What an opportunity! The brothers could sell Joseph. They would not be responsible for his death, but they would be rid of him. So they sold him for twenty pieces of silver.

> *His feet were hurt with fetters; his neck was put in a collar of iron. (Psalm 105:18)*

Joseph was now a slave in chains and an iron collar. Finally, his brothers were rid of him. Reuben was not around when the other brothers sold Joseph, and when he came back to rescue Joseph, he found that Joseph was gone! Would his father blame him, the oldest son? The brothers had to make up a story to tell their father. So, they killed a goat and dipped Joseph's robe in the blood. They brought the bloody robe to their father and pretended they had found it. They continued to deceive their father by acting like they didn't know if it was Joseph's robe or not. But Jacob recognized the torn, bloody robe. It was Joseph's robe! Just as the brothers had hoped, Jacob thought that a wild animal had killed Joseph and torn him to pieces. Jacob had lost his favorite son. He mourned Joseph's death, and no one could comfort him.

What had really happened to Joseph? The traders sold him as a slave in Egypt to a man named Potiphar. Potiphar was the captain of the king's guard. Joseph had been the favored son of a rich man, and now he was a slave! He was far from home with no hope of seeing his father again. But God was with Joseph. **God does not forsake or abandon His people**. In every way that Joseph served his master, he did well. This pleased Potiphar, who saw that God was with Joseph and that God caused all that Joseph did to succeed or turn out well. So, Potiphar made Joseph his "overseer" and put Joseph in charge of all he had. Joseph was in charge of Potiphar's home and all his fields *and the LORD blessed the Egyptian's house for Joseph's sake.* **God is faithful.** He had not forgotten Joseph.

But just as things were going well for Joseph, he had a problem in Potiphar's house. Joseph was young and handsome, and after a while, Potiphar's wife started looking at Joseph differently . . . as she would look at her own husband. She made sinful suggestions to Joseph about the two of them together.

But he refused and said to his master's wife, "Behold, because of me my master has no concern about anything in the house, and he has put everything that he has in my charge. He is not greater in this house than I am, nor has he kept back anything from me except you, because you are his wife. How then can I do this great wickedness and sin against God?" (Genesis 39:8-9)

Joseph would not sin against God or against his master. He would not "commit adultery"—take another man's wife and treat her like his own . . . even though day after day she kept asking him. Then one day Joseph found himself alone in the house with her, and she reached for him and grabbed his clothing. But Joseph would not give in and sin. He left his garment in her hands and immediately ran out of the house.

However, Potiphar's wife had his piece of clothing. She would get back at Joseph for refusing her, for turning her down. When Potiphar came home, she falsely accused Joseph. She told Potiphar that Joseph had treated her wrongly. Potiphar became furious! He took Joseph and threw him in prison. Joseph had done nothing wrong; he was innocent. But here he was in jail!

But the LORD was with Joseph and showed him steadfast love and gave him favor in the sight of the keeper of the prison. (Genesis 39:21)

The prison keeper put Joseph in charge of all the prisoners. Everything that Joseph was in charge of went well and was successful *because the LORD was with him.* **God is faithful.** He is always watching over His people and caring for them. Even when things don't seem right, He can be trusted. **God is sovereign over all things,** and **His plans never fail**. God had not forgotten Joseph. God was just carrying out His great plan of rescue.

Even when things don't seem to go well for you, if you are a child of God, you can be sure that God is still in charge. All His plans are good and right. *Has there ever been a time in your life (or a time for your family) when it was hard to trust God? Explain.*[1]

The LORD is a stronghold for the oppressed, a stronghold in times of trouble. And those who know your name put their trust in you, for you, O LORD, have not forsaken those who seek you. (Psalm 9:9-10)

MAKING YOU WISE FOR SALVATION

What does this chapter tell us about God? Talk about and apply the **biblical truths** in **bold** text.

Salvation Thread: God was at work in Joseph's life to make a way of salvation for His people. He was sovereignly keeping His covenant promise, even though Joseph's situation seemed like a mistake.

Joseph was innocent, and yet he was mistreated. Even so, Joseph still trusted God and was faithful in his duties. *How do you respond when you are mistreated? Do you trust that God is with you and is at work?*

Talk About: *The LORD is a stronghold for the oppressed, a stronghold in times of trouble. And those who know your name put their trust in you, for you, O LORD, have not forsaken those who seek you. (Psalm 9:9-10)*

Does trusting God mean that nothing bad will ever happen to you?

Pray: Praise God that He will never forsake those who look to Him. Thank God that He is a stronghold, and that He is with His people in times of trouble. Ask Him to help you trust Him.

Think About: *How can I keep trusting God when going through suffering or difficulty?*

Memorize: Psalm 9:10

1. You may want to teach your child the following rhyme by John Piper: "When things don't go the way they should, God always makes them turn for good." ("11 Truths John Piper Learned from His Father," June 17, 2012, desiringGod.org)

CHAPTER 18

FROM A COLLAR OF IRON TO A GOLD CHAIN

Joseph Rises to Power in Egypt—Genesis 40-41

This God—his way is perfect; the word of the LORD proves true; he is a shield for all those who take refuge in him. (Psalm 18:30)

Things had gone from bad to worse! Now Joseph was in prison in Egypt. What was the purpose of all this? Was God really with him? It is always good to wait to see what God is doing . . .

While in prison, Joseph met two men who had worked for Pharaoh, the Egyptian king. One was a baker, and the other was a cupbearer. (Cupbearers were responsible to personally fill the king's cup and hand it directly to him to make sure the king's drink hadn't been poisoned.) Both these men had troubling dreams, but they didn't know what the dreams meant. However, God gave Joseph a special understanding of these dreams. Joseph had good news for the cupbearer. His dream meant that in three days he would once again be Pharaoh's cupbearer. Joseph told the cupbearer his own story—that he was a Hebrew who had been kidnapped, and that he had done nothing wrong to deserve prison.

Then the chief baker asked Joseph the meaning of his dream. Joseph sadly had to tell the baker that his dream meant he would be hanged in three days. Sure enough, three days later, things happened just as God had shown Joseph. The baker was hanged, and the cupbearer got his job back.

Since the cupbearer filled Pharaoh's cup, he was with Pharaoh often. Joseph had asked the cupbearer to tell Pharaoh about him. But two years passed . . . and Joseph still remained in prison. Had the cupbearer forgotten him? Worse yet, had God forgotten about Joseph?

One night, Pharaoh had a dream about seven beautiful, fat cows. Then seven ugly, skinny cows came and ate up the fat cows. Pharaoh dreamed next about seven good ears of grain that were swallowed up by seven thin ears of grain. What could these dreams mean? They were very troubling. Pharaoh was so upset about his dreams that he called the magicians and the wise men of Egypt to tell him what his dreams meant. But no one could interpret Pharaoh's dreams.

This was God's appointed or set time for bringing Joseph to Pharaoh's attention. **God is sovereign**—He rules over all things, including dreams, cupbearers, and even kings. Everything was happening exactly according to God's plan. God caused the cupbearer to remember Joseph and tell Pharaoh about him. So, Pharaoh sent for Joseph and told him his strange,

troubling dreams. God gave Joseph understanding of the dreams as he listened to Pharaoh. *Then Joseph said to Pharaoh, "The dreams of Pharaoh are one; God has revealed to Pharaoh what he is about to do . . . . There will come seven years of great plenty throughout all the land of Egypt, but after them will arise seven years of famine . . . the famine will consume the land."*

Then Joseph boldly made a suggestion to Pharaoh. Pharaoh should appoint overseers in Egypt to store some of the food that grew in the seven good years. When the seven years of famine came, and no crops would grow, Egypt would have the stored food to use and to sell. Pharaoh liked Joseph's idea and said there was no man like Joseph *in whom is the Spirit of God.*

> *Then Pharaoh said to Joseph, "Since God has shown you all this, there is none so discerning and wise as you are. You shall be over my house, and all my people shall order themselves as you command. Only as regards the throne will I be greater than you." And Pharaoh said to Joseph, "See, I have set you over all the land of Egypt." Then Pharaoh took his signet ring from his hand and put it on Joseph's hand, and clothed him in garments of fine linen and put a gold chain about his neck. (Genesis 41:39-42)*

Joseph had come to Egypt as a slave in chains, with a collar of iron around his neck. Now Pharaoh had put him in charge of all of Egypt, and Pharoah even put a gold chain necklace on Joseph's neck! God had been with Joseph. God had been preparing Joseph for this important job in Egypt. All the things Joseph had learned as Potiphar's overseer, and all he had learned when he was in charge of the prisoners would now help him to be in charge of the whole land of Egypt. Joseph's years as a slave and prisoner were not wasted years. God had used them to teach Joseph how to organize, make things successful, and manage people. God had also used those years to humble Joseph, give him patience, and teach him to trust God. God's ways are always perfect. **God is wise. His plans always work out perfectly.** Joseph would not have learned these things as a spoiled younger brother in his father's home.

At thirty years old, Joseph was the second most powerful man in Egypt. During the seven good years, the crops grew so well that Joseph was able to store huge amounts of food. *Joseph stored up grain in great*

abundance, like the sand of the sea, until he ceased to measure it, for it could not be measured. Joseph also married and had two sons. *Joseph called the name of the firstborn Manasseh. "For," he said, "God has made me forget all my hardship and all my father's house." The name of the second he called Ephraim, "For God has made me fruitful in the land of my affliction."* **God is a faithful God**. He had been faithful to Joseph. Joseph was faithful to his God; he "took refuge" in God, and God protected him.

> *This God—his way is perfect; the word of the LORD proves true; he is a shield for all those who take refuge in him. (Psalm 18:30)*

Just as God had shown Joseph, the famine came. No crops grew in Egypt . . . but there was plenty of food, food that Joseph had wisely stored for years. But far away in Canaan, Jacob and Joseph's eleven brothers were in the middle of a great famine. What would they do? They had very little food. But Joseph had plenty of food in Egypt . . .

Do you believe God is faithful and has good plans for His people? How can even suffering and mistreatment be used for good? Give an example.

And we know that for those who love God all things work together for good, for those who are called according to his purpose. (Romans 8:28)

MAKING YOU WISE FOR SALVATION

What does this chapter tell us about God? Talk about and apply the **biblical truths** in **bold** text.

Salvation Thread: God's Word and His plans are perfect. If you trust in Him, He will be a refuge for you.

How can suffering serve the good purposes of God?

Talk About: *This God–his way is perfect; the word of the LORD proves true; he is a shield for all those who take refuge in him. (Psalm 18:30)*

Do you know anyone who is suffering or who has big problems now? What can you do to help?

Pray: Thank God that He is a shield and protector. Ask Him to help you to turn to Him at all times, especially times of difficulty.

Think About: God's ways are always perfect. Everything He plans, He does. Romans 8:28 is not a promise for everyone. For whom is this promise? What does this mean for your life?

Memorize: Romans 8:28

CHAPTER 19

GOD PRESERVES HIS CHOSEN PEOPLE

Joseph Is Reunited with His Family in Egypt—Genesis 42-50

"And God sent me before you to preserve for you a remnant on earth, and to keep alive for you many survivors. So it was not you who sent me here, but God." (Genesis 45:7-8a)

While Joseph was now prospering in Egypt and had an abundance of food during the famine, his father and brothers were experiencing something very different. They were hungry! They had little food, and the situation was getting more and more desperate every day. It didn't seem as if God's promise to make Jacob into a great nation was coming true. How would God provide for them?

Jacob had heard there was food in Egypt. So Jacob told his sons, *"Go down and buy grain for us there, that we may live and not die."* Jacob sent his ten sons to buy food in Egypt, but he wanted his youngest son, Benjamin, to stay home with him.

Joseph was in charge of selling the food in Egypt. One day he looked up and saw ten men who had come to buy food. They looked very familiar. Did he know them? Yes, they were his own

brothers! But his brothers did not recognize this Egyptian-looking man. Joseph remembered the dreams he had when he was a boy . . . now these dreams were coming true. To test his brothers, Joseph accused them of being spies and said he would keep Simeon locked up until they returned with their youngest brother. The brothers were sure this problem had come upon them because of what they had done to Joseph. Would Joseph's brothers abandon Simeon, as they had abandoned him?

The brothers had to leave Egypt without Simeon. Things got worse when one of them opened his sack on the journey and found his money in it. *They turned trembling to one another saying, "What is this that God has done to us?"* Strangely, when they opened their sacks at home, they all found that their money was in their sacks! How had it gotten there? They had paid the Egyptian man. What was going on? They were afraid to return to Egypt. But they had to bring Benjamin there so they could get Simeon.

Jacob would not allow it! He had already lost two sons, Joseph and Simeon. He would not lose Benjamin, too! No one was going back to Egypt . . . he thought. But the famine became so severe that once again Jacob's family was running out of food. So Jacob reluctantly had to let Benjamin go. Maybe if they brought presents to the Egyptian man, he would not be so rough with them.

However, when the brothers returned to Egypt to buy food, Joseph ordered them to be brought to his house. Now they were afraid. Why did this Egyptian want to bring them to his house? Was he going to make them servants? Would he beat them because of the money that was put in their sacks? The brothers tried to return the money to the Egyptian's overseer. But the man said he had received their money, and he brought Simeon to them.

When Joseph arrived home, the brothers gave him the presents they had brought. The eleven brothers bowed down before him—this great "Egyptian" man. He greeted them and left. Now what? They didn't know he was so affected by seeing Benjamin that he left to cry. When he returned, Joseph seated them at the table for a meal . . . from oldest to youngest. They were amazed. How did this Egyptian know in what order they were born?

After buying grain, the brothers left. But they didn't get far. Joseph had sent men after them to search their sacks for his silver cup. It was found in Benjamin's sack! They wondered how the cup got there. (The brothers didn't know that Joseph had ordered his cup be put in Benjamin's sack.) Did the Egyptian think Benjamin had stolen the cup? What would happen to Benjamin? Would Joseph put him in prison or make him a servant?

Then they tore their clothes, and every man loaded his donkey, and they returned to the city. They threw themselves down before Joseph and said they would be his servants. But Joseph said only the guilty one, Benjamin, would be his servant. The rest could go home. How could the brothers return without Benjamin? Their father would be so distressed about losing Benjamin that it would cause his death. They could not let this happen! Judah begged this Egyptian to take him instead and let Benjamin go free.

Now Joseph knew his brothers had changed. They were not the same men who had sold him into slavery.

. . . And he said, "I am your brother, Joseph, whom you sold into Egypt. And now do not be distressed or angry with yourselves because you sold me here, for God sent me before you to preserve life. For the famine has been in the land these two years, and there are yet five years in which there will be neither plowing nor harvest. And God sent me before you to preserve for you a remnant on earth, and to keep alive for you many survivors. So it was not you who sent me here, but God. He has made me a father to Pharaoh, and lord of all his house and ruler over all the land of Egypt." (Genesis 45:4b-8)

Joseph? How could this Egyptian-looking man be Joseph? But it was Joseph! Joseph was alive and he was an important man in Egypt. Joseph wanted them to return to Canaan and get their father and their families. They could live close to Joseph in the land of Goshen in Egypt. Joseph would care for them and their families, and they would not starve in the famine. Jacob's eleven sons hurried back to Canaan to tell Jacob all that had happened.

Imagine the tremendous surprise and joy Jacob felt when he heard that Joseph was alive! God had sent Joseph to Egypt to save them and to keep His promise to make of them a great nation.

Could Jacob leave the Promised Land, the land God had given him? *And Israel [Jacob] said, "It is enough; Joseph my son is still alive. I will go and see him before I die."* So, Israel started on the journey to Egypt.

And God spoke to Israel in visions of the night and said, "Jacob, Jacob." And he said, "Here am I." Then he said, "I am God, the God of your father. Do not be afraid to go down to Egypt, for there I will make you into a great nation. I myself will go down with you to Egypt, and I will also bring you up again, and Joseph's hand shall close your eyes." (Genesis 46:2-4)

It was enough—**God**, who **had been faithful** to Jacob all his life, had planned all this. **He was sovereign**, ruling over every part of His plan to fulfill His promise. God would be with Jacob and his family in Egypt. So Joseph's father, brothers, and all their families settled in Goshen, the best land in Egypt. There they had plenty of food and land for their animals. Joseph continued to serve Pharaoh and made him a very rich king. In Egypt, Joseph's family *gained possessions . . . and were fruitful and multiplied greatly.*

Jacob lived seventeen years in Egypt. Before he died, he blessed all his sons. Then his twelve sons brought him back to Canaan—the Promised Land—to bury him with Abraham, Sarah, Isaac, Rebekah, and Leah. When they returned, Joseph's brothers were afraid that, now that their father was gone, Joseph would hate them and punish them for the evil they did to him. They bowed down before him, asked his forgiveness, and promised to be his servants. Here were his brothers, the "stalks of grain," "the stars" bowing before him. Joseph could punish them for hating him and selling him as a slave. *Do you know what Joseph did?*

But Joseph said to them, "Do not fear, for am I in the place of God? As for you, you meant evil against me, but God meant it for good, to bring it about that many people should be kept alive, as they are today. So do not fear; I will provide for you and your little ones." Thus he comforted them and spoke kindly to them. (Genesis 50:19-21)

". . . you meant evil against me, but God meant it for good."

Joseph was able to see the big picture. He saw that he was one part in a big plan of God. Behind all that happened to him was the hand of God bringing about His great purposes, preserving a nation that would be a blessing to all peoples.

Just as God saved His chosen people from famine, He is still at work saving and caring for His people today. **God is always faithful to His people. He is always at work bringing about His grand purposes.** *Sometimes we don't see the big picture of what God is doing. What can help you to trust God when things don't seem like they are going well? Can you think of a time when you saw God's good and right plan for you or someone else?*

The counsel of the LORD stands forever, the plans of his heart to all generations. (Psalm 33:11)

MAKING YOU WISE FOR SALVATION

What does this chapter tell us about God? Talk about and apply the **biblical truths** in **bold** text.

Salvation Thread: God saved His people through Joseph. But this was just one part of God's plan to bring about an even greater salvation.

What did Joseph mean when he said that his brothers "meant evil against me but God meant it for good"? Does this mean that what the brothers did was not wrong? What is the solution for their sin and ours?

Talk About: *"And God sent me before you to preserve for you a remnant on earth, and to keep alive for you many survivors. So it was not you who sent me here, but God." (Genesis 45:7-8a)*

God is working in the world today. He does not just sit by and watch what is going on. Where do you see His hand at work?

Pray: Thank God for His amazing power to bring about His purposes. Ask Him to give you faith to believe that all His purposes are good and right. Confess any way in which you have sinned against others.

Think About: How does seeing the bigger purposes of God help you understand the problems or difficulties in your life?

CHAPTER 20

GOD HEARS THE GROANING OF HIS PEOPLE

Birth of Moses—Exodus 1-2:10

He remembers his covenant forever, the word that he commanded, for a thousand generations, (Psalm 105:8)

After Jacob and Joseph died, God blessed their descendants, the Hebrews, in Egypt. The Bible says, *they multiplied and grew exceedingly strong, so that the land was filled with them.* For years, the Hebrews worked, gave birth to new children, became grandparents, and grew in number in Egypt. Almost two hundred years had passed since Joseph had died. All the good that Joseph had done for Egypt was in the past long ago, probably forgotten by most Egyptians.

There was a new Pharaoh in Egypt who didn't know Joseph. But he knew about the Hebrews—these people who had come from Jacob, or Israel—and he was quite concerned. The people of Israel were stronger than the Egyptians . . . and there were so many of them! He had to do something to keep the Hebrews from growing even stronger!

> *And he said to his people, "Behold, the people of Israel are too many and too mighty for us. Come, let us deal shrewdly with them, lest they multiply, and, if war breaks out, they join our enemies and fight against us and escape from the land." (Exodus 1:9-10)*

Do you know what it means to "deal shrewdly"? It means to be clever. The Egyptians needed to figure out a smart plan to keep the Hebrews from growing stronger. So the Egyptians put men called overseers in charge of the Hebrews. The overseers treated the Hebrews badly and made them work very hard building cities for Pharaoh. The Hebrews became slaves with no rights.

But the plan wasn't *really* the Egyptians' plan or Pharaoh's plan. It was God's plan. *Do you know what Joseph said when he was going to die?* He promised that God would take care of the people of Israel and bring them out of Egypt to the land He promised to Abraham, Isaac, and Jacob. **God always keeps His promises.** He was keeping this promise in Egypt . . . even though it didn't look like it. He was keeping it because **God is faithful.**

Guess what God did? The more the people of Israel were treated badly, the more they grew in number! There were more and more Hebrews! The Egyptians not only hated the Hebrews, but they became very afraid of them. So, they made the Hebrews work even harder making bricks and working in the fields. But their plan to make the Hebrews weaker did not work.

So, Pharaoh came up with another plan, or at least he thought he did. He was only following God's plan to keep *His* promise, but Pharaoh didn't know that! He told the Hebrew midwives (women who help when a woman is having a baby) that when a baby boy was born to a Hebrew woman, they should kill the baby boy. They could let the girls live, but they must kill all the boys. *Do you think the Hebrew midwives would do this?*

The Hebrew midwives couldn't do such a horrible thing! They knew the one true God. They knew killing babies would be wrong. God was pleased that the midwives disobeyed Pharaoh and let the baby boys live. He was good to the midwives and gave them many children of their own.

Well, if the Hebrew midwives would not kill the babies, who would? Maybe the Egyptians would. Pharaoh gave an order to the Egyptians to throw every Hebrew baby boy into the Nile River to drown, but they could let the girls live. What would the Hebrews do now? Would all the baby boys be thrown in the river to die? Did God know what was happening? **God always knows what is happening . . . and His plans never fail.**

God was working His great purposes through something that seemed very ordinary. It started with a man "from the house of Levi." *Do you remember who Levi was?* He was one of Jacob's twelve sons. Everyone born from him—his sons, his grandson, and his great-grandson—all the people born from Levi—was a Levite. Well, this man married a Levite woman, and God gave these two people a baby . . . a baby *boy.* What would happen to this Hebrew baby boy? Would the Egyptians drown him?

The mother couldn't let the Egyptians throw her precious baby in the river, so she hid him. *Do you think it would be hard to hide a baby? Why would it be hard?* Babies are not quiet! And the bigger they get, the stronger—and LOUDER they get! Eventually, the mother could not hide this baby any longer. If he cried at the wrong time or cried too loudly, the Egyptians might discover him. She didn't know what to do.

But God knows everything. He knew just what to do about this noisy baby boy. God gave the mother the idea to make a basket—a basket that would float and would keep the water out. She would put the baby in the basket and put the basket in the reed plants at the edge of the river. What would happen to the baby? Would he drown? Would he get lost in the reeds? The baby's sister, Miriam, stayed to watch what would happen. God had a wonderful plan for this baby boy and for the people of Israel, and **whatever God plans, He does.**

An Egyptian lady went to the river and found the basket. *How did she get to just the right spot at just the right time?* God sent her! **God is in control of all things** . . . even Egyptian ladies and baskets and babies. When she opened the basket, she saw . . . the baby boy! The Egyptian lady knew it was a Hebrew baby, but God gave her a kind heart toward the baby. She decided to keep the baby and take care of him!

The baby's sister knew that the lady would not be able to nurse or feed the baby. So, Miriam asked if the Egyptian lady wanted her to find a Hebrew woman to care for the baby—and she did. Do you know whom the sister got to take care of the baby? The baby's mother! So, the baby's mother was able to take care of her own baby boy. And the Egyptian lady even paid her to do it! Aren't God's plans wonderful?

But the story gets even better. Guess who the Egyptian lady was? She was the daughter of Pharaoh! After the baby grew a little, the baby's mother brought him to Pharaoh's daughter to live in the palace and become her adopted son. The baby boy would be safe in the palace.

Pharaoh would not hurt his own adopted grandson. So the daughter of Pharaoh named the baby Moses, and he grew up as a prince of Egypt.

But this is just the beginning of God's plan to free the Hebrews and bring them to their own land as He promised. The story gets even better!

Pharaoh had an evil plan, but God protected Moses and even put him safely in Pharaoh's palace! Wasn't this an amazing plan of God? **God is always at work, and His plans are always good. He always has everything under His control.** *Why can you trust that God is working even when you don't see Him at work? Why don't we always understand what God is doing? How does reading about God's works in the Bible help you to see that He can be trusted?*

For my thoughts are not your thoughts, neither are your ways my ways, declares the LORD. For as the heavens are higher than the earth, so are my ways higher than your ways and my thoughts than your thoughts. (Isaiah 55:8-9)

MAKING YOU WISE FOR SALVATION

What does this chapter tell us about God? Talk about and apply the **biblical truths** in **bold** text.

Salvation Thread: God honors the covenant He has made with His people. He will fulfill every word He has promised. You can trust that God will never forsake His people.

Share with your child one of God's good plans in your own life.

Talk About: *For my thoughts are not your thoughts, neither are your ways my ways, declares the LORD. For as the heavens are higher than the earth, so are my ways higher than your ways and my thoughts than your thoughts. (Isaiah 55:8-9)*

What are some promises God makes to His people today?

Pray: Thank God for who He is.

Think About: God had a special plan for Moses. God has a plan for everyone. That means God has a plan for you, too.

C H A P T E R 2 1

A GREATER REWARD THAN THE TREASURES OF EGYPT

God Calls Moses to Rescue His People—Exodus 2-4

By faith Moses, when he was grown up, refused to be called the son of Pharaoh's daughter, choosing rather to be mistreated with the people of God than to enjoy the fleeting pleasures of sin. (Hebrews 11:24-25)

Moses grew up as an Egyptian prince with fine clothes, plenty of food, and a good education. It was a great honor to be an Egyptian prince. But not to Moses. He was a Hebrew by birth and a Hebrew at heart. When he was forty years old, he went out among his people. He saw how hard they worked and how badly they were treated. One day, he saw an Egyptian beating a Hebrew slave. *How do you think Moses felt?* Moses became very angry, so angry that he actually killed the Egyptian. Then to cover his deed, he hid the dead Egyptian in the sand. Moses thought no one knew what he had done. But he was wrong. The next day he found out that his deed wasn't a secret. When Pharaoh heard about it, he wanted to kill Moses.

So, Moses ran away to the land of Midian where Prince Moses became just plain Moses, a poor shepherd taking care of someone else's sheep. But he liked this new life. He got married and started a family, yet God had other plans for Moses . . .

The Hebrews in Egypt were still slaves even though Pharaoh had died. *Their cry for rescue from slavery came up to God. And God heard their groaning, and God remembered his covenant with Abraham, with Isaac, and with Jacob. God saw the people of Israel—and God knew.* **God is always attentive to the cries of His people**—He hears them when they call to Him for help. God was going to rescue His people. He would use a former prince of Egypt, a murderer, a shepherd to do it!

One day, Moses was watching his father-in-law's flocks on Mount Horeb when he saw a very strange sight. He saw a bush that looked like it was on fire . . . only it wasn't getting burned up! It just kept burning and burning. Then the voice of God Himself called to Moses from out of the bush.

> *"Moses, Moses!" And he said, "Here I am." Then he said, "Do not come near; take your sandals off your feet, for the place on which you are standing is holy ground." And he said, "I am the God of your father, the God of Abraham, the God of Isaac, and the God of Jacob." And Moses hid his face, for he was afraid to look at God. Then the LORD said, "I have surely seen the affliction of my people who are in Egypt and have heard their cry because of their taskmasters. I know their sufferings, and I have come down to deliver them out of the hand of the Egyptians and to bring them up out of that land to a good and broad land, a land flowing with milk and honey . . . Come, I will send you to Pharaoh that you may bring my people, the children of Israel, out of Egypt." (Exodus 3:4b-8a, 10)*

What do you think Moses thought of this? Even the ground around God was holy. Why would God call Moses, a sinful man, to deliver His people? *Moses said to God, "Who am I that I should go to Pharaoh and bring the children of Israel out of Egypt."* God's answer was very simple, *"But I will be with you."* It didn't matter who Moses was. It mattered who God is. **God is all-powerful and all-knowing**. God would deliver His people! One day, God's people would worship Him on that very same mountain where God called to Moses out of the burning bush.

But Moses still had questions for God. He wanted to know God's name. In the Bible, names had meaning—they told something important about the person. Abraham means "father of many nations." Isaac means "laughter," because Abraham and Sarah first laughed at the thought of having a son in their old age. God has many, many names because God is so great, so wonderful, so amazing that it takes many names just to begin to explain who He is! God answered Moses with His most personal, most important name.

> *God said to Moses, "I AM WHO I AM." And he said, "Say this to the people of Israel, 'I AM has sent me to you.'" God also said to Moses, "Say this to the people of Israel, 'The LORD, the God of your fathers, the God of Abraham, the God of Isaac, and the God of Jacob, has sent me to you.' This is my name forever, and thus I am to be remembered throughout all generations." (Exodus 3:14-15)*

God's personal name is I AM or *Yahweh*. In Hebrew, it was written YHWH with no vowels. In many of our English Bibles, it is written "LORD" with all capital letters. God was explaining the meaning of His special name Yahweh when He said, "I AM WHO I AM." Yahweh means God is who He is—we don't get to decide who God is. When God said, "I am who I am" He was saying something like, I have always been and always will be God. I am **eternal**—I have no beginning and no end. God also showed Moses the meaning of His name by using a burning bush that never burned up. The burning bush was a picture of God—He never wears out, He never runs out of power, He doesn't need anything, **He is unchanging**—just like the bush never changed or burned up, and the fire never died down. Yahweh is **self-existent** or **self-sufficient**—He doesn't need anything. He exists or is living without the help of anything. He is the source or beginning of all things. He is the **sovereign** LORD. He has the right, power, and wisdom to do all that He pleases. He is **almighty**—He is all-powerful; nothing is too hard for God.

This is the God who would deliver His people. This is the God who had chosen Moses to be His prophet. Moses would speak for God. Moses would deliver God's message to Pharaoh and tell him to let God's people go. God told Moses in advance exactly how Pharaoh would respond. Pharaoh would not let the people go, unless a "mighty hand" forced him to let them go. God would "strike" Egypt with "wonders." And when the Egyptians let the people go, they would give the Hebrews silver, gold jewelry, and clothes.

Moses was still unsure . . . *"But behold, they will not believe me or listen to my voice, for they will say, 'The LORD did not appear to you.'"* **God is understanding.** He gave Moses some signs of His power to show the people if they would not listen to Moses. He told Moses to throw his shepherd's staff onto the ground. When he did, the ordinary staff turned into a fearsome snake! Then God told him to pick it up by the tail. When Moses grabbed the tail, the snake turned back into a staff. God told Moses to put his hand inside his cloak, and it became white with leprosy (a disease). Then, when Moses put his hand back into his cloak, his hand became normal again. God even gave Moses a third sign to use if Pharaoh would not listen. Moses could pour some water from the Nile River onto the ground, and it would turn to blood.

Surely, with all these amazing signs of God's immense power, Moses would have the faith and courage to be God's messenger to Pharaoh. But Moses still hesitated and gave God the excuse that he couldn't speak very well. Moses said, *"I am slow of speech and of tongue."*

Then the LORD said to him, "Who has made man's mouth? Who makes him mute, or deaf, or seeing, or blind? Is it not I, the LORD? Now therefore go, and I will be with your mouth and teach you what you shall speak." (Exodus 4:11-12)

Surely now Moses would understand that God would go with him, and God Almighty would deliver His people. But Moses was still fearful and asked God to send someone else instead. God was angry with Moses, but He was also patient. He told Moses that Moses' brother Aaron was coming to meet him, and Aaron would speak for Moses. Moses could tell Aaron the words to say.

So Moses took the staff of God and headed back to Egypt. He had left the treasures of Egypt, but he was returning with a greater treasure; Yahweh, the God of Abraham, Isaac, and Jacob was with him. This was the God who would deliver His people. This was the eternal, self-sufficient, unchanging God Moses could trust and would follow.

If you have God, you have everything. Moses found God to be a greater treasure than the treasures of Egypt. But God had only just begun to reveal Himself to Moses. He would use Moses to show off more of Himself to the entire world. God reveals Himself to all people so that we might know and treasure Him above all things. *What are some of the things that tempt you to love the treasures of this world rather than see God as the greatest treasure?*

Thus says the LORD: "Let not the wise man boast in his wisdom, let not the mighty man boast in his might, let not the rich man boast in his riches, but let him who boasts boast in this, that he understands and knows me, that I am the LORD who practices steadfast love, justice, and righteousness in the earth. For in these things I delight, declares the LORD." (Jeremiah 9:23-24)

MAKING YOU WISE FOR SALVATION

What does this chapter tell us about God? Talk about and apply the **biblical truths** in **bold** text.

Salvation Thread: Moses had a personal encounter (experience) with the living God. Knowing God is the greatest treasure there is.

What does *Yahweh* mean? How can knowing this name of God help you to have confidence in Him?

Talk About: *Thus says the LORD: "Let not the wise man boast in his wisdom, let not the mighty man boast in his might, let not the rich man boast in his riches, but let him who boasts boast in this, that he understands and knows me, that I am the LORD who practices steadfast love, justice, and righteousness in the earth. For in these things I delight, declares the LORD." (Jeremiah 9:23-24)*

Are you amazed that God chose Moses? What does this tell you about God? How does this encourage you?

Pray: Thank God for being self-existent, unchanging, and eternal. Ask Him to give you a heart that sees Him as the greatest treasure.

Think About: *Do I care more about being important in this world than about understanding and knowing God?*

CHAPTER 22

YAHWEH PROMISES TO DELIVER HIS PEOPLE

Moses and Aaron Bring God's Message to Pharaoh—Exodus 5-7

"...I am God, and there is no other; I am God, and there is none like me, declaring the end from the beginning and from ancient times things not yet done, saying, 'My counsel shall stand, and I will accomplish all my purpose.'" (Isaiah 46:9b-10)

Moses had tried to help the Hebrews his own way—through angrily fighting with and killing an Egyptian. But now, he would do things God's way with God's help. God was not surprised that the Hebrews had been slaves for four hundred years. **God is never surprised. God knows everything,** even before it happens, because **God plans all things.** *Do you remember God's covenant promise to Abram?* When God made this promise, He told Abram his descendants would be slaves.

> *... "Know for certain that your offspring will be sojourners in a land that is not theirs and will be servants there, and they will be afflicted for four hundred years. But I will bring judgment on the nation that they serve, and afterward they shall come out with great possessions." (Genesis 15:13-14)*

God was unfolding history according to His plan, and He was now going to fulfill the promise He made to Abraham. Egypt would be judged, and the descendants of Abraham, Isaac, and Jacob (Israel) would leave with great possessions.

Moses and Aaron went to the elders of Israel. Aaron spoke for Moses and told them the words the LORD had spoken to Moses. Then Moses showed the people the signs God gave him.

> *And the people believed; and when they heard that the LORD had visited the people of Israel and that he had seen their affliction, they bowed their heads and worshiped. (Exodus 4:31)*

Now it was time to go to Pharaoh. God had said that Pharaoh would not let the people go unless a "mighty hand" forced him to let them go. What would happen in this battle between God and Pharaoh? *Moses and Aaron went and said to Pharaoh, "Thus says the LORD, the God of Israel, 'Let my people go, that they may hold a feast to me in the wilderness.'"*

What would hardened, stubborn Pharaoh say about this? Surely, he could not stand against the God who made the world and everything in it! *But Pharaoh said, "Who is the LORD, that I should obey his voice and let Israel go? I do not know the LORD, and moreover, I will not let Israel go."* Then, to make things worse, Pharaoh told the Egyptian taskmasters and the

Hebrew foremen not to give the Hebrews straw anymore. They used the straw to make bricks, and the slaves had to make a certain number of bricks every day. They would still need to make the same number of bricks . . . and they would have to gather the straw, too! When they complained to Pharaoh, he told them they were just lazy. He would not change his orders. Now the Hebrews were mad at Moses and Aaron! They had made things worse, not better, it seemed.

> *Then Moses turned to the LORD and said, "O Lord, why have you done evil to this people? Why did you ever send me? For since I came to Pharaoh to speak in your name, he has done evil to this people, and you have not delivered your people at all." (Exodus 5:22-23)*

How did God answer Moses? Did He say, "Oh, I didn't know this would happen"? Did He say, "This wasn't what I planned. Now what will I do?" No, **God is totally in control of all things at all times.** He absolutely knew this would happen. He had told Moses that He would harden Pharaoh's heart. It was part of His plan. Moses needed to trust God . . . no matter how things looked.

> *But the LORD said to Moses, "Now you shall see what I will do to Pharaoh; for with a strong hand he will send them out, and with a strong hand he will drive them out of his land." (Exodus 6:1)*

Then God reminded Moses of the sure covenant He had made with Abraham, and God told Moses:

> *"Say therefore to the people of Israel, 'I am the LORD, and I will bring you out from under the burdens of the Egyptians, and I will deliver you from slavery to them, and I will redeem you with an outstretched arm and with great acts of judgment. I will take you to be my people, and I will be your God, and you shall know that I am the LORD your God, who has brought you out from under the burdens of the Egyptians. I will bring you into the land that I swore to give to Abraham, to Isaac, and to Jacob. I will give it to you for a possession. I am the LORD.'" (Exodus 6:6-8)*

How did God start and end His promise to the people? He said, "I am the LORD." **God is Yahweh, the sovereign, self-existent, eternal, almighty, unchanging God.** All His promises would come true because **God is who He says He is**! No Pharaoh can stand against a God who doesn't need anything, a God who is all-powerful, a God who controls all things, a God who keeps His promises to His people!

Pharaoh had said, *"Who is the LORD, that I should obey his voice and let Israel go?"* Pharaoh was about to find out who the God of Israel is! God sent Moses and Aaron back to Pharaoh with these instructions:

> *"You shall speak all that I command you, and your brother Aaron shall tell Pharaoh to let the people of Israel go out of his land. But I will harden Pharaoh's heart, and though I multiply my signs and wonders in the land of Egypt, Pharaoh will not listen to you. Then I will lay my hand on Egypt and bring my hosts, my people the children of Israel, out of the land of Egypt by great acts of judgment." (Exodus 7:2-4)*

Still Pharaoh scoffed at Moses and Aaron. He wanted them to do a miracle to prove they had power. Moses and Aaron had no power, but the LORD did. The LORD had told them what to do. Aaron threw down his staff in front of Pharaoh, and it became a slithering serpent. But Pharaoh was not impressed. He called his magicians, and they did the same thing using

their secret arts. Now there were a lot of wiggling serpents, but Aaron's swallowed up all the others! Still, Pharaoh would not give in.

But this was just the beginning of the wonders God would do in Egypt. It was just the beginning of what God would do to free His people. And it was the beginning of God's display of His power and His glorious deeds. God's wonders would show that **Yahweh is the LORD, the sovereign, self-existent, eternal, almighty, unchanging God!**

> *"The Egyptians shall know that I am the LORD, when I stretch out my hand against Egypt and bring out the people of Israel from among them." (Exodus 7:5)*

What reason can you give for believing that God is eternal, almighty (all-powerful), unchanging, and self-existent (He is the true God who doesn't need anything)? How do you know that God will keep His promises and do what He says He will do?

"I have spoken, and I will bring it to pass; I have purposed, and I will do it." (Isaiah 46:11b)

MAKING YOU WISE FOR SALVATION

What does this chapter tell us about God? Talk about and apply the **biblical truths** in **bold** text.

Salvation Thread: God is almighty and sovereign. He is willing and able to save His people.

Share with your child about a time when you prayed, and things got worse. How was God faithful?

Talk About: *"...I am God, and there is no other; I am God, and there is none like me, declaring the end from the beginning and from ancient times things not yet done, saying, 'My counsel shall stand, and I will accomplish all my purpose.'" (Isaiah 46:9b-10)*

Where do you see the truth of Isaiah 46:9b-10 in this story?

Pray: Praise God for being Yahweh—self-existent, eternal, almighty, and unchanging. Ask Him to give you the faith to believe in Him and in all His promises.

Think About: What would life be like if God were not self-existent, eternal, almighty, and unchanging?

Memorize: Isaiah 46:9b-10

CHAPTER 23

"YOU SHALL KNOW THAT I AM THE LORD"

God Shows His Power in Egypt—Exodus 7-10

"But for this purpose I have raised you up, to show you my power, so that my name may be proclaimed in all the earth." (Exodus 9:16)

What mighty acts would God do when He "stretched out his hand against Egypt to bring his people out"? He sent Moses to Pharaoh with these powerful words, *"Thus says the LORD, 'By this you shall know that I am the LORD.'" What sign would God do to show Pharaoh that He is Yahweh?* Aaron held out his staff over the waters of Egypt . . . and the water turned to blood! The fish in the rivers died, the Nile River stank, and the water was undrinkable. There was blood in all the waters of Egypt. But the magicians of Egypt did similar things with their secret arts. So, Pharaoh just ignored Moses' words.

Seven days later, God sent Moses to Pharaoh with His message again, *"Thus says the LORD, 'Let my people go, that they may serve me. But if you refuse to let them go, behold, I will plague all your country with frogs.'"* Again, Aaron stretched out his staff. This time, the mighty hand of God covered Egypt with frogs. There were frogs in the river, in the houses, in the bedrooms . . . even on the beds! There were frogs in the ovens and in the bowls. There were frogs everywhere! Again, the magicians of Egypt were able to do the same thing. But . . . they couldn't make the frogs go away. How would they get rid of all these pesky frogs? Pharaoh called Moses and Aaron to plead with the LORD to take the frogs away. Then he would let the people go. *Moses said, "Be it as you say, so that you may know that* ***there is no one like the LORD our God****."*

> *And the LORD did according to the word of Moses. The frogs died out in the houses, the courtyards, and the fields. And they gathered them together in heaps, and the land stank. But when Pharaoh saw that there was a respite, he hardened his heart and would not listen to them, as the LORD had said. (Exodus 8:13-15)*

Then God told Moses to tell Aaron to *stretch out [his] staff and strike the dust of the earth, so that it may become gnats in all the land of Egypt.* And all the dust became tiny gnat bugs covering the people and animals. The magicians of Egypt tried to copy this, but they couldn't make gnats appear. Finally, they told Pharaoh, *"This is the finger of God."* Pharaoh had not listened to Moses and Aaron. Would he now listen to his own magicians? Not at all! His heart was so hardened!

Then God sent the plague of flies. However, the flies only covered the land of the Egyptians. The Hebrew land of Goshen was "set apart" from this plague—there were no flies there. God had put a dividing line between the Egyptians and the Hebrews. The land of Egypt was ruined by the swarms of flies, and Pharaoh began to bend just a little. He said the Hebrews could offer sacrifices to God, but in Egypt not in the wilderness. The people were not allowed to leave Egypt. This was not what God had promised, so Moses rightly refused this offer.

However, buzzing flies were still swarming everywhere. Pharaoh had to do something! So, Pharaoh said the Hebrews could go into the wilderness . . . but not very far. *What do you think happened as soon as Moses prayed and God removed the flies? Pharaoh hardened his heart this time also, and did not let the people go.*

Again, God sent Moses to warn Pharaoh. This time, if Pharaoh would not let the people go, God would cause a "very severe plague" on the animals, but only on the animals of the Egyptians. The animals of the Hebrews would be safe. But once more, Pharaoh ignored God's warning. So, the next day, the horses, donkeys, camels, sheep, and goats of the Egyptians all became sick, but not one animal of the Hebrews was touched. Now, you would think Pharaoh would give in. But even after this, stubborn, hard-hearted Pharaoh would not let the people go.

The LORD told Moses and Aaron to take handfuls of ashes from the oven. *What would God do with these ashes?* Moses threw the ashes in the air in front of Pharaoh, and it became boils—puffy sores—on the Egyptians and their animals. But even after this sixth plague, Pharaoh still would not give up.

What would happen next? God was kind to the Egyptians and sent a warning through Moses:

> *. . . "Thus says the LORD, the God of the Hebrews, 'Let my people go, that they may serve me. For this time I will send all my plagues on you yourself, and on your servants and your people, so that you may know that there is none like me in all the earth. For by now I could have put out my hand and struck you and your people with pestilence, and you would have been cut off from the earth. But for this purpose I have raised you up, to show you my*

power, so that my name may be proclaimed in all the earth. You are still exalting yourself against my people and will not let them go. Behold, about this time tomorrow I will cause very heavy hail to fall, such as never has been in Egypt from the day it was founded until now. Now therefore send, get your livestock and all that you have in the field into safe shelter, for every man and beast that is in the field and is not brought home will die when the hail falls on them.'" Then whoever feared the word of the LORD among the servants of Pharaoh hurried his slaves and his livestock into the houses, but whoever did not pay attention to the word of the LORD left his slaves and his livestock in the field. (Exodus 9:13b-21)

God could have wiped out the Egyptians in one big blow. But even evil Pharaoh's stubbornness had a purpose. *"But for this purpose I have raised you up, to show you my power, so that my name may be proclaimed in all the earth."* Each plague showed more of God's mighty power and greatness. Again, Moses stretched out his hand, and the LORD sent crashing thunder, pounding hail, and flashing lightning, just as He said He would. It was the fiercest storm that had ever struck Egypt, sent by the **God** who **controls all things**, even storms. The hail destroyed the plants in the field and even the trees—everywhere in Egypt. *Only in the land of Goshen, where the people of Israel were, there was no hail.*

Pharaoh sent for Moses and Aaron and said, *"This time I have sinned; the LORD is in the right, and I and my people are in the wrong. Plead with the LORD, for there has been enough of God's thunder and hail. I will let you go."* But Moses was not fooled. He knew the Egyptians did not fear or respect the LORD. Moses knew that when God stopped the storm, Pharaoh's hard heart would refuse to let them go.

When Moses warned Pharaoh of the eighth plague—the plague of locusts (a kind of grasshopper)—even Pharaoh's servants were begging him to let Israel go. They told Pharaoh, *"Do you not yet understand that Egypt is ruined?"* The locusts would eat every tree and would fill every house. Even then, Pharaoh thought he could bargain with God and just let the men go, leaving their families behind. But God would keep His promise, His whole promise—every person of Israel would be freed. So God sent an east wind that blew in dense swarms of locusts. They covered the entire land and ate every plant and any fruit left from the hailstorm, so there was not one green living plant left in Egypt. What a disaster! Egypt was ruined!

Once again, Pharaoh said he had sinned and asked for forgiveness. But this was not a **true repentance, a turning away from sin**. It was a very short sorrow for the consequences of his sin. As soon as the locusts left, Pharaoh again stubbornly refused to let the people go.

Next came three days of pitch-black darkness in Egypt. The Egyptians couldn't do anything. It was so dark that they couldn't even see each other. But there was light in Goshen. Now Pharaoh was furious! This time, Pharaoh threatened to kill Moses if he ever saw him again, but *still* he would not let all the Israelites and all their flocks and herds leave.

Pharaoh was rebellious, stubborn, and foolish. His hard heart had caused not only damage to himself but ruin to his country. He refused to submit to God or recognize God's greatness. **No one can fight against God and win.**

We, too, can be stubborn and foolish. But the Bible warns us about being stubborn and not learning from the discipline God brings to us.

> *He who is often reproved, yet stiffens his neck, will suddenly be broken beyond healing. (Proverbs 29:1)*

What does it mean to fear the LORD? (It is different from being afraid of God.) Why is a person who fears the LORD blessed? What does it mean to harden your heart? What is the danger of hardening your heart?

Blessed is the one who fears the LORD always, but whoever hardens his heart will fall into calamity. (Proverbs 28:14)

MAKING YOU WISE FOR SALVATION

What does this chapter tell us about God? Talk about and apply the **biblical truths** in **bold** text.

Salvation Thread: Fear the LORD, and do not harden your heart against Him.

What does it mean to harden your heart? (Make sure your child understands what it means to resist the things of God, to be slow to confess sin, to take His commands lightly, to neglect time in His Word, etc.)

What is the difference between true repentance and worldly sorrow? (Make sure your child understands that dismay over the consequences of sin is not the same as true repentance over sin.)

Talk About: *"But for this purpose I have raised you up, to show you my power, so that my name may be proclaimed in all the earth." (Exodus 9:16)*

Why does God want His name "proclaimed in all the earth"? How do the plagues show God's greatness? *How can you let others know how great God is?*

Pray: Praise God for His mighty acts. Ask Him to give you a soft heart and help you to submit to Him.

Think About: Why is someone blessed when he fears (respects) God? *Am I hardening my heart in any way?*

CHAPTER 24

GOD'S PASSOVER RESCUE

The Plague of Death of the Firstborn and God's Rescue of Israel—Exodus 11-12

Every word of God proves true; he is a shield to those who take refuge in him. (Proverbs 30:5)

What was God doing with these nine plagues? Why didn't He just send one big plague and be done with it? **God is always doing more than one thing at a time.** Yes, He was rescuing His people. But He was also bringing His righteous judgment on a very evil nation. He was demonstrating His power so that all might know that **He is Yahweh the sovereign, self-existent, eternal, almighty, unchanging God who rules over all.** God was showing that He is greater than all the gods of Egypt.

The Egyptians worshiped thousands of gods—a god with the head of a frog, one with the head of a fly, another with a head of a cow, the sun, a god of storms, and thousands of others. *So why did God choose the particular plagues He sent on Egypt?* Every plague was showing not only Egypt, but even God's own people, who had lived in Egypt for hundreds of years, that He is greater than all the gods—that He alone is God Almighty. **Yahweh is the one true God and the only One worthy of worship.**

There was one more act of justice, power, and deliverance that God would do in Egypt—one more dreadful plague—and then Pharaoh would let the people go. Not only would Pharaoh let the people go, but God's words to Moses were that Pharaoh *will drive you away completely.* Pharaoh would be eager to get rid of Israel! God told Moses to tell the Israelites to ask for silver and gold jewelry from their neighbors. *What would happen to make Pharaoh and the Egyptians so eager for the Israelites to leave that they would give the Israelites their wealth?*

God is patient and gracious. He gives men the opportunity to repent. God sent Moses to warn Pharaoh of God's just punishment:

> *"Thus says the LORD: 'About midnight I will go out in the midst of Egypt, and every firstborn in the land of Egypt shall die, from the firstborn of Pharaoh who sits on his throne, even to the firstborn of the slave girl who is behind the handmill, and all the firstborn of the cattle. There shall be a great cry throughout all the land of Egypt, such as there has never been, nor ever will be again. But not a dog shall growl against any of the people of Israel, either man or beast, that you may know that the LORD makes a distinction between Egypt and Israel.'" (Exodus 11:4-7)*

The consequence of Egypt's rebellion was death. What a final and awful blow this would be! The Israelites would be spared God's judgment, but only if they obeyed God's special instructions. It would require the death of a perfect lamb, a year old. The Israelites must paint the lamb's blood on the top and sides of the doorframes of their houses. They were to roast the lamb and eat it with a special flat bread (unleavened bread) and bitter herbs (plant leaves). But they should eat the meal quickly and with their traveling clothes on. What did all this mean?

". . . It is the LORD's Passover. For I will pass through the land of Egypt that night, and I will strike all the firstborn in the land of Egypt, both man and beast; and on all the gods of Egypt I will execute judgments: I am the LORD. The blood shall be a sign for you, on the houses where you are. And when I see the blood, I will pass over you, and no plague will befall you to destroy you, when I strike the land of Egypt." (Exodus 12:11b-13)

Israel would be saved by the blood of the lamb. *Why would God require the blood of a lamb?* The punishment for sin is death, and the Israelites were sinners, too. God accepted the Israelites, not for their goodness but because of a perfect lamb's blood. Putting blood on their doorframes was a mark of faith in God's provision and willingness to save them from destruction. Moses gave God's instructions to the people and told them to stay in their houses until morning.

"For the LORD will pass through to strike the Egyptians, and when he sees the blood on the lintel and on the two doorposts, the LORD will pass over the door and will not allow the destroyer to enter your houses to strike you. You shall observe this rite as a statute for you and for your sons forever. And when you come to the land that the LORD will give you, as he has promised, you shall keep this service. And when your children say to you, 'What do you mean by this service?' you shall say, 'It is the sacrifice of the LORD's Passover, for he passed over the houses of the people of Israel in Egypt, when he struck the Egyptians but spared our houses.'" And the people bowed their heads and worshiped. (Exodus 12:23-27)

God would judge the Egyptians for their sin, but He would pass over the Hebrews, saving them from death. God not only wanted the Israelites in Egypt to remember His deliverance from death. He also wanted their children and their grandchildren—all their descendants—to know His mighty saving power. They were to remember God's mercy and deliverance with a special ceremony every year. The Israelites were to eat unleavened (flat) bread for seven days, and then celebrate the Passover meal of the perfect Passover lamb.

Pharaoh and the Egyptians had killed the baby sons of the Israelites. Now their firstborn sons would die. *At midnight the LORD struck down all the firstborn in the land of Egypt... And Pharaoh rose up in the night, he and all his servants and all the Egyptians. And there was a great cry in Egypt, for there was not a house where someone was not dead.*

Pharaoh desperately called for Moses and Aaron and "drove them out completely," just as God had said. The Egyptian people were also very eager for Israel to leave immediately. They gave the Israelites everything they asked for—silver, gold jewelry, and clothing. Every word God spoke had come true. **God is the King above all kings! God is Yahweh—the sovereign, self-existent, eternal, almighty, unchanging God.** God had shown His power and control over all the gods of the most powerful ruler and nation of the world at that time. He had delivered His people as He promised, and He had given them the Passover to remember His mighty salvation. Someday God would bring a greater Passover Lamb to save His people by His own blood!

God wants His mighty deeds to be remembered. It is one way we learn to trust Him. *What mighty deeds of God's faithfulness have you seen? How can this help you to trust God? Just as God was a refuge, or safe place, for Israel, so He can be a refuge for you.*

Every word of God proves true; he is a shield to those who take refuge in him. (Proverbs 30:5)

MAKING YOU WISE FOR SALVATION

What does this chapter tell us about God? Talk about and apply the **biblical truths** in **bold** text.

Salvation Thread: God's people were saved through the blood of a lamb. The Passover helped the Israelites remember God's deliverance from judgment and pointed forward to the time when God would send a permanent Passover Lamb.

What is the Passover? Why did the blood of the lamb keep the people safe? (You might want to read Exodus 11-12 and see how every word of God came true.)

Talk About: *Every word of God proves true; he is a shield to those who take refuge in him. (Proverbs 30:5)*

Pray: Praise God for His faithfulness and His rescue. Ask Him to be your shield.

Think About: What do I need to be rescued from? Why can God pass over the sins of His people and rescue them from eternal death?

Memorize: Proverbs 30:5

CHAPTER 25

GOD BRINGS HIS PEOPLE OUT OF EGYPT WITH SINGING

God Defeats Egypt and Protects His People—Exodus 13-15

"Who is like you, O LORD, among the gods? Who is like you, majestic in holiness, awesome in glorious deeds, doing wonders?" (Exodus 15:11)

Wouldn't you love to be able to watch the scene of the Israelites marching triumphantly out of Egypt? What a day of victory it was! But now what? Where would they go now? **God is always present to help His people**. When God brought Israel out of Egypt with His mighty power, *the LORD went before them by day in a pillar of cloud to lead them along the way, and by night in a pillar of fire to give them light.* God not only rescued His people, but He stayed with them and continued to show them where to go—*the pillar of cloud by day and the pillar of fire by night did not depart from before the people.* **God is faithful**; He never abandons (leaves) His people.

God led the people to the Red Sea. There, God told Moses to set up camp facing the sea. With the wilderness behind them and the sea in front of them, where could they go? They were stuck. Did God make a mistake . . . or was this part of His grand plan of rescue, of judgment on Egypt, and to demonstrate His control and power over all things?

God, who **knows all things,** knew exactly what Pharaoh would think of the grand escape of Israel. He told Moses,

"...Pharaoh will say of the people of Israel, 'They are wandering in the land; the wilderness has shut them in.' And I will harden Pharaoh's heart, and he will pursue them, and I will get glory over Pharaoh and all his host, and the Egyptians shall know that I am the LORD"... (Exodus 14:3-4)

Just as God had said, when the king of Egypt was told that the Israelites had fled, Pharaoh and his servants changed their minds. Why did they let the slaves leave? Who would serve them now? So Pharaoh took his mighty army and more than six hundred chariots and horses and horsemen and chased hard after Israel. When they got near the camp of the Israelites, the people of Israel saw the Egyptians charging toward them. They were terrified and cried out to the LORD. But they did not cry out in faith. Believing that they would die in the wilderness, they blamed Moses. They cried that it would have been better to stay and serve the Egyptians.

And Moses said to the people, "Fear not, stand firm, and see the salvation of the LORD, which he will work for you today. For the Egyptians whom you see today, you shall never see again. The LORD will fight for you, and you have only to be silent." (Exodus 14:13-14)

God is the Deliverer of His people. The LORD would protect His people and fight for them! *Then the angel of God who was going before the host of Israel moved and went behind them, and the pillar of cloud moved from before them and stood behind them, coming between the host of Egypt and the host of Israel.* God Himself protected Israel from the army of Pharaoh! God stood between His people and danger. He commanded Moses to stretch out his hand over the sea and divide it, and the LORD sent a strong wind all night long. The wind of God was amazing! It piled up the water like walls on either side of a perfect path through the sea for His people! In the morning, Israel crossed the sea along God's path while God held back the walls of water with His mighty hand.

The Egyptians followed Israel, but they did not have the protection of God, and God *threw the Egyptian forces into a panic, clogging their chariot wheels.* Now the Egyptians wanted to run *away* from Israel because they saw that God Almighty fought for Israel. But it was too late! God told Moses to stretch out his hand over the sea so the water would crash back into place . . . covering the Egyptians. Not one Egyptian survived God's just judgment, but all of Israel crossed on dry land. God had delivered His people from slavery in Egypt and brought them to safety.

> *Thus the LORD saved Israel that day from the hand of the Egyptians, and Israel saw the Egyptians dead on the seashore. Israel saw the great power that the LORD used against the Egyptians, so the people feared the LORD, and they believed in the LORD and in his servant Moses. (Exodus 14:30-31)*

What had the people of Israel seen about God? They saw His protection and care for His people, His power over the wind and water, His judgment on those who rebel against Him and do evil, and His sovereign or supreme rule over all things to bring about His purposes. When God is seen in all His magnificence and glory, the appropriate response is praise. And that is just what Moses and Israel did. They praised God by joyfully singing about His greatness:

> *. . . "I will sing to the LORD, for he has triumphed gloriously; the horse and his rider he has thrown into the sea. The LORD is my strength and my song, and he has become my salvation; this is my God, and I will praise him, my father's God, and*

I will exalt him. The LORD is a man of war; the LORD is his name. Pharaoh's chariots and his host he cast into the sea, and his chosen officers were sunk in the Red Sea. The floods covered them; they went down into the depths like a stone. Your right hand, O LORD, glorious in power, your right hand, O LORD, shatters the enemy. In the greatness of your majesty you overthrow your adversaries . . . ***Who is like you, O LORD, among the gods? Who is like you, majestic in holiness, awesome in glorious deeds, doing wonders?*** *You stretched out your right hand; the earth swallowed them. You have led in your steadfast love the people whom you have redeemed; you have guided them by your strength to your holy abode . . .* ***The LORD will reign forever and ever.****" (Exodus 15:1-7a, 11-13, 18)*

The Egyptians were destroyed because they refused to worship the one true God, Yahweh. But God kept His promise to Abraham, Isaac, and Jacob to make of them a great nation and to be their God. **God always keeps His promises. God always defeats His enemies. And God always cares for His people. He is the Deliverer and the King who reigns forever!**

God is worthy of our admiration. *What characteristics about God can you list? How do these characteristics make God worthy of our admiration? How can you praise God for His greatness and faithfulness?*

"The LORD is my strength and my song, and he has become my salvation; this is my God, and I will praise him, my father's God, and I will exalt him." (Exodus 15:2)

MAKING YOU WISE FOR SALVATION

What does this chapter tell us about God? Talk about and apply the **biblical truths** in **bold** text.

Salvation Thread: God is the Deliverer of His people. He is the supreme King of kings who reigns forever. He is worthy of praise, honor, and admiration.

Was it "right" for God to destroy Pharaoh and his army? Explain. What does this tell you about those who do not put their trust in God but ignore, reject, or rebel against Him?

Talk About: *"Who is like you, O LORD, among the gods? Who is like you, majestic in holiness, awesome in glorious deeds, doing wonders?" (Exodus 15:11)*

God's deliverance of His people from slavery in Egypt points forward to a greater deliverance for man. What is that deliverance?

Pray: Praise God for who He is. Thank Him for His care for His children. Ask Him to show you whether you truly worship Him in your heart.

Think About: *How do you know if God is your God? How can you have a personal relationship with Him?* (See John 14:6.)

C H A P T E R 2 6

ISRAEL'S HEALER, PROVIDER, AND PROTECTOR

Food and Water in the Wilderness; Victory over the Amalekites—Exodus 15-17

For the LORD will not forsake his people; he will not abandon his heritage; (Psalm 94:14)

Israel had been in Egypt for hundreds of years surrounded by the worship of thousands of false gods. God had shown them His amazing power through the mighty plagues He brought on Egypt. He rescued Israel from slavery and miraculously delivered them from Pharaoh's army at the Red Sea. Now they needed to know and learn to trust Yahweh as the one true God. After Israel left the Red Sea, God led them with the pillar of cloud by day and pillar of fire by night into the barren wilderness on the way to the Promised Land.

Why would God lead them into the wilderness? The wilderness was a dry and deserted place where there was little food or water. After three days of travel, their water was gone. Almost two-and-a-half million Israelites left Egypt in the Exodus. Where would they get water for so many people? *Would God lead them into the wilderness just to let them die?* God was testing them. Would Israel trust Him? Would they depend on Him to care for them? Did they believe that He is faithful?

The Israelites finally came to a place called Marah where there was water. Just think how glad they must have been! But the water tasted horribly bitter, and they couldn't drink it. How disappointing! The people bitterly complained to Moses. What would they drink now? But Moses had learned to trust God. He prayed, and God showed him a log. Moses threw the log into the water "and the water became sweet"! Even more important than the water was the promise that God gave His people there:

> *..."If you will diligently listen to the voice of the LORD your God, and do that which is right in his eyes, and give ear to his commandments and keep all his statutes, I will put none of the diseases on you that I put on the Egyptians, for I am the LORD, your healer." (Exodus 15:26)*

God would not abandon or leave His people. He would care for them and be faithful to them. But they must trust and obey Him. It wasn't long before they were tested again in the wilderness. This time, the people grumbled because they were hungry. They complained that it would have been better to die in Egypt where they had food than to die in the wilderness.

Then the LORD said to Moses, "Behold, I am about to rain bread from heaven for you, and the people shall go out and gather a day's portion every day, that I may test them, whether they will walk in my law or not. On the sixth day, when they prepare what they bring in, it will be twice as much as they gather daily." (Exodus 16:4-5)

Would the people trust God to give them food every day? Would they obey Him and only gather enough for one day? Would they gather twice as much on the sixth day and rest on the seventh day?

And the LORD said to Moses, "I have heard the grumbling of the people of Israel. Say to them, 'At twilight you shall eat meat, and in the morning you shall be filled with bread. Then you shall know that I am the LORD your God.'" (Exodus 16:11-12)

In the evening, birds called quail flew in and covered the camp of the Israelites. In the morning, there was a "fine, flake-like thing" on the ground. *What was this strange substance*? It was "manna" or bread that God had sent for them to eat. Just as God had promised, He gave the Israelites meat and bread. *What did this tell them about God?* Did they now know that **Yahweh is the one true God**? Did they understand that **God always keeps His promises**? Would Israel trust Him? Would they depend on Him to care for them?

Sadly, not all the people obeyed God's commands. They did not trust Him for each day's food. Some of them kept leftovers for the next day . . . and in the morning, it smelled terrible and had slimy worms in it! Only on the sixth day could they have leftover manna that would not be smelly and wormy. This leftover manna they could eat on the seventh day, the Sabbath. However, some of the people went to gather manna on the seventh day anyway . . . but there was none. Still, they did not trust God's word. It made God angry that the people would not obey His commands.

God had miraculously fed the Israelites in the wilderness with manna. As a reminder of His goodness and faithfulness, God commanded them to keep a jar of manna for all generations. But Israel did not remember God's faithfulness to provide for them. Once again, when there was no water, they grumbled and demanded that Moses give them water. Why couldn't they just trust God to know what they needed and to provide for them? Instead, they accused

Moses of bringing them into the wilderness to die. This time, when Moses cried out to the LORD, God told him *"Behold I will stand before you there on the rock at Horeb, and you shall strike the rock, and water shall come out of it, and the people will drink."* Moses took his staff and struck the rock, and fresh water came gushing out! Once again, God had proven His faithfulness and goodness to His grumbling people.

> *He made streams come out of the rock and caused waters to flow down like rivers. Yet they sinned still more against him, rebelling against the Most High in the desert. They tested God in their heart by demanding the food they craved. They spoke against God, saying, "Can God spread a table in the wilderness?" (Psalm 78:16-19)*

God had graciously given them food and water in the wilderness . . . He had "spread a table in the wilderness." He also protected them from their enemies. Though other nations were in great fear of the Hebrews because of God's mighty acts in Egypt, the Amalekites came to fight against Israel. So, Moses told Joshua to choose some men to fight the Amalekites. Moses would stand on the top of the hill with the "staff of God" in his hand. He was praying for God to give them victory and showing Israel that their victory would come through God's help.

Whenever Moses held his hand up to God, Israel was winning. And whenever Moses lowered his hand . . . the Amalekites began to succeed in the battle. But Moses couldn't hold his arms up all the time because they would get so tired and start to ache. So, Aaron and Hur got a

stone for Moses to sit on, and they held up his hands. They did this until the sun went down and Joshua and Israel won the battle. God had given them a mighty victory! He had shown the Israelites that He was with them, and He would fight for them. So, Moses built an altar and called it "The LORD is my banner," or the LORD is my victory.

God led His people into the wilderness to show them their helplessness, to show them that they needed Him every day. He showed them wonders—flocks of quail and manna covering the ground, water from a rock, and victory over their enemies—so they would learn to trust Him. He gave them many opportunities to see His faithfulness.

You, too, need God. Without Him, you are helpless. *Will you trust Him, or trust in yourself? The verse below is a good verse to pray for ourselves.*

Teach me your way, O LORD, that I may walk in your truth;
unite my heart to fear your name. (Psalm 86:11)

MAKING YOU WISE FOR SALVATION

What does this chapter tell us about God? Talk about and apply the **biblical truths** in **bold** text.

Salvation Thread: Man does not deserve any mercy from God. But God is gracious and pours out His kindness, though it is undeserved.

How did God show His faithfulness to Israel? Did the Israelites deserve God's kindness? Why not? What was their attitude toward God's kindness?

Talk About: *For the LORD will not forsake his people; he will not abandon his heritage; (Psalm 94:14)*

It is easy to see Israel's sin. But we have the same sinful hearts. *How are you like Israel?*

Pray: Psalm 86:11 is a prayer that God will teach you His truth, that you would obey Him, and that you would love and fear Him. Can you pray this prayer?

Think About: Many of the people of Israel had "divided hearts"—not fully trusting God. *Do I have a divided heart?*

Memorize: Psalm 86:11

CHAPTER 27

GOD'S TREASURED POSSESSION

God Makes a Covenant with Israel at Mount Sinai—Exodus 19-20

"Now therefore, if you will indeed obey my voice and keep my covenant, you shall be my treasured possession among all peoples..." (Exodus 19:5)

Israel had been wandering—and grumbling—in the wilderness for three long months. But now, God had brought Israel to Mount Sinai,[1] where He had met Moses earlier in the burning bush. God had faithfully kept His promise. At the burning bush, God had promised Moses that He would be with him to bring the people out of Egypt, and they would worship Him on this same mountain. ***Every word of God proves true.***

While Israel camped at the bottom of the mountain, Moses went up the mountain to meet with God.

> *...The LORD called to him out of the mountain, saying, "Thus you shall say to the house of Jacob, and tell the people of Israel: 'You yourselves have seen what I did to the Egyptians, and how I bore you on eagles' wings and brought you to myself. Now therefore, if you will indeed obey my voice and keep my covenant, you shall be my treasured possession among all peoples, for all the earth is mine; and you shall be to me a kingdom of priests and a holy nation.' These are the words that you shall speak to the people of Israel." (Exodus 19:3b-6)*

God was making a covenant or agreement with Israel. In the covenant, He promised that Israel would be His treasured possession—His own special people. Israel would be a kingdom of priests—a blessing to all nations, leading others to know God. God would also make Israel into a holy, righteous, and good nation—a people set apart, blessed in a special way and different from all the other nations. These were wonderful promises! But God's covenant promises came with a requirement. Israel had to make a promise, too. God expected Israel to obey Him and keep His covenant commands or law. If they obeyed Him and kept His covenant, then He would keep His covenant promises to them.

God's prophet, Moses, told the people all that the LORD had told him. Yahweh had judged the Egyptians with mighty signs and faithfully brought Israel out from slavery. Would they now be the people of God and keep His covenant?

> *All the people answered together and said, "All that the LORD has spoken we will do." And Moses reported the words of the people to the LORD. (Exodus 19:8)*

Then God told Moses to "consecrate" the people—to tell them to prepare their hearts and minds to meet with Yahweh, the holy God who is like nothing else. They were to wash their clothes and be ready because in three days God would "come down on Mount Sinai in the sight of all the people." God told Moses to instruct the people not to go up the mountain or even "touch the edge of it." God is perfect and separate from sin. If the people even touched the mountain, they would be put to death. When the people heard a long trumpet blast, it would be time to come near the mountain.

On the third day, there was loud thunder and flashing lightning. A thick cloud fell on the mountain, and a loud trumpet blast sounded. *How do you think the Israelites reacted to this?* They were terrified! All the people trembled as they gathered near the mountain. God had come down on the mountain in fire, and thick smoke flew upward. The whole mountain trembled and quaked, and the trumpet grew louder and louder! The presence of God Almighty was powerful, astonishing, and fearsome. But Yahweh called to Moses to come up to the top of the mountain. Moses was God's chosen prophet who spoke God's words to the people and spoke to God for the people.

Then God spoke from the mountain to the people of Israel saying, *"I am the LORD your God, who brought you out of the land of Egypt, out of the house of slavery."* God was going to give Israel His commands, but first He reminded Israel that He is **Yahweh, the sovereign, almighty, unchanging, eternal, self-sufficient One**. Yahweh was promising to be Israel's God and to have a special relationship with Israel. He reminded the Israelites that He had been their **Deliverer** or **Savior** who brought them out of slavery in Egypt. This is the God who was making a covenant promise with Israel. This is the God who gave His good commands to the people of Israel. Some of the commandments He gave the Israelites to keep are:

1. *"You shall have no other gods before me.*
2. *You shall not make for yourself a carved image, or any likeness of anything . . . You shall not bow down to them or serve them, for I the LORD your God am a jealous God . . .*
3. *You shall not take the name of the LORD your God in vain . . .*
4. *Remember the Sabbath day, to keep it holy.*
5. *Honor your father and your mother, that your days may be long in the land that the LORD your God is giving you.*
6. *You shall not murder.*
7. *You shall not commit adultery.*
8. *You shall not steal.*
9. *You shall not bear false witness against your neighbor.*
10. *You shall not covet your neighbor's house; you shall not covet your neighbor's wife, or his male servant, or his female servant, or his ox, or his donkey, or anything that is your neighbor's." (Exodus 20:3-5, 7-8, 12-17)*

God's commands show His good and holy character. God was commanding His people to be like Him—good and righteous and holy. They were to worship only Yahweh, the one true God. They were to honor and respect Him. As His people, they were not to bring dishonor on His name. They were to treat their parents and others with respect by not murdering, taking another person's husband or wife, stealing, or lying. The Israelites were to find God as their greatest treasure and to be content in what He provided for them. **God's commandments showed them the attitudes and actions that were good, right, and pleasing to God.** Israel was to **keep all of these commands perfectly** and to be a holy, righteous, and good people.

What do you think the people thought about the mighty presence of God? The people were terrified of the thunder, lightning, the smoking mountain, and the loud trumpet blasts. They said to Moses, *"You speak to us, and we will listen; but do not let God speak to us, lest we die." Moses said to the people, "Do not fear, for God has come to test you, that the fear of him may be before you, that you may not sin."* God did not want the people to die. In love, He was warning them of the danger of sinning against Him and breaking His covenant with them. **All of God's actions toward His people are done in love.**

Israel was called to be a "set-apart" people—to be different from all the other nations. They had a special covenant relationship with the one true God. God's holy character requires His people to be a holy people, living in obedience to His commands. Sin would separate them from their God.

Sin will also separate you from God. *Do you know how to receive forgiveness for your sin? Do you fear breaking God's good commands? How are God's commands for our good?*

> **Give me understanding, that I may keep your law and observe it with my whole heart. Lead me in the path of your commandments, for I delight in it . . . Great peace have those who love your law; nothing can make them stumble. (Psalm 119:34-35, 165)**

MAKING YOU WISE FOR SALVATION

What does this chapter tell us about God? Talk about and apply the **biblical truths** in **bold** text.

Salvation Thread: God is calling people to be a people of His own. God is holy and righteous. God demands obedience to His righteous commands.

Talk about the meaning of each of the Ten Commandments.

Talk About: *"Now therefore, if you will indeed obey my voice and keep my covenant, you shall be my treasured possession among all peoples . . ." (Exodus 19:5)*

How is God's law a reflection of His character?

Pray: Thank God for His holy and righteous character. Ask Him to give you a love for His law and His way. Ask God to give you love for Him and trust in Him.

Think About: God is still calling people to be His children. *Do you know how to become a child of God?* (See John 1:12.)

Memorize: The Ten Commandments

1. Most biblical scholars believe Mount Sinai and Mount Horeb are the same mountain.

THE TEN COMMANDMENTS EXPLAINED

(Take several days to explain, discuss, make personal application, and pray about each commandment.)

I am the LORD your God, who brought you out of the land of Egypt, out of the house of slavery.

God's law shows us His perfect and righteous character which should lead us to worship Him. It also provides a right code of conduct and a standard of justice. God's perfect law shows us our sinfulness, our inability to keep God's law perfectly, and our need for redemption. For those who have been redeemed by faith, it shows us what is pleasing to God so that we can live under His blessing and enjoy the righteous life that God desires.

1. **You shall have no other gods before me. (Exodus 20:3)**

   God is greater than all other gods. He alone is worthy of our worship. To worship or serve anything other than Yahweh is idolatry. This includes any desires for other things that grow to occupy a position of too much importance in our hearts. We are all worshipers. Whom or what will you worship and treasure?

2. **You shall not make for yourself a carved image, or any likeness of anything . . . You shall not bow down to them or serve them, for I the LORD your God am a jealous God . . . (Exodus 20:4-6)**

   God is incomprehensible. No manmade form can adequately represent Him. God is a jealous God. All images, whether physical or mental, that lead to false worship or false ideas of God are prohibited.

3. **You shall not take the name of the LORD your God in vain . . . (Exodus 20:7)**

   God commands that His name and reputation be honored. Dishonoring God's name by using it carelessly is prohibited. Do you speak and live in a way that brings honor to God?

4. **Remember the Sabbath day, to keep it holy. (Exodus 20:8-11)**

   The Sabbath is a gift from God to man, given for man's mental, physical, and spiritual refreshment. Resting from our labor acknowledges God as our Provider. Resting from working for our salvation acknowledges faith in the saving work of Jesus.

5 Honor your father and your mother, that your days may be long in the land that the LORD your God is giving you. (Exodus 20:12)

God commands that parents and others in authority be honored—obeyed, respected, supported, and appreciated with gratitude for them. Disrespect for superiors and elders is prohibited. Dishonoring those in authority is prohibited.

6 You shall not murder. (Exodus 20:13)

God commands the protection of human life. Not only does God prohibit murder ("unlawful killing"), but also all wrong attitudes of the heart that could lead to murder (anger, bitterness, resentment, envy, hatred, and revenge).

7 You shall not commit adultery. (Exodus 20:14)

God's faithfulness to His covenant people serves as our example in covenant relationships. God commands the faithful commitment between a man and woman in marriage, forbidding lust and requiring purity of thought, attitudes, and actions.

8 You shall not steal. (Exodus 20:15)

Stealing, in any form, is forbidden. The roots of stealing are heart issues, such as greed, pride, covetousness, and unbelief in God.

9 You shall not bear false witness against your neighbor. (Exodus 20:16)

God commands that our speech be truthful and loving. Therefore, speaking evil against another is forbidden. God hates lies.

10 You shall not covet your neighbor's house; you shall not covet your neighbor's wife, or his male servant, or his female servant, or his ox, or his donkey, or anything that is your neighbor's. (Exodus 20:17)

God is our greatest treasure, and we are to be content with what He provides. In forbidding coveting, God is claiming authority over our hearts. Is God your greatest treasure, or are you laying "up treasures on earth"?

CHAPTER 28

I WILL DWELL AMONG THEM

God Instructs Moses about the Tabernacle and Priests—Exodus 21-31

"I will dwell among the people of Israel and will be their God." (Exodus 29:45)

The Ten Commandments were not the only laws that God gave Israel. Moses went back up the mountain to hear from God. God had some very important laws, instructions, and customs or practices to command Israel to follow—laws about altars, the Sabbath and other special festival days, and the right way to treat others. God also promised to bring them to Canaan, the Promised Land, and to drive out all the people who lived there. But He gave them a warning about the people in Canaan, *"You shall make no covenant with them and their gods. They shall not dwell in your land, lest they make you sin against me; for if you serve their gods, it will surely be a snare [a trap] to you."* Moses wrote all this in the Book of the Covenant, which he went down and read to the people. Again, the people said, *"All that the LORD has spoken we will do, and we will be obedient."*

God once again called His prophet to come up to meet with Him on the mountain. This time, God was going to give Moses the commandments written on tablets of stone. God had promised to be with Israel, to protect them, and make of them a special nation. But Israel had to keep His laws perfectly. *Do you think Israel could do this?*

God knew that the Israelites had Adam's sin nature and would not be able to perfectly obey His commands all the time. How could a holy God live among sinful people? When they disobeyed God's commands, they would deserve punishment. *Do you remember what the punishment for sin is?* **Death is the punishment for sin**. So, would all the Israelites have to die because of their sin? How could they become "a kingdom of priests and a holy nation"?

God is a God of steadfast, never-ending love and mercy, who wants to be in relationship with man. There was **nothing man could do to solve his sin problem** and be in the presence of a holy God. But God made a way for Israel to be in a relationship with Him. He told Moses to ask the people for gold, silver, and bronze metals; yarns and linen fabric; goat hair; animal skins; acacia wood; oil and spices; and precious stones . . . *And let them make me a sanctuary, that I may dwell in their midst.* A sanctuary is a "holy place" or a "set-apart place." This was a home or "dwelling place" where God would live among His covenant people and have a special relationship with them.

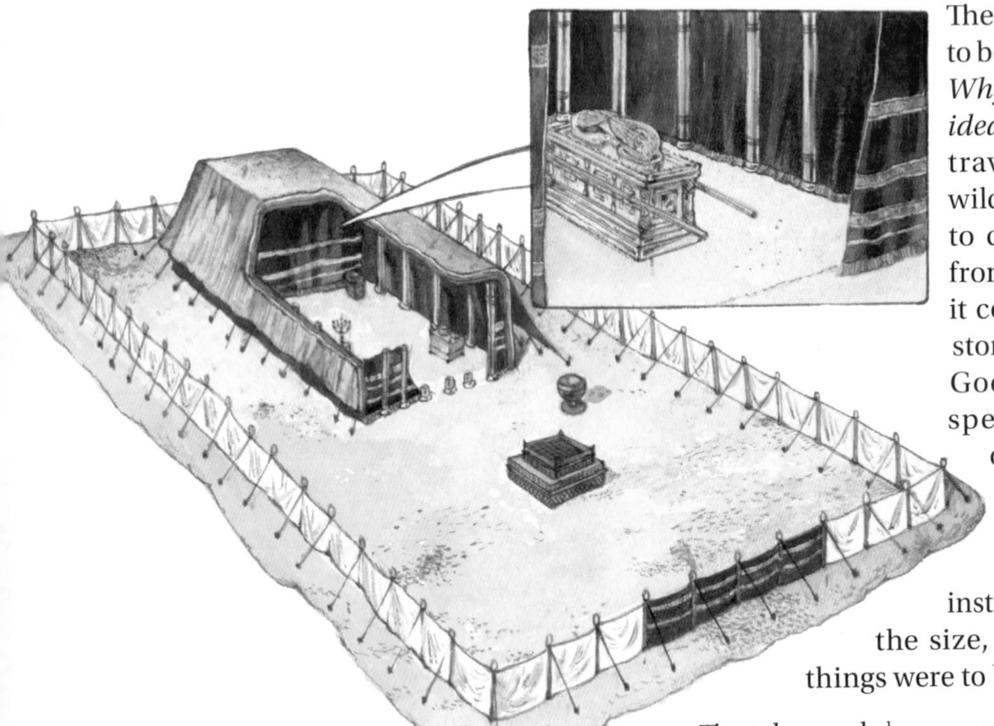

The first sanctuary was to be a tabernacle or tent. *Why was a tent a good idea?* The Israelites were traveling through the wilderness, and they had to carry the sanctuary from place to place. So, it could not be made of stone or be permanent. God gave Moses very specific instructions on how to make the tabernacle and all its furniture. They must follow these instructions exactly about the size, materials, and how things were to be made.

The tabernacle[1] was surrounded by an outside wall made of curtains hung between pillars. There was no roof—only curtain walls. Inside the walls, there was a large open space. This was called the outer court, or the courtyard. *Can you find the outer court on the drawing?* At the entrance to the courtyard, there was a bronze altar for making sacrifices. This is where the priests would offer dead animals as payment for sin. Beyond the altar was a bronze basin for washing.

Inside the outer court beyond the basin was a tent, the actual tabernacle, with walls and a roof. It was made of fabric and animal skin, and it had two rooms—one larger and one smaller. The first room, the larger one, was called the Holy Place. There were three things in this room. *Do you know what they were?* On one side was a golden lampstand. On the other side was the table of bread holding twelve loaves of bread. *Why do you think there were twelve loaves?* Each loaf represented one of the twelve tribes of Israel. At the end of the room was the altar of incense. Incense is a mixture of spices and oils that smells nice when burned. The smoke that went up from the burning incense represented, or was a picture of, the prayers of the people going up to God.

The second room, the smaller one, was separated from the larger room by a long, thick curtain or veil. It was the most special and beautiful place of all. It was called the Most Holy Place or the Holy of Holies. God's special presence would fill this room. Even though God is everywhere all the time, here God would be with His people in a special way. What a wonderful promise!

The Most Holy Place only had one piece of furniture in it. *Do you know what that piece of furniture was?* In the Most Holy Place was the Ark of the Covenant. This was a special box made of acacia wood and covered with gold. After it was made, it would hold the stone tablets of the covenant or the Ten Commandments, Aaron's rod, and a pot of manna.

The Ark of the Covenant had a special lid. It was called the mercy seat and was made of pure gold. Two gold angels called cherubim knelt on the lid with their wings stretched out over the top. *Do you remember when the cherubim separated Adam and Eve from God by guarding the entrance of the Garden of Eden?* God was now making a way for sinful Israel to come to Him. The mercy seat is where God would come down to be present with His people and where He would show mercy to His sinful people.

Every part of the tabernacle was to be made exactly as God said—the number of loops on the curtains, the size of each curtain, the materials used for each piece of furniture, the colors in the veil, the exact decorations—everything had to be made according to God's precise instructions. Every detail was given to Moses to make a most beautiful tabernacle where God's presence would be with His people.

God also gave Moses instructions about setting apart Aaron and his sons to be priests. The priests were to have special clothes, and they had special instructions about making offerings. They were to make an offering of two one-year-old lambs every day as a covering for sin—one in the morning and one in the evening.

"It shall be a regular burnt offering throughout your generations at the entrance of the tent of meeting before the LORD, where I will meet with you, to speak to you there. There I will meet with the people of Israel, and it shall be sanctified by my glory . . . I will dwell among the people of Israel and will be their God. And they shall know that I am the LORD their God, who brought them out of the land of Egypt that I might dwell among them. I am the LORD their God." (Exodus 29:42-43, 45-46)

God also gave instructions about the Sabbath. The Sabbath, or the seventh day, was to be treated as a holy day of rest and worship. It was a sign or a remembrance that God created the world in six days and rested on the seventh.

And he gave to Moses, when he had finished speaking with him on Mount Sinai, the two tablets of the testimony, tablets of stone, written with the finger of God. (Exodus 31:18)

God did not have to make a way for sinful man to have a relationship with Him. But **God is merciful and loving and wants to have a special relationship with man.** Adam and Eve lived in the Garden of Eden with God. But sin separated man from a holy God. In His tabernacle, God was once again choosing to dwell, or live, among His people.

Our sin separates us from God. It is only through God's mercy that we can receive forgiveness from sin and have a relationship with God. *Do you know someone who has a relationship with the living God? Ask that person how he or she came to be a child of God. Decide in your heart to seek God.*

"You will seek me and find me, when you seek me with all your heart." (Jeremiah 29:13)

MAKING YOU WISE FOR SALVATION

What does this chapter tell us about God? Talk about and apply the **biblical truths** in **bold** text.

Salvation Thread: God is holy, and yet He has made a way for sinful man to be in relationship with Him.

Why do you think God's instructions about the tabernacle were so specific? Why did Israel have to follow them exactly?

Talk About: *"I will dwell among the people of Israel and will be their God." (Exodus 29:45)*

Pray: Admit to God that you are a sinner. Thank Him for making a way for sinful man to be forgiven and have a relationship with Him. Ask Him to show you if you are depending on your own goodness to save you.

Think About: Why was the top of the Ark of the Covenant called the mercy seat? What does this tell you about salvation from sin?

Memorize: The Ten Commandments

1. Help your child to check the illustraton and find all these elements of the tabernacle.

CHAPTER 29

A JEALOUS GOD IS FAITHFUL TO A STIFF-NECKED PEOPLE

Israel Makes a Golden Calf, Yet God Renews the Covenant—Exodus 32-34

But you, O Lord, are a God merciful and gracious, slow to anger and abounding in steadfast love and faithfulness. (Psalm 86:15)

Moses had been on the mountain for a long time—forty days and forty nights. The people of Israel wondered what had happened to him. Was he going to return? They didn't have Moses to lead them, so they approached Aaron and asked him to make gods for them. Aaron, the man set apart to be God's priest, did not remind them of the first two commandments or of God's covenant with them. Instead, he foolishly told them to give him the gold jewelry they had received from the Egyptians—the gold God had graciously given them in the Exodus!

> *And he received the gold from their hand and fashioned it with a graving tool and made a golden calf. And they said, "These are your gods, O Israel, who brought you up out of the land of Egypt!" When Aaron saw this, he built an altar before it. (Exodus 32:4-5a)*

Aaron even proclaimed the next day as a feast day to their god! *What do you think the one true God thought of this?*

> *And the LORD said to Moses, "Go down, for your people, whom you brought up out of the land of Egypt, have corrupted themselves. They have turned aside quickly out of the way that I commanded them. They have made for themselves a golden calf and have worshiped it and sacrificed to it and said, 'These are your gods, O Israel, who brought you up out of the land of Egypt!'" And the*

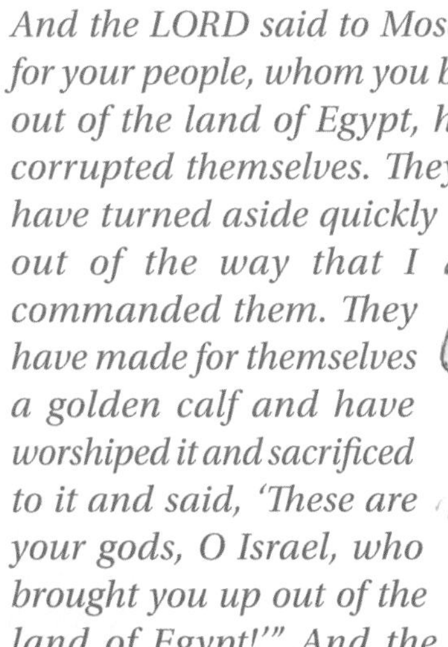

LORD said to Moses, "I have seen this people, and behold, it is a stiff-necked people. Now therefore let me alone, that my wrath may burn hot against them and I may consume them, in order that I may make a great nation of you." (Exodus 32:7-10)

How quickly the people of Israel had broken their covenant with God! Did they not remember the fierce thunder, the flashing lightning, the shaking mountain, and their trembling fear at the presence of God when they heard these words?

"I am the LORD your God, who brought you out of the land of Egypt, out of the house of slavery. You shall have no other gods before me. You shall not make for yourself a carved image or any likeness of anything . . . You shall not bow down to them or serve them, for I the LORD your God am a jealous God . . . (Exodus 20:2-4a, 5a)

How quickly they had forgotten their promise, *"All that the LORD has spoken we will do, and we will be obedient."* How quickly they turned to other gods instead of following Yahweh, who had brought them out of Egypt. God had not only rescued them from slavery, but He had also redeemed them from the worship of false gods. Yet they so quickly turned right back to their old ways and idolatry. They were a stiff-necked people, a stubborn people who deserved God's fierce anger and destruction!

Moses could have proudly delighted in the idea of God making a great nation from him. After all, Moses was a descendant of Abraham. God would still be keeping His promise. But God had called Moses to be a *mediator*—a go-between or someone to represent the people before God and to receive and tell God's words to the people, someone who would be in the middle between God and the people to make peace between them. As a mediator, Moses pleaded with God not to destroy the people. He reminded God of His glorious deeds—that He had brought the people out of Egypt with His mighty hand. He appealed to God's glory and the honor of His great name. *"Why should*

the Egyptians say, 'With evil intent did he bring them out, to kill them in the mountains and to consume them from the face of the earth.'" And he reminded God of His great promise to Abraham, Isaac, and Jacob to make this people a great nation. Moses had become the great mediator, the great *intercessor* who *prayed* for God's favor on Israel . . . as God had called him to be. So, God respected the prayer of Moses and turned away from destroying the people.

Joshua had accompanied Moses partway up the mountain and, as they started down, he thought he heard the sound of war in Israel's camp. But Moses knew what the sound was—it was the sickening, horrifying sound of singing and celebrating the worship of an idol. *And as soon as he came near the camp and saw the calf and the dancing, Moses' anger burned hot, and he threw the tablets out of his hands and broke them at the foot of the mountain. He took the calf that they had made and burned it with fire and ground it to powder and scattered it on the water and made the people of Israel drink it.* Moses' horrified anger was a very small picture of the fierce anger of God at sin.

The broken tablets were a symbol of God's law horribly broken by rebellious Israel. Moses asked Aaron what the people had done to him that he had brought this great sin on them. Instead of confessing his sin and repenting, Aaron blamed the people and made excuses for himself. He also lied. He said that he just threw the gold in the fire and out came the calf! Aaron had not acted as a priest to Israel. He had not encouraged the people to repent and trust Yahweh. Instead of being a priest who asked God to forgive the sins of the people, he sinned along with them.

. . . then Moses stood in the gate of the camp and said, "Who is on the LORD's side? Come to me." And all the sons of Levi gathered around him. And he said to them, "Thus says the LORD God of Israel, 'Put your sword on your side each of you, and go to and fro from gate to gate throughout the camp, and each of you kill his brother and his companion and his neighbor.'" And the sons of Levi did according to the word of Moses. And that day about three thousand men of the people fell. (Exodus 32:26-28)

Sin is serious. Rebellion and idolatry must be punished. Three thousand men died because of their horrific sin. God was rightly angry with the people. The next day, Moses went back up the mountain to pray for the people again. They deserved to be punished and rejected by God forever. But God had made Moses a great mediator and intercessor, and he continued to pray for the people and plead for God's mercy. As the people mourned the loss of their relationship with God, Moses continued to meet with God on the mountain and in a tent outside the camp called the tent of meeting. *When Moses entered the tent, the pillar of cloud would descend and stand at the entrance of the tent, and the LORD would speak with Moses.* Moses found favor before God. His continued obedience and faithfulness to his calling to lead the people and pray for them was pleasing to God.

God told Moses to cut two new tablets. God would again write the words on the tablets. The LORD passed before Moses on Mount Sinai and proclaimed:

"The LORD, the LORD, a God merciful and gracious, slow to anger, and abounding in steadfast love and faithfulness, keeping steadfast love for thousands, forgiving iniquity and transgression and sin, but who will by no means clear the guilty, visiting the iniquity of the fathers on the children and the children's children, to the third and the fourth generation." (Exodus 34:6b-7)

Sin is serious. Yet merciful, gracious, faithful Yahweh renewed His covenant with His unfaithful, rebellious people. Once again, He promised His blessing. He promised to give them the land of Canaan, and He reminded them of their covenant-keeping responsibility. The **Israelites could not be righteous in God's eyes by obeying the law.** They would never be able to keep God's law perfectly. But they were blessed to have Yahweh, the one true God, as their covenant-keeping God, who would provide atonement for sins.

The LORD is merciful and gracious, slow to anger and abounding in steadfast love. *He will not always chide, nor will he keep his anger forever.* ***He does not deal with us according to our sins,*** *nor repay us according to our iniquities. (Psalm 103:8-10)*

We can look at the Israelites and think how foolish they were to worship a golden calf. But all of us have inherited Adam's sin nature. We are all foolish, rebellious, prideful, and stubborn deep in our hearts—and we all need God's grace.

When we look into the perfect law of God, we see that we cannot keep God's law and be righteous through our obedience. Why is it good for us to see this? What should this cause us to do?

For by works of the law no human being will be justified in his sight, since through the law comes knowledge of sin. (Romans 3:20)

MAKING YOU WISE FOR SALVATION

What does this chapter tell us about God? Talk about and apply the **biblical truths** in **bold** text.

Salvation Thread: God is a jealous God and will not allow worship of any other gods.

How have you broken God's law this week? What do you deserve? How did Moses pray for the people when they were disobedient? How does this help you to know how to pray?

Talk About: *But you, O Lord, are a God merciful and gracious, slow to anger and abounding in steadfast love and faithfulness. (Psalm 86:15)*

Pray: Confess your sin to God. Thank God that He is merciful and gracious. Ask Him to give you a heart to love and trust Him.

Think About: Since you cannot keep God's commands perfectly, what hope is there for you to receive God's favor and inherit eternal life? (See 1 Peter 1:3-4.)

Memorize: The Ten Commandments

CHAPTER 30

GOD'S COVERING FOR ISRAEL

Sacrifices—Exodus 35, 40; Leviticus 1

...without the shedding of blood there is no forgiveness of sins. (Hebrews 9:22b)

Do you like to draw, sew, or make things? The Israelites needed all of these skills to make the tabernacle, its furniture, and clothing for the priests. God had renewed His covenant with His rebellious people. Now they were ready to make the tabernacle—the place where God would be with His people in a special way. The Israelites drew artistic designs and engraved them in gold, silver, and bronze metal. They cut stones, carved wood, wove cloth, spun yarn, and embroidered beautiful designs on fabric. Everyone with a willing heart brought materials for the tabernacle. In fact, they brought *more* contributions than were needed for the tabernacle and its furniture. They were willing and eager to make this special earthly dwelling place for God. Israel made the tabernacle (or tent of meeting), bronze altar, basin, lampstand, table, altar of incense, the Ark of the Covenant and mercy seat, the thick dividing curtain, and all the clothing for the priests exactly as God had instructed Moses.

And Moses saw all the work, and behold, they had done it; as the LORD had commanded, so had they done it. Then Moses blessed them. (Exodus 39:43)

Moses put everything in the tabernacle exactly as God had said they should. Then Moses "anointed" Aaron and his sons with oil—he poured oil on their heads. *Why did Moses do this?* Moses was following God's instructions to show that Aaron and his sons were chosen by God to be priests. They were not like the other people. They were set apart to serve God in a special way. *Then the cloud covered the tent of meeting, and the glory of the LORD filled the tabernacle.* God's presence was with His people.

How could God live among a people who had rejected Him and worshiped a golden calf? How could sinful people who had broken God's law be in the presence of a holy God? The Israelites' sin had caused a separation between them and their God. **Sin must be judged** and paid for. It is not easily forgiven. There was only one way to receive forgiveness.

> *. . . without the shedding of blood there is no forgiveness of sins. (Hebrews 9:22b)*

God is merciful. He did not want to destroy His people; He wanted to forgive them. *Do you remember how God covered Adam and Eve's sins?* He covered their shame with the skins of animals. The blood of innocent animals had been the temporary payment for their sin. Israel's sins could be covered through sacrifices, too. Instead of putting the people to death for their sin, **God was willing to accept a substitute.** *What was the substitute?* The substitute was an animal—such as a lamb, goat, or bull. It had to be a male animal, and it had to be perfect. It could not be sick, scarred, bruised, or imperfect in any way.

God gave the Israelites the tabernacle and priests, and exact instructions about making sacrifices so they could be forgiven. The relationship between Israel and God could be restored. But Israel had to do things God's way. When a person made an offering, he had to bring the animal to the entrance of the courtyard of the tabernacle.

> *He shall lay his hand on the head of the burnt offering, and it shall be accepted for him to make atonement for him. (Leviticus 1:4)*

Why do you think the person had to put his hand on the head of the animal? Laying a hand on the animal's head was a symbol or picture God gave the Israelites to help them understand that they were putting their sin on the animal. The guilty person's sin was *transferred* or passed to the innocent animal. Though the guilty person deserved to die, the animal would die in his place. The animal was a *substitute.* The person would confess his sin and then kill the animal, shedding its blood. But the person could not draw close to God by himself. He needed the help of the priests. He had to give the animal's blood to the priests, who would

throw it on the bronze altar. Then he would cut up the animal, and the priests would burn it on the altar. They did all this in the outer court of the tabernacle.

Every morning and every evening, the priests were to make animal sacrifices to cover the sins of Israel. They had to make these sacrifices every morning, every evening, every day, every week, all year long, year after year. *Why do you think they had to make these sacrifices continually?* The people continued to sin, and **animal sacrifices were only a temporary covering for sin**. They did not take away sin, but only covered it. On the Sabbath, more sacrifices were made. In addition, each person could make an offering for sin. This was a continual reminder to Israel that **sin is serious** and that **sin must be covered**.

This sounds strange and horrible to us. But this is the way God provided for Israel's sin in His covenant with them. The sacrifices taught them that **sin brings death, and only through the shedding of blood can sinful man be at peace with God** again.

> *"For the life of the flesh is in the blood, and I have given it for you on the altar to make atonement for your souls . . ." (Leviticus 17:11a)*

To make atonement means "to cover over." The blood of animals made it possible for sinful man to be at peace with God by covering over sin. It was God's good way for the Israelites to live in peaceful friendship with a holy God, even though they broke His law. But Israel had to have faith in God and trust that His way is right.

Just like Israel, we are to be holy, righteous, and good in all that we want, think, say, and do. And just like Israel, we cannot keep God's law perfectly. God's perfect law shows us that we are sinners. But God is merciful and eager to forgive those who come to Him His way, by faith.

Why would God be eager to forgive sinners? What examples have you seen of His justice? Of His mercy? How has God shown you His kindness? What kind of heart is pleasing to God?

The sacrifices of God are a broken spirit; a broken and contrite heart, O God, you will not despise. (Psalm 51:17)

MAKING YOU WISE FOR SALVATION

What does this chapter tell us about God? Talk about the **biblical truths** in **bold** text.

Salvation Thread: Sin brings death. Only through the shedding of blood can sinful man be at peace with God.

Discuss why blood is necessary for the forgiveness of sin.

There was no chair in the tabernacle for the priest. Why do you think this was so? What does this tell you about the work of the priests? What does this tell you about sin? Why is God's mercy so wonderful?

Talk About: *The sacrifices of God are a broken spirit; a broken and contrite heart, O God, you will not despise. (Psalm 51:17)*

Do you see your sin as serious? Explain.

Pray: Ask God for a "broken and contrite heart." Confess your sin to Him and ask Him to give you a heart to love and trust Him.

Think About: Why don't we sacrifice animals for our sin anymore? What did God do that changed our need for animal sacrifices?

CHAPTER 31

BEING AT PEACE WITH A PURE, POWERFUL GOD

The Day of Atonement—Leviticus 16

For as high as the heavens are above the earth, so great is his steadfast love toward those who fear him; as far as the east is from the west, so far does he remove our transgressions from us. (Psalm 103:11-12)

H*ow many animals do you think the Israelites had to kill to cover their sin?* Remember that they had to sacrifice an animal every morning and every evening. They had to make more sacrifices every Sabbath and on special feast days. On the Passover, every household sacrificed a lamb . . . and then there were all the individual offerings. They sacrificed *thousands* of animals every year, year after year. This would be a continual reminder to the Israelites of their sin and the serious payment necessary to cover their sin. But it was only a temporary covering, which was repeated over and over because the blood of bulls, lambs, and goats could never truly pay for their sins. All of this reminded them that sin brought death into God's once perfect world.

The priests had other duties besides offering the people's sacrifices on the altar. They made other offerings, such as the grain offering to thank God and praise Him for His goodness.

They had to keep the fire on the altar burning continually, so they were constantly adding more wood. Only the priests could go inside the tabernacle and enter the Holy Place. Before they did this, they had to wash their hands and feet at the bronze basin. **They had to be clean to come into the presence of God.**

Inside the tabernacle, all the furniture was made of precious gold.[1] The golden lampstand had seven bowls of oil, which must be kept filled and burning so there was constant light in the Holy Place. Every Sabbath, the twelve loaves of bread on the table of bread must be replaced with fresh bread. Sweet-smelling incense must be burned at the altar of incense every morning and evening. The priests also taught the people God's commands and settled difficult cases when the people had disagreements with each other.

The tribe of Levi was set apart to lead the people in praises to God and to take care of the tabernacle. Some of the sons of Aaron were priests, but one priest, the high priest, was most special and had special duties. Aaron was the first high priest of Israel. Whenever Aaron entered the Holy Place, he wore eight very special garments. There were twelve precious stones attached to his breastplate, each inscribed with a name of one of the twelve tribes of Israel. *Can you find these twelve stones?* On each shoulder, he wore a special gold setting with a precious onyx stone in it. The names of the tribes of Israel were engraved in birth order on these stones also. These were called "Remembrance Stones."

"And you shall set the two stones on the shoulder pieces of the ephod [a special garment], as stones of remembrance for the sons of Israel. And Aaron shall bear their names before the LORD on his two shoulders for remembrance." (Exodus 28:12)

When the high priest entered the Holy Place, God saw the names of all the tribes of Israel on the ephod. This was a symbol of God remembering to have mercy on His people. The priests, especially the high priest, had an important duty to represent the people before God—to stand before God to plead for His mercy on His people and to be a reminder of the covenant relationship He had with them.

Do you remember what separated the Holy Place from the Most Holy Place, or the Holy of Holies? A thick, heavy curtain separated the two rooms of the tabernacle. It separated the people and even the priests from the presence of God. Even though God is everywhere all the time, God was present in a special way in the Most Holy Place. The priests could go into the first room . . .

. . . but into the second only the high priest goes, and he but once a year, and not without taking blood, which he offers for himself and for the unintentional sins of the people. (Hebrews 9:7)

Every sin, every disobedience, every rebellion of every Israelite could not be covered by individual sacrifices, so once a year a special sin offering was made for the whole nation of Israel. This special sacrifice was made on the Day of Atonement. On this day, the Israelites did not work, but instead they fasted, prayed, and mourned over their sin the whole day.

The Day of Atonement was the one and only day of the year that the high priest could enter the Most Holy Place. If the high priest entered the Most Holy Place at any other time, he would die before the pure and powerful presence of God. On the Day of Atonement, the high priest washed not only his hands and feet in the basin but his whole body. Instead of wearing his special colorful garments, on the Day of Atonement the high priest wore a white robe. Once a year, on this day only, the high priest went beyond the thick curtain and entered the Most Holy Place. *What did he do there?*

First, he entered carrying hot burning coals from the altar in one hand and a dish of incense in the other. He scattered the incense on the coals, and sweet-smelling smoke filled the room. This was to dim or hide the glory of God so that the high priest could stand before Him. Then, the high priest returned a second time with the blood of a bull that had been sacrificed for his own sin. He sprinkled the blood on the mercy seat. The third time, the high priest entered with the blood of a goat that had been sacrificed to cover the sin of the people. This, too, was sprinkled on the mercy seat. The blood of the animals made "atonement" for sin—it made it possible for Israel to be at peace with God and live in relationship with a holy and perfect God.

Then the high priest bathed again and dressed in his regular regal clothing. But the ceremonies of the Day of Atonement were not over. One perfect male goat had been sacrificed for the people, but another perfect male goat had been chosen to live. *Do you know what happened to this goat?* The high priest laid both of his hands on the live goat. He confessed the sin, disobedience, rebellion, and wickedness of the people, transferring or putting them on the goat. But this goat was not killed. Instead, it was sent far away into the wilderness, never to be seen again. This goat, called the "scapegoat," was a physical example of what was happening spiritually. It was a symbol or picture of God's merciful heart. It showed **God's desire to take away sin and its consequences from His people so that they could be at peace with Him and have a relationship with Him.**

Then, in the evening, they made the regular sacrifice again—the constant cycle of sacrifices never ended. Even though the Old Testament sacrifices were given by God so that His people

could be at peace with Him, they could not remove sin forever. It was a temporary covering of sin. Would the day come when God would provide a permanent provision for man's sin problem?

After the evening sacrifice and the setting of the sun, the fast ended and the people feasted. They rejoiced that their sins had been covered—the sacrifices had been made, and the scapegoat carrying their sin had been sent far away. The Day of Atonement was a reminder of God's mercy to His people and His loving and forgiving heart. The scapegoat showed Israel that God wanted to put their sin far away, never to remember it again. This is the heart of Yahweh.

> *For as high as the heavens are above the earth, so great is his steadfast love toward those who fear him; as far as the east is from the west, so far does he remove our transgressions from us. (Psalm 103:11-12)*

One day, God would send a greater High Priest to bring His mercy and grace to His people. Because of that, our sins can be carried far away, and we can be forgiven. Our sins can be covered and we can be at peace with God. *Are you trusting in Yahweh's heart of love and mercy and His provision that has made a way for sinful people to be forgiven and at peace with Him? How has God made that possible?*

Blessed is the one whose transgression is forgiven, whose sin is covered. (Psalm 32:1)

MAKING YOU WISE FOR SALVATION

What does this chapter tell us about God? Talk about the **biblical truths** in **bold** text.

Salvation Thread: God desires to take sin and its consequences away from His people so that they can be at peace with Him and have a relationship with Him.

Explain the meaning of the Day of Atonement and the scapegoat.

Talk About: *For as high as the heavens are above the earth, so great is his steadfast love toward those who fear him; as far as the east is from the west, so far does he remove our transgressions from us. (Psalm 103:11-12)*

Why do you think that the furnishings in the outer court were made of bronze and the furnishings in the tabernacle's two rooms were made of gold? What does this tell you about God and about man?

Pray: Thank God for His steadfast love for His people. Confess your sin and ask God for His forgiveness.

Think About: Why would the high priest die if he entered the Most Holy Place except on the Day of Atonement? What does this tell you about God? About man? Why is there a need for a greater High Priest?

1. Parents: You may want to turn back to the illustration of the tabernacle in chapter 28 and ask your child to point out the different elements as you read this paragraph.

C H A P T E R 3 2

GRUMBLING IN THE CAMP

Israel Complains about God; Miriam and Aaron Complain about Moses—Numbers 9-12

Then they despised the pleasant land, having no faith in his promise. They murmured in their tents, and did not obey the voice of the LORD. (Psalm 106:24-25)

The Israelites had been camped at Mount Sinai about a year. They had been given the law and had entered into a covenant with God. They had also constructed the tabernacle and all its furnishings. Finally, it was now time to leave for the Promised Land of Canaan! What excitement must have run through the camp! The people would have a land of their very own! The promise made to Abraham so many years ago would finally be fulfilled.

On the day that the tabernacle was set up, the cloud covered the tabernacle, the tent of the testimony. And at evening it was over the tabernacle like the appearance of fire until morning . . . And whenever the cloud lifted from over the tent, after that the people of Israel set out, and in the place where the cloud settled down, there the people of Israel camped. (Numbers 9:15, 17)

When the cloud moved from the tabernacle, the Israelites packed up their tents and all their belongings. The Levites packed up the tabernacle and all its furniture. God had given very special instructions on how to carry the Ark of the Covenant. The Ark was holy and represented the presence of God to Israel. The Levites couldn't even come near the Ark until the priests had covered it with a cloth. Each side of the Ark had two rings. Each set of rings had a pole between them. The Levites picked up the two poles and carried the Ark on their shoulders whenever Israel moved. These instructions were very important, and Moses warned the Levites of God's command that *they must not touch the holy things, lest they die.*

The people of Israel traveled until the cloud stopped. Sometimes they traveled for days, and sometimes they stayed in the same place for days. But every time they stopped, the camp was set up in the same way.[1] The tabernacle was in the middle of the camp with the tribe of Levi encamped around it on all four sides. Then the other tribes of Israel—the ten tribes and the two half-tribes of Joseph (Ephraim and Manasseh)—camped around the tribe of Levi, three on each side making a rectangle.

It didn't take long before a familiar pattern started again. The Israelites started complaining. They forgot about what it was like to be slaves in Egypt. They were craving the fish, cucumbers, melons, onions, and other food they had eaten in Egypt. They were tired of God's manna! They were not just complaining. They were even weeping about it!

Once again, they were not grateful for God's goodness to them. Once again, they did not trust Him to care for them in the best way. It was not just a pattern of complaining and ingratitude. It was a pattern of not trusting God, of not being satisfied with God's plan for them, of not treasuring His covenant friendship with them. They were rejecting God. Even Moses, the great intercessor, was frustrated with Israel. How could he give meat to millions

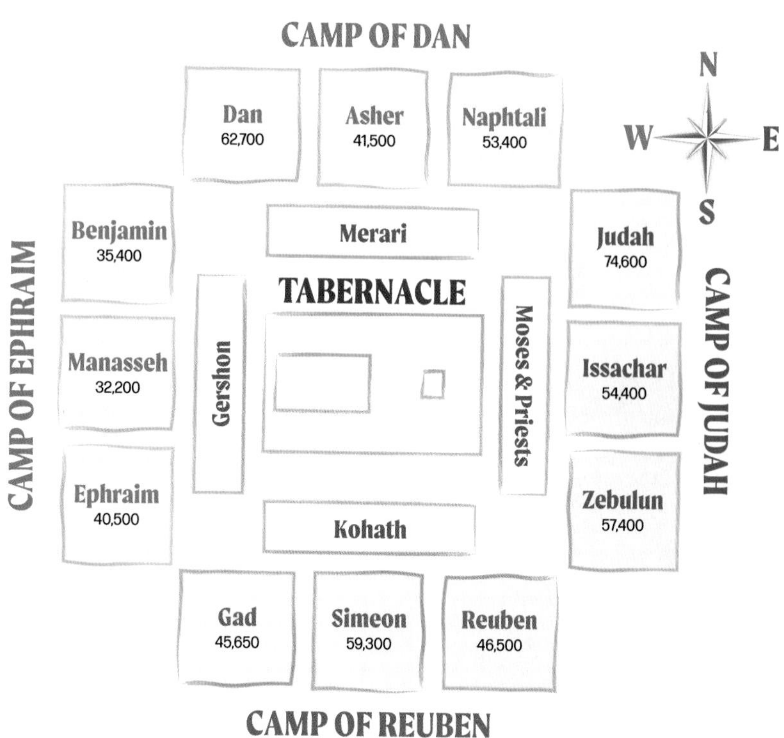

Jacob's son, Levi, had three sons: Gershon, Kohath, and Merari. Their descendants became the tribe of Levi. Each of these family groups—the Gershonites, Kohathites, and Merarites—held different roles in caring for the tabernacle and its furnishings, as well as assisting in Israel's worship of Yahweh.

of people? He was tired of caring for this ungrateful, rebellious people. Not only did Moses hate Israel's grumbling, but **God hates grumbling**.

What do you think God did? First, He graciously gave Moses helpers—seventy elders. This is what God promised Moses, *"And I will take some of the Spirit that is on you and put it on them, and they shall bear the burden of the people with you, so that you may not bear it yourself alone."* He also told Moses to tell the people that He had heard their crying. God was going to give the people what they demanded.

> *"You shall not eat just one day, or two days, or five days, or ten days, or twenty days, but a whole month, until it comes out at your nostrils and becomes loathsome to you, because you have rejected the LORD who is among you and have wept before him, saying, 'Why did we come out of Egypt?'" (Numbers 11:19-20)*

God gave them what they wanted. He brought a wind that blew quail from the sea and dropped the quail beside the camp. *How much quail did He bring?* God brought enough quail to cover the ground a day's journey in every direction from the camp! It took the people all day—and all night—and all the next day to gather the quail. They had baskets and baskets and baskets of quail! Yet, this quail did not satisfy them. Before they had even eaten all the quail . . . *While the meat was yet between their teeth, before it was consumed, the anger of the LORD was kindled against the people and the LORD struck down the people with a very great plague.* So those who craved Egypt and its food were buried in the wilderness.

But this was not the end of the discontentment. This time, it was Aaron and Miriam who grumbled. *Do you know why they were upset?* They complained about their brother, Moses. It started with them criticizing him for marrying a Cushite woman. The Cushites were descendants of Noah's son, Ham. They were not Canaanites, which the Israelites were forbidden to marry. So, Moses had not broken God's law.

But that wasn't the only reason they spoke against Moses. *And they said, "Has the LORD indeed spoken only through Moses? Has he not spoken through us also?"* They were jealous of Moses and wanted more recognition, power, and authority. Moses was a humble man who did not seek leadership. *Who would defend Moses?*

God Almighty defended His prophet Moses. The LORD came down in a pillar of cloud and called Aaron and Miriam to the entrance of the tent of meeting. Then, with Moses there, God defended him.

> *And he said, "Hear my words: If there is a prophet among you, I the LORD make myself known to him in a vision; I speak with him in a dream. Not so with my servant Moses. He is faithful in all my house. With him I speak mouth to mouth, clearly, and not in riddles, and he beholds the form of the LORD. Why then were you not afraid to speak against my servant Moses?" And the anger of the LORD was kindled against them, and he departed. (Numbers 12:6-9)*

When the cloud moved away, Aaron saw that Miriam had leprosy. Aaron was horrified! Leprosy was a dreadful skin disease that eats away at a person's flesh. Aaron begged Moses not to let them be punished for their sin. *What do you think Moses did for this brother and sister who had sinned so terribly against him?*

He did what only a humble man would do. He prayed to God to heal Miriam. Once again, God was gracious, and He removed Miriam's awful disease. But she would have to stay outside the camp for seven days as part of her punishment. This was also God's way of restoring Miriam back into leadership. Being alone for seven days would give her time to think about her sin and God's mercy. **God is both just and merciful.** He punishes sin, and yet **He is a God of steadfast love. He keeps His covenant even when His people are unfaithful.**

Why is it so much easier for us to complain rather than to be grateful? When has it been hard for you to trust God this week? How has God shown you compassion this week? Thank God that His Word says that He can give us a heart to trust Him and fight our sin nature.

For the Lord will not cast off forever, but, though he cause grief, he will have compassion according to the abundance of his steadfast love; (Lamentations 3:31-32)

MAKING YOU WISE FOR SALVATION

What does this chapter tell us about God? Talk about and apply the **biblical truths** in **bold** text.

Salvation Thread: God is both just and merciful.

Talk about God's goodness to your family. Are you grateful for all His mercies?

Talk About: *For the Lord will not cast off forever, but, though he cause grief, he will have compassion according to the abundance of his steadfast love; (Lamentations 3:31-32)*

Why is grumbling so sinful? What does it say about a person's heart? What does it say about a person's trust in God's wisdom and goodness?

Pray: Thank God for His steadfast love. Ask Him to give you a grateful heart that trusts in His goodness and wisdom.

Think About: *Am I a grateful person?* Read 1 Timothy 6:6 and Philippians 4:11. *What do these verses tell you about contentment?*

1. Help your child to identify the tribes on the diagram.

CHAPTER 33

REBELLION AND UNBELIEF LEAD TO FORTY YEARS OF WANDERING

Israel Refuses to Trust God and Possess the Land—Numbers 13-14

"Because you have turned back from following the LORD, the LORD will not be with you." (Numbers 14:43b)

Once again, the people set out following the cloud of God and stopped in the wilderness of Paran. There, Moses chose twelve men, one from each tribe, to spy out the land of Canaan as God had instructed him. They were about to enter the land God had promised to give them!

The spies spent forty days checking out the people and the land. Were the people strong, or weak? Were there a few of them, or many? Did they live in tents, or fortified cities? Was the land good, or bad? Did it have trees and good crops?

When they returned to the camp of Israel, the spies showed Moses, Aaron, and the people the big, luscious fruit from the land of Canaan. The land was very good, "flowing with milk and honey," just as God had said. But the people were large and powerful, and the cities were strongly fortified. This made ten of the spies very fearful, and their fear spread to the people. But Caleb, one of the spies, quieted them and suggested that they "go up at once and occupy" the land because they were "well able" to do so. The ten spies strongly disagreed with him. They didn't believe they could fight the fierce people of Canaan, who were stronger than the people of Israel. They agreed that the land was good, but there were other

problems, *"The land, through which we have gone to spy it out, is a land that devours its inhabitants, and all the people that we saw in it are of great height . . . and we seemed to ourselves like grasshoppers . . ."*

What was wrong with the report of the ten spies? They were looking at the size of the people instead of the size, the greatness, the power of their God! They made their decision because of their feelings of grasshopper-like smallness, instead of trusting in the truth of who God is and the promises He made to them. They looked at themselves, rather than at their great, wonder-working God!

How do you think the people of Israel reacted to the report? They fell into their typical pattern. They "raised a loud cry," wept, and grumbled against Moses and Aaron. *What do you think they said to Moses and Aaron? "Would that we had died in the land of Egypt! Or would that we had died in this wilderness! Why is the LORD bringing us into this land, to fall by the sword? . . . Would it not be better for us to go back to Egypt?"* It was the same old words again! Again, their response was unbelief! Again, they refused to believe God's word and His promise! Again, they gave in to despair instead of standing strong in faith!

But two spies believed the promise of God. Joshua and Caleb had faith in God's mighty power, His faithful character, and His unfailing word. They were so distressed at the rebellion and unbelief that they tore their clothes and said to the people:

> *"If the LORD delights in us, he will bring us into this land and give it to us, a land that flows with milk and honey. Only do not rebel against the LORD. And do not fear the people of the land, for they are bread for us. Their protection is removed from them, and the LORD is with us; do not fear them." (Numbers 14:8-9)*

Would Israel listen to these words of faith and confidence in God? No, instead they wanted to stone Joshua and Caleb—to kill them by throwing stones at them! But God rescued His faithful servants, Joshua and Caleb.

> *. . . the glory of the LORD appeared at the tent of meeting to all the people of Israel. And the LORD said to Moses, "How long will this people despise me? And how long will they not believe in me, in spite of all the signs that I have done among them?" (Numbers 14:10b-11)*

Once again, God tested Moses, saying He would disinherit Israel and make a greater, mightier nation from Moses. And once again, Moses was a faithful mediator between the people and God. Once again, Moses, the intercessor, pleaded for mercy by reminding God of the glory of His great name. What a dishonor it would bring on God's name if the nations thought that God was not able to keep His promise! Moses also pleaded for mercy on the basis of God's character—that God is *"slow to anger and abounding in steadfast love, forgiving iniquity and transgression, but he will by no means clear the guilty . . . Please pardon the iniquity of this people according to the greatness of your steadfast love, just as you have forgiven this people, from Egypt until now."*

How do you think God responded to Moses' intercession—his prayer for the people? Just as God had been so many times before, **God was both just and merciful**. Over and over, God had forgiven His people, and yet, **God is just and must punish rebellion and sin.**

Then the LORD said, "I have pardoned, according to your word. But truly, as I live, and as all the earth shall be filled with the glory of the LORD, none of the men who have seen my glory and my signs that I did in Egypt and in the wilderness, and yet have put me to the test these ten times and have not obeyed my voice, shall see the land that I swore to give to their fathers. And none of those who despised me shall see it. But my servant Caleb, because he has a different spirit and has followed me fully, I will bring into the land into which he went, and his descendants shall possess it . . . not one shall come into the land where I swore that I would make you dwell, except Caleb . . . and Joshua . . . But your little ones, who

> *you said would become a prey, I will bring in, and they shall know the land that you have rejected. But as for you, your dead bodies shall fall in this wilderness. And your children shall be shepherds in the wilderness forty years and shall suffer for your faithlessness . . . I, the LORD, have spoken. Surely this will I do to all this wicked congregation who are gathered together against me . . ." (Numbers 14:20-24, 30-33, 35a)*

Again, the people mourned their sin. Just as they had done so many times before, they regretted their sin and tried to make things right on their own. They decided to do what God had asked them. They would go up, fight the people in Canaan, and take the land, but it was too late. They would be going on their own, without God's help. Moses warned them, *"Because you have turned back from following the LORD, the LORD will not be with you."* But they stubbornly refused to listen and went anyway.

What do you think happened? They were defeated! It was true. The people of Canaan were too strong for them. But they were not too strong for the LORD—something Israel had refused to believe.

What you believe about God affects the way you act. Joshua and Caleb believed the truth that **God is trustworthy, truthful, and all-powerful**. So, they could face the men of Canaan confident of God's help. *God has shown us that we can hold fast to His promises because of who He is. What do you believe about God? How can you look to God for help?*

I lift up my eyes to the hills. From where does my help come? My help comes from the LORD, who made heaven and earth. (Psalm 121:1-2)

MAKING YOU WISE FOR SALVATION

What does this chapter tell us about God? Talk about and apply the **biblical truths** in **bold** text.

Salvation Thread: God's Word can be trusted because God is trustworthy. Failing to trust God's Word is sin.

Talk about the difference between Joshua and Caleb and the other spies. Read Deuteronomy 1:29-30. How does remembering what God has done in the past strengthen our faith?

Talk About: *I lift up my eyes to the hills. From where does my help come? My help comes from the LORD, who made heaven and earth. (Psalm 121:1-2)*

Why was God right to punish the people of Israel? Why was Israel's sin so grave?

Pray: Praise God for being both just and merciful. Confess any rebellion or unbelief in your heart. Thank God for making a way for our sins to be forgiven through His Son.

Think About: Why is it good that God is both just and merciful? What if He was only just? What if He was only merciful?

Memorize: Psalm 121:1-2

CHAPTER 34

GOD DEFENDS HIS CHOSEN LEADERS

Korah, Dathan, Abiram, and Others Rebel—Numbers 16

"Therefore it is against the LORD that you and all your company have gathered together." (Numbers 16:11a)

So Israel began forty years of wandering in the wilderness. Every day, they would be reminded that they could be in the Promised Land, but their sin of unbelief and rebellion had kept them from it. Except for Joshua and Caleb, all those who were twenty years old or older would die in the wilderness, but their children would inherit the Promised Land.

However, God never left His people alone in the wilderness. His presence in the pillar of fire and the cloud led them, camped over the tabernacle when they stopped, and filled the Most Holy Place in a special way. Every day, the Israelites had to depend on God to bring them manna, and **God never failed** to provide it. Perhaps the Israelites would learn humility and trust in God through their years of wandering. Perhaps . . .

Or perhaps not—at least not all of them. The Levites had been especially chosen by God to lead the people in praise to God, to carry and care for the tabernacle and its furnishings, and to camp closest to the tabernacle and the visible presence of God with Israel. They were helpers to Aaron and his sons, the priests. It was a great honor to be a Levite. But one Levite, Korah, who was Moses and Aaron's cousin, wasn't satisfied with his special position. Neither were Dathan, Abiram, and On from the tribe of Reuben (Jacob's first-born son). They started to complain to others. They asked questions like these: What made Moses and Aaron better than everyone else? Why should they lead Israel? Why should they have honored positions? Why couldn't the other Levites be priests and enter the tabernacle, too?

Moses and Aaron were not the leaders of Israel because they wanted to be. They were chosen by God to be the leaders Israel needed. **God has the right and wisdom to choose how each person fits in His eternal plan**. Sadly, Korah, Dathan, Abiram, and On did not honor God's right or trust His wisdom. These men spread their poisonous thoughts to others, and soon 250 other leaders joined their rebellion against God's chosen leaders.

When Moses heard this, he trusted the LORD to show the people "who is His, and who is holy." He told Korah and each of his followers to come the following day with a censer filled with burning coals. A censer was a gold container used in the tabernacle for burning incense. Aaron would also bring a censer, and they would all throw incense on their coals before God. God would show them whom He had chosen to be holy—who was chosen to enter the tabernacle and offer incense.

Then Moses sent for Dathan and Abiram, who refused to come. They said it was Moses and Aaron's fault that they were not living in the Promised Land. They accused Moses of wanting to kill them in the wilderness so he could become a prince over Israel. What a wicked thing to think and say! Moses was angry, but instead of defending himself, he asked the LORD to humble the people.

The next morning, everyone met at the entrance of the tent of meeting—Korah had *assembled all the congregation against them . . . And the glory of the LORD appeared to all the congregation.* What would happen? Korah, Dathan, Abiram, and the 250 leaders were grumbling against Moses and Aaron, but they were really rebelling against God. They were questioning God's wisdom, goodness, and His right to rule. They were not content with the position God gave them. They wanted Aaron's job and Moses' authority—they wanted to be in charge. *Does this sound familiar?* It was the same rebellion and discontentment found in Satan, in Eve, in Joseph's brothers . . . and in all sinful hearts.

Again, Israel had rebelled against God. And again, God threatened to destroy all Israel in a moment. Once again, Moses, along with Aaron, pleaded with God not to punish them all. And still another time, God who is ***merciful and gracious, slow to anger and abounding in steadfast love*** did not destroy Israel.

But **sin and rebellion against God is very serious and brings consequences.** God instructed Moses to tell the people to move away from the tents of Korah, Dathan, and Abiram. While Israel did this, Korah, Dathan, and Abiram with their families stood defiantly at the door of their tents. Then Moses spoke:

> *"If these men die as all men die, or if they are visited by the fate of all mankind, then the LORD has not sent me. But if the LORD creates something new, and the ground opens its mouth and swallows them up with all that belongs to them, and they go down alive into Sheol, then you shall know that these men have despised the LORD." (Numbers 16:29-30)*

What do you think happened? As soon as Moses finished speaking, the ground suddenly split apart and these rebellious, discontent, ungrateful, prideful men and their families were swallowed up! The rest of Israel ran away in terror! And then fire came from the LORD to consume the 250 men offering incense. God, with great mercy, spared Israel, but in justice punished those who sinfully rebelled.

Do you think that now Israel finally learned to be content? The very next day, the people of Israel who were mercifully spared from judgment grumbled against Moses and Aaron again! This time, they accused Moses and Aaron of killing those who had died. The Israelites still did not see their rebellion as serious and worthy of judgment. Did they think God would be patient with them forever? Why shouldn't He destroy them all and start over with Moses and Aaron? Had they no fear of the wrath of God? The LORD was rightly angry with them and sent a plague—a serious illness—among the people. Once again, Moses and Aaron fell on their faces before the LORD and pleaded for mercy.

God mercifully allowed Aaron to carry burning incense in his censer and bring it to the Israelites to make atonement for the people. He stood as a mediator between God and the people to make peace between them and God. In response to the prayers of Moses and Aaron—their work as mediators and intercessors—God stopped the plague. Though 14,700 people died in the plague, God spared millions of Israelites. **God never punishes more than is necessary. His heart is to cause repentance and restore His people.**

When Korah and his friends rebelled against Moses and Aaron, they really rebelled against God who placed Moses and Aaron in positions of leadership. **God has the right, wisdom, and goodness to rule His world, to work out His purposes in His own way, and to choose whomever He wills.**

You can either recognize God's authority over you, or you can rebel against it. You can choose to trust God's goodness and wisdom, or to resist Him. *What are some examples of how you can trust God's goodness and wisdom? What are some examples of resisting Him?*

"Yours, O LORD, is the greatness and the power and the glory and the victory and the majesty, for all that is in the heavens and in the earth is yours. Yours is the kingdom, O LORD, and you are exalted as head above all." (1 Chronicles 29:11)

MAKING YOU WISE FOR SALVATION

What does this chapter tell us about God? Talk about the **biblical truths** in **bold** text.

Salvation Thread: God has authority over all things.

What were the sinful heart attitudes that Korah, Dathan, and Abiram expressed? Why was this such an offense to God?

Talk About: *"Yours, O LORD, is the greatness and the power and the glory and the victory and the majesty, for all that is in the heavens and in the earth is yours. Yours is the kingdom, O LORD, and you are exalted as head above all." (1 Chronicles 29:11)*

Are you content with how God has made you? Can you trust God to know what is best for you?

Pray: Praise God that He can be trusted to rule the world well. Thank Him for the blessings He has given you and for making you who you are. Ask Him to give you a grateful heart.

Think About: God has the right, power, wisdom, and righteousness to rule the world well. What does this practically mean in everyday life? *Does this give me comfort, concern, or both?*

CHAPTER 35

THE END OF THE JOURNEY

Moses Dishonors God; the Bronze Serpent; and the Death of Moses—Numbers 20-21, 26-27, Deuteronomy 34

"For the LORD your God has blessed you in all the work of your hands. He knows your going through this great wilderness. These forty years the LORD your God has been with you. You have lacked nothing." (Deuteronomy 2:7)

The Israelites had been wandering almost forty years in the wilderness. In all this time, God protected, guided, and cared for them. God's presence in the cloud and pillar of fire was continually with them. **Never once did God fail** to give them food and water. He even kept their clothes from wearing out! One by one, those who refused to believe that God would fight for them and give them the Promised Land died. Miriam also died in the wilderness, and Moses was now 120 years old.

Once again, God tested Israel. Again, there was no water. Would Israel trust Yahweh to provide for them? Would they remember His forty years of faithfulness?

> *And the people quarreled with Moses and said, "Would that we had perished when our brothers perished before the LORD! Why have you brought the assembly of the LORD into this wilderness, that we should die here, both we and our cattle?" (Numbers 20:3-4)*

Such familiar words! Such unbelief after so many signs of God's care! Moses and Aaron fell on their faces in humble prayer before the entrance of the tent of meeting. Did God refuse to help His complaining, unbelieving people this time? No, **God** proved once again that He **is slow to anger and patient.** He told Moses to speak to the rock, and God would bring water out of it for the people and their animals.

But Moses was angry with the people and said, *"Hear now, you rebels; shall we bring water for you out of this rock?"* Then he hit the rock with his staff twice, and water gushed out. Moses did not speak to it as God told him. Instead, he struck out in anger.

> *And the LORD said to Moses and Aaron, "Because you did not believe in me, to uphold me as holy in the eyes of the people of Israel, therefore you shall not bring this assembly into the land that I have given them." (Numbers 20:12)*

Moses and Aaron did not model faithful obedience and trust in God's word. They were God's appointed leaders to show the people what God is like—but they failed to do that, too. God did not respond in anger but in love and patience, giving His people water. But

this is not the picture of God that Moses represented to the people; He showed them anger and impatience instead of love. **Whenever God punished His people, it was to bring them to repentance and to teach them to have faith in Him.** It was never just because He was angry and wanted to express His anger.

How very sad that after forty years of wandering and leading the complaining, unbelieving, rebellious Israelites, Moses and Aaron could not enter the Promised Land. Instead, another leader would have to lead them. Another high priest would have to mediate between Israel and God. Before long, Aaron died, and God appointed Aaron's son, Eleazar, to become the new high priest.

Because the people of Edom would not allow Israel to pass through their land, the Israelites had to take a detour around Edom, making the journey even longer. They became impatient and *spoke against God and Moses. What do you think they said?* They had the same old complaints: *"Why have you brought us up out of Egypt to die in the wilderness? For there is no food and no water, and we loathe this worthless food."*

God had protected them from danger for forty years—the danger of starvation, thirst, destruction by their enemies, scorpions, poisonous snakes, wild animals, and all kinds of

danger. But now God pulled back His hand of blessing, and *sent fiery serpents among the people*. After some of the people were bitten by the poisonous snakes and died, the people repented. *And the people came to Moses and said, "We have sinned, for we have spoken against the LORD and against you. Pray to the LORD, that he take away the serpents from us." So Moses prayed for the people.*

After all Israel's failures and ingratitude, do you think God was done with them? No, He wasn't, because **God is a God of steadfast love and faithfulness**. But He saved them in a strange way to teach them something very important. He told Moses to make a fiery serpent of bronze metal and put it on a pole. Then God said something really strange: *"Everyone who is bitten, when he sees it, shall live."* That's it—all they had to do was to look at the snake on the pole and they would be healed! *Do you think a bronze snake can heal a poisoned person?* Not at all! The bronze snake couldn't heal, but God Almighty heals. God was asking Israel to have faith—to trust Him, believe in Him, and obey His word. **Faith alone would bring salvation and life.** The people who looked at the snake in faith were healed and lived! All they had to do was to trust God and look!

By now, Moses was nearing the end of his life. Before getting to the Jordan River, God gave Israel victory over the Amorites and Moabites. Their land would belong to the tribes of Reuben, Gad, and the half-tribe Manasseh. Moses and Eleazar counted the number of adults (age twenty years and older) in each tribe and made a record of them. Not one of the adults counted at Sinai were on the list... except Joshua and Caleb. All the rest had died, just as God had said. **God's word never fails!** Moses' work was almost done. He told the people God's good commands and wrote them in a book to be put beside the Ark of the Covenant. Then he reminded Israel of the covenant between God and Israel and God's commitment to keep His covenant.

There was just one thing left for Moses to do—to pass on the leadership to the next leader of Israel.

> *So the LORD said to Moses, "Take Joshua the son of Nun, a man in whom is the Spirit, and lay your hand on him. Make him stand before Eleazar the priest and all the congregation, and you shall commission him in their sight. You shall invest him with some of your authority, that all the congregation of the people of Israel may obey." (Numbers 27:18-20)*

Then Moses went up Mount Nebo, and from there Yahweh showed him all the land He was giving to Israel. There Moses, the prophet *whom the LORD knew face to face*, died. The people of Israel wept for Moses for thirty days. A prophet like no other had died, a mediator between God and man, the great intercessor who prayed and pleaded for mercy on sinful Israel.

Moses was a great prophet, speaking God's word to the people. Before He died, God gave Moses a picture of a great work He would do. Looking at the bronze serpent was more than a cure for snakebites. It was a picture of the great work God would do in sending the Promised One, who would take away the sin of anyone who looked to Him in repentance and faith. Just as the serpent was cursed in the Garden of Eden, Satan would one day be crushed by the Promised One who would take the curse of sin upon Himself and be lifted up for all to look to for salvation.

Isn't God's faithfulness, goodness, and power amazing? Why is it so wonderful that faith alone brings salvation from sin? Can you pray with the writer of this psalm?

> O Lord, hear my voice! Let your ears be attentive to the voice of my pleas for mercy! If you, O LORD, should mark iniquities, O Lord, who could stand? But with you there is forgiveness, that you may be feared. (Psalm 130:2-4)

MAKING YOU WISE FOR SALVATION

What does this chapter tell us about God? Talk about the **biblical truths** in **bold** text.

Salvation Thread: Salvation is by faith alone.

Why were the Israelites healed by simply looking at the bronze snake? Why is this so important to understand?

Talk About: *"You shall love the LORD your God with all your heart and with all your soul and with all your might. And these words that I command you today shall be on your heart." (Deuteronomy 6:5-6)*

What does it mean to "have faith in God"?

Pray: Praise God for being a faithful God. Ask Him to give you faith in Him.

Think About: How would you describe God? What is He like?

CHAPTER 36

STANDING FIRMLY ON GOD'S PROMISE

Spying Out Jericho and Crossing the Jordan River—Joshua 1-4

"Have I not commanded you? Be strong and courageous. Do not be frightened, and do not be dismayed, for the LORD your God is with you wherever you go." (Joshua 1:9)

God had spoken to Moses face to face. Moses then spoke God's words to Israel. Moses was a great prophet, leader, mediator, and intercessor. How could Joshua hope to fill Moses' position? But it isn't the skill of the leader that is important—it is the favor of God that is important. And God's favor was on Joshua.

"No man shall be able to stand before you all the days of your life. Just as I was with Moses, so I will be with you. I will not leave you or forsake you." (Joshua 1:5)

What a wonderful promise God had given Joshua! God commanded Joshua to cross the Jordan River and take the Promised Land, defeating all the enemies of Israel. This was a big and frightening task. But with His command God also gave Joshua a great promise. He promised Joshua that He would be *with him*. Yahweh, the **sovereign, self-existent, eternal, almighty, unchanging God**, who had helped Moses, would help Joshua.

Again, Israel sent men to spy out the land, and especially the city of Jericho. What would happen this time? Would they come back and say they felt "like grasshoppers"? Would they say that Israel could not take the land? Would Israel fail to trust God's promise again?

The two spies entered the walled city of Jericho and went to the house of a woman named Rahab. She was used to entertaining different men, so it was not strange for two men to enter her house. But these were Israelites, so they must be spies wanting to check out Jericho. Someone told the king of Jericho about the men, and he ordered Rahab to bring out these spies of Israel. But she had cleverly hidden them under stalks of grain on the roof of her house.

Then she helped the spies even more. She told the king that the men had left Jericho just before the gates of the city closed that evening. If the men from Jericho hurried, they would be able to catch the two men. *Why did Rahab do this?* She told the two spies:

..."I know that the LORD has given you the land, and that the fear of you has fallen upon us, and that all the inhabitants of the land melt away before you. For we have heard how the LORD dried up the water of the Red Sea before you when you came out of Egypt, and

what you did to the two kings of the Amorites... And as soon as we heard it, our hearts melted, and there was no spirit left in any man because of you, for the LORD your God, he is God in the heavens above and on the earth beneath." (Joshua 2:9-11)

Although she was a Canaanite, Rahab believed that Yahweh is the one true God. She knew Israel would be victorious in battle. Rahab asked the spies to save her family. The men promised that, because of her kindness, she and her family would be protected if they stayed in her house when Israel attacked. The spies thought they were just repaying Rahab for her kindness, but **God had a bigger, eternal plan**—for Rahab later married Salmon, one of the spies, and became the mother of a man named Boaz... someone we will read about in another story.

Then Rahab, whose house was built into the Jericho wall, let the two spies down through a window. She told them to hide in the hills for three days, until the men who were looking for them returned to Jericho. Then it would be safe to travel back to where Israel was camped. Before they left, the men told Rahab to tie a red rope in her window so the Israelites would know which home to protect.

After hiding for three days, the spies returned to Joshua. *And they said to Joshua, "Truly the LORD has given all the land into our hands. And also, all the inhabitants of the land melt away because of us."* What a different report this was from the report the ten spies brought back to Moses and Aaron! This time, Israel was standing firmly on God's promise to give them the land. This time, Israel was trusting in Yahweh!

The next day, Joshua and Israel set out for the Jordan River and camped there. After three days, Joshua told Israel, *"As soon as you see the ark of the covenant of the LORD your God being carried by the Levitical priests, then you shall set out from your place and follow it . . . for tomorrow the LORD will do wonders among you."*

Israel would see more of God's mighty wonders! What would God do? The next day, Joshua called the people together to hear the word of the LORD their God. They would know the living God was among them and that He would defeat all the enemies of Israel when they saw the wonders He would do that day. *What miracle would God do?*

Then Joshua commanded the priests to carry the Ark of the Covenant and step into the Jordan River. As soon as the feet of the priests stepped into the edge of the water, God stopped the water from flowing! It *rose up in a heap very far away,* and the priests stood firmly on dry ground. The whole nation of Israel then passed across the Jordan River on dry ground. **God is almighty. He can do anything. Nothing is too hard for God.**

Do you know what happened next? God told Joshua to choose twelve men, one from each tribe, to each take a stone from the place where the priests stood in the river. *What were they going to do with these stones?* Each stone would be a stone of remembrance[1] for Israel. So, Joshua set up the twelve stones to show God's mighty work in bringing Israel into the Promised Land.

When the priests reached the dry ground on the other side of the river, the waters rushed back in. But the stones stood as a sign, or reminder, to Israel:

> *. . . "When your children ask their fathers in times to come, 'What do these stones mean?' then you shall let your children know, 'Israel passed over this Jordan on dry ground.' For the LORD your God dried up the waters of the Jordan for you until you passed over, as the LORD your God did to the Red Sea, which he dried up for us until we passed over,* ***so that all the peoples of the earth may know that the hand of the LORD is mighty, that you may fear the LORD your God forever."*** *(Joshua 4:21b-24)*

God gave Israel these twelve stones for a reason. He wanted Israel—and all the peoples of the earth, including you—to know that He is mighty so that you might fear or honor Him forever. *What has God done to show you that He is mighty and worthy to be honored?*

I will remember the deeds of the LORD; yes, I will remember your wonders of old. I will ponder all your work, and meditate on your mighty deeds. Your way, O God, is holy. What god is great like our God? You are the God who works wonders; you have made known your might among the peoples. (Psalm 77:11-14)

MAKING YOU WISE FOR SALVATION

What does this chapter tell us about God? Talk about the **biblical truths** in **bold** text.

Salvation Thread: God is the living God who accomplishes His purposes and works for His people.

Talk about the wonders of God your family has seen—both the everyday ones and the unusual ones.

Talk About: *"Have I not commanded you? Be strong and courageous. Do not be frightened, and do not be dismayed, for the LORD your God is with you wherever you go." (Joshua 1:9)*

What does it mean to "fear God"?

Pray: Praise God for being almighty. Thank Him for being with His people. Ask Him to help you to fear Him.

Think About: What is the significance of God being "with you"?

Memorize: Joshua 1:9

1. "Stone of remembrance" in Hebrew is transliterated into English as "Ebenezer."

C H A P T E R 3 7

BY FAITH WALLS FALL DOWN

God Gives Israel Victory over Jericho—Joshua 5-6

By faith the walls of Jericho fell down after they had been encircled for seven days. (Hebrews 11:30)

After the Israelites passed over the Jordan River, they camped at Gilgal and celebrated the Passover. *And the day after the Passover, on that very day, they ate of the produce of the land . . . And the manna ceased the day after they ate of the produce of the land. And there was no longer manna for the people of Israel.* God had miraculously provided what Israel needed to survive in the wilderness for forty years. But now He was giving them the plentiful land of Canaan, the Promised Land, and all its fruits and grains. The Israelites had often despised the manna, wanting the fish, cucumbers, melons, and other foods of Egypt—but God had something so much better for them. He saved them from slavery and the false gods of Egypt and promised to be their God. Would the Israelites now have faith in their God and His promise?

Jericho was the first city the Israelites needed to conquer in order to occupy the land of Canaan. It was a very well-protected city, surrounded by not one, but two massive walls—both very high and very wide. Normally, the gates of the ancient cities were open during the day and closed at night. But after the Israelites crossed the Jordan River, orders were given to keep the gates of Jericho closed. No one could go in or out of the city. *Why do you think this order was given?*

As soon as all the kings of the Amorites who were beyond the Jordan to the west, and all the kings of the Canaanites who were by the sea, heard that the LORD had dried up the waters of the Jordan for the people of Israel until they had crossed over, their hearts melted and there was no longer any spirit in them because of the people of Israel. (Joshua 5:1)

The people of Jericho were terrified of Israel, and Israel's God. They knew Israel's God was powerful and worked wonders! But their strong walled city was a good defense against the army of Israel. They had just harvested their crops, so there was plenty of food within the walls, and the city had springs of water. The only way an invading army could defeat them was to starve them to death or attack them by tunneling under the walls, making a ramp, using ladders or battering rams, or setting fires. This could take months and months. *How would Israel defeat this strongly fortified city?*

Just as God spoke to Moses, who then told God's words to the people, God spoke to Joshua. He was the new mediator between God and His people. Yahweh gave Joshua a *very unusual* battle strategy—march around the city for seven days! That was not the way to defeat a walled city! Israel had refused to trust God forty years ago when He told them to take the land of Canaan. Would they have faith in Yahweh now and obey His command? Would they trust that **God will do what He says He will do**? Or would they trust in what seemed right and best to them?

Here was God's very strange battle plan: Armed men were at the head of the procession of people. Then came the seven priests of Israel blowing trumpets of ram's horns with the Ark of the Covenant following them. After them came another group of armed men following the Ark. The people were not to speak but just march around the city one time each day for

six days. God, in His graciousness, would give the people of Jericho six days to turn to Him. Then, on the seventh day, the Israelites were to march around the city seven times, and then all the people were to shout, and the walls would fall down. Really? It sounded like a crazy strategy! Sometimes God's ways seem so strange to us. But **God's plans are higher or better than our plans.**

Would the Israelites follow God's strange commands? What if the enemy shot arrows or spears at them as they marched around the city? God was testing Israel. It would take faith to trust that God would protect them and give them victory—faith that **Yahweh is the LORD, the sovereign, self-existent, eternal, almighty, unchanging God**!

The Israelites marched around the city the first day . . . and then left. *What must the people of Jericho have thought about this?* Israel circled the city again the second day . . . and left. Again, what a strange strategy this was! Israel did this for six days, just as God had commanded. By then, the people of Jericho must have thought the Israelites were crazy! Then came the seventh day and a real test of Israel's faith in God. On the

seventh day, they were to march around the city seven times and then the priests were to blow a long blast on the trumpets, and the walls would fall down. *What was the significance of the trumpets?* The Israelites used these special trumpets at their feasts to proclaim or announce the presence of God. So God was showing Israel and Jericho that it was God Almighty who would defeat Jericho.

The city of Jericho and all in it was to be "devoted to the LORD for destruction"—except Rahab and her family. Israel was commanded to completely destroy everything except the things of silver, gold, bronze and iron. The precious metals would be put into the treasury of the LORD for the building of a permanent sanctuary someday. God also gave Israel a warning against taking anything else or sparing anyone except Rahab and her family.

> *"But you, keep yourselves from the things devoted to destruction, lest when you have devoted them you take any of the devoted things and make the camp of Israel a thing for destruction and bring trouble upon it." (Joshua 6:18)*

Why do you think God commanded Israel to completely destroy Jericho? The nations of Canaan were extremely evil, yet God had been merciful, sparing them from judgment. But they continued in their wicked ways—worshiping false gods, sacrificing babies to their gods, and doing other acts of violence and all kinds of horrible things. **God is patient, giving man many opportunities to repent.** Yet, the Canaanites were not repentant and did not turn away from their evil ways. It was time for God to stop their wickedness. It was time to bring judgment on them. **God's judgment against evil is always right.** By completely destroying Jericho, God was also protecting His people from the evil ways of the Canaanites. If they lived among the Canaanite people, the Israelites might begin to worship Canaan's false gods and do the same wicked things as the Canaanites did.

Would Israel have faith in God's wisdom and righteous judgment? Would Israel obey God's command completely? On the seventh day, they marched around Jericho one . . . two . . . three . . . four . . . five . . . six . . . seven times. The fighting men were in front, then the priests carrying the Ark of the Covenant and blowing the trumpets, and finally another group of fighting men. As they finished the seventh march around the city, the priests blew a long blast on the trumpets. Then *Joshua said to the people, "Shout, for the LORD has given you the city". . . the people shouted a great shout, and the wall fell down flat, so that the people went up into the city, every man straight before him, and they captured the city.*

God had knocked down the walls of Jericho with a loud crash! Yahweh had given His covenant-people a spectacular victory! God was fulfilling His promise to Abraham, Isaac, and Jacob to give them the land of Canaan. Joshua and Israel trusted God and followed His command. In the past, Israel had often failed to trust God, but this time they trusted and obeyed God! *By faith the walls of Jericho fell down after they had been encircled for seven days. By faith Rahab . . . did not perish with those who were disobedient because she had given a friendly welcome to the spies.*

It takes faith to obey God . . . especially when things don't seem to make sense to us. But **God is wise, faithful, and good. He can be trusted at all times. He is powerful** enough to bring down a walled city and to do all that He has planned or purposed. *Do you believe this about God? How should this mighty act of God give you confidence to trust God even when things look impossible?*

> "It is the LORD who goes before you. He will be with you; he will not leave you or forsake you. Do not fear or be dismayed." (Deuteronomy 31:8)

MAKING YOU WISE FOR SALVATION

What does this chapter tell us about God? Talk about the **biblical truths** in **bold** text.

Salvation Thread: God is faithful in keeping His promises and victorious in all He does.

Why was it right for God to punish the nations of Canaan? Why did Jericho have to be completely destroyed?

Talk About: *"It is the LORD who goes before you. He will be with you; he will not leave you or forsake you. Do not fear or be dismayed." (Deuteronomy 31:8)*

What does faith in God look like when things look impossible or very hard?

Pray: Praise God for being a faithful God and providing for His people. Praise Him for being righteous, just, almighty, and victorious. Ask God to give you faith to believe in who He is.

Think About: *Do I have faith that God has good in store for His people—that He is wise, gracious, strong, and faithful?*

CHAPTER 38

A CURSE AND A BLESSING

Israel's Defeat at Ai; Achan's Sin; and Victory over Ai—Joshua 7-8

"See, I am setting before you today a blessing and a curse: the blessing, if you obey the commandments of the LORD your God ... and the curse, if you do not obey the commandments of the LORD your God, but turn aside from the way that I am commanding you today, to go after other gods that you have not known." (Deuteronomy 11:26-28)

The defeat of Jericho was a great victory for Israel and a clear demonstration of the mighty power and sure faithfulness of God to Israel, *but*... Whenever the Bible uses the word, "but," it is important to pay close attention to what the Bible is teaching us.

> *But the people of Israel broke faith in regard to the devoted things, for Achan ... of the tribe of Judah, took some of the devoted things. And the anger of the LORD burned against the people of Israel. (Joshua 7:1)*

Joshua didn't know about Achan's sin or God's anger toward Israel. So he confidently sent men to spy out the town of Ai. When the men returned, they told Joshua he didn't need to send all the fighting men to defeat Ai. It was a small city with a small army. It would be easy to defeat Ai with only two thousand to three thousand men. Israel had just defeated the mighty city of Jericho! God Almighty was on their side.

So, Joshua sent a small army of three thousand fighting men to defeat Ai. This looked like an easy victory! *But guess what happened?* The men of Israel turned around and fled from the men of Ai. The men of Ai chased the men of Israel, killing thirty-six of Israel's soldiers. *And the hearts of the people melted and became as water.* The Israelites were suddenly filled with great fear. How could they defeat all their powerful enemies when they couldn't even defeat small unimportant Ai?

In desperation, Joshua tore his clothes and fell on his face before the Ark of the LORD. Why had God let Israel be disgraced? Would they be destroyed in Canaan? Joshua prayed just as Moses had prayed, asking God to protect His great name. *"O Lord, what can I say, when Israel has turned their backs before their enemies! For the Canaanites and all the inhabitants of the land will hear of it and will surround us and cut off our name from the earth. And what will you do for your great name?"*

What do you think God told Joshua?

> *"Israel has sinned; they have transgressed*
> *my covenant that I commanded them; they have*
> *taken some of the devoted things; they have stolen and lied*
> *and put them among their own belongings. Therefore the people of Israel cannot stand before their enemies . . . I will be with you no more, unless you destroy the devoted things from among you." (Joshua 7:11-12)*

Israel's sin had caused their defeat. The Israelites had broken their covenant with Yahweh. Without God, Israel was powerless before her enemies. So, the next morning, Joshua called all Israel before him, and the LORD showed him that the sin was in the tribe of Judah. Then each clan, and then each household of Judah came before Joshua . . . until it came down to a man named Achan. *What had Achan done to bring such judgment on Israel?*

> *And Achan answered Joshua, "Truly I have sinned against the LORD God of Israel, and this is what I did: when I saw among the spoil a beautiful cloak from Shinar, and 200 shekels of silver, and a bar of gold weighing 50 shekels, then I coveted them and took them. And see, they are hidden in the earth inside my tent, with the silver underneath." (Joshua 7:20-21)*

Achan disobeyed God's clear command and took things he coveted from Jericho. **Israel must take breaking God's covenant seriously**. Achan's sin harmed all Israel. It was up to Israel to deal with the sin and restore their relationship with Yahweh. So, Joshua and all Israel took the cloak, the silver, the gold, Achan's household, and all he had—including his animals and his tent—and stoned them with rocks and burned them. Achan had brought God's curse upon himself and his household for loving the treasures of this world more than loving and obeying God.

Then the LORD told Joshua, *"Do not fear and do not be dismayed. Take all the fighting men with you, and arise, go up to Ai. See, I have given into your hand the king of Ai, and his people, his city, and his land."* This time, God allowed the Israelites to take the possessions of their enemies for themselves. And God gave Joshua a clever battle plan for taking Ai.

Joshua chose 30,000 brave men to sneak behind the city of Ai and quietly hide there during the night. In the morning, Joshua came with another group of fighting men to face the city. The king and all the men of Ai left the city to meet Israel in battle—not one man was left in the city. Joshua and the Israelites with him ran away from the men of Ai, just as Israel had done before. But this time it was part of God's clever battle plan. While chasing Joshua's group, the men of Ai left the city unprotected. *Then the LORD said to Joshua, "Stretch out the javelin [spear] that is in your hand toward Ai, for I will give it into your hand."* When Joshua

pointed his spear toward the city, the Israelites who were hiding behind the city rose up, seized the city, and set it on fire.

When the men of Ai looked back, they saw their city in flames! An army of Israel was behind them . . . and then Joshua and his men turned around in front of them. They were trapped between the two armies of Israel! *Joshua did not draw back his hand with which he stretched out the javelin until he devoted all the inhabitants of Ai to destruction. Only the livestock and the spoil of that city Israel took as their plunder, according to the word of the LORD that he commanded Joshua.*

Once again, God was with His people and had given Israel victory. God, in **righteous justice**, had put an end to the wickedness of the people of Ai. **Yahweh, the faithful, covenant-keeping God**, was fulfilling His promise to His covenant people to give them the land of Canaan.

So, Joshua built an altar of uncut stones to the LORD, and Israel offered sacrifices for sin and sacrifices of thanks to God. Joshua wrote on the stones a copy of the law of Moses and read *all the words of the law, the blessing and the curse,* to everyone in Israel—the men, women, children, and foreigners among them.

> *"If you obey the commandments of the LORD your God that I command you today, by loving the LORD your God, by walking in his ways, and by keeping his commandments and his statutes and his rules, then you shall live and multiply, and the LORD your God will bless you in the land that you are entering to take possession of it. But if your heart turns away, and you will not hear, but are drawn away to worship other gods and serve them, I declare to you today, that you shall surely perish. You shall not live long in the land that you are going over the Jordan to enter and possess. I call heaven and earth to witness against you today, that I have set before you life and death, blessing and curse. Therefore choose life, that you and your offspring may live," (Deuteronomy 30:16-19)*

Loving and obeying God brings great blessing. *What are some of the blessings Israel received from God? What are some of the promises God made to Israel? God is unchanging. He still offers life to those who love Him, walk in His ways, and keep His commandments.*

"I call heaven and earth to witness against you today, that I have set before you life and death, blessing and curse. Therefore choose life, that you and your offspring may live," (Deuteronomy 30:19)

MAKING YOU WISE FOR SALVATION

What does this chapter tell us about God? Talk about and apply the **biblical truths** in **bold** text.

Salvation Thread: God is righteous in His judgments and faithful in keeping His covenant.

In what ways did Achan disobey God's law? How was Achan's sin similar to the sin in the Garden of Eden? [He saw the forbidden item; he coveted it–he wanted it; and he disobeyed and took it. He valued the items more than he valued his relationship with God.]

Talk About: *"See, I am setting before you today a blessing and a curse: the blessing, if you obey the commandments of the LORD your God ...and the curse, if you do not obey the commandments of the LORD your God, but turn aside from the way that I am commanding you today, to go after other gods that you have not known." (Deuteronomy 11:26-28)*

What are the blessings of loving God and obeying Him? How has God blessed your family?

Pray: Praise God for being a just God and for destroying evil in the world. Thank Him for His patience. Confess your sin to Him.

Think About: *Do I obey God's Word? What do I do when it is hard to obey?*

C H A P T E R 3 9

THE LORD FIGHTS FOR ISRAEL

God Gives Israel Victory over the Armies of Southern and Northern Canaan—Joshua 9-11

. . ."Hear, O Israel, today you are drawing near for battle against your enemies: let not your heart faint. Do not fear or panic or be in dread of them, for the LORD your God is he who goes with you to fight for you against your enemies, to give you the victory." (Deuteronomy 20:3-4)

What do you think the other nations of Canaan thought about the Israelites? The Bible says that their "hearts melted"—they were filled with terror! *Was this because the Israelites were fierce fighters or great in number?* No, it was because God was at work, ruling the hearts of men and fulfilling all His purposes. God had already told Israel through Moses that He would bring fear upon the Canaanite people:

"I will send my terror before you and will throw into confusion all the people against whom you shall come, and I will make all your enemies turn their backs to you." (Exodus 23:27)

So, it wasn't that the Israelites were such great soldiers, but that Yahweh, the one true God is the *LORD, strong and mighty, the LORD, mighty in battle!* God was not only fulfilling His promise to give Israel the land, but He was also bringing judgment on the evil nations of Canaan. Just as Yahweh had defeated all the gods of Egypt, He was defeating the false gods of Canaan and proving that He is the one true God.

Before Joshua had led the Israelites in battle against Jericho, a man with a sword in his hand appeared before Joshua. *And Joshua went to him and said to him, "Are you for us, or for our adversaries [enemies]?"* The "man" was really a mighty warrior angel—the commander of the army of the LORD. He was neither for Israel nor for their enemies, but rather he was on the LORD's side. What was important was if Joshua and Israel were on God's side. God was fighting this battle, and whoever was on His side would win. So, the size of the army didn't matter, because **Yahweh is great, mighty, and always victorious.**

As soon as they heard about Israel's victories in Jericho and Ai, *all the kings of the hill country and in the lowland all along the coast . . . the Hittites, the Amorites, the Canaanites, the Perizzites, the Hivites, and the Jebusites . . . gathered together as one to fight against Joshua and Israel.* This one big army would try to defeat Israel.

But one group, the Gibeonites, decided not to fight Israel. They feared for their lives because they were certain God would give Israel the land and destroy the people. So, they dressed up in worn-out clothes and patched sandals. They carried torn sacks and dried, crumbly bread to make it look they had been traveling for a long time. The Gibeonites went to Joshua and said they came from a faraway country. They wanted to make a peace agreement with Israel. They were very cunning, and the men of Israel *did not ask counsel from the LORD.* So, Israel was deceived and agreed to let them live. Later, Joshua and Israel found out that they were really some of their Canaanite neighbors. But Israel had made a peace agreement that they needed to honor. Like Rahab, the Gibeonites were spared.

When the five kings of the Amorites heard of the peace agreement between Israel and the Gibeonites, they gathered their armies and went to attack Gibeon. So, Joshua and the fighting men of Israel, "the mighty men of valor," went to help Gibeon. *And the LORD said to Joshua, "Do not fear them, for I have given them into your hands. Not a man of them shall stand before you."* God would surely give Israel victory. **God always defeats His enemies.**

Joshua and his army marched all night and surprised the Amorite armies, coming upon them suddenly. *And the LORD threw them into a panic before Israel who struck them with a great blow.* Then God worked in another amazing way. As the Amorites were fleeing from the Israelites, *the LORD threw down large stones from heaven on them . . . There were more who died because of the hailstones than the sons of Israel killed with the sword.* **Yahweh is sovereign—He rules over all things**—even hailstones! He brought the hail at just the right time and in just the right place!

But the sun was going down. It would soon be dark, which would keep Israel from gaining a complete victory over the Amorites. *What could Joshua do?* Joshua couldn't do anything about the sun going down, but God Almighty, the Ruler of all could! So, *Joshua spoke to the LORD . . . and he said in the sight of Israel, "Sun, stand still at Gibeon, and moon, in the Valley of Aijalon" And the sun stood still, and the moon stopped, until the nation took vengeance on their enemies . . . There has been no day like it before or since, when the LORD obeyed the voice of a man, for the LORD fought for Israel.* **God, who is sovereign over all things, rules the sun and the moon.** He wins battles for His people and **He accomplishes all His purposes**.

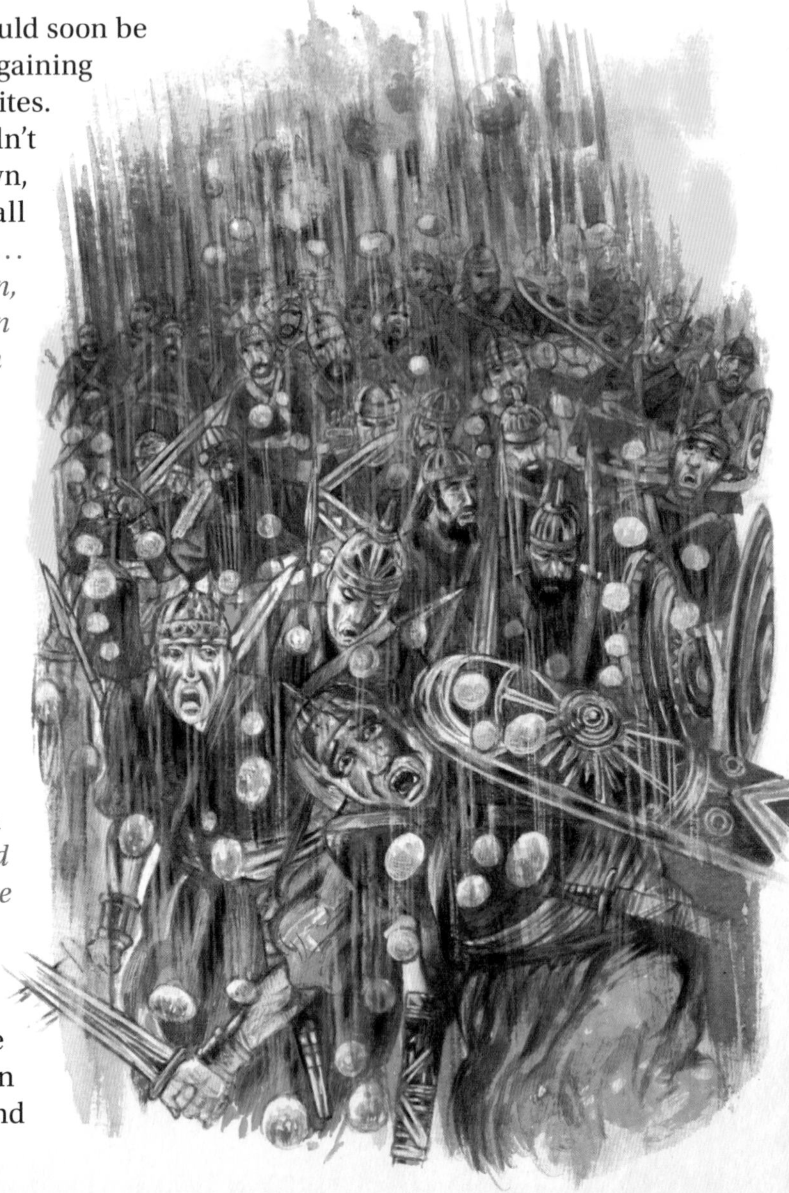

Joshua and Israel continued to battle the kings of the southern part of Canaan. *And Joshua captured all these kings and their land at one time, because the LORD God of Israel fought for Israel.* Then, the army of Israel marched toward the northern part of Canaan, and the LORD gave them victory after victory. Even though the kings joined together and *came out with all their troops, a great horde, in number like the sand that is on the seashore, with very many horses and chariots . . .* they could not defeat the army of Israel and their all-powerful God. *So Joshua took the whole land, according to all that the LORD had spoken to Moses.* **God is the Most High, the King of kings who reigns victorious!** He gave Israel full victory over all the kings of southern and northern Canaan.

Just as He had promised, God had given Israel the Promised Land. *By faith, you can trust that God is who He says He is, and that He will keep every promise in His Word. What are you facing today? If you are a child of God, the LORD will fight for you.*

The LORD is my rock and my fortress and my deliverer, my God, my rock, in whom I take refuge, my shield, and the horn of my salvation, my stronghold. (Psalm 18:2)[1]

MAKING YOU WISE FOR SALVATION

What does this chapter tell us about God? Talk about and apply the **biblical truths** in **bold** text.

Salvation Thread: God is always victorious.

What does it mean that God is "sovereign"? [God has the right, power, and wisdom to rule the world and do all He pleases.] How does this personally apply to your life?

Talk About: *The LORD is my rock and my fortress and my deliverer, my God, my rock in whom I take refuge, my shield, and the horn of my salvation, my stronghold. (Psalm 18:2)*

What are some ways God has acted for your family?

Pray: Praise God for being almighty. Thank Him that He works for His people. Give Him all your concerns.

Think About: God does not just stand by and watch things happen. God is at work in the world and in the lives of people.

1. A horn is a symbol of power, much like an animal's horn is powerful.

The 12 TRIBES of ANCIENT ISRAEL

C H A P T E R 4 0

CHOOSE THIS DAY WHOM YOU WILL SERVE

Joshua's Farewell and the Next Generation —Joshua 23-24; Judges 1-2

"... choose this day whom you will serve, whether the gods your fathers served in the region beyond the River, or the gods of the Amorites in whose land you dwell. But as for me and my house, we will serve the LORD." (Joshua 24:15b)

Have you ever read a story that ends, "And they lived happily ever after"? It might seem like the history of Israel would end this way. **God had been so faithful to the Israelites** and had done so many mighty acts for them. He saved them from slavery. He kept them safe on their journey and gave them food and water in the wilderness. And He fulfilled His wonderful promise to give them their own land. Near the end of the book of Joshua, it sounds like there will be a "happily ever after" ending:

Thus the LORD gave to Israel all the land that he swore to give to their fathers. And they took possession of it, and they settled there. And the LORD gave them rest on every side just as he had sworn to their fathers. Not one of all their enemies had withstood them, for the LORD had given all their enemies into their hands. Not one word of all the good promises that the LORD had made to the house of Israel had failed; all came to pass. (Joshua 21:43-45)

But we must remember about the **sin nature passed on by Adam to all people**. Joshua remembered it. After dividing the land among the tribes and giving the Levites forty-eight cities in which to live, Joshua made a speech. *Can you find the challenge and the warning in his speech?*

> *"Therefore, be very strong to keep and to* ***do all that is written in the Book of the Law*** *of Moses, turning aside from it neither to the right hand nor to the left, that* ***you may not mix with these nations remaining among you*** *or make mention of the names of their gods or swear by them or serve them or bow down to them, but you shall cling to the LORD your God just as you have done to this day." (Joshua 23:6-8)*

> *"But just as all the good things that the LORD your God promised concerning you have been fulfilled for you, so the LORD will bring upon you all the evil things, until he has destroyed you from off this good land that the LORD your God has given you,* ***if you transgress the covenant of the LORD*** *your God, which he commanded you, and go and serve other gods and bow down to them.* ***Then the anger of the LORD will be kindled against you****, and you shall perish quickly from off the good land that he has given to you." (Joshua 23:15-16)*

He pleaded with Israel to follow Yahweh, who had been so faithful to them. He warned the people not to worship the false gods of the Canaanites or follow their evil ways. Israel was to be a "set-apart people"—different from the other nations. Israel had conquered much of Canaan. But there were still many Canaanite people living in parts of Canaan. God commanded the Israelites not to marry or live among the Canaanites. *Why did God do this?*

God was protecting His people from becoming like the Canaanites—worshiping other gods and doing all kinds of evil. He knew that if His people married the Canaanite people and lived among them, they would turn away from Him and do what is evil. **God would bless the Israelites if they were faithful to Him, but if they turned away from Yahweh, He would bring destruction on them**.

By now, Joshua was an old man. He had fought many battles for Israel and had stayed faithful to his God. He was a good leader. Israel *served the LORD all the days of Joshua, and all the days of the elders who outlived Joshua and had known all the work that the LORD did for Israel.*

God had wisely told Israel to conquer the closest nations of Canaan first. The rest should be conquered little by little, as Israel grew larger in number. *Why was it wise for God to tell them this?* There were not enough Israelites to fill all of Canaan yet. If the Israelites defeated all their enemies at once, much of the land would be empty. The wild animals would multiply quickly without anyone to control them. So many wild animals would be a great danger to Israel.

As the Israelites grew in number, God was willing to give Israel the rest of the land of Canaan. But instead of finishing the job of driving out the evil nations, Israel wanted to rest. Joshua, Israel's great military leader, had died, and Israel was afraid of the nations of the valleys. These nations had great armies with chariots. Surely, this was no problem for God! But instead of trusting God to help them conquer these nations, the Israelites began to live among the Canaanites. They let their fear keep them from obeying God and receiving all the land God would give them.

Joshua and all the people of his age had died. They had lived through the conquering of the northern and southern parts of Canaan and had seen God's mighty acts for His people. But now they were gone. *And there arose another generation after them who did not know the LORD or the work that he had done for Israel. And the people of Israel did what was evil in the sight of the LORD and served the Baals.*

The younger generation (those who came after Joshua) broke God's command and did not break down the altars to the false gods of the Canaanites. They did not think of the Canaanites as enemies—enemies of the LORD, and therefore enemies of Israel. So, they married Canaanite men and women and began to worship the false gods of the Canaanites—Baal and Asherah. They still worshiped Yahweh, but He was one god among many gods that they worshiped. They broke the first commandment: ***You shall have no other gods before me***. They didn't care that **God is a jealous God** who commands His people to worship Him alone. Just as God had said, the Canaanites had become a *snare and a trap* for them. **God's words always prove true.** How very foolish and sinful Israel was to worship idols and turn away from the one true God alone.

> *The idols of the nations are silver and gold, the work of human hands. They have mouths, but do not speak; they have eyes, but do not see; they have ears, but do not hear, nor is there any breath in their mouths. Those who make them become like them, so do all who trust in them. (Psalm 135:15-18)*

Israel, God's chosen people, had promised to be faithful to Yahweh and His covenant. They were called to be a distinct, different, separate people, keeping God's good laws and living holy lives, so they could show other nations what God is like. Instead of showing other nations the kindness, goodness, and faithfulness of God, and being a blessing to them, they became like the other nations. They followed the sinful, wicked ways of the Canaanites because they were foolish and they were deceived. They were tricked by Satan and his demons to believe these idols had real power.

Moses had been a great prophet—He spoke the words of God to the people. He was a great mediator between God and man, and a great intercessor praying for the people. Joshua was a great military leader, trusting God to give Israel success in battle. He was a godly leader who encouraged the people to have faith in God and obey His commands. But now there was no leader in Israel, no one to pray for them, no one to call them to repentance. *In those days there was no king in Israel. Everyone did what was right in his own eyes.*

Israel did not see **God's good law as a protection and blessing.** And so the nation of Israel began sinking further and further into sin. A pattern, or cycle, began. The people fell into deep sin, rejecting Yahweh and worshiping false gods. God allowed other nations to conquer them and oppress them (treat them badly), so that they would call out to God and turn back to Him. Eventually, the people repented, and God raised up a judge or leader to deliver them. Then there was peace. But it didn't last long. And soon the cycle started over again. Sin . . . oppression . . . repentance . . . deliverance . . . peace. Sin . . . oppression . . . repentance . . . deliverance . . . peace . . . on and on . . . over and over. The peace was very temporary. Israel needed a greater peace, a greater prophet, a greater deliverance.

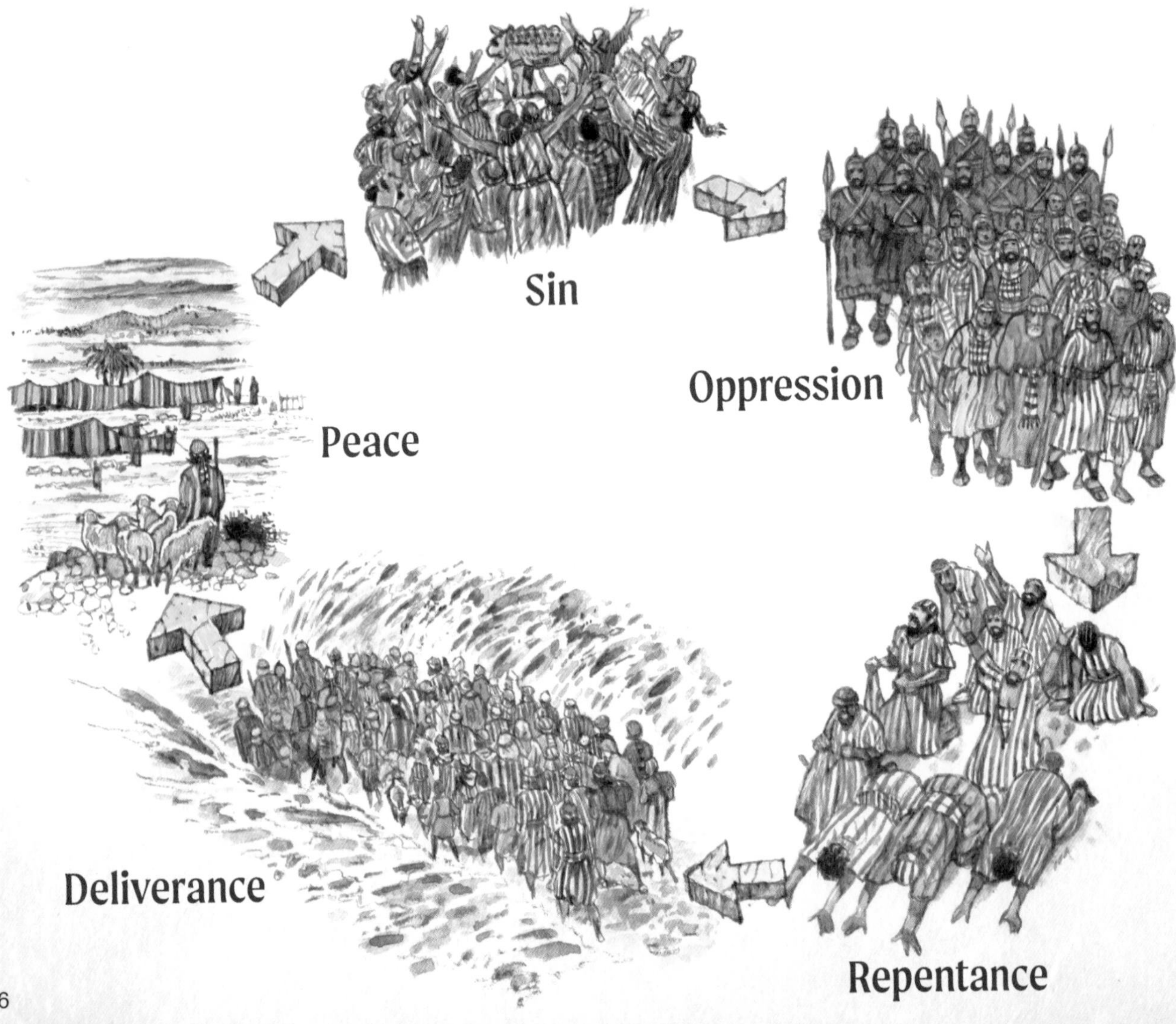

Joshua's challenge to *choose this day whom you will serve* is a challenge not just for Israel, but for us today as well. We, too, live among people who want us to turn away from God. *Who are your closest friends? How do they affect you? (How do you think, talk, and act when you are with them?) Who are the leaders, friends, and other people in your life who encourage you to follow God and obey His good commands? Is anyone leading you away from God?*

"Hear, O Israel: The LORD our God, the LORD is one. You shall love the LORD your God with all your heart and with all your soul and with all your might. And these words that I command you today shall be on your heart." (Deuteronomy 6:4-6)

MAKING YOU WISE FOR SALVATION

What does this chapter tell us about God? Talk about and apply the **biblical truths** in **bold** text.

Salvation Thread: God is a jealous God—He will not share His glory, or the honor and praise He deserves.

Read Psalm 78:5-7. What is God's command in these verses? Why did He give this command? How does this story about Israel show you the importance of parents teaching, and children accepting God's Word?

Talk About: "... *choose this day whom you will serve ... as for me and my house, we will serve the LORD." (Joshua 24:15b)*

Do you have a plan as a family to read and discuss the Bible?

Pray: Praise God for His good and holy ways. Thank Him for His Word and His good commands. Ask Him to give you a heart to follow Him and obey His good commands.

Think About: *Do I truly follow God?*

Memorize: Deuteronomy 6:4-6

CHAPTER 41

GOD DOES NOT FORSAKE HIS UNFAITHFUL PEOPLE

God Calls Gideon —Judges 6

..."Arise, for the LORD has given the host of Midian into your hand." (Judges 7:15b)

So the people of Israel were living in *caves*. These were the covenant people of God, the chosen people. *Why in the world would they be living in caves?* They were living in caves because they were afraid of the Midianites. *The people of Israel did what was evil in the sight of the LORD, and the LORD gave them into the hand of Midian seven years.* Israel was living in the Promised Land, but they had rebelled against God, worshiped false gods, and copied the wicked ways of the Canaanites. Now they were being oppressed once again.

God is holy and does not ignore sin. Because He loved the Israelites, Yahweh was confronting their sin—He was giving them the consequences of sin so they would turn back to Him and to what is good, right, and holy. God was using the Midianites to bring His people to repentance. **God punishes those He loves to cause them to repent.**

The Midianites were nomads. They didn't live in one place or in cities. They lived in tents and moved around. So they couldn't grow crops. When they needed food, they often just stole it from other people. They raided the Israelites at harvest time. They swooped down upon Israel "like locusts in number" to "devour the produce of the land." Not only did they steal the Israelites' crops, but they also stole their sheep, oxen, donkeys, and cattle! Because of this, Israel became very poor, and lived in fear of the Midianites.

When the people of Israel cried out to God, He sent a judge to remind them of what He had done for Israel. God had brought them out of slavery in Egypt, showing them both His love and His power. God had driven out their enemies and given them the Promised Land, showing them that **He is faithful to keep His promises**. He had warned them not to worship false gods. Yet they had disobeyed Him and turned away from Him. *Why would God help disobedient, rebellious Israel?*

God is merciful and faithful. He is attentive to the cries of His people. So the angel of the LORD appeared to an Israelite named Gideon with a message, *"The LORD is with you, O mighty man of valor [courage]."* This "mighty man of valor" didn't seem very brave. He was hiding in a winepress beating out his wheat instead of beating it out in the open field. A

winepress was a big pit dug into stone—an easy place to hide from the Midianites. *Do you know what Gideon said to the angel?*

And Gideon said to him, "Please, sir, if the LORD is with us, why then has all this happened to us? And where are all his wonderful deeds that our fathers recounted to us, saying, 'Did not the LORD bring us up from Egypt?' But now the LORD has forsaken us and given us into the hand of Midian." (Judges 6:13)

God had not forsaken Israel. **God never forsakes His people,** but He does allow them to experience the consequences of their sin. This is what was happening to Israel—yet God was mercifully going to deliver Israel again!

And the LORD turned to him and said, "Go in this might of yours and save Israel from the hand of Midian; do not I send you?" And he said to him, "Please, Lord, how can I save Israel? Behold, my clan is the weakest in Manasseh, and I am the least in my father's house." And the LORD said to him, "But I will be with you, and you shall strike the Midianites as one man." (Judges 6:14-16)

But Gideon wanted a sign that it was the LORD who was speaking with him. Gideon brought goat meat and flat bread to the angel of the LORD. Instead of eating this food, the angel of the LORD reached out his staff and fire sprang up, burning the meat and bread as a sacrifice.

That night, God told Gideon to take his father's two bulls and pull down the altar of Baal, and then cut down the Asherah pole[1] beside it. Destroying the worship place of

the false gods was a step toward peace with God and deliverance. Next, Gideon should build an altar to Yahweh, the one true God, and offer the seven-year-old bull to the LORD. What would his father or the rest of Israel do about this? Would Gideon, "the mighty man of valor," be brave and obedient enough to do this? Yes! God gave Gideon the courage to obey Him.

Gideon took ten of his servants and followed God's instructions—but he did it at night *because he was too afraid of his family and the men of the town to do it by day*. The next day, the men of the town wanted to kill Gideon for what he had done! *What do you think Gideon's father did?* He said that if Baal really was a god he could fight for himself—which of course Baal, the false, powerless god, could not do!

After this, the "Spirit of the LORD" came upon Gideon. God was giving Gideon the courage and strength to fight the Midianites. He was making Gideon "a mighty man of valor"! Gideon sent messengers to some of the tribes of Israel to ask them to fight the Midianites with him.

But Gideon's faith was still weak. He needed reassurance that God would save Israel through him—that God would be with him and make him able to lead the battle. So he asked God for a sign. He put a piece of sheep's wool on the ground. He told the LORD that he would know that God would save Israel through him if the wool was wet and the ground was dry in the morning. When he checked the next morning, the wool was wet and the ground was dry! Gideon squeezed enough water out of the wool to fill a bowl. This was God's assurance that He was with Gideon. Yet Gideon wanted another sign from God. This time he asked God to let the wool be dry and the ground wet. The next morning, the wool was dry but all around it the ground was wet. Wasn't God kind to give Gideon this sign? God was with Gideon, and He would give him the power and courage to fight the Midianites.

God would deliver His undeserving people. Yahweh was the same **loving and powerful God** who had rescued the Israelites from slavery—the same **faithful God** who gave them the Promised Land. Now He would rescue them from the Midianites—through the "least in the weakest clan."

God does not need mighty men of valor—God *makes* mighty men of valor. It is God who gives us the power to do hard things. It is God who gives us the courage to step out in faith and face what we fear. And it is God who goes with His children and never forsakes them.

God strengthens those who belong to Him so they can do hard things, turn from sin, and become mighty men or women of valor! Do you know someone with that kind of faith and confidence in God?

For the eyes of the LORD run to and fro throughout the whole earth, to give strong support to those whose heart is blameless toward him. (2 Chronicles 16:9a)

MAKING YOU WISE FOR SALVATION

What does this chapter tell us about God? Talk about and apply the **biblical truths** in **bold** text.

Salvation Thread: God is faithful and disciplines His children to bring them to repentance.

How is punishment an act of love? (See Hebrews 12:5-11.) *What is your attitude toward discipline? Do you or your parents know someone who repented because of God's discipline?*

Talk About: *For the eyes of the LORD run to and fro throughout the whole earth, to give strong support to those whose heart is blameless toward him. (2 Chronicles 16:9a)*

Why would God choose the least in the weakest clan? What does this tell you about what is needed to fight hard battles? Why was it important for Gideon to destroy the altar of Baal and the Asherah pole?

Pray: Praise God for His steadfast love and faithfulness. Thank God for His presence with His people.

Think About: *Do I trust God when I am facing hard things?*

1. An Asherah pole was a sacred tree or pole placed at worship places to honor the Canaanite goddess Asherah.

CHAPTER 42

I HAVE GIVEN THEM INTO YOUR HAND

God Leads Gideon in Victory over the Midianites—Judges 7

…"Arise, go down against the camp, for I have given it into your hand." (Judges 7:9b)

How does an army defeat another army? By having more men? Better weapons? Do you think a trumpet or a torch would make a good weapon? Maybe having a better plan is the way to win a battle.

God gave Gideon a battle plan to defeat the Midianites, but it wasn't the plan that defeated the Midianites, or a strong army, or even better weapons—It was the power of Yahweh. Let's see what happened…

Gideon and his men camped near a spring of water about three or four miles from the camp of the Midianites. Gideon had an army of 32,000 men, which sounds like a lot of fighting men. But the Midianite army had 135,000 men! So, Gideon's army was outnumbered—by a lot!

> *The LORD said to Gideon, "The people with you are too many for me to give the Midianites into their hand, lest Israel boast over me, saying, 'My own hand has saved me.'" (Judges 7:2)*

God wanted Gideon's army to be smaller to fight the LARGE Midianite army! *Smaller? Why did God do this?* God wanted the Israelites to know that they would not win the battle on their own. God would give Israel the victory. God was fighting for them! God told Gideon to tell the men that whoever was afraid should go home… and 22,000 men left. Now Gideon only had 10,000 men! How would they win against such a big army of Midianite men?

However, God said that there were *still* too many men with Gideon! God told Gideon to take the men to the water where He would test them to show who should be in Gideon's army. Every man who scooped water in his hand and lapped it like a dog would be in one group. The men who knelt down by the water to drink would be in the other group. There were only 300 men in the group that lapped the water . . . and this was the group God chose. *And the LORD said to Gideon, "With the 300 men who lapped I will save you and give the Midianites into your hand, and let all the others go every man to his home."* So, Gideon sent all the rest of the men—the 9,700 men—home.

This doesn't sound like a great battle plan. The Israelites could look down on the army of the Midianites—and the Amalekites who joined them—and all the people of the East who *lay along the valley like locusts in abundance, and their camels were without number, as the sand that is on the seashore in abundance.* Locusts can come in great swarms and cover the ground, eating everything in sight. Gideon's army wasn't like "locusts in abundance." It was only a little group of 300 men now. There was only one Israelite for about every 450 Midianite soldiers! This doesn't sound like a good way to win a battle. *Would you be afraid to be on Israel's side in this battle? Do you think this was a good battle plan?*

> *That same night the LORD said to him, "Arise, go down against the camp, for I have given it into your hand." (Judges 7:9)*

It was a GREAT battle plan because Yahweh was on Israel's side. **Yahweh, the sovereign, self-existent, eternal, almighty, unchanging God,** would give Israel the victory! An army of 135,000 men cannot win against 300 men who have Yahweh on their side!

God knows we are weak. The Bible says, *For he knows our frame; he remembers that we are dust.* So, God graciously told Gideon, *"But if you are afraid to go down, go down to the camp with Purah your servant. And you shall hear what they say, and afterward your hands shall be strengthened to go down against the camp."* Oh, the kindness of God! He reassured fearful Gideon once again. Instead of Gideon asking for a sign, God just graciously gave him one.

Gideon and his servant went down to the Midianite camp and heard a man telling a fellow soldier his dream. He dreamt that a cake of barley bread rolled into the camp, knocked into the tent, and flattened it. The soldier answered, *"This is no other than the sword of Gideon the son of Joash, a man of Israel; God has*

given into his hand Midian and all the camp." How could he possibly think that a cake of bread was Gideon? God had given the soldier this meaning of the dream and caused the Midianites to fear Gideon and his army.

What do you think Gideon did when he heard the dream and its interpretation? He worshiped. He saw the greatness of God and praised Him for His greatness. Then he returned to the camp and told his tiny army that God had given them victory over the Midianites. He divided the men into three groups and gave each man a trumpet and a torch inside a jar. He told the men to watch him and do what he did. When he blew his trumpet, they were to blow theirs and shout, *"For the LORD and for Gideon."*

So the three Israelite groups went down to the enemy's camp. At Gideon's example, they blew their trumpets, broke the jars, and shouted, *"A sword for the LORD and for Gideon!"* The men of Israel stood in place around the camp. *When they blew the 300 trumpets, the LORD set every man's sword against his comrade and against all the army. And the army fled.* The Midianites were so confused they didn't know what they were doing!

The Midianites fought their own army! Then they ran away. But Israel followed them and defeated their enemy, just as God had promised. God had given them victory! **Salvation comes from God alone.** The Israelites did not win this battle themselves—*the LORD set every man's sword against his comrade and against all the army.* God won the battle for Israel. Yahweh had clearly shown

His greatness and worth—His glory! **God is worthy to be worshiped.** He had rescued Israel again, and Israel had forty years of rest, or peace.

Gideon didn't need a great army to defeat a great enemy. Gideon needed God. God showed Gideon and Israel that He is more than enough for anything they faced. **God always helps His people when they cry out to Him.** It doesn't matter how smart or brave you are. **If you have God as your heavenly Father, you have all you need.** *How have the chapters you have read shown you that God is more than able to handle any situation His children face? In what ways can you see that you need God?*

Now I know that the LORD saves his anointed; he will answer him from his holy heaven with the saving might of his right hand. Some trust in chariots and some in horses, but we trust in the name of the LORD our God. (Psalm 20:6-7)

MAKING YOU WISE FOR SALVATION

What does this chapter tell us about God? Talk about and apply the **biblical truths** in **bold** text.

Salvation Thread: Salvation comes from God alone.

Why did God make Gideon's army smaller? Why didn't God want the Israelites to boast that they had gotten the victory themselves?

Talk About: *Now I know that the LORD saves his anointed; he will answer him from his holy heaven with the saving might of his right hand. Some trust in chariots and some in horses, but we trust in the name of the LORD our God. (Psalm 20:6-7)*

Why does God want to show His greatness and worth (His glory)?

Pray: Praise God for His mighty acts! Praise Him for being all-powerful! Praise Him for showing us His glory!

Think About: Why are we so tempted to trust in "horses and chariots"?

CHAPTER 43

TAKING REFUGE IN THE GOD OF ISRAEL

Ruth Leaves Moab and Puts Her Trust in God—Ruth 1-2

He who dwells in the shelter of the Most High will abide in the shadow of the Almighty. I will say to the LORD, "My refuge and my fortress, my God, in whom I trust." (Psalm 91:1-2)

It would be great if we could say that Israel repented and trusted in God without fail after the defeat of the Midianites. But that isn't true. As soon as Gideon died, the people again worshiped false gods. The pattern, or cycle, started all over again.

Do you remember what the cycle is? The people sinned, rejecting God and worshiping false gods. Then God allowed other nations to conquer and oppress them (treat them badly), so that Israel would call out to God and turn back to Him. Then the people repented. Then God raised up a judge or leader to deliver them. Then there was peace or rest—and then the cycle started all over again. Sin . . . oppression . . . repentance . . . deliverance . . . peace. This cycle lasted almost three hundred years. Yet Yahweh, the covenant-keeping God, did not destroy His people, even though they constantly rebelled against Him and broke their covenant with Him. Instead, God raised up fifteen judges to deliver His people time after time.

During one of the times of oppression or suffering, there was a famine in Israel. *Do you remember what a famine is?* It is when there is very little food in the land. So a man from the tribe of Judah named Elimelech, his wife Naomi, and their two sons left Israel and went to the land of Moab. Elimelech died there, and the two sons married Moabite women—Orpah and Ruth. They lived there ten years, and then the two sons died. *What do you think this must have meant for Naomi?* She came to Moab with her husband and two sons, and she had buried them all. What a deep grief Naomi must have had.

There was no reason to stay in Moab. Who would care for Naomi now? When Naomi heard that there was food in Israel again, she decided to return to Israel. Her two daughters-in-law (wives of her sons) wanted to go with her. Naomi had nothing to offer them. She was too old to marry again and have sons for them to marry. Besides, even if that were possible, the sons would be little children! Naomi convinced Orpah to stay in Moab, but Ruth would not leave Naomi.

> *But Ruth said, "Do not urge me to leave you or to return from following you. For where you go I will go, and where you lodge I will lodge. Your people shall be my people, and your God my God. Where you die I will die, and there will I be buried. May the LORD do so to me and more also if anything but death parts me from you." (Ruth 1:16-17)*

Ruth was determined to go with Naomi. Ruth wanted to worship the one true God of Israel, not the false gods of the Moabites. So the two women made the long journey back to Bethlehem. When Naomi's old friends saw her, she told them not to call her Naomi (which means "pleasant"), but Mara (which means "bitter"). *Why would Naomi say this?* She felt that God had taken everything away from her and treated her bitterly. Naomi did not have the faith to see that God was at work accomplishing His grand plan for Naomi, Ruth, Israel, and all peoples.

Naomi and Ruth were very poor when they arrived in Bethlehem. They had no husbands or sons to care for them. But **God's law** given to Moses **is good, perfect, and righteous**. His law made a way for poor people to get food. Poor people could pick and eat any grain or fruit

left behind after a field was picked. This was called "gleaning." It was not stealing. This was God's kind way to provide for those in need. Even if a whole bundle of grain was accidentally left in a field, the owner could not go back to get it; he had to leave it for the poor.

> *"When you reap the harvest of your land, you shall not reap your field right up to its edge, neither shall you gather the gleanings after your harvest. And you shall not strip your vineyard bare, neither shall you gather the fallen grapes of your vineyard. You shall leave them for the poor and for the sojourner: I am the LORD your God." (Leviticus 19:9-10)*

Naomi and Ruth arrived in Bethlehem just when the barley crop was being harvested. Barley could be used in making bread, soup, or stew. So, Ruth went to glean in the fields after the workers gathered the crops. *She happened to come to the part of the field belonging to Boaz.* Ruth didn't know it, but Boaz was a close relative of Naomi's husband.

Ruth worked very hard gathering the leftover barley and only took one very short break. Boaz noticed Ruth and how hard she worked. When Boaz found out that Ruth was Naomi's daughter-in-law, he told her to keep gleaning in his field. Then he told his workers to protect her and give her water. He even told them to pull out some barley from the bundles of grain and leave them in the field for Ruth. Later, Boaz offered her lunch. Ruth could not understand why Boaz would show such kindness to her.

> *But Boaz answered her, "All that you have done for your mother-in-law since the death of your husband has been fully told to me, and how you left your father and mother and your native land and came to a people that you did not know before. The LORD repay you for what you have done, and a full reward be given you by the LORD, the God of Israel, under whose wings you have come to take refuge!" (Ruth 2:11-12)*

Naomi and Ruth did not *just happen* to arrive in Bethlehem when the crops were ready to be picked. Ruth didn't *just happen* to glean in Boaz's field. God quietly *directed* Naomi and Ruth. Ruth had rejected the Moabite false gods and put her trust in the God of Israel. She had "taken refuge under His wings." And the faithful God of Israel, the one true God, guided, protected, and cared for her.

When Ruth got home from gleaning, she gave Naomi the leftover food from her lunch and the grain she had gleaned. She told Naomi about the kindness Boaz had shown her. This was good news to Naomi! *And Naomi said to her daughter-in-law, "May he be blessed by the LORD, whose kindness has not forsaken the living or the dead!" Naomi also said to her, "The man is a close relative of ours, one of our redeemers."*

Naomi had returned to Bethlehem thinking God had "dealt bitterly" with her—but Naomi was wrong. Perhaps God had a great and marvelous plan for Naomi and her family. Perhaps there was reason for Naomi to have hope—hope in the steadfast love of Yahweh.

Sometimes when things happen that we don't understand, we wonder if God remembers us. We wonder if He has forgotten to be gracious to us. But it is at those times that we must remember who God is—He is Yahweh, **the sovereign, self-existent, eternal, almighty, unchanging, faithful, gracious God, who always accomplishes His purposes.** God is actively at work in this world bringing about His marvelous purposes. *Do you trust God to have the best plan for your life? Do you have faith to believe that God works for the good of His children even when things seem confusing and hard? How can you "find refuge" in God?*

For God alone, O my soul, wait in silence, for my hope is from him. He only is my rock and my salvation, my fortress; I shall not be shaken. On God rests my salvation and my glory; my mighty rock, my refuge is God. Trust in him at all times, O people; pour out your heart before him; God is a refuge for us. (Psalm 62:5-8)

MAKING YOU WISE FOR SALVATION

What does this chapter tell us about God? Talk about and apply the **biblical truths** in **bold** text.

Salvation Thread: God has an eternal, sovereign plan and is a refuge for His people.

Why did Ruth leave Moab? (Think of the many reasons for leaving.)

Talk About: *For God alone, O my soul, wait in silence, for my hope is from him. He only is my rock and my salvation, my fortress; I shall not be shaken. On God rests my salvation and my glory; my mighty rock, my refuge is God. Trust in him at all times, O people; pour out your heart before him; God is a refuge for us. (Psalm 62:5-8)*

Does being a child of God (a Christian) mean life will be easy? Will only happy things happen to Christians? Explain.

Pray: Praise God that He is actively at work in the world. Thank God for His good, perfect, and righteous law. Ask God for the faith to believe that His laws are good and that He can be trusted even when things are hard. Confess any bitterness you have in your heart.

Think About: God is working in your life—even though you might not be aware of it. Everyday things that seem unimportant are part of God's plan for you and the whole world.

CHAPTER 44

GOD PROVIDES A KINSMAN REDEEMER

God Rescues Naomi and Ruth through Boaz—Ruth 3-4

Know therefore that the LORD your God is God, the faithful God who keeps covenant and steadfast love with those who love him and keep his commandments, to a thousand generations, (Deuteronomy 7:9)

D*o you know what a "kinsman" is?* A kinsman is a relative. It can be an uncle, a brother, a cousin—anyone in your family. *Do you remember what Naomi said when Ruth told her that the man who had shown her kindness was Boaz?* Naomi said, *"The man is a close relative of ours, one of our redeemers."* Not only was Boaz a close relative—a kinsman—but he was also a "redeemer." *What did Naomi mean?*

Naomi was thinking about another one of Yahweh's good and righteous laws given to His covenant people—the law of the kinsman redeemer. The law of the kinsman redeemer was a law to protect widows without sons. (A widow is a woman whose husband has died.) Among God's people, it was very important to have your family line continue. Abraham had a son, Isaac, to continue his family line. Then Isaac's son, Jacob, continued his father's line. But if a man died and had no sons, or if his sons died, then the family line would stop. Elimelech had died, and his sons had died. So there was no one to carry on the family name . . . and no one to care for Naomi and Ruth, the wife of Elimelech's son.

Remember that Naomi had told her old friends to call her Mara instead of Naomi, *for the Almighty has dealt very bitterly with me.* Naomi had no husband, no sons, and no way to earn a living. She had no way to carry on her family name and keep their family's place among the people of Israel. But a kinsman redeemer could change all that. A redeemer is a savior, or rescuer. When Naomi heard about Boaz, she had hope. Maybe God had not abandoned her. Maybe there were future joys for her. Maybe, just maybe, she was wrong about being dealt with bitterly.

God's kinsman redeemer law commanded that if a man died without leaving any sons for his wife, it was the duty and the privilege of the man's nearest male relative to marry the dead man's wife. Their son would then carry on the dead man's family name. If the dead man's land had been sold,[1] the redeemer was responsible to buy the land back. If the closest relative refused to do this, the next closest relative could be the redeemer.

This is why Naomi was hopeful. Boaz was an Israelite from the same tribe as Elimelech—the tribe of Judah—and of the same family. He could be a redeemer for her family! So, Naomi told Ruth to go to Boaz in private and ask him to be their redeemer. Ruth agreed to obey her mother-in-law and went at night to talk to Boaz in private. She bravely asked Boaz to be the redeemer of Elimelech's family, *"Spread your wings over your servant, for you are a redeemer."*

What did Boaz think of this idea? Boaz was pleased with Ruth's request. He saw her as a "worthy woman." However, there was one problem. A closer relative would have the first chance to redeem Elimelech's land and family. Would this man decide to be the redeemer?

The next day Boaz went to the gate of the city where important agreements were made. The city gate was the center of activity. There Boaz met the city leaders and it *just happened* that the closer relative came by. But he was not interested in being the redeemer. So Boaz agreed to be the kinsman redeemer. He would claim Elimelech's land and marry Ruth. If God gave them a son, that son would carry on the family name of Elimelech and his son, Mahlon, who had been Ruth's husband. Then those at the city gate prayed that God would "build up the house of Israel"—that He would give Boaz and Ruth children.

So Boaz married Ruth, and the LORD gave them a son. Now Naomi had a grandson! Naomi's friends came to her with great excitement, praising Yahweh.

> *Then the women said to Naomi, "Blessed be the LORD, who has not left you this day without a redeemer, and may his name be renowned in Israel! He shall be to you a restorer of life*

and a nourisher of your old age, for your daughter-in-law who loves you, who is more to you than seven sons, has given birth to him." (Ruth 4:14-15)

Elimelech's name and family line would continue through this child. It was true that it seemed like Naomi had come back from Moab with nothing. But she had the greatest blessing of all! Yahweh was her God. He had given her Ruth, and then Boaz . . . and now this beautiful grandson. God had not abandoned her. He was restoring her family. He was giving her back an even greater family. **Yahweh is *the faithful God who keeps covenant and steadfast love with those who love him and keep his commandments, to a thousand generations.* God never forsakes His children.**

This would be a great ending to the story of Ruth—but it gets even better:

> *And the women of the neighborhood gave him a name, saying, "A son has been born to Naomi." They named him Obed. He was the father of Jesse, the father of David. (Ruth 4:17)*

Do you remember Rahab, the Canaanite woman who hid the spies? She was saved when Israel defeated Jericho. Rahab, the Canaanite, had trusted in the one true God and became part of Israel. Later, she married Salmon, one of the spies she hid on her roof, and they had a son. That son was Boaz, the man who showed kindness to Ruth, became the kinsman redeemer, and rescued Ruth and Naomi. Boaz married Ruth, the Moabite who trusted in the God of Israel, and had a son named Obed. Obed was the father of Jesse . . . who was the

father of King David of Israel! God had not only saved Elimelech's name and family line—but God was also creating a royal line! All the ordinary things, and even the hard things in Naomi's life, were part of God's great plan of redemption for the whole world—of rescuing sinful men and making a people of His own through a greater Redeemer.

God is a God of great providence—providing for His world. **God is always watching and working in the world.** He is attentive to everything that happens in your life. He is not sitting around bored or uninterested. He is always paying attention. **He is always working all things to serve His great purposes. He is working out all His plans for His glory and the good of His children.**

Everything in your life is part of an eternal plan of God. There are no accidents, no coincidences—nothing that *just happens.* If you are a child of God, God is actively working for your good—even when things seem hard, even when there are great losses. *Will you trust the ever-faithful God who works for His children? Will you guard your mouth and your heart from bitterness and complaining . . . and wait for God to show Himself faithful?*

> From of old no one has heard or perceived by the ear, no eye has seen a God besides you, who acts for those who wait for him. (Isaiah 64:4)

MAKING YOU WISE FOR SALVATION

What does this chapter tell us about God? Talk about and apply the **biblical truths** in **bold** text.

Salvation Thread: God sovereignly works to bring about His eternal purposes and provide redemption for His people.

What is a kinsman redeemer? How does this show God's good care for those who need help? Boaz was Naomi's and Ruth's kinsman redeemer. How does this story point forward to a greater Redeemer who would save His people?

Talk About: *From of old no one has heard or perceived by the ear, no eye has seen a God besides you, who acts for those who wait for him. (Isaiah 64:4)*

How have you or your family seen God work "all things for good" for His children? List all the amazing pieces God fit together in Ruth's life. What does this tell you about God? How does this show you that His wisdom and goodness can be trusted?

Pray: Praise God for faithfully fulfilling His good purposes. Thank God that He can be trusted. Bring Him any problems you have and ask Him to give you the faith to trust Him.

Think About: *Do I sometimes have a hard time trusting God when things happen that I don't like?*

1. When land was sold in Israel, it was in effect rented, as the title to the land would still belong to the owner. What was actually sold were the profits from crops that the land produced. In the year of Jubilee, the land would return to the original owner or family.

CHAPTER 45

THE GLORY DEPARTS, YET THERE IS HOPE

God Raises Up Samuel and Brings Judgment on Eli and Israel—1 Samuel 1-4

"...those who honor me I will honor, and those who despise me shall be lightly esteemed." (1 Samuel 2:30b)

Do you know what the Bible says about the time of the judges? *In those days there was no king in Israel. Everyone did what was right in his own eyes.* What a sad and distressing report! The Israelites were not following God's good laws and doing what was right in God's eyes. They had their own idea of what was right—and it certainly wasn't right! Surely, things could not turn out well for rebellious Israel.

Eli was a judge who was also the high priest. He had two sons, Hophni and Phinehas, who were also priests. But, unlike Eli, they stole from the offerings given to the LORD and did other wicked things. How wickedness had grown in Israel, that two priests would sin so terribly! But there was hope. It came through the answer to a woman's prayer. The woman was Hannah. She was one of the two wives of a man named Elkanah. Elkanah's other wife, *Peninnah, had children, but Hannah had no children.* The situation was very much like it was with Leah and Rachel—one wife was more loved, Hannah, but the other, Peninnah, had children.

The tabernacle and Ark of the Covenant were in the city of Shiloh. Every year, Elkanah went to Shiloh to worship and make a sacrifice. There Hannah wept bitterly as she prayed to the LORD, *"O LORD of hosts, if you will indeed look on the*

affliction of your servant and remember me and not forget your servant, but will give to your servant a son, then I will give him to the LORD all the days of his life." Hannah was deeply troubled and though her lips moved, no sound came out. Eli saw her and thought there was something wrong with her. But Hannah explained that she was pouring out her great sadness to God. *Then Eli answered, "Go in peace, and the God of Israel grant your petition that you have made to him."* Just imagine how grateful and excited Hannah must have been!

God answered Hannah's prayer and gave her a son. She called him Samuel. When Samuel was still a young child, Hannah brought him to Eli. She reminded Eli that she was the woman who prayed for a child.

> *"For this child I prayed, and the LORD has granted me my petition that I made to him. Therefore I have lent him to the LORD. As long as he lives, he is lent to the LORD." (1 Samuel 1:27-28a)*

Hannah kept her promise to the LORD and left Samuel to help Eli in his priestly duties. Every year, she brought Samuel a new robe when she went with Elkanah to make their sacrifice. God kindly gave Hannah three more sons and two daughters. But Samuel stayed with Eli and *continued to grow both in stature and in favor with the LORD and also with man.* Not only did he grow bigger, but, more than that, the LORD's kindness was on Samuel.

However, the sons of Eli continued in their wicked ways. Sadly, Eli allowed them to continue in their wickedness. He showed more honor to his sons than to his God. This could not turn out well! Eli's sons were more important to him than doing what is right and being a faithful priest. So one day, "a man of God" came to warn Eli. He told Eli that God would remove him as a priest and raise up a faithful priest in his place. Eli's sons would die, and Eli's family would no longer be priests.

It was rare in those days for God to speak to His people in a dream or vision. His people had ignored His message so many times. But one night, the LORD called Samuel. The boy had been lying down and thought that Eli had called him. So he ran to Eli. But Eli had not called him. This happened a second time. The third time it happened, Eli realized that the LORD was calling Samuel. So he told Samuel to tell the LORD that he was listening. The next time the LORD called, Samuel said, *"Speak, for your servant hears."* Then God told Samuel that judgment was coming upon Eli and his sons:

> *"And I declare to him that I am about to punish his house forever, for the iniquity that he knew, because his sons were blaspheming God, and he did not restrain them." (1 Samuel 3:13)*

The next morning, Samuel was afraid to tell Eli the vision God had given him. But Eli encouraged him not to hide what God had said. So Samuel was faithful to speak God's message. *What do you think Eli said then?* He did not complain, argue, or get upset. He knew God's judgment was right. He said, *"It is the LORD. Let him do what seems good to him."*

Samuel became a man, and it was obvious to all that the LORD was with him. He became a prophet, speaking the LORD's word to the people. But disaster came to Eli and his household, and to Israel. Israel went to battle with the Philistines who were trying to take their land.

Israel was defeated, and four thousand Israelites died in battle.

Then the elders of Israel had a terrible idea. Israel would bring the precious Ark of the Covenant into battle with them! Hophni and Phinehas brought the Ark, and all the Israelites shouted when they saw it. When the Philistines found out that the Ark of the LORD was in the Israelite camp, they were afraid. They said,

"Woe to us! Who can deliver us from the power of these mighty gods? These are the gods who struck the Egyptians with every sort of plague in the wilderness. Take courage, and be men, O Philistines, lest you become slaves to the Hebrews as they have been to you; be men and fight." (1 Samuel 4:8-9)

They were right to be afraid, for Yahweh is all-powerful. He is the one true God who defeated Pharaoh, his army, and all the gods of Egypt. But God was not fighting for Israel that day because Israel had not been faithful to God. So the Philistines defeated Israel in a horrible way. It was a terrible battle, and thirty thousand Israelite soldiers were killed. The two sons of Eli were also killed, just as God had said. But worst of all, the most horrible, awful thing happened. The Ark of God was captured by the Philistines!

Eli was waiting for news of the battle for *his heart trembled for the ark of God.* However, the news was not good. Israel had been defeated, and Eli's sons were dead. But when Eli heard that the Ark of God had been captured, he fell over backward, broke his neck, and died. When his pregnant daughter-in-law heard the news, her labor pains immediately started, and she gave birth to a baby boy. But her strength was gone and, as she was dying, she said, *"The glory has departed from Israel, for the ark of God has been captured."* Because of Israel's foolishness and disrespect, they lost the Ark of the Covenant, the symbol of God's presence with them. The Israelites had rejected the worship of God, dishonored Him, and broken their covenant with Him. Now God's protection, His glorious presence, His mighty works, and His blessing were no longer among them.

What a terribly sad ending to this part of Israel's history. But, as always, **God gives hope to His people**, even in the tragedies. For He had raised up a great prophet, priest, and judge—the godly man, Samuel. Though the Ark was gone, **God is everywhere all the time. Yahweh, the covenant-keeping God, does not abandon His people.**

Samuel honored God when so many of the rest of the Israelites turned away from God. You, too, live in a time when many have turned away from God. *How can you show honor to God like Samuel did? What have you read in the Bible that you can act on? Will you pray that God would make you a faithful follower of Him?*

Blessed is the man who walks not in the counsel of the wicked, nor stands in the way of sinners, nor sits in the seat of scoffers; but his delight is in the law of the LORD, and on his law he meditates day and night. (Psalm 1:1-2)

MAKING YOU WISE FOR SALVATION

What does this chapter tell us about God? Talk about and apply the **biblical truths** in **bold** text.

Salvation Thread: God is worthy of worship and honor. To disrespect God is a serious sin with grave consequences.

Why did judgment come upon Eli? Why was Eli's response right?

Talk About: *Blessed is the man who walks not in the counsel of the wicked, nor stands in the way of sinners, nor sits in the seat of scoffers; but his delight is in the law of the LORD, and on his law he meditates day and night. (Psalm 1:1-2)*

Why was it so wrong to send the Ark into battle?

Pray: Thank God for always giving hope to His people. Ask God to help you to honor (respect) Him and to keep His good commands.

Think About: *How can I honor God?*

Memorize: Psalm 1:1-2

CHAPTER 46

GOD'S PRESENCE— A BLESSING OR A CURSE?

God Destroys the Idol Dagon, and Samuel Calls Israel to Return to the LORD—1 Samuel 5-7

Thus says the LORD, the King of Israel and his Redeemer, the LORD of hosts: "I am the first and I am the last; besides me there is no god." (Isaiah 44:6)

The Philistines had captured the special Ark of the Covenant. What would they do now? Would they worship the one true God? Not at all! In their minds, the God of Israel was not powerful enough to help the Israelites win the battle. But their god, Dagon, had given them victory. At least that is what they thought. But they were wrong.

They didn't understand that the Israelites had lost the battle because they had disobeyed God and broken their covenant with Him. Israel had not treated God as holy. They had not valued God's presence, and they had sent the Ark of the Covenant into battle. So God had not fought for them. All of Israel's victories in the past were really Yahweh's victories. Without God's help, Israel could not defeat her enemies.

The Philistines brought the Ark of God to the city of Ashdod and put it in the temple of their god, Dagon. Dagon was an idol that was part man and part fish. It had the head, body, and hands of a man, but the tail of a fish. *Does this seem like a very strange idol to you?* The Philistines worshiped this false god and even brought the Ark as an offering to Dagon. They thought that the God of Israel was a weaker god who could serve Dagon. Oh, how very wrong they were! So they set the Ark right beside Dagon. But the next morning, the Philistines found that *Dagon had fallen face downward on the ground before the ark of the LORD.*

Do you think the Philistines now understood the power of the one true God, Yahweh? No, the Philistines just put Dagon back in his place. The next morning, they found Dagon face down on the ground before the Ark of the LORD again. But this time Dagon was broken! His head and hands had been cut off. Only the body was left. Yahweh's message was clear. He was more powerful than the false god, Dagon. **The LORD alone is God.**

> *Thus says the LORD, the King of Israel and his Redeemer, the LORD of hosts: "I am the first and I am the last; besides me there is no god." (Isaiah 44:6)*

All the gods of the nations are powerless before the one true God.

> *Their idols are silver and gold, the work of human hands. They have mouths, but do not speak; eyes, but do not see. They have ears, but do not hear; noses, but do not smell. They have hands, but do not feel; feet, but do not walk; and they do not make a sound in their throat. Those who make them become like them; so do all who trust in them. (Psalm 115:4-8)*

Then the LORD brought a plague of tumors, or painful lumps, on the people of Ashdod. They were terrified and said, *"The ark of the God of Israel must not remain with us, for his hand is hard against us and against Dagon our god."* So they sent the Ark to the city of Gath. But *the hand of the LORD was against the city.* The people of Gath were in a panic—they were terrified. Tumors broke out on the men of the city, and rats devastated the city. So they sent the Ark to the city of Ekron. But the people of Ekron cried out, *"They have brought around to us the ark of the God of Israel to kill us and our people."* The Ark, which had been a blessing to the people of Israel, was a curse to the Philistines. The panicked people told the leaders of the Philistines to send the Ark away before it killed all the people. It is true that **unholy people cannot stand in the presence of the holy God and live.**

After seven months, the Philistines decided to return the Ark to Israel. But they wanted to send it with a guilt offering. So they made five golden tumors and five golden rats to send with the Ark. Perhaps then, the God of Israel would not be angry with them. They did not want to harden their hearts like Pharaoh and the Egyptians and experience the full fury of God's wrath.

They put the Ark on a cart pulled by two cows. They decided that if the cows headed for Israel, then their troubles had come from the hand of God. But if the cows returned, it would be a sign that their troubles happened by chance. When they released the cows, the cows went straight toward Israel and stopped in the town of Beth-shemesh.

The people of Beth-shemesh rejoiced when they saw the Ark. The Ark of God was back in Israel! They broke apart the cart and offered the cows as a burnt offering to the LORD. However, some of the men of Beth-shemesh did an unthinkable thing. They opened the Ark and looked inside it—the Ark that was holy and special. God had warned His people of the danger of looking in the ark: *". . . they shall not go in to look on the holy things even for a*

moment, lest they die." But these men disobeyed, and the LORD struck seventy of them dead. *Then the men of Beth-shemesh said, "Who is able to stand before the LORD, this holy God?"*

The Ark was then brought to the house of Abinadab. And for twenty years, the people of Israel mourned because they thought God had abandoned them. After these twenty years, Samuel challenged Israel:

> *..."If you are returning to the LORD with all your heart, then put away the foreign gods and the Ashtaroth from among you and direct your heart to the LORD and serve him only, and he will deliver you out of the hand of the Philistines." So the people of Israel put away the Baals and the Ashtaroth, and they served the LORD only. (1 Samuel 7:3-4)*

The people of Israel repented of their sin, and Samuel prayed for them. He offered a burnt offering to the LORD and *cried out to the LORD for Israel, and the LORD answered him.* Though His people had broken their covenant with Him, Yahweh forgave Israel. **God is faithful to His covenant even when His people are not.** Then God fought for Israel and defeated the Philistines, so the land taken from Israel was restored to them.

It is a wonderful blessing to have God as your God. But it is a great horror to have God against you. *What have you read so far that shows these statements to be true? What caused Israel to turn away from God? What can you learn from this?*

For great is the LORD, and greatly to be praised; he is to be feared above all gods. For all the gods of the people are worthless idols, but the LORD made the heavens. (Psalm 96:4-5)

MAKING YOU WISE FOR SALVATION

What does this chapter tell us about God? Talk about and apply the **biblical truths** in **bold** text.

Salvation Thread: The LORD alone is God.

Why did Dagon fall before the Ark of God? Why did God send a plague on the Philistines? What does this tell you about God?

Talk About: *For great is the LORD, and greatly to be praised; he is to be feared above all gods. For all the gods of the people are worthless idols, but the LORD made the heavens. (Psalm 96:4-5)*

Why is the fear of the LORD a good thing?

Pray: Thank God for being everywhere all the time. Thank Him for His great power and for fighting for His people. Ask God to show you if you are truly a child of God.

Think About: *How have I personally seen God's power?*

Memorize: Deuteronomy 10:12-13

CHAPTER 47

REJECTING GOD, DEMANDING A KING

Israel Demands a King—1 Samuel 8-12

"But there shall be a king over us, that we also may be like all the nations, and that our king may judge us and go out before us and fight our battles." (1 Samuel 8:19b-20)

Samuel had been a faithful prophet, judge, and priest "all the days of his life." As a prophet, he spoke God's words to the people of Israel—reminding them of His covenant, warning them to repent, and instructing them to obey and follow God. As a judge, he made sure that people were treated fairly, and he judged difficult disagreements. As a priest, he made sacrifices for the people and was an intercessor, praying for the people. In all these roles, Samuel was very faithful.

By now, Samuel was an old man. The elders, or leaders, of Israel met together and said to him, *"Behold, you are old and your sons do not walk in your ways. Now appoint for us a king to judge us like all the nations." **What do you think Samuel thought of this?*** The Bible says that Samuel was "displeased." He was disappointed and upset. Why would Samuel be upset? God had told Moses long ago that Israel could one day have a king, and yet Samuel was very upset and prayed to the LORD about it.

And the LORD said to Samuel, "Obey the voice of the people in all that they say to you, for they have not rejected you, but they have rejected me from being king over them . . . Now then, obey their voice; only you shall solemnly warn them and show them the ways of the king who shall reign over them." (1 Samuel 8:7, 9)

Why did the LORD say that the people were rejecting Him? The people of Israel were the covenant people of God. They were a "set-apart people." They were not like the other nations. Yahweh had told them His personal name. He had been faithful to keep His covenant with them even when they had not been faithful to Him. But now Israel wanted to be like the other nations. They wanted an earthly king. *Why was this so foolish?*

Yahweh had fought their battles for them and given them victory after victory—with hailstones, trumpets, and torches, and even making the sun stand still! But now, Israel wanted a man to fight their battles and rule over them! Israel's enemy, the Philistines, were becoming a mighty people, and Israel's fear of the Philistines was greater than their trust in God. They were rejecting God as their king and their mighty warrior. They did not want the faithful and just God to rule over them. And, even more foolishly, they trusted *a* king instead of *the* King over all other kings! They did not trust **Yahweh, the sovereign, self-existent, eternal, almighty, unchanging God, the Victorious One, God Almighty!**

Samuel warned the people that a king would take their sons to be part of his army, to work his fields, to make weapons, and to serve him as cooks and in other ways. He would also take some of their servants and some of their animals. *But the people refused to obey the voice of Samuel. And they said, "No! But there shall be a king over us, that we also may be like all the nations, and that our king may judge us and go out before us and fight our battles."* So God told Samuel, *"Obey their voice and make them a king."*

However, **God rules over all**—even when His people don't want His rule. So God would be the One to choose Israel's king, and He told Samuel His plan. *"Tomorrow about this time I will send to you a man from the land of Benjamin, and you shall anoint him to be prince over my people Israel. He shall save my people from the hand of the Philistines. For I have seen my people, because their cry has come to me."* How would God send this man to Samuel? God can use anything, and He used lost donkeys!

A wealthy man of the tribe of Benjamin had a tall, handsome son named Saul. Saul's father sent him and a servant to look for some lost donkeys. Saul looked for three days, but the donkeys were not to be found. By now, Saul knew his father would be worried that something had happened to him. So Saul decided it was time to head home—without the donkeys.

But Saul's servant had an idea. There was a prophet in the city where they were. Maybe this prophet or "seer" could tell him where the donkeys were. So, before returning home, Saul and his servant went to find the prophet and, as they were entering the city, they saw the prophet Samuel. When Samuel saw Saul coming toward him, *the LORD told him, "Here is the man of whom I spoke to you! He it is who shall restrain my people."*

Samuel invited Saul to eat with him and stay the night. Surprisingly, Samuel had good news for Saul. The donkeys had been found. *How did Samuel know this? Did someone come and tell him?* Samuel was God's special prophet, and God revealed or showed this to Samuel. Then Saul knew that Samuel was a true prophet of God.

Samuel had even more shocking news for Saul—God had chosen Saul as the king of all Israel! Samuel took a bottle of oil and poured it on Saul's head. *Do you remember another time when someone was anointed with oil?* Moses anointed Aaron as God's priest. Being anointed with oil was a sign of being chosen by God. Samuel told Saul that God would give him three signs. These signs would prove to Saul that God had chosen him to be the king and that God would be with him. All three signs happened just as Samuel had said they would. The Bible also tells us that God changed Saul's heart. God was working in Saul to make him a leader of His people.

Even so, when later, Samuel called the people of Israel together to reveal God's chosen king of Israel, Saul could not be found. He was hiding! *Do you know where he was hiding?* Saul was hiding with the baggage. Leading Israel would be very difficult. Surely, Saul was nervous! When Saul was found, Samuel presented him to the people, and the people responded, *"Long live the king!"* They now had their king.

In just a short time, God showed His faithfulness to Saul. Saul heard that the Ammonites wanted to take one of Israel's cities and make the people their servants. *The Spirit of God rushed upon Saul when he heard these words, and his anger was greatly kindled.* Saul called the men of Israel to fight the Ammonites with him, and God gave them a big victory over their enemies. Now Israel had their king to fight for them—but really, God had fought for Israel and given them victory.

It was time for Samuel to let Saul lead the Israelites as their king. But Samuel would still be their priest and prophet. Always faithful to his duty to speak God's words, Samuel gave Israel these words of warning and promised to pray for them:

> *If you will fear the LORD and serve him and obey his voice and not rebel against the commandment of the LORD, and if both you and the king who reigns over you will follow the LORD your God, it will be well. But if you will not obey the voice of the LORD, but rebel against the commandment of the LORD, then the hand of the LORD will be against you and your king . . ."do not turn aside from following the LORD, but serve the LORD with all your heart. And do not turn aside after empty things that cannot profit or deliver, for they are empty. For the LORD will not forsake his people, for his great name's sake, because it has pleased the LORD to make you a people for himself. Moreover, as for me, far be it from me that I should sin against the LORD by ceasing to pray for you, and I will instruct you in the good and the right way." (1 Samuel 12:14-15, 20b-23)*

Even though the Israelites had sinned in rebelling against God, God gave them another chance to follow Him. You, too, have rebelled against God and disobeyed His commands, yet God is willing and eager to receive anyone who turns away from sin and comes to Him in faith. *Do you want to put your trust in the LORD, serve Him, obey His voice, and follow Him?*

"And now, Israel, what does the LORD your God require of you, but to fear the LORD your God, to walk in all his ways, to love him, to serve the LORD your God with all your heart and with all your soul, and to keep the commandments and statutes of the LORD, which I am commanding you today for your good?" (Deuteronomy 10:12-13)

MAKING YOU WISE FOR SALVATION

What does this chapter tell us about God? Talk about and apply the **biblical truths** in **bold** text.

Salvation Thread: God, the King over all kings, established a kingly line in Israel.

What wisdom is there in God's command regarding a king in Deuteronomy 17:14-17?

Read about the three signs God gave Saul in 1 Samuel 10:2-9. *Why did God give Saul these signs?*

Talk About: *And now, Israel, what does the LORD your God require of you, but to fear the LORD your God, to walk in all his ways, to love him, to serve the LORD your God with all your heart and with all your soul, and to keep the commandments and statutes of the LORD, which I am commanding you today for your good. (Deuteronomy 10:12-13)*

What can you learn about God and about Samuel from Samuel's speech in 1 Samuel 12?

Pray: Praise God for being a faithful God. Praise Him for His willingness to receive all who come to Him. Ask Him to give you a heart to follow Him.

Think About: What are "empty things that cannot profit or deliver" (1 Samuel 12:21)? *Why don't they profit or deliver? Am I going after those things?*

C H A P T E R 4 8

DISHONORING GOD AND LOSING THE KINGDOM

Saul Fails to Trust God, but Jonathan Shows Confidence in God—1 Samuel 13-14

..."You have not kept the command of the LORD your God, with which he commanded you. For then the LORD would have established your kingdom over Israel forever." (1 Samuel 13:13b)

Saul and his men had defeated the Ammonites, but the Philistines were still a problem. Jonathan, Saul's son, along with 1,000 other men, defeated a troop of Philistines in the town of Geba. *What do you think the Philistines thought of this?* This small defeat made the Philistine nation very angry with the Israelites. The Bible says that Israel "had become a stench" or a terrible smell to the Philistines! What would happen now?

The Philistines gathered to fight Israel—the mighty Philistines with 30,000 chariots, 6,000 horsemen, and troops *like the sand on the seashore in multitude. What do you think the Israelites thought when they saw the Philistine army?* They thought they were in really big trouble! *Can you guess what they did? The people hid themselves in caves and in holes and in rocks and in tombs and in cisterns.* Some even fled, crossing the Jordan River. *Saul was still at Gilgal, and all the people followed him trembling.* This sounds like a hopeless situation, *doesn't it?* But remember, the Israelites had Yahweh as their God. He would fight for them if they would trust Him.

Would their new king, Saul, encourage them to trust God and fight the Philistines? Samuel had told Saul to wait seven days at Gilgal for him. When Samuel arrived, he would offer a sacrifice to God. Saul waited . . . and waited . . . and waited . . . until the seventh day. But Samuel did not come. Little by little, the men with Saul started to leave. Saul's army was getting smaller and smaller. Would Saul obey the word of God spoken through Samuel?

Finally, Saul told the people to bring the burnt offering and the peace offering. Saul was going to offer the sacrifices himself! *What would Samuel say? More importantly, what would God say?* The priests made offerings, and Saul was not a priest. Besides, God had given Saul a command through Samuel to wait seven days. But Saul went ahead and offered the burnt offering himself.

As soon as Saul was done, Samuel showed up! Now what would Saul do? He had disobeyed the law of Moses and the command of God. Maybe Saul would admit his sin and repent. But, no, he made an excuse for his sin of disobedience. *"When I saw that the people were scattering from me, and that you did not come . . . and that the Philistines had mustered [gathered] . . . I said, 'Now the Philistines will come down against me at Gilgal, and I have not sought the favor of the LORD.' So I forced myself and offered the burnt offering."* He *forced* himself? *What do you think Samuel said about that?*

> *And Samuel said to Saul, "You have done foolishly. You have not kept the command of the LORD your God, with which he commanded you. For then the LORD would have established your kingdom over Israel forever. But now your kingdom shall not continue. The LORD has sought out a man after his own heart, and the LORD has commanded him to be prince over his people, because you have not kept what the LORD commanded you." (1 Samuel 13:13-14)*

Then Samuel left, and Saul went to meet Jonathan at Geba. Saul had a huge problem. He had dishonored the LORD, and the LORD would cut off his family line from ruling Israel. What a huge price he would pay for dishonoring God!

Saul also had another problem. There were no blacksmiths in Israel. Blacksmiths are men who make things with iron. So Saul's army had no metal weapons, no swords, and no spears. Only Saul and Jonathan had iron weapons. Now Saul was facing this very strong enemy, having dishonored the LORD—and without weapons! He was really terrified now!

But Jonathan was not like his father. Jonathan had great confidence in God. He suggested to his armor bearer that the two of them go over to the Philistine camp. He knew that the Philistines were not the chosen, covenant people of God. God might still give Israel victory over them—*"It may be that the LORD will work for us, for* ***nothing can hinder the LORD from saving by many or by few.****"* Jonathan was a young man of great courage, because he had great faith in God's saving power. Jonathan's armor bearer agreed—*"Do all that is in your heart. Do as you wish. Behold, I am with you heart and soul."*

Jonathan's plan was to get closer to the Philistines and let the Philistines see them. If the Philistines told them to wait because they were coming, then Jonathan and his armor bearer would stay put. But if the Philistines told them to come, Jonathan said, *"Then we will go up, for the LORD has given them into our hand."*

When Jonathan and his armor bearer showed themselves, the Philistines started mocking them. *"Look, Hebrews are coming out of the holes where they have hidden themselves . . . Come up to us and we will show you a thing."* So, with confidence in God and the strength of the LORD, Jonathan and his armor-bearer climbed up and killed twenty Philistines. *And there was a panic in the camp, in the field, and among all the people. The garrison and even the raiders trembled, the earth quaked, and it became a very great panic.*

God had placed a great fear in the Philistines. When the men with Saul saw the Philistines fleeing, they turned and joined the battle. The Philistines were so confused that they even fought their own men!

> *So the LORD saved Israel that day. (1 Samuel 14:23a)*

Even though Saul had disobeyed God, God was faithful to Israel and gave Israel victory over the Philistines. Jonathan was right. **Nothing can stop the LORD**! *When Saul had taken the kingship over Israel, he fought against all*

his enemies on every side, against Moab, against the Ammonites, against Edom, against the kings of Zobah, and against the Philistines. Wherever he turned he routed them . . . and delivered Israel out of the hands of those who plundered them. But there would be grave consequences for Saul's rebellion and lack of faith. God would raise up a king who would honor Him. **God honors those who have faith in Him.**

Saul was more afraid of the enemy than he was afraid of disobeying God. He should have feared God and trusted God. But Jonathan had great confidence in God. He knew that **nothing can hinder the LORD.** *What was the difference between how Saul and how Jonathan faced fearful situations? What kinds of situations are fearful to you? What would confidence in God look like in your life? Do you want God to give you the kind of confidence in Him that Jonathan had?*

I sought the LORD, and he answered me and delivered me from all my fears. Those who look to him are radiant, and their faces shall never be ashamed. (Psalm 34:4-5)

MAKING YOU WISE FOR SALVATION

What does this chapter tell us about God? Talk about and apply the **biblical truths** in **bold** text.

Salvation Thread: God would build the kingly line through those who honored Him.

Why was Saul's sin so serious? What lies did Saul believe?

Talk About: *I sought the LORD, and he answered me and delivered me from all my fears. Those who look to him are radiant, and their faces shall never be ashamed. (Psalm 34:4-5)*

How was Jonathan's focus different from his father's?

Pray: Praise God that nothing can hinder Him. Thank Him for being worthy of our trust. Confess your fears to God. Ask Him to give you a confidence in Him that is greater than your fears. Ask Him to give you a fear of Him—a fear of disobeying Him, turning away from Him, and dishonoring Him.

Think About: What great truths did Jonathan believe? How did this give him confidence in God?

CHAPTER 49

TO OBEY IS BETTER THAN SACRIFICE

Saul Disobeys Again, and God Chooses David—1 Samuel 15-16

..."Has the LORD as great delight in burnt offerings and sacrifices, as in obeying the voice of the LORD? Behold, to obey is better than sacrifice, and to listen than the fat of rams." (1 Samuel 15:22)

Maybe after disobeying God by making the sacrifice himself, Saul had learned his lesson. Maybe now he would trust God and obey Him. Once again, the LORD sent Samuel to Saul with a command. This time, the command was to *strike Amalek and devote to destruction all that they have.* Nothing was to be spared—everything was to be destroyed. *Why would God command this?*

The Amalekites were descendants of Esau's grandson. They were an evil nation, known for killing children when they attacked their enemies. Many times, they had attacked Israel, the nation God had chosen to bless. They had tried to wipe out Israel, but they had failed. God had been patient. God had given Amalek many chances to repent. Now it was time for God's justice on the Amalekites for all the evil they had done. It was time to destroy the Amalekites completely before they destroyed Israel. **God's judgment is always right.**

But there was a tribe called the Kenites living among the Amalekites. Saul warned them to leave before Amalek was destroyed. God's judgment was not on the Kenites, and Israel did not need protection from the Kenites. After giving the Kenites time to leave, Saul and more than 200,000 Israelites attacked the evil nation of Amalek.

> *But Saul and the people spared Agag and the best of the sheep and of the oxen and of the fattened calves and the lambs, and all that was good, and would not utterly destroy them. All that was despised and worthless they devoted to destruction. (1 Samuel 15:9)*

Again, Saul had disobeyed God! He spared Agag, the king of the Amalekites, and kept the best animals. Not only that, but Saul set up a monument to himself. Saul could not be trusted to be a faithful king who would honor the LORD and follow His commands.

> *The word of the LORD came to Samuel: "I regret that I have made Saul king, for he has turned back from following me and has not performed my commandments." And Samuel was angry, and he cried to the LORD all night. (1 Samuel 15:10-11)*

In the morning, Samuel met Saul. *Do you know what Saul told Samuel?* Saul told Samuel, *"I have performed the commandment of the LORD."* Can you believe that he said this? Well, he did! Not only had he disobeyed God's command, but he also tried to deceive Samuel! But Samuel was not deceived. He simply said to Saul, *"What then is this bleating of the sheep in my ears and the lowing of the oxen that I hear?"* Saul was caught in his lie. He could not hide the sounds of the animals.

How did Saul respond? He tried to blame the people. *Saul said, "They have brought them from the Amalekites, for the people spared the best of the sheep and of the oxen to sacrifice to the LORD your God, and the rest we have devoted to destruction."* But Samuel wouldn't listen. *"Stop!" he said.* The LORD had given him a message for Saul:

> *..."Though you are little in your own eyes, are you not the head of the tribes of Israel? The LORD anointed you king over Israel. And the LORD sent you on a mission ...Why then did you not obey the voice of the LORD? Why did you pounce on the spoil and do what was evil in the sight of the LORD?" (1 Samuel 15:17-19)*

Samuel had heard enough! God had given Saul the privilege of leading His people. He had given him the mission of destroying the Amalekite nation. Why hadn't Saul obeyed? Why had he taken the best things from Amalek and done what was evil?

Saul again defended himself. He insisted he had obeyed God by defeating the Amalekites. He made an excuse for sparing the animals. *Do you know how he excused this disobedience?* Saul said that the animals were spared as a sacrifice to God. But Samuel responded with a stern word:

> *"Has the LORD as great delight in burnt offerings and sacrifices, as in obeying the voice of the LORD? Behold,* ***to obey is better than sacrifice****, and to listen than the fat of rams." (1 Samuel 15:22)*

Rebellion against God's command is always serious. Saul's boldness in thinking that his way was better than God's instructions was sinful. A heart of obedience and trust was more precious to God than sacrifices made through disobedience. Finally, Saul saw his sin of rebellion, unfaithfulness, and pride. He admitted that he disobeyed God because he wanted to please the people and obey their wishes. He wanted the praise of the people more than he wanted the approval of God.

God had given Saul two chances to prove himself to be a faithful king—and Saul had failed both times. Samuel had to finish the task God had given Saul and kill Agag, the king Saul had spared. Because Saul "rejected the word of the LORD," Yahweh rejected him from being king over Israel. **There are always consequences for disobedience.** God would now choose a king whose heart was faithful to Him.

Samuel followed God's instructions to go to the home of Jesse in Bethlehem for a new king. God had provided a king for Israel from among Jesse's sons. When Samuel saw the oldest son, Eliab, he thought that surely this fine-looking man was God's choice. *But the LORD said to Samuel, "Do not look on his appearance or on the height of his stature, because I have rejected him. For the LORD sees not as man sees: man looks on the outward appearance, but the LORD looks on the heart."*

Abinadab was also rejected, Shammah was rejected—seven of Jesse's sons were rejected. None of them was God's choice. Were these all the sons of Jesse? No, there was one more,

the youngest son, David, who was looking after the sheep. How could he be the one God would choose? But when they brought David before Samuel, *the LORD said: "Arise, anoint him, for this is he."* So Samuel anointed David, and *the Spirit of the LORD rushed upon David from that day forward.*

But just the opposite happened to Saul—*the Spirit of the LORD departed from Saul*—and instead, an evil spirit tormented or troubled him. Saul's servants encouraged him to find a man who could play the lyre well to soothe him when the evil spirit tormented him. One of his servants suggested a young man *"who is skillful in playing, a man of valor, a man of war, prudent in speech, and a man of good presence, and the LORD is with him." Guess who this young man was?* It was Jesse's son, David!

So David brought his lyre, a small U-shaped instrument like a harp, to serve Saul. David also became Saul's armor bearer. And whenever the evil spirit was upon Saul, David played his lyre. David's playing comforted Saul, and the evil spirit left him.

God looks at the heart of a person. Does that person love Him and His ways? Does he want to please God or man? Does he trust God's wisdom and command, or does he think his

own ideas are best? Saul was rejected as king because his heart was not true toward God. So, God chose David, "a man after his own heart." Though David was not yet the king, God was preparing him to be the king someday.

God sees your heart, too. Do you trust Him—even when you don't understand what He is doing? Do you want to please Him, or be popular with your friends and others? What does God see when He looks at your heart? Is there a way to be accepted by God, even though we are sinners?

…"For the LORD sees not as man sees: man looks on the outward appearance, but the LORD looks on the heart." (1 Samuel 16:7b)

MAKING YOU WISE FOR SALVATION

What does this chapter tell us about God? Talk about and apply the **biblical truths** in **bold** text.

Salvation Thread: God looks at man's heart. The person who honors God pleases God.

Where do you see God's mercy and His justice in this story?

Talk About: … *"For the LORD sees not as a man sees: man looks on the outward appearance, but the LORD looks on the heart." (1 Samuel 16:7b)*

Why must there be consequences for disobedience?

Pray: Praise God for being a God of mercy and of justice. Thank Him for His patience. Confess the sin in your heart. Ask God to show you how to be acceptable to Him even though you are a sinner.

Think About: What does it mean that God "looks on the heart"? What did God see in Saul's heart? *What does God see in my heart?*

C H A P T E R 5 0

FACING A BIG ENEMY WITH A BIGGER GOD

Goliath is Defeated by a Youth with Faith in God—1 Samuel 17

..."The LORD who delivered me from the paw of the lion and from the paw of the bear will deliver me from the hand of this Philistine." (1 Samuel 17:37a)

Do you remember when Israel defeated the Midianites with torches and trumpets? Why did God reduce the army to just three hundred men? He wanted Israel, the nations, and us to see that He is **Yahweh who is sovereign, self-existent, eternal, all-powerful, unchanging, and victorious.** God doesn't need big armies or smart people to accomplish His purposes. **God doesn't need anyone or anything. And nothing can stop His mighty works**—including a large Philistine army and a giant of a man.

Saul and the men of Israel were on one mountain and the Philistines on another with a valley between them. The Philistines had a champion. He was a very large man—a huge giant of a man. He was mean, vicious, and insulting—and his name was Goliath. With his helmet of bronze, a coat of mail, armor on his legs, and a javelin, Goliath stood where he could be clearly seen. He mockingly shouted his challenge to the army of Israel. Goliath would fight an Israelite soldier, and whichever side lost would be the servants of the winning army. Not one

of the Israelite men volunteered to fight Goliath. They wanted to stay far away from this battle! Saul and all the men of Israel were "dismayed and greatly afraid." Would no one fight Goliath? Saul had promised riches and his daughter in marriage to the man who defeated Goliath—but no man stepped up to fight Goliath.

The three oldest sons of Jesse—Eliab, Abinadab, and Shammah—had joined Saul to fight the Philistines. They were standing on Israel's battle line, with Saul's army facing the Philistine battle line, when David came with grain, bread, and cheese for his brothers. While David was talking to his brothers, Goliath appeared, shouting his challenge again. When they saw Goliath, the men of Israel "fled from him and were much afraid." But David had a very different view of things—he was indignant! He was irritated and offended—*"Who is this . . . Philistine, that he should defy the armies of the living God?"* Goliath had mocked Israel and Israel's God. David was furious! Israel was the army of Yahweh, who fights for His people! How could this Philistine think he could resist the army of God?

Saul sent for David when he heard about the brave words David had said. Imagine what he thought when David showed up. David was just a youth, probably about sixteen years old. And here he was, reassuring Saul, *"Let no man's heart fail because of him. Your servant will go and fight with this Philistine." What do you think Saul thought of this?*

Saul was not convinced. Goliath had been a "man of war" since his youth. He was an experienced soldier, while David was just a young shepherd boy. Saul knew David as a palace musician, but he did not know that David had been anointed to be the next king. David insisted, telling Saul that he had rescued his father's sheep from the mouths of lions and bears. This Philistine would be just like one of the lions and bears he had killed, for Goliath had defied the armies of the living God. David had great confidence in God. He had seen God work in the past. He knew that the **unchanging God** would be with him. *And David said, "The LORD who delivered me from the paw of the lion and from the paw of the bear will deliver me from the hand of this Philistine." And Saul said to David, "Go and the LORD be with you!"*

Saul put his own armor on David—his helmet, his coat of mail, and his sword. But David couldn't move around in them. He wasn't used to the bulky, heavy armor. So David took the armor off and picked up his staff. He chose five smooth stones from the stream, which he put in his shepherd's pouch. He took his sling in his hand . . . and he walked out to meet the giant, Goliath.

What do you think Goliath thought when he saw David coming to fight him? He was insulted! He said to David, *"Am I a dog, that you come to me with sticks?" And the Philistine cursed David by his gods. The Philistine said to David, "Come to me, and I will give your flesh to the birds of the air and to the beasts of the field."* How dare the Israelites send a boy to fight against him! Goliath was arrogant and self-confident. He was already boasting of his victory.

But David, full of confidence in the LORD, looked right at Goliath and said,

> *"You come to me with a sword and with a spear and with a javelin, but I come to you in the name of the LORD of hosts, the God of the armies of Israel, whom you have defied. This day the LORD will deliver you into my hand, and I will strike you down and cut off your*

head. And I will give the dead bodies of the host of the Philistines this day to the birds of the air and to the wild beasts of the earth, that all the earth may know that there is a God in Israel, and that all this assembly may know that the LORD saves not with sword and spear. For the battle is the LORD's, and he will give you into our hand." (1 Samuel 17:45-47)

David spoke words of faith. He was not facing the enemy alone. The LORD of hosts—the God of the armies of heaven—was with him! Goliath was not fighting David; he was fighting Yahweh, who never loses a battle! David was full of confidence—but his confidence was not in himself but in his God. He saw how big Goliath was, but he knew his God was so much bigger!

When Goliath started to approach, David ran quickly toward the battle line. He would face this Philistine with the strength of the LORD! David took a stone out of his bag. He put it in his sling, swung it around . . . and let it go. God gave David perfect aim . . . and the stone of God struck Goliath smack in the middle of his forehead! It hit him with such a force that it sank into his forehead "and he fell on his face to the ground." *So David prevailed over the Philistine with a sling and a stone, and struck the Philistine and killed him.*

When the Philistines saw that their hero, their champion, Goliath, was dead, they turned and fled! The men of Israel and Judah "rose with a shout." They chased the Philistines for about twelve miles, striking down the Philistines on the way. Then they raided the Philistine camp on the way back, taking whatever was valuable.

God does not need an army to defeat His enemies! He can use a boy with a sling and a stone to kill a giant and defeat His enemies. **God is the LORD of hosts, who is always victorious!** God defeats His enemies with hailstones, confusion, marches around city walls, and even a stone. **Nothing is too hard for God!**

Why did God give David victory over Goliath? So *that all the earth may know that there is a God in Israel.* God's mighty acts show that He is God Almighty. Every act of God is intended to show us His glory—His greatness and worth—so that we might put our trust in Him. When God is on your side, you do not need to fear the giants in your life. *Do you truly believe that God can do anything? Do you know in your heart that God is bigger than anything you face? Have you put your full confidence and trust in Him?*

> Those who trust in the LORD are like Mount Zion, which cannot be moved, but abides forever. As the mountains surround Jerusalem, so the LORD surrounds his people, from this time forth and forevermore. (Psalm 125:1-2)

MAKING YOU WISE FOR SALVATION

What does this chapter tell us about God? Talk about and apply the **biblical truths** in **bold** text.

Salvation Thread: Faith is trusting that God is who He says He is. The kingdom of Satan is at war with the Kingdom of God, but God always defeats His enemies.

Why was David able to defeat Goliath? (Give a complete, well-thought-out answer.)

Talk About: *Those who trust in the LORD are like Mount Zion, which cannot be moved, but abides forever. As the mountains surround Jerusalem, so the LORD surrounds his people, from this time forth and forevermore. (Psalm 125:1-2)*

What does faith in God look like in your everyday life?

Pray: Praise God for being the LORD of hosts, who is always victorious. Thank God that He is bigger than anything else is, and that He has promised to help His people. Ask God to give you an unshakable faith in His goodness, love, power, and wisdom.

Think About: *How can I have the kind of confidence in God that David had? How does "remembering the deeds of the LORD" strengthen my faith?*

Memorize: Psalm 125:1-2

CHAPTER 51

TRUSTING GOD AND SPARING SAUL

David Flees from Saul but Clings to God—1 Samuel 18-26

The LORD rewards every man for his righteousness and his faithfulness... (1 Samuel 26:23a)

After defeating the Philistines, Saul sent David into many battles. God was with David and gave him victory every time. So Saul made David in charge of Israel's fighting men. This pleased the people of Israel very much. To them, David was a great hero.

But Saul was beginning to feel differently about David. When David and Saul had come back from defeating the Philistines, they passed through city after city of cheering crowds celebrating Israel's victory. The women were dancing and singing, *"Saul has struck down his thousands, and David his ten thousands." What do you think Saul thought of the words of their song?* He was angry! He was jealous of David! What would happen next? Would David want to be king? All these thoughts stirred around in Saul's mind and heart, making him more and more jealous of David. Oh, how he hated David now! Saul began to look for an opportunity to get rid of David.

One day, Saul was troubled by an evil spirit. David was playing his lyre to comfort Saul. But Saul was not comforted. He had his spear in his hand. This was his chance to kill David. Suddenly he hurled his spear at David! But God helped David dodge the spear. Saul had lost the LORD's favor. But he knew that the LORD was with David. That made Saul afraid of David.

How could Saul get rid of David? He would not give up. He came up with a cunning plan. Saul demanded the death of one hundred of his Philistine enemies. If David did this, he could marry Saul's other daughter. Saul was sure that David would die fighting the Philistines. Instead, God gave David victory—he and his men killed *two* hundred Philistine soldiers—and David was a hero again! Saul only hated David more. He plotted again to kill David, but David's wife lowered him down through a window, and David escaped. Again, Saul failed to kill David.

Saul's son, Jonathan, was David's close and faithful friend. He loved David like a brother. Jonathan warned David that Saul still wanted to kill him. It would never be safe for David to return. Even so, David and Jonathan made a promise to each other to remain faithful friends, saying *"The LORD shall be between me and you, and between my offspring and your offspring, forever."*

So David was an outcast, a fugitive, a man without a home hiding in caves, living in the wilderness, and moving from place to place to escape Saul. Once he even went to hide in the land of the Philistines. He pretended he had lost his mind so the Philistines would not harm him. A crazy man wasn't much of an enemy. Later, David left Philistia and returned to Judah (the southern part of Israel). There he lived in a cave. But he wasn't alone. His brothers, his family, *and everyone who was in distress, and everyone who was in debt, and everyone who was bitter in soul [discontent], gathered to him. And he became captain over them. And there were with him about four hundred men . . . Saul sought him every day, but God did not give him into his hand.*

Once, Saul chased David in the wilderness and almost caught him. But God protected David. David was rushing to escape with Saul close behind him. Saul was getting closer and closer . . . but then a messenger caught up to Saul to tell him that the Philistines had attacked Israel. **God's timing is perfect,** and it saved David. Saul had to turn back to fight the Philistines, and David got away. After the battle, Saul took three thousand men to hunt down David. Saul would not give up! He must capture David!

Another time, David and his men were hiding in the dark shadows in the back of a cave . . . and who should come into the cave but Saul! However, Saul didn't know David and his men were quietly hiding in the darkness. *And the men of David said to him, "Here is the day of which the LORD said to you, 'Behold, I will give your enemy into your hand, and you shall do to him as it shall seem good to you.'"* Here was David's chance to get rid of his enemy and claim the throne as God had promised him! *What should he do?*

David quietly got up. He slowly crept up close to Saul. He reached out and cut off . . . a corner of Saul's robe. Saul's robe? Not his head? No! David would not kill God's anointed king. David was a man of noble character who feared the LORD. **The fear of the LORD gives man wisdom.**

> *And afterward David's heart struck him, because he had cut off a corner of Saul's robe. He said to his men, "The LORD forbid that I should do this thing to my lord, the LORD's anointed, to put out my hand against him, seeing he is the LORD's anointed." So David*

persuaded his men with these words and did not permit them to attack Saul. And Saul rose up and left the cave and went on his way. (1 Samuel 24:5-7)

Imagine Saul's surprise when David stepped outside the cave and called out to him. David respectfully addressed Saul as "my lord the king," and bowed down to him. David pleaded with Saul not to believe those who said he wanted to harm Saul. He then told Saul how he had spared his life in the cave and promised not to harm Saul in the future. He would not lift his hand against Saul. The LORD would judge Saul, but David would not.

And Saul lifted up his voice and wept. He said to David, "You are more righteous than I, for you have repaid me good, whereas I have repaid you evil." Saul admitted that David would be king someday and asked David not to destroy his family. Again, David repaid Saul with good and promised to protect Saul's offspring.

But Saul's change of heart didn't last. He was not able to truly repent from his sin of jealousy and hatred. Before long, he again wanted to kill David. **Only God can give man true repentance.** David continued to flee from Saul, and Saul continued to hunt for David. Once again, David had the opportunity to kill Saul—this time, when Saul was camped in the wilderness where David was hiding. In the dark of the night, while Saul and his men were sleeping, David and one of his mighty men, Abishai, quietly snuck down to Saul's camp. They found Saul with his spear near his head. All they had to do was pick up the spear and drive it through Saul. That would be the end of the constant fleeing and hiding. Abishai wanted to strike Saul with

Saul's own spear, but David stopped him saying, *"Do not destroy him, for who can put out his hand against the LORD's anointed and be guiltless? . . . As the LORD lives, the LORD will strike him, or his day will come to die, or he will go down into battle and perish."* Then David picked up Saul's spear and a jar of water and left. Saul never even knew David and Abishai were there because God had put Saul and his men into a deep sleep.

Standing far away, David called down to Saul's camp. He held up Saul's spear and the water jug. It was clear that David had been close enough to kill Saul, but once again, David had spared Saul's life. Saul admitted again that he had sinned and promised not to harm David. But David knew he could not trust Saul. His trust was in the LORD, and he left Saul with these words:

> *"The LORD rewards every man for his righteousness and his faithfulness, for the LORD gave you into my hand today, and I would not put out my hand against the LORD's anointed.*

Behold, as your life was precious this day in my sight, so may my life be precious in the sight of the LORD, and may he deliver me out of all tribulation." (1 Samuel 26:23-24)

David could have killed Saul and come out of hiding. But he refused to sin against God by harming the man God had anointed as king. His fear of the LORD was greater than his fear of danger. Though Samuel had anointed David as the next king, David would not wrongly take the throne. He waited for God to give him the throne. He had great faith in God's good plan. He would wait for God to work in His own time. **Faith is believing that God's word is true and waiting for Him to act.**

Like Abraham who wanted a son, we too sometimes want to act on our own instead of waiting for God to act. David was not sinless, but he was wise and patient in waiting for God to make him king. He faced many fearful situations, but he trusted God to be with him. *What fears do you have? Do you sometimes find it hard to wait for God to act? Do you have the faith to do what is right and trust God to deal with the situation?*

"But this is the one to whom I will look: he who is humble and contrite in spirit and trembles at my word." (Isaiah 66:2b)

MAKING YOU WISE FOR SALVATION

What does this chapter tell us about God? Talk about and apply the **biblical truths** in **bold** text.

Salvation Thread: True repentance is a deep sorrow for sin and a turning away from it. Man is unable to repent on his own. Faith is believing that God's word is true—that God can be trusted.

What in this story shows you that David feared God more than he feared Saul? Why is the fear of the LORD a very good thing? What shows you that David trusted God? What would trust in God look like in your situation?

Talk About: *"But this is the one to whom I will look: he who is humble and contrite in spirit and trembles at my word." (Isaiah 66:2)*

Are you waiting for an answer to prayer, or for God to work in some situation in your life? What verses can encourage you to trust God?

Read in 1 Samuel 25 about how God protected David through Abigail and about David's wisdom and humility in listening to advice.

Pray: Thank God that He rewards those who are righteous and faithful. Ask Him to make you a righteous, faithful follower of Him.

Think About: *Am I jealous of anyone? What might my jealousy lead to? With God's help, will I let go of my jealousy?*

C H A P T E R 5 2

THE SHEPHERD OF GOD'S PEOPLE

Saul Dies, and David Becomes King—1 Samuel 27-2 Samuel 5

"You shall be shepherd of my people Israel, and you shall be prince over Israel." (2 Samuel 5:2b)

David knew that Saul would not stop hunting him down as long as he was in Israel. *So, can you guess where David went to live?* He went to live among the Philistines, Israel's enemy. Saul surely would not look for him there! David now had six hundred men following him. One of the five kings of the Philistines gave David the city of Ziklag, which was right on the border with Judah.

How would David live among Israel's enemies? He could not fight *against* Israel—he would not harm his own people—but he would fight *for* Israel. So David and his men often made secret raids on the enemies of Israel far away from the land of the Philistines. He had to be very careful that the Philistines didn't find out what he was doing. He did this for more than a year, fooling the Philistines.

One day, the five Philistine kings and their armies gathered to fight against Israel. When Saul saw the army of the Philistines, "he was afraid, and his heart trembled greatly." Saul asked the LORD what he should do about the Philistines. But the LORD had turned away from Saul and would not answer him. Samuel had died, so he couldn't ask Samuel what to do. Once more, Saul disobeyed God's law. He went to a woman who claimed she could speak to the spirits of dead people. Maybe she could find out what Samuel's spirit would tell Saul. This was a very wicked thing for Saul to do. It was one more act of rebellion against God and His commands. The woman told Saul that the Philistines would defeat Israel. And he and his sons would die. These words filled Saul with terror!

The Philistines attacked Israel with great might, defeating one man after another. When the men of Israel saw they were losing the battle, they fled from the Philistines. Many of them were struck down as they fled. The Philistines caught up with Saul and his sons. They killed three of Saul's sons, including David's beloved friend, Jonathan. Saul received deadly arrow wounds but did not want to die by the hand of the Philistines. That would be an insult. Instead, Saul wanted his armor-bearer to kill him. But the man refused to do this wickedness. So Saul fell on his own sword and died. What a horrible end for Saul.

When the Israelites living beyond the Jordan River learned that Israel had fled and that Saul and his sons had died, they fled in terror. Then the Philistines came, took the Israelite cities, and lived in them. It was a dreadful day of defeat for Israel.

Saul, the first king of Israel, was dead. He had not stayed faithful to the LORD, so the LORD had turned away from Him. **Disobedience and rebellion bring grave consequences**. Saul's bones were buried along with his sons' bones.

So Saul died for his breach of faith. He broke faith with the LORD in that he did not keep the command of the LORD . . . Therefore the LORD put him to death and turned the kingdom over to David the son of Jesse. (1 Chronicles 10:13a, 14)

What do you think David did when he heard of the death of Saul? David and his men *mourned and wept and fasted until evening for Saul and for Jonathan his son and for the people of Israel, because they had fallen by the sword.* David could have been glad that maybe now he would be the king of Israel. But David never wanted to take the kingdom from Saul. He was loyal to

Saul as God's anointed king, even though Saul had treated him so badly. David loved Israel, and Israel's defeat was a great sorrow to him.

What would David do now? He had been a fugitive running from Saul, hiding in caves, living in the wilderness, and even among the Philistines for eight years. *How would David know what to do?* David turned to the LORD and asked him, *"Shall I go up into any of the cities of Judah?"* David was "a man after God's heart"—He loved God and His law. He loved the ways of God and wanted to honor God.

The LORD answered David and told him to go to the city of Hebron. In Hebron, the men of Judah *anointed David king over the house of Judah.* David became king fifteen years after Samuel had anointed him. **God's word had proven true**. But this was just the beginning of the fulfillment of God's promise to make David king, for David was only king over the tribe of Judah—not over all Israel. Abner was the commander of Saul's army. He made Saul's son, Ish-bosheth, king of the other eleven tribes of Israel. Israel was now a divided nation. Would Israel ever become a strong nation again after being disgraced and defeated by the Philistines? Would David ever reign over all of Israel?

Abner started a war with Judah. Now the chosen people of God were fighting each other! Abner wanted to conquer Judah and make Israel one nation again. But he wanted Ish-bosheth to be the king. He would not submit to God's choice of David as king.

David had to defend Judah. But that meant fighting against the other tribes of Israel. What a difficult thing for David to have to do. A bitter war between Judah and the rest of Israel dragged on for more than seven years. David and his kingdom grew stronger because the LORD was with him. But Ish-bosheth and his kingdom grew weaker and weaker. In the end, Abner and Ish-bosheth both died.

By this time, David had several wives and many children. He had made peace agreements with some of the countries around Israel. Now the elders of all the tribes came to David. They were finally ready to accept David as God's choice:

> *"Behold, we are your bone and flesh. In times past, when Saul was king over us, it was you who led out and brought in Israel. And the LORD said to you, 'You shall be shepherd of my people Israel, and you shall be prince over Israel.'" (2 Samuel 5:1b-2)*

So David the shepherd boy became the king of all Israel. Once he had protected, cared for, and guided sheep. Now he would be protecting, caring for, and leading God's people. It took twenty-two years for God's promise made through Samuel to be fulfilled. But God was faithful to His word. **God always keeps His promises, and He always fulfills His purposes**.

God had been moving all of history to fulfill His grand purposes. The spies didn't *just happen* to go to the house of Rahab. God led them there. Rahab, a Moabite, trusted in the God of Israel and was rescued from destruction to become the mother of Boaz. Elimelech and Naomi didn't *just happen* to go to Moab; and their son didn't *just happen* to marry Ruth. God had sovereignly chosen Ruth, a Moabite, to be one of His covenant people. God led Ruth to Israel and to Boaz, the kinsman redeemer. Boaz and Ruth were the parents of Obed,

who was the father of Jesse, who was the father of David. For generations, God had been establishing a line from the tribe of Judah—the royal line of David, the line of the future Messiah. Nothing *just happens* by chance. **Everything God does has a purpose.** There are no mistakes, coincidences, or unexpected problems in God's plans.

Saul was not faithful to God, and God turned away from him. David was faithful to the LORD, and God's favor was on him. *Will you be like Saul who trusted his own wisdom and did things his own way? Or will you be like David who trusted God and waited for the fulfillment of God's promise? Do you have faith in the God who accomplishes all His plans and fulfills all His purposes?*

God is not man, that he should lie, or a son of man, that he should change his mind. Has he said, and will he not do it? Or has he spoken, and will he not fulfill it? (Numbers 23:19)

MAKING YOU WISE FOR SALVATION

What does this chapter tell us about God? Talk about and apply the **biblical truths** in **bold** text.

Salvation Thread: God always fulfills His purposes. God raised up the royal line of David—the line of the coming Messiah.

What pattern do you see in Saul's life? Everyone is a sinner. Even godly people sin. What made Saul's sin especially serious? What is a *pattern of sin? Why is it a fearful thing when God turns away from a person?*

Talk About: *God is not a man, that he should lie, or a son of man, that he should change his mind. Has he said, and will he not do it? Or has he spoken, and will he not fulfill it? (Numbers 23:19)*

Are God's promises for all people, or just for His people? Why?

Pray: Praise God for being a promise-keeping God. Praise Him for His power to accomplish all His purposes. Thank Him for the goodness He has shown you. Ask Him to give you faith in Him.

Think About: *What should my response be to a God who is all-powerful, wise, loving, just, and sovereign over all things?*

CHAPTER 53

AN ETERNAL THRONE

David Brings the Ark to Jerusalem, and God's Covenant to Establish David's Eternal Throne —2 Samuel 5-7

"And your house and your kingdom shall be made sure forever before me. Your throne shall be established forever." (2 Samuel 7:16)

How would David make Israel one nation again? One of the first things he did was to choose a capital city—a city that would be his home and the most important city in Israel. *What city did he choose?* David was wise. He didn't choose a city in Israel or one in Judah. Instead, he chose Jerusalem. Jerusalem was close to the border between Israel and Judah, but the Israelites had never conquered it. So it didn't belong to either Israel or Judah. If David could conquer this city, it would unite Israel and Judah under David's rule.

But there was a problem. Jerusalem was considered unconquerable. It was protected by walls more than ten stories high. In three hundred years, no one had conquered this Canaanite city. But God gave David a clever plan. David's men wouldn't go *over* the wall. They would go *under* the wall. David would use the city's secret water system. He sent Joab and his men through a water tunnel under the wall and up into the city. They quietly snuck through the city to the city gate. Then they threw open the gates for the rest of David's mighty men to come in! David and his men conquered the city, and Jerusalem became the city of David. David built his palace there and built up the city. He also took more wives and had more children. *And David became greater and greater, for the LORD, the God of hosts, was with him.*

When the Philistines heard that David had become Israel's king, they gathered to fight Israel. *What do you think David did?* He didn't just gather his army and march out to fight them. Instead, he asked the LORD *if* he should fight them. *And the LORD said to David, "Go up, for I will certainly give the Philistines into your hand."* **God,** who **always does what He says he will do**, gave David a great victory over the Philistines. *And [David] said, "The LORD has broken through my enemies before me like a bursting flood."* God was the One who gave David and his army victory. It wasn't David and his might that defeated the enemy but God and His almighty power. *And the fame of David went out into all lands, and the LORD brought the fear of him upon all nations.*

David was a great military leader—a great soldier. But he was also the shepherd of God's people. He cared for them and protected them just as he had done as a shepherd for his sheep. Most importantly, he encouraged the people to worship Yahweh alone. He wanted to bring the Ark of the Covenant, the symbol of God's presence with His people, to Jerusalem. So David took thirty thousand men to get the Ark from the house of Abinadab and bring it to Jerusalem. But they made a very big mistake. They put the Ark on an ox cart. *Do you remember God's instructions about moving the Ark?* God's very careful instructions about the Ark were a way of showing the Israelites that He is holy. The priests were first to cover the Ark with three layers of cloth to protect others from seeing it. Only the priests could carry the Ark. The priests were to carry the Ark on their shoulders by its poles, and everyone else had to stay one thousand yards away. (That's ten football fields, or 2/3 of a mile!) The priests were forbidden from touching the Ark, lest they die. They could only touch the poles. *So, how many of God's instructions were the Israelites disobeying?*

David and the people were singing and playing instruments in praise to God as they were moving the Ark, and then the oxen stumbled. Surely, the cart carrying the Ark rocked and

swayed. So a man named Uzzah reached out and "took hold" of the Ark. But he didn't grab the poles; he grabbed the actual Ark. *And the anger of the LORD was kindled against Uzzah, and God struck him down there because of his error, and he died there beside the ark.* *Why would God do this?*

The Ark was to be treated with respect and a holy fear. Coming near the Ark would be coming near the presence of God. A sinful person should be fearful of being in the presence of a holy God, who cannot accept sin. God warned His people not to touch the Ark to protect them from death. Uzzah knew the law of God and the correct way to treat the holy Ark. Yet he dared to touch the Ark of God. His disobedience and disrespect for the holiness of God brought sudden death. **God's warnings are always right.**

David *was afraid of the LORD that day* and was not willing to bring the Ark to Jerusalem. So he brought it to the house of a man named Obed-edom. *And the LORD blessed Obed-edom and all his household.* The Ark, treated respectfully, brought blessing. When David saw that the Ark brought the LORD's blessing on Obed-edom and his family, David decided to bring the Ark to Jerusalem. But this time, he followed God's commands. David asked the priests to carry the Ark, telling them that *"Because you did not carry it the first time, the LORD our God broke out against us, because we did not seek him according to the rule."*

This time, David and "all Israel" brought the Ark of the Covenant to Jerusalem with great rejoicing, singing, dancing, and shouts of joy "to the sound of the horn, trumpets, and cymbals," along with the music of harps and lyres. They stopped several times to offer sacrifices to God along the way. They set the Ark inside a tent and made more burnt offerings and peace offerings.

David lived in a beautiful palace. Surely, the Ark of the Covenant should have a beautiful permanent home, not a tent. The prophet, Nathan, thought this was a good idea when David told him about it. But that night, the LORD told Nathan that David was not the man to build a house for Him. How sad and disappointing this must have been for David. Though God did not allow David to build the temple, He did have an amazing promise for Nathan to pass on to David:

> *"...you shall say to my servant David, 'Thus says the LORD of hosts, I took you from the pasture, from following the sheep, that you should be prince over my people Israel. And I have been with you wherever you went and have cut off all your enemies from before you. And I will make for you a great name, like the name of the great ones of the earth. And I will appoint a place for my people Israel and will plant them, so that they may dwell in their own place and be disturbed no more... When your days are fulfilled and you lie down with your fathers, I will raise up your offspring after you... and I will establish his kingdom. He shall build a house for my name, and I will establish the throne of his kingdom forever... my steadfast love will not depart from him... And your house and your kingdom shall be made sure forever before me. Your throne shall be established forever.'" (selections from 2 Samuel 7:8-10a, 12-13, 15a, 16)*

God was making an everlasting covenant with David. Some of these promises David would see in his lifetime—a great name, a place for God's people, and rest from Israel's enemies. Though David would not build a special temple for the LORD, his son would. But God's promise was not just for David's son and grandson. It was also a promise for far into the future and forever. God would establish David's royal line forever. **God would raise up from David's descendants a new and Greater King who would rule forever in an eternal Kingdom!** What an amazing promise from Yahweh, the faithful covenant-keeping God of Israel!

Why should God make such a promise to David, a simple shepherd boy, who said, *"Who am I, O LORD GOD, and what is my house, that you have brought me thus far?"* Why should David's throne be an eternal throne? David was unworthy of such an honor. But God had set His favor on David. It was pure grace—undeserved blessing. What response could David make to such a wonderful promise?

> *"Therefore you are great, O LORD God. For there is none like you, and there is no God besides you..." (2 Samuel 7:22a)*

David's response was gratitude, humility, amazement, and worship. Our response to God should be the same. *Have you expressed your sincere gratitude to God? Have you seen your unworthiness before the great God of the universe? Are you amazed that God would choose a people for Himself and have a personal relationship with them? Do you see Him as the greatest treasure and the only One worthy of worship?*

Ascribe to the LORD the glory due his name; bring an offering and come before him! Worship the LORD in the splendor of holiness; tremble before him, all the earth; yes, the world is established; it shall never be moved. Let the heavens be glad, and let the earth rejoice, and let them say among the nations, "The LORD reigns!" (1 Chronicles 16:29-31)

MAKING YOU WISE FOR SALVATION

What does this chapter tell us about God? Talk about and apply the **biblical truths** in **bold** text.

Salvation Thread: God would raise up an eternal King and an eternal Kingdom from the line of David.

What does the story about moving the Ark tell you about the holiness of God? What does it tell you about the seriousness of sin and disobeying God's commands? Why can't sinful man be in the presence of God?

Talk About: *Ascribe to the LORD the glory due his name; bring an offering and come before him. Worship the LORD in the splendor of holiness; tremble before him, all the earth; yes, the world is established; it shall never be moved. Let the heavens be glad, and let the earth rejoice, and let them say among the nations, "The LORD reigns!" (1 Chronicles 16:29-31)*

Read 2 Samuel 7:8-16. What are the promises God makes to David? Why are these such amazing promises?

Pray: Praise God for His holiness–there is none like God. Thank Him for His covenant love and everlasting promises. Ask Him to give you a fear of Him and a heart to worship Him above all else. Ask Him to show you the importance of His commands and the preciousness of His promises

Think About: *Do I really know what it means to worship God?*

DAVID'S SONG OF THANKS

*Oh give thanks to the LORD; call upon his name; make known his
deeds among the peoples! [9]Sing to him; sing praises to him; tell of all
his wondrous works! [10]Glory in his holy name; let the hearts of those
who seek the LORD rejoice! [11]Seek the LORD and his strength; seek his presence
continually! [12]Remember the wondrous works that he has done, his miracles
and the judgments he uttered, [13]O offspring of Israel his servant, children of
Jacob, his chosen ones! [14]He is the LORD our God; his judgments are in all the
earth. [15]Remember his covenant forever, the word that he commanded, for a
thousand generations, [16]the covenant that he made with Abraham, his sworn
promise to Isaac, [17]which he confirmed to Jacob as a statute, to Israel as an
everlasting covenant, [18]saying, "To you I will give the land of Canaan, as your
portion for an inheritance." [19]When you were few in number, and of little account,
and sojourners in it, [20]wandering from nation to nation, from one kingdom to
another people, [21]he allowed no one to oppress them; he rebuked kings on their
account, [22]saying, "Touch not my anointed ones, do my prophets no harm!"
[23]Sing to the LORD, all the earth! Tell of his salvation from day to day. [24]Declare
his glory among the nations, his marvelous works among all the peoples! [25]For
great is the LORD, and greatly to be praised, and he is to be held in awe above
all gods. [26]For all the gods of the peoples are worthless idols, but the LORD made
the heavens. [27]Splendor and majesty are before him; strength and joy are in his
place. [28]Ascribe to the LORD, O clans of the peoples, ascribe to the LORD glory
and strength! [29]Ascribe to the LORD the glory due his name; bring an offering
and come before him! Worship the LORD in the splendor of holiness; [30]tremble
before him, all the earth; yes, the world is established; it shall never be moved.
[31]Let the heavens be glad, and let the earth rejoice, and let them say among the
nations, "The LORD reigns!" [32]Let the sea roar, and all that fills it; let the field
exult, and everything in it! [33]Then shall the trees of the forest sing for joy before
the LORD, for he comes to judge the earth. [34]Oh give thanks to the LORD, for
he is good; for his steadfast love endures forever!*

*Say also: "Save us, O God of our salvation, and gather and deliver us from
among the nations, that we may give thanks to your holy name, and glory in your
praise. [36]Blessed be the LORD, the God of Israel, from everlasting to everlasting!"
Then all the people said, "Amen!" and praised the LORD. (1 Chronicles 16:8-36)*

C H A P T E R 5 4

GOD'S MERCIFUL DISCIPLINE

David's Sin Brings Judgment on His Household—2 Samuel 8, 10-12

For I know my transgressions, and my sin is ever before me. Against you, you only, have I sinned and done what is evil in your sight, so that you may be justified in your words and blameless in your judgment. (Psalm 51:3-4)

So much of Israel's history was filled with wars—wars to take the Promised Land, wars to protect the land, even a war between Israel and Judah. But one of the covenant promises God made to David was that someday He would give Israel rest from all its enemies. God was keeping this promise by making David a great military leader. Yet it was Yahweh defeating the enemies of His people. Each victory brought more gold, silver, and bronze into David's kingdom, as well as servants, cities, land, and money from taxes. *And the LORD gave victory to David wherever he went.*

In those days, kings usually led their armies in battles. They didn't stay home in their comfortable palaces. So David led Israel in battle, even though Joab was the captain of his army. But one spring, David sent Joab to lead his army in battle, and David stayed home in Jerusalem. David was walking on the roof of his house one afternoon and saw a startling sight. He saw a beautiful woman bathing.

What should David have done? David should have looked away, left the roof, and put the woman out of his mind. Sin was "crouching at the door" waiting to capture David. *Did David rule over it?* Sadly, David didn't rule sin; he let sin rule him. Taking a step toward sin, David asked about the woman. He found out she was Bathsheba, the wife of Uriah the Hittite, one of his men on the battlefield. Then he took one more step toward sin. He sent a messenger to get her—and when she came, he treated her as though she was his wife. David disobeyed God's good command *not* to commit adultery. Though David was "a man after God's own heart," he ignored his conscience, rejected God's law, and deliberately sinned. David already had seven wives and many children. Why did he think he needed to take Uriah's wife, too? How could he think that having Bathsheba was better than having the favor of his God? How could he offend **Yahweh, the sovereign, self-sufficient, eternal, unchanging, almighty, holy, gracious, faithful** God with whom he had a personal relationship?

Later, Bathsheba sent David an alarming message. She was pregnant with his baby. David's people would know about his sin. What would David do now? Would he confess his sin and repent? Once again, David took another sinful step. He tried to cover up his sin. He sent a message to Joab on the battlefield: "Send me Uriah the Hittite." David would ask Uriah about the battle, and then Uriah would go home and be with his wife. People would think the baby was Uriah's baby—and David's sin would be hidden. But Uriah did not go home to see his wife. He stayed with the servants. Now what would David do?

One sin led to another sin. *In the morning David wrote a letter to Joab and sent it by the hand of Uriah. In the letter he wrote, "Set Uriah in the forefront of the hardest fighting, and then draw back from him, that he may be struck down, and die."* Many men die in battle, but David was asking Joab to make sure that Uriah would be killed! *Why would David do such an evil thing?*

Sin had grabbed hold of David's heart. It would have been better to confess his sin and repent. Instead, in trying to hide his sin, David sank deeper and deeper into sin. He had disobeyed and dishonored his God, the God who had made wonderful covenant promises to him.

Joab obeyed David's command, and David added murder to his list of sins. *When the wife of Uriah heard that Uriah her husband was dead, she lamented over her husband. And when the mourning was over, David sent and brought her to his house, and she became his wife and bore him a son. But the thing that David had done displeased the LORD.* How David's sin must have grieved the heart of Yahweh, the holy God who had been faithful to David.

Perhaps David thought that all would be well now. He had hidden his sin and married Bathsheba. He had gotten what he wanted. *But can anything ever be hidden from God?* **God is all-knowing.** He sees even the secret things. Because He is just, He must deal with sin. Because He loves His children, He disciplines them for their good. So God, who is faithful in all His ways, sent Nathan the prophet to David.

Nathan told David a story about two men. One man was quite rich and had many flocks and herds of animals. But the other man was poor. He only had one little pet lamb. He loved his lamb and even treated it like a member of the family. One day the rich man had a visitor. Instead of eating one of his many sheep for dinner, he took the one little pet lamb of the poor man and served it to his guest!

When David heard this, he was furious! The rich man had done a despicable thing! David told Nathan, *"As the LORD lives, the man who has done this deserves to die."* It was very easy for David to see this man's sin. He knew this man deserved to be punished severely. Then came Nathan's shocking words:

> *"You are the man! Thus says the LORD, the God of Israel, 'I anointed you king over Israel, and I delivered you out of the hand of Saul. And I gave you your master's house and your master's wives into your arms and gave you the house of Israel and of Judah. And if this were too little, I would add to you as much more. Why have you despised the word of the LORD, to do what is evil in his sight? You have struck down Uriah the Hittite with the sword and have taken his wife to be your wife and have killed him with the sword of the Ammonites. Now therefore the sword shall never depart from your house, because you have despised me and have taken the wife of Uriah the Hittite to be your wife.' Thus says the LORD, 'Behold, I will raise up evil against you out of your own house.'" (2 Samuel 12:7-11a)*

How did David respond to this word from the LORD? This time David admitted his sin. He didn't try to deny it, blame others, or make excuses. Deep down, David truly was "a man after God's own heart." *David said to Nathan, "I have sinned against the LORD."* He didn't plead with God to take away the consequences. He knew he was guilty and deserved the wrath of God. He had broken God's holy law. He had offended his God and hurt others. He humbled himself before God, admitted his sin, and accepted the consequences.

> *For I know my transgressions, and my sin is ever before me. Against you, you only, have I sinned and done what is evil in your sight, so that you may be justified in your words and blameless in your judgment. (Psalm 51:3-4)*

God is gracious and merciful to undeserving sinners. And God gave Nathan these amazing words of grace for David:

> *"The LORD also has put away your sin; you shall not die. Nevertheless, because by this deed you have utterly scorned the LORD, the child who is born to you shall die." Then Nathan went to his house. And the LORD afflicted the child that Uriah's wife bore to David, and he became sick. (2 Samuel 12:13b-15)*

God was gracious to forgive David's sin. However, **sin always brings consequences**. David did not eat anything, and he pleaded with God for seven days to spare his sick child. But the child died. **God's judgment is real and sure.** David's sin had brought judgment on his household.

Even in His sure and right judgment, God is gracious to those who are humble in heart and repent from sin. In His kindness, God gave David and Bathsheba another son. David *called his name Solomon. And the LORD loved him.*

Do you find this statement amazing? And the LORD loved him. God loved the son from a relationship that started in sin. *What does this tell you about the heart of God?* There were terrible consequences to David because of his sin, but there was also amazing grace from God.

You can hide sin from others for a while, but **you can never hide sin from God**. The wonderful news is that God is eager to forgive those who come to him with humble and repentant hearts. *Is there any sin that you are trying to hide? Is there anything you must confess to God and to others? There may be consequences, but there is also great freedom and peace in confession. Like David, you can experience God's grace toward undeserving sinners.*

> Have mercy on me, O God, according to your steadfast love; according to your abundant mercy blot out my transgressions. Wash me thoroughly from my iniquity, and cleanse me from my sin! ...Create in me a clean heart, O God, and renew a right spirit within me. (Psalm 51:1-2, 10)

MAKING YOU WISE FOR SALVATION

What does this chapter tell us about God? Talk about and apply the **biblical truths** in **bold** text.

Salvation Thread: God sees and judges man's sin. God forgives those who repent.

Does receiving forgiveness mean there are no consequences? What are the consequences Nathan said would come because of David's sin? Why do there have to be consequences to sin?

Talk About: *Have mercy on me, O God, according to your steadfast love; according to your abundant mercy blot out my transgressions. Wash me thoroughly from my iniquity, and cleanse me from my sin! ... Create in me a clean heart, O God, and renew a right spirit within me. (Psalm 51:1-2, 10)*

Think of the Ten Commandments. *Which commandments did David break?*

Pray: Thank God that He is merciful and forgiving. Confess your sin to the LORD. Ask God to give you a clean heart and renew a right spirit in you—a desire to please Him and to love what is right.

Think About: Why does confession and repentance bring peace?

DAVID'S PRAYER OF CONFESSION

Psalm 51 : A Model of Confessional Prayer[1]

To the choirmaster. A Psalm of David, when Nathan the prophet went to him, after he had gone in to Bathsheba.

1 *Have mercy on me, O God, according to your steadfast love; according to your abundant mercy blot out my transgressions.*

Remember who God is. Recognize that you have no right to be forgiven; forgiveness is an undeserved mercy. Appeal to God on the basis of His character (ask God to act according to His merciful nature).

2 *Wash me thoroughly from my iniquity, and cleanse me from my sin!*

Recognize that your sin is serious and makes you unacceptable to a holy God; your sin deserves God's condemnation (punishment). Admit that only God has the right and power to forgive your sin and wash away your guilt before Him; there is nothing you can do to make yourself acceptable to God.

3 *For I know my transgressions, and my sin is ever before me.*

Admit your sin. Until you humbly confess your sin, it will trouble your heart.

4 *Against you, you only, have I sinned and done what is evil in your sight, so that you may be justified in your words and blameless in your judgment.*

Admit that you have offended God, who is righteous and demands obedience to His holy and righteous law. Recognize that any consequence God gives you is deserved and right.

5 *Behold, I was brought forth in iniquity, and in sin did my mother conceive me.* **6** *Behold, you*
delight in truth in the inward being, and you teach me wisdom in the secret heart.

Do not excuse your sin but look at your sinful heart. Confess your inborn sin nature that draws you away from God and what He desires. Thank God for the gift of conscience and the Holy Spirit, which bring conviction, making you recognize sin in your heart. Confess that you cannot live a sinless life in obedience to God, and plead for His help and grace.

7 *Purge me with hyssop[2], and I shall be clean; wash me, and I shall be whiter than snow.* **8** *Let*
me hear joy and gladness; let the bones that you have broken rejoice. **9** *Hide your face from*
my sins, and blot out all my iniquities.

Pray earnestly for pardon from sin, which is only possible through the shedding of blood. Ask God for the forgiveness and pardon from sin bought by the death of Jesus on the cross.

10 *Create in me a clean heart, O God, and renew a right spirit within me.* **11** *Cast me not away*
from your presence, and take not your Holy Spirit from me. **12** *Restore to me the joy of your*
salvation, and uphold me with a willing spirit.

Ask God to give you an undivided heart—a heart that desires Him above all else, a heart that finds its satisfaction in God and true joy in salvation. Pray for a heart that loves righteousness and hates sin. Pray for God's protection over your heart and soul, and for a restored relationship with Him.

13 *Then I will teach transgressors your ways, and sinners will return to you.* **14** *Deliver me*
from bloodguiltiness, O God, O God of my salvation, and my tongue will sing aloud of your
righteousness. **15** *O Lord, open my lips, and my mouth will declare your praise.*

Make a commitment to be righteous and to encourage others to walk in obedience to God's good commands and ways. Commit yourself to praise God for who He is and for the goodness of His ways.

16 *For you will not delight in sacrifice, or I would give it; you will not be pleased with a burnt*
offering. **17** *The sacrifices of God are a broken spirit; a broken and contrite heart, O God,*
you will not despise.

Admit that true repentance involves a heart crushed with the seriousness of sin and a humble spirit that leaves no room for excuses or blame. Ask God to continue to make your heart broken and repentant over sin.

18 *Do good to Zion in your good pleasure; build up the walls of Jerusalem;* **19** *then will you*
delight in right sacrifices, in burnt offerings and whole burnt offerings; then bulls will be
offered on your altar.

Pray for spiritual blessing on others.

1. The language and concepts in this explanation will be difficult for many children. Carefully explain this prayer little by little, and help your child to put these biblical principles into practice. Pray for humble and repentant hearts for you and your child.
2. Hyssop is a bushy plant that was used to sprinkle blood on the altar.

CHAPTER 55

THE TERRIBLE CONSEQUENCES OF SIN

Absalom Starts a Revolution, and David Flees—2 Samuel 13-19

"Now therefore the sword shall never depart from your house . . ." (2 Samuel 12:10a)

Sometimes if you pull the wrong thread on a sweater, it starts to come apart—to unravel. Well, that is what happened in David's life. His sin of rebellion, adultery, deception, and murder brought consequences that made his life come apart. God had said, *"Behold, I will raise up evil against you out of your own house"* and *"the sword shall never depart from your house,"* and it was beginning . . .

First, David's son, Amnon, horribly abused his half-sister. Then, another son, Absalom, was so furious that he murdered Amnon. Then Absalom fled from Jerusalem and his heartbroken father. Evil rose up within David's own house—just as God had said it would. David grieved the loss of Amnon. But after three years, David allowed Absalom to return to Jerusalem. However, he did not allow Absalom to live with him. It was two more years before David finally asked to see Absalom. By this time, Absalom hated his father. But the unraveling in David's life was just beginning.

Absalom was the most handsome man in Israel. He had long thick hair—and a rebellious, proud, deceitful heart. He got a chariot and had fifty men run ahead of him when he went out. In a way, he was "showing off," making himself look important. He also had a very cunning plan to take David's throne. He started listening to people's complaints at the city gate, boasting that he would make things better if he were king. *Thus Absalom did to all of Israel who came to the king for judgment. So Absalom stole the hearts of the men of Israel.* Absalom was becoming very popular with the people, and more unraveling was happening.

Next, Absalom asked David if he could go to the city of Hebron to make a sacrifice to the LORD. This sounds like a good thing. But Absalom was not thinking about God. This was really part of his plot to take David's throne. *Absalom sent secret messengers throughout all the tribes of Israel, saying, "As soon as you hear the sound of the trumpet, then say, 'Absalom is king at Hebron!'"* He brought two hundred men with him from Jerusalem, and that number grew. More and more people joined Absalom. Now things were unraveling very fast.

And a messenger came to David, saying, "The hearts of the men of Israel have gone after Absalom." Instead of being loyal to David, their king who had conquered their enemies, the people wanted Absalom to be king. ***How do you think David felt? What do you think David did?*** David, the great warrior and king, fled from Jerusalem with his servants and friends. Among them were the Levites and two priests who brought the Ark of the Covenant. But David still had hope in God, so he sent the priests and the Ark back to Jerusalem: *"Carry the ark of God back into the city. If I find favor in the eyes of the LORD, he will bring me back and let me see both it and his dwelling place. But if he says, 'I have no pleasure in you,' behold, here I am, let him do to me what seems good to him."* ***What was David's attitude?*** David trusted God. He knew that **God is both merciful and sovereign.** God would determine who would be king. David also knew that his troubles were a just judgment from God. David would submit to God's wisdom and rule.

David and his loyal followers traveled toward the wilderness, weeping as they went. How much sadness had come to so many from David's sin! Along the way Shimei, a relative of King Saul, threw rocks at David and insulted him. David learned that his close friend and trusted advisor Ahithophel[1] betrayed him and became Absalom's advisor. What kind of evil advice would Ahithophel give Absalom? Whom could David trust? David trusted God, who can always be trusted. **God is always faithful to His children.** *And David said, "O LORD, please turn the counsel of Ahithophel into foolishness."*

David's friend, Hushai, met David on the way and wanted to join him. But David sent him back to Jerusalem. Hushai could be his spy and speak against Ahithophel's advice to Absalom. Hushai came into the city just as Absalom was entering Jerusalem.

> *Morever, Ahithophel said to Absalom, "Let me choose twelve thousand men, and I will arise and pursue David tonight. I will come upon him while he is weary and discouraged and throw him into a panic, and all the people who are with him will flee. I will strike down only the king, and I will bring all the people back to you as a bride comes home to her husband. You seek the life of only one man, and all the people will be at peace." And the advice seemed right in the eyes of Absalom and all the elders of Israel. (2 Samuel 17:1-4)*

David's own son wanted him dead! Surely evil had come against David "out of [his] own house." But God had sent Hushai to protect David. Hushai strongly disagreed with Ahithophel's advice. He told Absalom not to chase David that night. He said that Absalom's men wouldn't find David because David wouldn't camp among the people. David would hide in a pit. He warned Absalom that David and his mighty men were experts in war. Absalom should wait until he could gather a big army to fight against David.

God answered David's prayer to *turn the counsel of Ahithophel into foolishness*. Absalom took Hushai's advice instead of Ahithophel's advice. God used Hushai to give David time to escape. Hushai quickly sent a message to David to cross the Jordan River instead of staying in the wilderness. David would have time to gather his men and be ready for Absalom and his men when they came.

When Absalom's army arrived, David was ready to join his men in battle. But his men convinced him to stay behind, saying, *"You shall not go out. For if we flee, they will not care about us. If half of us die, they will not care about us. But you are worth ten thousand of us. Therefore it is better that you send us help from the city."* David agreed but gave the order to *"Deal gently for my sake with the young man Absalom."* Though his rebellious son wanted to kill him, David still had compassion on Absalom.

So the two armies fought in the field and in the forest. *And the men of Israel were defeated there by the servants of David, and the loss there was great on that day, twenty thousand men. The battle spread over the face of all the country, and the forest devoured more people that day than the sword. How could the forest "devour" Absalom's men?* The forest was rough and hilly with bushes and rocks. It was a dangerous place to fight. It would be easy to fall into a pit, to fall against rocks, or to trip over stumps while fighting. The men in David's small army were experienced fighters. They knew the dangers of the forest. But Absalom's men were not used to the dangers of fighting in a forest. They could get lost and eventually die from wounds, thirst, or exhaustion, or even be killed by wild animals. They could be separated from each other and be easy targets for David's men hiding in the forest.

What happened to Absalom in the fighting? Absalom was riding his mule and went under the gnarly branches of a large oak tree. Absalom's thick, long hair, which he was so proud of, was caught in the branches, and he was pulled off the mule! His own hair trapped him, and he hung from the branches. One of David's men found Absalom, but he would not kill him and go against David's wishes. However, Joab, the captain of David's army, threw three

spears through the heart of rebellious Absalom. Then Joab blew the victory trumpet and the troops came back. The battle was over. They threw Absalom's body into a pit and covered it with stones. **God's word had come true**: *"the sword shall never depart from your house."* Once again, death came to David's house.

A messenger brought David the good news that God had given them victory. But David asked, *"Is it well with the young man Absalom?"* When he heard that Absalom was dead, *the king was deeply moved and went up to the chamber over the gate and wept. And as he went, he said, "O my son Absalom, my son, my son Absalom! Would I had died instead of you, O*

Absalom, my son, my son!" Such great sadness had come upon David and his family. **The consequences of sin are always painful.**

The remaining men of Israel all fled to their homes. Absalom was dead. They were without a king, without a leader. The people decided to make David their king again, but the tribe of Judah was not ready to accept David as their king at first. Once again, God was merciful and put David on the throne. David returned to Jerusalem. He pardoned his enemies—even Shimei—and united Israel and Judah.

David's son and his trusted advisor had both betrayed him, but God had been faithful to David. In love, God had disciplined David for his good. But David's sin had brought terrible consequences on his family and his people. Even David, "a man after God's own heart," was a very sinful man. David was a good king, but Israel needed a greater King.

Sin always brings great consequences. The enjoyment that sin brings is very short, but the consequences can be long lasting. God is good and brings painful consequences to His children as a warning to turn away from sin. *Do you learn from consequences and turn away from sin? Do you see discipline as a loving and merciful act?*

My son, do not despise the LORD's discipline or be weary of his reproof, for the LORD reproves him whom he loves, as a father the son in whom he delights. (Proverbs 3:11-12)

MAKING YOU WISE FOR SALVATION

What does this chapter tell us about God? Talk about and apply the **biblical truths** in **bold** text.

Salvation Thread: Sin always brings consequences. God disciplines His children to bring them to repentance. King David's sin pointed to the need for a greater King.

Ask Dad or Mom to share with you a consequence of sin he or she experienced. How did discipline save your dad or mom from further sin? Why is discipline a blessing?

Talk About: *My son, do not despise the LORD's discipline or be weary of his reproof, for the LORD reproves him whom he loves, as a father the son in whom he delights. (Proverbs 3:11-12)*

What does this story tell you about the consequences of sin? Have you ever been grateful for discipline? Tell about that time. Why should you be grateful when your parents discipline you?

Pray: Thank God for His discipline. Ask Him to reveal any rebellion in your heart. Confess your sins to the LORD and ask Him to give you a humble, repentant heart.

Think About: *Why does God discipline those He loves? Why is discipline a mercy? Why must there be consequences to sin?*

1. Ahithophel had been David's chief counselor for many years, so he was the most trusted man in his cabinet. Interestingly, he was the grandfather of Bathsheba. David betrayed Uriah and took his wife; Bathsheba's grandfather betrayed David. David was reaping the consequences of his sin.

CHAPTER 56

SONGS OF JOY AND TEARS IN A BOTTLE

The Songs and Prayers of God's People—Psalms

The LORD is my shepherd; I shall not want. (Psalm 23:1)

How do you think David felt when he left Jerusalem and ran from Absalom? We know he was sad. He was probably discouraged, scared, and even angry. But he also told himself great truths *when he fled from Absalom his son.* We can read about them in Psalm 3:

> *O LORD, how many are my foes [enemies]! Many are rising against me; many are saying of my soul, "There is no salvation for him in God." But you, O LORD, are a shield about me, my glory, and the lifter of my head. I cried aloud to the LORD, and he answered me from his holy hill. (Psalm 3:1-4)*

A very large group of enemies was chasing David and his small group of followers—yet he had confidence in God. Through all the problems in his life, David never lost his faith in God. He knew that **God is faithful and can be trusted**. No matter what the situation, David found his comfort, confidence, and hope in God. Even though he failed many times, he was a man who longed for friendship with God.

> *O God, you are my God; earnestly I seek you; my soul thirsts for you; my flesh faints for you, as in a dry and weary land where there is no water. So I have looked upon you in the sanctuary, beholding your power and glory. Because your steadfast love is better than life, my lips will praise you. (Psalm 63:1-3)*

Because David was a musician, he put many of his prayers to music. As a young shepherd boy, he would play his lyre and sing his prayers to the LORD. He continued to sing his prayers and praises throughout his whole life—during Saul's fits of madness, while hiding in the wilderness, after victories over his enemies, and as the king of Israel longing for a Greater King. These songs are included in the book of Psalms. They tell us David's experiences of seeing God's glory, power, and faithfulness in all kinds of situations—even the hard ones.

> *Now I know that the LORD saves his anointed; he will answer him from his holy heaven with the saving might of his right hand. Some trust in chariots and some in horses, but we trust in the name of the LORD our God. They collapse and fall, but we rise and stand upright. O LORD, save the king! May he answer us when we call. (Psalm 20:6-9)*

David wrote almost half of the psalms. Asaph, the sons of Korah, and other worship leaders in the temple wrote many of the other psalms. *Do you remember who Korah was?* Korah, Dathan, and Abiram rebelled against Moses and Aaron. *Do you remember what happened then?* The ground split beneath them and swallowed them up, along with their families and possessions. This was God's judgment for their rebellion. But remember that **God is just, and He is also merciful**. God spared some of the sons of Korah, and God had a plan and purpose for Korah's descendants. Many of them became worship leaders in Israel, using both instruments and singing. *What does this tell you about God's mercy and faithfulness to His people?*

The book of Psalms became the worship songs, prayers, and poems of Israel. They show the honest emotions of God's people: joy, sorrow, desperation, discouragement, thanksgiving, praise, trust, fear, all kinds of feelings.

> *I will bless the LORD at all times; his praise shall continually be in my mouth. My soul makes its boast in the LORD; let the humble hear and be glad. Oh, magnify the LORD with me, and let us exalt his name together! (Psalm 34:1-3)*

> *My God, my God, why have you forsaken me? Why are you so far from saving me, from the words of my groaning? O my God, I cry by day, but you do not answer, and by night, but I find no rest. Yet you are holy, enthroned on the praises of Israel. In you our fathers trusted; they trusted, and you delivered them. To you they cried and were rescued; in you they trusted and were not put to shame. (Psalm 22:1-5)*

But the psalms are not just Israel's book of worship. They are also worship songs and prayers of God's people used throughout the world today. They help us tell our thoughts and emotions to God. They give us words to praise God. They help us remember the greatness and goodness of God. They give us truth and wisdom. They strengthen our faith. And they remind us of the coming King. Many of the psalms tell us about the Messiah, the Savior who will defeat all evil and bring salvation to His people. This King from the line of David will fulfill God's promise to Abraham to bring God's blessing to all nations. He will someday return as the victorious King, who will put a final end to evil and establish God's Kingdom rule over all the nations of the world!

It is easy to forget who God is and be stuck feeling sad or afraid. So the book of Psalms also teaches us a very important pattern. Sometimes we can see the whole pattern in a psalm, and sometimes we see just part of it. This three-part pattern shows us how to respond to everything in life:

POUR OUT YOUR HEART

Trust in him at all times, O people; pour out your heart before him; God is a refuge for us. (Psalm 62:8)

We have the same emotions as the psalmists did. So we can learn from the psalmists how to respond in faith to our circumstances. Instead of just stuffing our feelings—pretending they aren't there—we can bring them to God. As long as we don't sin with our words, we can tell God honestly how we feel—no matter what we feel. The psalms show us people with all kinds of feelings:

My tears have been my food day and night, while they say to me all the day long, "Where is your God?" (Psalm 42:3)

Fear and trembling come upon me, and horror overwhelms me. And I say, "Oh, that I had wings like a dove! I would fly away and be at rest;" (Psalm 55:5-6)

But we don't just stay stuck in our emotions. We don't have to be controlled by our feelings. The psalms tells us next to:

LIFT UP YOUR EYES: SEE GOD

I lift up my eyes to the hills. From where does my help come? My help comes from the LORD, who made heaven and earth. (Psalm 121:1-2)

When we see LORD written in all capital letters, what name of God is that? LORD is the way the English Bible writes Yahweh, God's personal name. The writer of this psalm knows Yahweh. He has a personal relationship with God. *What does Yahweh mean?* The name Yahweh tells us that **God is sovereign, self-sufficient, eternal, almighty, and unchanging.** He is the covenant God of Israel. No matter how we feel, God's people can look to God and remember who He is and what He has promised His children. We can remind ourselves of the truth. When we see Yahweh, our problems and feelings become very small compared to the greatness and goodness of God. God will work for His children! That leads to the next step in the pattern:

OPEN YOUR MOUTH: PRAISE GOD

I have not hidden your deliverance within my heart; I have spoken of your faithfulness and your salvation; I have not concealed your steadfast love and your faithfulness from the great congregation. (Psalm 40:10)

Pour out your heart to God. Lift up your eyes to see the greatness of God and His sure promises. Then open your mouth in praise to God for His faithfulness, help, and deliverance. The psalms show us that if we are a child of God, we always have a reason to praise Him. **He is the faithful, unchanging God, the great and mighty warrior who fights for His people, and the coming King who will rule with goodness forever!**

Do you have a personal relationship with Yahweh? Can you tell him your hurts, fears, failures, frustrations, victories, joys, and hopes? Do you believe that there are always reasons to trust and praise God?

Make a joyful noise to the LORD, all the earth! Serve the LORD with gladness! Come into his presence with singing! Know that the LORD, he is God! It is he who made us, and we are his; we are his people, and the sheep of his pasture. Enter his gates with thanksgiving, and his courts with praise! Give thanks to him; bless his name! For the LORD is good; his steadfast love endures forever, and his faithfulness to all generations. (Psalm 100)

MAKING YOU WISE FOR SALVATION

What does this chapter tell us about God? Talk about and apply the **biblical truths** in **bold** text.

Salvation Thread: God is worthy of praise. God promised to send the Messiah, who would rule forever in righteousness.

Ask Dad or Mom to share a favorite psalm. Share one of your favorites. Why is it a favorite?

Talk About: *The LORD is my shepherd; I shall not want. (Psalm 23:1)*

There are different kinds of psalms—thanksgiving, praise, remembrance (tell of God's work), lament (express suffering or struggles), wisdom, trust, celebration. *Why are there different kinds?* Can you find some of these kinds of psalms?

Pray: Thank God for giving us His Word and the book of Psalms.

Think About: Why is there always reason to praise God? Put into practice the pattern in the psalms.

Memorize: Psalm 23, 100, or 121

CHAPTER 57

A HOUSE FOR THE KING AND A HOUSE FOR THE KING OF KINGS

Solomon Becomes King and Builds the Temple—1 Kings 1-9

"But will God indeed dwell on the earth? Behold, heaven and the highest heaven cannot contain you; how much less this house that I have built!" (1 Kings 8:27)

D*o you remember why the tabernacle was made with curtain walls that could be folded?* The Israelites had to carry the tabernacle while they traveled through the wilderness. But now they lived in their own land. Ever since he became king in Jerusalem, David had wanted to build a permanent house for the LORD. But God would not let him do this good thing. *Do you know why?*

David was a man of war. God told David, *"You have shed much blood and have waged great wars. You shall not build a house to my name, because you have shed so much blood before me on the earth."* Death was the result of sin. The shedding of blood was necessary to make sacrifices and to fight just wars. But death was never God's desire.

David was now an old man. For many years, he had been storing up materials for the temple—gold, silver, brass, bronze, iron, great cedar trees, large building stones, marble, onyx, and precious stones. *For David said, ". . . the house that is to be built for the LORD must be exceedingly magnificent, of fame and glory throughout all lands."* Even though David could not build the temple, God had given David a wonderful promise:

> *"Behold, a son shall be born to you who shall be a man of rest. I will give him rest from all his surrounding enemies. For his name shall be Solomon, and I will give peace and quiet to Israel in his days. He shall build a house for my name. He shall be my son, and I will be his father, and I will establish his royal throne in Israel forever." (1 Chronicles 22:9-10)*

Do you remember who Solomon was? Solomon was the son of David and Bathsheba. David had eight wives and many sons, but from all these sons God chose a son of Bathsheba to be the next king, to build the temple, and to establish God's throne forever. This is amazing! David had sinned greatly in wanting Bathsheba more than God's favor. He had covered that sin with murder. Yet God loved and chose Solomon. *What does this tell you about God?*

However, another one of David's sons, Adonijah, wanted to be king. Adonijah had a big feast and invited many important people. But he did not invite Solomon, David's mighty men, or Nathan the prophet. At the feast, Adonijah declared himself king.

But David knew that God had chosen Solomon to be king. So he quickly came up with a plan to stop Adonijah. David asked some trusted men to have Solomon ride through the streets of Jerusalem on David's personal mule. At that time, kings rode on mules to show their role as a servant of their people. Just outside the city, Nathan and another prophet anointed Solomon as king. Then they blew the trumpet, which was a sign that Solomon was the official king of Israel—not Adonijah.

David knew he would soon die, so he gave Solomon very clear instructions about building the temple. He also gave Solomon some final words encouraging him to follow God:

> *"I am about to go the way of all the earth. Be strong, and show yourself a man, and keep the charge of the LORD your God, walking in his ways and keeping his statutes, his commandments, his rules, and his testimonies, as it is written in the Law of Moses, that you may prosper in all that you do and wherever you turn." (1 Kings 2:2-3)*

> *"And you, Solomon my son, know the God of your father and serve him with a whole heart and with a willing mind, for the LORD searches all hearts and understands every plan and thought. If you seek him, he will be found by you, but if you forsake him, he will cast you off forever." (1 Chronicles 28:9)*

Then King David praised God before the people he had ruled for forty years.

> *And David said: "Blessed are you, O LORD, the God of Israel our father, forever and ever.* ***Yours, O LORD, is the greatness and the power and the glory and the victory and the majesty, for all that is in the heavens and in the earth is yours****. Yours is the kingdom, O LORD, and you are exalted as head above all. Both riches and honor come from you, and* ***you rule over all****. In your hand are power and might, and in your hand it is to make great and to give strength to all. And now we thank you, our God, and praise your glorious name." (1 Chronicles 29:10b-13)*

After this, David, the shepherd boy, the king of Israel, "a man after God's own heart," a repentant sinner, *slept with his fathers and was buried in the city of David.* What would young King Solomon do now? Would he follow the LORD, or turn away? He was still a very young man. Would he know how to rule such a great nation?

God was still watching over His people. He came to Solomon in a dream one night and said, *"Ask what I shall give you." If God asked you what you would want from Him, what would you ask for? Do you know how Solomon answered God? ". . . you have made me king over a people as numerous as the dust of the earth. Give me now wisdom and knowledge to go out and come in before this people, for who can govern this people of yours, which is so great?"*

The LORD was pleased that Solomon did not ask for possessions, wealth, honor, revenge on his enemies, or a long life. Solomon's unselfish desire was to rule his people well. God promised to give Solomon the wisdom and knowledge he wanted—and to give even more blessings: *"I will also give you riches, possessions, and honor, such as none of the kings had who were before you, and none after you shall have the like."*

Solomon's fame for wisdom and knowledge spread to all the surrounding nations. He gave fair judgments that made his people in awe of him. They knew it was the wisdom of God. Judah and Israel grew in number and lived in safety and great peace. Solomon was *greater in riches and wisdom than all the other kings of the earth.* He built fleets of ships and many cities.

And yes, Solomon also built the beautiful temple his father wanted to build. He used the tabernacle as a model. Like the tabernacle, the temple had two rooms separated by the thick curtain. It also had an outer court. But it was twice the size of the tabernacle. Solomon built the temple of stone blocks, and covered the walls inside with gold. He built it *with stone prepared at the quarry, so that neither hammer nor axe nor any tool of iron was heard in the house while it was being built.* ***Why were the temple parts made in a different place, away from the temple?*** The temple was built in hushed quietness, because there was great respect for the house of the LORD.

It took seven years to build the magnificently beautiful and costly temple. The temple truly was *exceedingly magnificent, of fame and glory throughout all lands.* Then it took another thirteen years to make the temple furnishings and to build a beautiful palace for Solomon. King Solomon had built a house for himself and a house for Yahweh, the King of kings. When the temple was done, the Ark was carefully placed in the Most Holy Place. Then Solomon spread his hands toward heaven and prayed a prayer of dedication for the temple:

> *"O LORD, God of Israel, there is no God like you, in heaven above or on earth beneath, keeping covenant and showing steadfast love to your servants who walk before you with all their heart . . . But will God indeed dwell on the earth? Behold, heaven and the highest heaven cannot contain you; how much less this house that I have built!" (1 Kings 8:23, 27)*

Certainly, no building, no matter how expensive, splendid, and magnificent could fully contain God's presence. The temple was a small glimpse of something greater and more magnificent to come. Yet Solomon prayed that God's presence would be in this earthly temple. He thanked God for His faithfulness. He asked God to forgive His people when they confessed their sins and to bless them. Then Solomon blessed the people, reminding them that **not one word of God's promises had failed**:

> *"The LORD our God be with us, as he was with our fathers. May he not leave us or forsake us, that he may incline our hearts to him, to walk in all his ways and to keep his commandments, his statutes, and his rules, which he commanded our fathers." (1 Kings 8:57-58)*

Can you imagine the joy of the people in having a permanent temple? What a sense of awe and honor they must have felt watching the priests take the Ark into the temple! They held a fourteen-day feast where Solomon sacrificed a peace offering of 220,000 oxen and 120,000 sheep. *Can you imagine what that must have been like?*

As soon as the buildings were finished, God appeared to Solomon in a dream again. God had heard Solomon's prayer and promised that His special presence would be in the temple. He would make it a holy place. But the LORD also gave Solomon a promise and a warning. If Solomon worshiped the LORD and obeyed Him, Solomon's descendants would rule forever. But if Solomon or any of his descendants turned away from Yahweh and worshiped other gods, God would remove Israel from the land, and the temple would be destroyed.

God blessed Solomon generously, giving him wisdom, knowledge, riches, and honor. You, too, have received many blessings from God. God's warning to Solomon is also His warning to us today. *Will you worship the King of kings and walk obediently in His ways? Or will you turn away from God and find grave consequences?*

> "...for the LORD searches all hearts and understands every plan and thought. If you seek him, he will be found by you, but if you forsake him, he will cast you off forever." (1 Chronicles 28:9b)

MAKING YOU WISE FOR SALVATION

What does this chapter tell us about God? Talk about and apply the **biblical truths** in **bold** text.

Salvation Thread: God's presence was in the temple, but there would be a greater temple someday—a dwelling place for God's Spirit, a temple made from living stones (1 Peter 2:4-6).

Read about the wisdom that God gave Solomon in 1 Kings 3:16-28. With your family, talk about the many blessings God has brought into your lives.

Talk About: "*. . . for the LORD searches all hearts and understands every plan and thought. If you seek him, he will be found by you, but if you forsake him, he will cast you off forever." (1 Chronicles 28:9b)*

What does it mean to seek God? What does it mean to forsake Him?

Pray: Praise God for keeping His promises. Praise Him for being gracious, generous, and faithful to His people. Thank Him for the blessings He has given you, naming them specifically. Ask Him to help you to seek Him.

Think About: Why is God worthy to be worshiped? Do I truly worship Him?

C H A P T E R 5 8

A TREASURE MORE PRECIOUS THAN JEWELS

Seek Wisdom and Reject Foolishness—Proverbs

Blessed is the one who finds wisdom, and the one who gets understanding, for the gain from her is better than gain from silver and her profit better than gold. She is more precious than jewels, and nothing you desire can compare with her. (Proverbs 3:13-15)

Do you know what the word abundance means? Abundance means plenty, a great amount of something. If you have an abundance of something, you have more than you need. Solomon prayed for wisdom, and God gave Solomon an *abundance* of wisdom. **God always keeps His promise.** This is what the Bible tells us about Solomon's wisdom:

> *And God gave Solomon wisdom and understanding beyond measure, and breadth of mind like the sand on the seashore, so that Solomon's wisdom surpassed the wisdom of all the people of the east and all the wisdom of Egypt. For he was wiser than all other men . . . and his fame was in all the surrounding nations. He also spoke 3,000 proverbs, and his songs were 1,005. He spoke of trees, from the cedar that is in Lebanon to the hyssop that grows out of the wall. He spoke also of beasts, and of birds, and of reptiles, and of fish. (1 Kings 4:29-33)*

What do these verses tell you about God?

Some of Solomon's wise sayings are recorded for us in the book of Proverbs. A proverb is a short, wise saying that is *generally* true. It is not *absolutely* true. It is true most of the time, but not always. It is not a promise, but an observation about what is usually true in life. Here are some examples:[1]

- *A soft answer turns away wrath, but a harsh word stirs up anger. (Proverbs 15:1)*
- *A joyful heart is good medicine, but a crushed spirit dries up the bones. (Proverbs 17:22)*
- *Good sense makes one slow to anger, and it is his glory to overlook an offense. (Proverbs 19:11)*
- *Whoever keeps his mouth and his tongue keeps himself out of trouble. (Proverbs 21:23)*
- *Train up a child in the way he should go; even when he is old he will not depart from it. (Proverbs 22:6)*
- *For lack of wood the fire goes out, and where there is no whisperer, quarreling ceases. (Proverbs 26:20)*
- *Whoever conceals his transgressions will not prosper, but he who confesses and forsakes them will obtain mercy. (Proverbs 28:13)*
- *One's pride will bring him low, but he who is lowly in spirit will obtain honor. (Proverbs 29:23)*

Can you think of some other proverbs from the Bible?

The book of Proverbs tells us that **wisdom is a great treasure**—more precious than gold, silver, or jewels. *If you heard of a great treasure buried in your backyard, what would you do?* You would probably eagerly look for it! We should do the same thing with wisdom. We should *seek it like silver and search for it as for hidden treasures.* Knowledge is knowing about things—knowing a lot of facts, like Solomon knew about animals, birds, trees, and fish. But wisdom is more than knowledge. It is understanding what to do with knowledge. It is seeing people and situations the way God sees them, and then acting on that understanding. It is knowing that what God says is good and right, and doing it. So if wisdom is seeing things the way God sees them, then the first step to getting wisdom is to know God.

The fear of the LORD is the beginning of wisdom, *and the knowledge of the Holy One is insight. (Proverbs 9:10)*

To fear the LORD is not to be terrified of Him. It is to be in awe of who God is—the Creator, Sovereign Ruler, Judge, and King. It is to be amazed at His love, and to honor or respect Him because of His great character. We should be afraid of disobeying God because it dishonors Him. Since God's ways are always good and right, we should also be afraid of disobeying God's good commands. **God, our Creator, knows what is best for us,** so disobedience leads to sorrow and destruction. *The fear of the LORD is [also] hatred of evil.*

The book of Proverbs talks about two kinds of people—the wise person and the fool. A wise person seeks knowledge and understanding. He delights in God's commands, so he turns away from evil immediately. *Can you think of a wise person who turned away from evil immediately?* One wise person was Joseph, who ran from Potiphar's wife. *One who is wise is cautious and turns away from evil, but a fool is reckless and careless.*

A wise person listens to good advice and accepts instruction. *When someone gives you godly advice or instruction, do you listen respectfully and follow it, or do you pridefully ignore it?* The book of Proverbs tells us, *"Listen to advice and accept instruction, that you may gain wisdom in the future." When your mother or father instruct you, what do you do?*

> *My son, keep your father's commandment, and forsake not your mother's teaching. Bind them on your heart always; tie them around your neck. When you walk, they will lead you; when you lie down, they will watch over you; and when you awake, they will talk with you. For the commandment is a lamp and the teaching a light, and the reproofs of discipline are the way of life, (Proverbs 6:20-23)*

A wise person also accepts correction, like David did when Nathan rebuked him. He didn't argue or get angry. He accepted Nathan's correction and repented. David also showed wisdom when his men wanted him to kill his enemy, Saul. David had self-control and refused to kill Saul. He was wise and trusted God rather than himself. He trusted God's promise, timing, and wisdom.

> *Trust in the LORD with all your heart, and do not lean on your own understanding. In all your ways acknowledge him, and he will make straight your paths. (Proverbs 3:5-6)*

The other person the book of Proverbs tells us about is the fool. A fool does not fear God. A fool loves what is bad and wrong, and does it. *The fear of the LORD is the beginning of knowledge; fools despise wisdom and instruction.*

There are different kinds of fools. There is the *mocking fool* who makes fun of God and the things of God. Maybe you know someone like this—someone who makes fun of others for believing in God or for doing what is right. He does not respect God or love what is good and right. Another fool is the *rebellious fool.* This person is stubborn, refuses to repent, and continues in evil. *Can you think of a rebellious fool in the Bible?* Maybe you thought of Absalom, who rebelled against his father and God. *A wise son makes a glad father, but a foolish son is a sorrow to his mother.* Absalom brought great grief to David.

The *godless fool says in his heart, "There is no God." They are corrupt, they do abominable deeds, there is none who does good.* This fool has no room for God in his heart. He only has room for himself, and he says that there is no God. You might recognize the last kind of fool—the *simple fool.* This person doesn't think. He just steps into what is wrong without thinking about what God says or about the consequences. He believes bad advice and follows it. *The prudent [wise] sees danger and hides himself, but the simple go on and suffer for it.* Saul became a fool. He was a rebellious fool, dishonoring God and disobeying His commands. He became a simple fool, listening to the people's desire to keep what God had told them to destroy. In the end, Saul destroyed himself.

Probably no one wakes up in the morning and says, "I want to be a fool." But because of the fall and our inborn sin nature, the human heart is bent toward foolishness. The only way to keep from being a fool is to seek God. Ask Him to give you a fear of Him and a love for Him and His ways. Only God can change foolish hearts, but choosing godly friends is a helpful encouragement to follow God's ways:

> *Whoever walks with the wise becomes wise, but the companion of fools will suffer harm. (Proverbs 13:20)*

You can grow up with godly parents, go to church all your life, choose good friends, and still become a fool. Only God can rescue us from our own foolish hearts. Seeking God is an active thing—it takes prayer, discipline (self-control), and diligence (hard work). *What do you love most of all? Do you want to be a wise person? How can you actively seek God?*

My son, if you receive my words and treasure up my commandments with you, making your ear attentive to wisdom and inclining your heart to understanding; yes, if you call out for insight and raise your voice for understanding, if you seek it like silver and search for it as for hidden treasures, then you will understand the fear of the LORD and find the knowledge of God. (Proverbs 2:1-5)

MAKING YOU WISE FOR SALVATION

What does this chapter tell us about God? Talk about and apply the **biblical truths** in **bold** text.

Salvation Thread: Everyone is born with a foolish heart. Only God can rescue us from our own foolishness.

Discuss with your family the proverbs on the first page of this chapter.

Talk About: *Keep your heart with all vigilance, for from it flow the springs of life. (Proverbs 4:23)*

Read Proverbs 2:1-5. *What actions and heart attitudes do we need in order to understand the fear of the LORD and find the knowledge of God?*

Describe the wise person and the foolish person.

Pray: Thank God for His Word that teaches us what is good and right. Ask God to help you love Him and to love wisdom.

Think About: *Am I wise or foolish? Am I actively seeking God?*

1. You may want to read through these slowly and discuss them.

CHAPTER 59

A DIVIDED HEART AND A DIVIDED KINGDOM

Solomon Turns from God, and the Kingdom is Divided—1 Kings 9-12

So Solomon did what was evil in the sight of the LORD and did not wholly follow the LORD, as David his father had done. (1 Kings 11:6)

Someone can know all about baseball, but never play a game of baseball. A person can also know all about wisdom, but not live wisely. This is what Solomon did. He wrote many wise proverbs and gave very good advice. But he lived foolishly. Sadly, Solomon did not do what is good and right. Instead, he slowly turned away from God.

How did this happen? Solomon gained enormous wealth, formed a huge army, and built great cities. But he couldn't build his magnificent buildings without help. So he forced other nations to be his slaves. Then, to protect and grow his own kingdom even more, he married the daughters of kings from other nations. These kings then would not attack Israel, because their daughters lived there. God had forbidden the Israelites from marrying women from these nations. *Why did God make this law?* Solomon's wives brought their false beliefs and false gods with

them. And Solomon began to worship those gods. Solomon broke God's good law given to protect him, and the result was disaster!

> *Now King Solomon loved many foreign women . . . from the nations concerning which the LORD had said to the people of Israel, "You shall not enter into marriage with them, neither shall they with you, for surely they will turn away your heart after their gods." Solomon clung to these in love. He had 700 wives . . . And his wives turned away his heart . . . after other gods, and his heart was not wholly true to the LORD his God, as was the heart of David his father. For Solomon went after Ashtoreth the goddess of the Sidonians, and after Milcom the abomination of the Ammonites. So Solomon did what was evil in the sight of the LORD and did not wholly follow the LORD, as David his father had done. (1 Kings 11:1-6)*

God's law is good and protects His people. Disobedience only brings heartache and destruction. Solomon did not follow the good and wise counsel of his father, David:

> *"And you, Solomon my son, know the God of your father and serve him with a whole heart and with a willing mind, for the LORD searches all hearts and understands every plan and thought. If you seek him, he will be found by you, but if you forsake him, he will cast you off forever." (1 Chronicles 28:9)*

Even though Solomon wrote the words to "make your ear attentive to wisdom" and "turn your heart to understanding," he didn't follow the wisdom God gave him. God had poured out love, kindness, goodness, blessing, and wisdom on Solomon, yet Solomon turned away from Yahweh. He even built altars to idols on the mountains near Jerusalem. Jerusalem was the worship center of Israel, but Solomon polluted, or poisoned, Jerusalem with his false gods. God had given Solomon so much and had been so faithful to Solomon, yet Solomon was not faithful to God. Just as Lot's wife turned away from the greater promises of God to the things of this world, Solomon loved power, wealth, and women more than he loved God or feared Him. *What does this tell you about the human heart?*

> *"And the LORD was angry with Solomon, because his heart had turned away from the LORD, the God of Israel, who had appeared to him twice and had commanded him concerning this thing, that he should not go after other gods. But he did not keep what the LORD commanded. Therefore the LORD said to Solomon, "Since this has been your practice and you have not kept my covenant and my statutes that I have commanded you, I will surely tear the kingdom from you and will give it to your servant. Yet for the sake of David your father I will not do it in your days, but I will tear it out of the hand of your son. However, I will not tear away all the kingdom, but I will give one tribe to your son, for the sake of David my servant and for the sake of Jerusalem that I have chosen." (1 Kings 11:9-13)*

Where do you see God's justice and His mercy in His judgment against Solomon? God would take away the great kingdom Solomon had wrongly tried to build up without God. But He would not do it during Solomon's lifetime. God foretold how he would divide the kingdom after Solomon's death, giving one tribe to Solomon's son, Rehoboam. Ten of the tribes, it was prophesied, would be given to a man named Jeroboam. Those of the priestly tribe of Levi would continue to live in forty-eight cities throughout Israel.

God sent a prophet to tell Jeroboam that He was about to tear the kingdom apart. This prophet acted out God's message. He took off his robe and tore it into twelve pieces—one for each tribe of Israel—and said, *"Take for yourself ten pieces for thus says the LORD, the God of Israel, 'Behold, I am about to tear the kingdom from the hand of Solomon and will give you ten tribes . . . because they have forsaken me and worshiped [other gods], and they have not walked in my ways, doing what is right in my sight and keeping my statutes and my rules, as David his father did.'"* When Solomon heard the prophecy about the kingdom, he tried to have Jeroboam killed. But Jeroboam fled to Egypt, where he stayed until Solomon died. **No one can stop the purposes of God.**

Solomon reigned for forty years and built a grand kingdom, but he turned away from the LORD, who had kept His promise to give Solomon wisdom, riches, possessions, and honor. Sadly, Solomon had enjoyed the gifts of God while on earth, but he ended his life as a fool.

After Solomon's death, Jeroboam and the leaders of Israel said to Rehoboam, *"Your father made our yoke heavy. Now therefore lighten the hard service of your father and his heavy yoke on us, and we will serve you."* Rehoboam asked for counsel from the old men who had served Solomon. They told him not to work the people so hard. But the young men who grew up with Rehoboam told him to make things even *harder* for the people—to add more work for them and treat them harshly! Rehoboam foolishly did not listen to the wise, experienced counselors. Instead, he took the advice of the young men. So Rehoboam told the people, *"My father disciplined you with whips, but I will discipline you with scorpions." What do you think the people thought of this?*

Sure enough, the ten northern tribes rebelled against Rehoboam and made Jeroboam their leader—just as God had said. **God's judgment is sure, and all His words prove to be true.** The Northern Kingdom became known as Israel. In time, Samaria became the capital city of Israel. Jeroboam built two new temples—one in the southern part of Israel (Bethel) and

one in the northern part (Dan). But he didn't build these temples for the worship of Yahweh. Jeroboam did something very foolish and wicked. *Do you know what he put in each temple for the people to worship?* A golden calf! *What does this tell you about the direction the Northern Kingdom was going?*

God was **faithful to His promise** to David. He did not cut off the line of David. Rehoboam ruled over the Southern Kingdom, which was called Judah, and Jerusalem remained the capital. Once again, God's words proved true, and the word of prophecy was fulfilled:

> *"Yet to his son I will give one tribe, that David my servant may always have a lamp before me in Jerusalem, the city where I have chosen to put my name." (1 Kings 11:36)*

The tribe of David had been humbled, the kingdom had been divided, and the grandeur of Israel faded. Instead of being a great and powerful nation ruled by one king, Israel was now two smaller, weaker nations. Yet there was still hope because of the promise made to David by **Yahweh,** ***the faithful God who keeps covenant and steadfast love.*** There was the hope of a greater King and a greater Kingdom.

God gave Solomon great wisdom, but Solomon didn't follow it. He seemed to have forgotten that his blessings came from God. He started to trust his own understanding, skill, and power. He brought judgment on his royal line because of his sin of pride and idolatry. God had warned the Israelites about this through Moses before they went in to take the land:

> *Beware lest you say in your heart, 'My power and the might of my hand have gotten me this wealth.' You shall remember the LORD your God, for it is he who gives you power to get wealth, that he may confirm his covenant that he swore to your fathers, as it is this day. (Deuteronomy 8:17-18)*

Success, pride, and bad companions are all dangerous. Solomon failed to thank God for all that God had given him. He allowed his wives to encourage him to worship their idols and did not honor the God of his father. But **God will not allow anyone to steal His glory. He is a jealous God, who deserves to be worshiped alone.**

Anything good in your life has come as a gift from God—your abilities; any good quality such as generosity, kindness, or perseverance; your family and friendships; food and clothing; even the air you breathe every day. *Do you recognize God's blessing in your life? Do you give God the glory and praise for all that He is and all He has done?*

Pride goes before destruction, and a haughty spirit before a fall. (Proverbs 16:18)

MAKING YOU WISE FOR SALVATION

What does this chapter tell us about God? Talk about and apply the **biblical truths** in **bold** text.

Salvation Thread: The heart is desperately wicked and fails to thank God and worship Him alone. God's judgment for sin is sure, and His promise to redeem His people is unfailing.

Read Deuteronomy 17:14-20, God's guidelines for kings. How did Solomon measure up?

Talk About: *Pride goes before destruction, and a haughty spirit before a fall. (Proverbs 16:18)*

How do you react when people compliment you or recognize that you have done something well? How can you give God the glory He deserves?

Pray: Praise God for His attributes–His qualities, what He is like. Thank Him for the kindness He has shown you and your family. Ask Him to give you a humble heart that wants to bring glory to Him.

Think About: *Do I just know the Bible, or do I follow its wise counsel?*

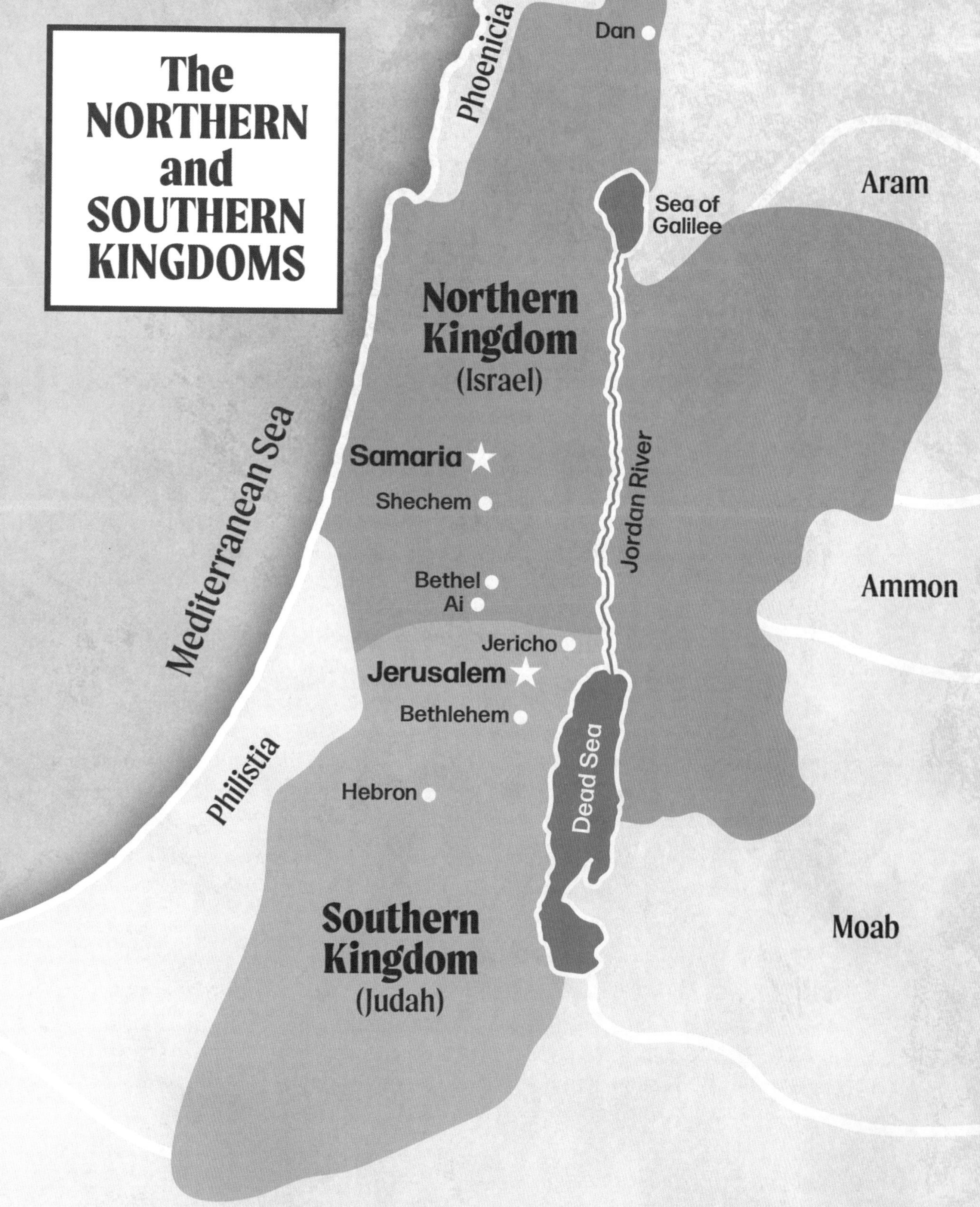
The NORTHERN and SOUTHERN KINGDOMS
Phoenicia
Dan
Aram
Sea of Galilee
Northern Kingdom
(Israel)
Mediterranean Sea
Samaria
Shechem
Jordan River
Bethel
Ai
Ammon
Jericho
Jerusalem
Bethlehem
Philistia
Dead Sea
Hebron
Moab
Southern Kingdom
(Judah)

CHAPTER 60

TROUBLE IN THE NORTHERN KINGDOM

God Warns Ahab and Israel through the Prophet Elijah—1 Kings 14-18

He did what was evil in the sight of the LORD and walked in the way of Jeroboam and in his sin which he made Israel to sin. (1 Kings 15:34)

Once more sin had caused brokenness in the world. The people of God were now two nations ruled by two different kings. When the nation split, the Northern Kingdom of Israel was larger, richer, and more powerful than the Southern Kingdom of Judah. Before long, the people of Israel and Judah went to war against each other. Here were God's people fighting each other! But even worse, king after king ruling Israel (the Northern Kingdom) *did what was evil in the sight of the LORD.* Worst of all, the people followed the bad example of these evil kings. God sent prophets to warn them about their rebellion, idolatry, and injustice (the wrong way they treated others). But sadly, the kings didn't listen:

> *"Go, tell Jeroboam, 'Thus says the LORD, the God of Israel . . . you have not been like my servant David, who kept my commandments and followed me with all his heart, doing only that which was right in my eyes, but you have done evil above all who were before you and have gone and made for yourself other gods and metal images, provoking me to anger, and have cast me behind your back,'" (1 Kings 14:7-9)*

> *Nadab the son of Jeroboam began to reign over Israel . . . He did what was evil in the sight of the LORD and walked in the way of his father, and in his sin which he made Israel to sin. (1Kings 15:25-26)*

> *Baasha . . . began to reign over all Israel . . . He did what was evil in the sight of the LORD and walked in the way of Jeroboam and in his sin which he made Israel to sin. (1 Kings 15:33b-34)*

Each of the next three kings was evil. The last one, Omri, *did more evil than all who were before him.* Surely, the Israelites needed a godly king who would encourage them to worship Yahweh alone, follow His good commands, and do what is right! Omri's son was Ahab—maybe he would listen to God's prophet and lead Israel to repent.

But the Bible gives us a very sad report about Ahab, too. It says, *And Ahab...did what was evil in the sight of the LORD, more than all who were before him.* Ahab did even more evil than his father, who had been the most evil king yet. Things were getting worse! But there was even more trouble. Ahab married a wicked foreign princess named Jezebel, who worshiped the false god Baal. Jezebel was determined to make the people stop worshiping Yahweh and worship false gods like Baal instead. She even planned to kill the true prophets of God! Ahab built an altar and a temple for Baal in Samaria. He chose evil men to be priests, who would make sacrifices to Baal. Ahab also put up an Asherah pole to honor the false goddess Asherah. And he wickedly encouraged Israel to worship these false gods. *Ahab did more to provoke the LORD, the God of Israel, to anger than all the kings of Israel who were before him.*

But God was faithful. **God's heart is always to warn and restore His people**. So Yahweh sent the prophet Elijah to Ahab. The name Elijah means, "Yahweh is my God." Elijah's mission was to show Ahab and Israel that Yahweh is the one true God. Elijah went to Ahab with a warning from God. *"As the LORD the God of Israel lives, before whom I stand, there shall be neither dew nor rain these years except by my word."*

God had already warned Israel during the time of Moses that if Israel served other gods He would *shut up the heavens, so that there will be no rain, and the land will yield no fruit.* The drought, the dry time with no rain, was God's discipline on the Israelites so they would repent from their evil and turn back to Him. This must have made Ahab very angry. But he was probably angry for another reason, too. People believed Baal was the god of rain. Now this prophet came to warn Ahab that Yahweh would hold back the rain. So who is more powerful—Ahab's Baal, or Elijah's Yahweh?

Ahab was so angry that he wanted to kill Elijah. But God warned Elijah to hide in the wilderness by a brook. *Where would Elijah get food in the wilderness?* Would God send more manna? God did not send manna, but He did feed Elijah in an unusual way. God sent very large black birds called ravens to bring Elijah bread and meat every morning and evening. Isn't it amazing that God commands even the birds? Elijah stayed in the wilderness until the brook dried up. *Why did the brook dry up?* It was dry because it hadn't rained. Not even a drop! **God does whatever He says He will do.** Yahweh was showing His power to His people. He was showing that Baal, the false god of rain, was powerless. God was proving that **He is all-powerful and sovereign. He rules over all**—even over birds and raindrops!

Then God told Elijah, *"Arise, go to Zarephath ... and dwell there. Behold, I have commanded a widow there to feed you."* Elijah obeyed God and found the widow gathering sticks. There was a famine in the land because there had been no rain to water the crops. This poor woman only had a "handful of flour and a little oil" left to feed herself and her son. But Elijah asked her for water and bread. How could she give Elijah her last bit of food? Elijah gave her God's promise, *"Thus says the LORD the God of Israel, 'The jar of flour shall not be spent, and the jug of oil shall not be empty until the day that the LORD sends rain upon the earth.'"*

So the woman made bread for Elijah. Perhaps she had faith in the word of the LORD, or perhaps she thought, "What was one last meal anyway?" Whatever her reason, she shared her food and water with Elijah. And God honored His word, as He always does. *And she and he and her household ate for many days. The jar of flour was not spent, neither did the jug of oil become empty, according to the word of the LORD that he spoke by Elijah.* God, the Provider, kept flour and oil in her jars day after day, without fail!

After this, her son became sick—so sick that he died. Elijah prayed to His all-powerful God and asked Him to bring the boy back to life. The LORD answered Elijah's prayer, and "the life of the child came into him again." It was another amazing miracle! Elijah brought the boy to his mother, and she said, *"Now I know that you are a man of God, and that the word of the LORD in your mouth is truth."* Elijah was a true prophet who spoke God's words. These mighty miracles didn't happen because Elijah had special powers, but because **God is all-powerful.**

Finally, God told Elijah, *"Go, show yourself to Ahab, and I will send rain upon the earth."* It had been more than three years since it had rained. The famine was very severe, especially in Samaria where Ahab was. On the way to see Ahab, Elijah met Obadiah, who was in charge of Ahab's household. Jezebel had brought more than eight hundred prophets of Baal and Ashera to Israel. When the prophets of Yahweh stood against the worship of Baal, Jezebel had them killed. But Obadiah feared the LORD and cleverly hid one hundred prophets of God in a cave. He secretly brought them food and water during the famine.

Elijah told Obadiah to tell Ahab that he had returned. This struck fear in Obadiah's heart. Ahab had looked for Elijah everywhere. There was not a nation or kingdom where Ahab had not searched for Elijah. If Obadiah brought the news of Elijah's return, Ahab might kill him, especially if Elijah disappeared again. But Elijah would not disappear. He was God's prophet with God's message for a very ungodly king.

How do you think Ahab greeted Elijah when he saw him? Did he repent and tell Elijah he had learned from God's discipline? Did he agree to get rid of all the idol worship in Israel? No, this evil, proud king said, *"Is it you, you troubler of Israel?"*

How do you think Elijah responded to this greeting? He responded with bold truth as a faithful prophet: *"I have not troubled Israel, but you have, and your father's house, because you have abandoned the commandments of the LORD and followed the Baals. Now therefore send and gather all Israel to me at Mount Carmel, and the 450 prophets of Baal and the 400 prophets of Asherah, who eat at Jezebel's table."* What did Elijah have in mind? What was he up to? Or rather, what was the one true God, Yahweh, up to?

Both Ahab and Elijah are well-known men from the Bible, but for different reasons. Ahab is remembered as a wicked, ungodly man. Elijah is remembered as a man who feared God and boldly proclaimed the truth. Unless Ahab truly repented, he will experience the judgment of God forever in hell. Elijah will receive a heavenly reward. You, too, will be remembered, maybe not for hundreds of years, but at least for a while—by men. But God will never forget you. And in the end, you will receive His everlasting reward or His eternal punishment. *Do you want to stand with Elijah? Do you listen to God's warnings in His Word? How can you honor the LORD and boldly proclaim the truth in this world?*

The eyes of the LORD are toward the righteous and his ears toward their cry. The face of the LORD is against those who do evil, to cut off the memory of them from the earth. (Psalm 34:15-16)

MAKING YOU WISE FOR SALVATION

What does this chapter tell us about God? Talk about and apply the **biblical truths** in **bold** text.

Salvation Thread: Sin causes trouble and punishment. God's heart is that man would repent. In the end, everyone will receive either an eternal reward or eternal punishment.

Did Elijah cause trouble? Why did Ahab and Israel have trouble? What is the right response when we experience the consequences of our choices? What is the wrong response?

Talk About: *The eyes of the LORD are toward the righteous and his ears toward their cry. The face of the LORD is against those who do evil, to cut off the memory of them from the earth. (Psalm 34:15-16)*

God did not punish His people without first warning them of the consequences of turning away from Him. He warned them through His word to Moses. *Why did God send prophets to warn Israel again? How does God warn us today?*

Pray: Praise God for His faithfulness and mercy to warn us of sin. Thank Him for keeping His Word and for His steadfast love. Ask Him to make you a faithful follower of Him and a bold proclaimer of truth.

Think About: *Do I have the courage to stand up for God, even if I have to stand alone when others dislike me or make fun of me for it?*

CHAPTER 61

THE LORD, HE IS GOD

God Proves He is God to Israel and the Prophets of Baal—1 Kings 18-19

"How long will you go about limping between two different opinions? If the LORD is God, follow him; but if Baal, then follow him." (1 Kings 18:21b)

W*hy did God want all the prophets of the false gods Baal and Asherah to meet at Mount Carmel?* The people of Israel (the Northern Kingdom) hadn't stopped worshiping God. They just worshiped Him as one of *many* gods. This wasn't true worship of Yahweh. If they had truly worshiped God, they would honor Him as the one true God and keep His commands, including the command not to worship any other gods. They would trust in Him alone and trust everything He said. So Elijah challenged the people who had gathered with the false prophets at Mount Carmel saying, *"How long will you go about limping between two different opinions. If the LORD is God, follow him; but if Baal, then follow him."* Elijah challenged them to make a choice, a decision, a commitment. *And the people did not answer him a word.*

Elijah suggested a demonstration or a contest. On one side were the 450 prophets of Baal, on the other side was Elijah. Actually, on one side there were 450 false prophets and their false god. And on the other side, there was a true prophet and the one true God, Yahweh, who is **sovereign, self-sufficient, almighty, eternal, and unchanging.** That really wasn't much of a contest, was it?

Each side would choose a bull, cut it in pieces, and put it on a pile of wood. But they would not put fire under it. The prophets of Baal would call on their god, and Elijah would call on the name of the LORD, *"and the God who answers by fire, he is God."* The prophets of Baal called out to Baal from morning to noon. *But there was no voice, and no one answered.* At noon, Elijah started to mock them. Maybe their god was busy thinking . . . or on a journey . . . or asleep? Maybe they needed to wake him up! The prophets of Baal cried aloud, and even cut themselves

with swords and spears. Maybe that would get Baal's attention. They did this until the middle of the afternoon . . . *but there was no voice. No one answered; no one paid attention.*

Then it was Elijah's turn. He built an altar in the name of the LORD using twelve stones. *Why did he choose twelve?* He chose one stone for each of the twelve tribes that had made a covenant with Yahweh. Then he dug a trench or a ditch around the altar. He put the wood and the pieces of the bull on the altar. But he didn't call out to the LORD . . . yet. He told the people to fill four large jars with water to pour on the offering and the wood, and then do it again . . . and again. Three times, they drenched the offering and wood with water. It was soggy, soaking wet, and the trench was filled with water. How can a fire burn something that is wet? The water would make it hard for fire to consume the bull and the wood on the altar, but Yahweh is the God of the impossible! Then Elijah called out to his **covenant-keeping God, Yahweh**:

> *. . . "O LORD, God of Abraham, Isaac, and Israel, let it be known this day that you are God in Israel, and that I am your servant, and that I have done all these things at your word. Answer me, O LORD, answer me, that this people may know that you, O LORD, are God, and that you have turned their hearts back." Then the fire of the LORD fell and consumed the burnt offering and the wood and the stones and the dust, and licked up the water that was in the trench. And when all the people saw it, they fell on their faces and said, "The LORD, he is God; the LORD, he is God." (1 Kings 18:36b-39)*

God's fire came down and completely burned the drenched offering. It burned the wood and the stones, and even dried up the water in the trenches. **Nothing is too hard for God. He is the real and living God.** God had proven that He is God Almighty—the **covenant-keeping God** who hears His people, the God who has **power and authority** over all things including fire from heaven, the God who is **always attentive** and never sleeps or goes on vacation, the **one true God who alone is worthy to be worshiped, honored, and loved.** Oh, that all people would praise Him!

Then Elijah told the people to grab every one of the evil, false prophets, and Elijah put them to death by the sword. The people obeyed God's command given to Moses to devote to destruction those who tempt others to serve other gods.

How did Ahab respond to all this? Did he finally see that Yahweh is the one true God? Did he repent? God utterly defeated the prophets of Baal! It would seem that Ahab would be amazed at what happened and would eagerly accept Yahweh as the one and only God. But his heart was hardened. He stubbornly refused to believe in God.

Elijah told Ahab that now, after three and a half years without rain, there would be a heavy rainstorm. Then Elijah prayed for rain and sent his servant to look toward the sea for rain clouds. He did this seven times. The seventh time, Elijah's servant saw a small cloud. So Elijah told his servant to warn Ahab to get in his chariot and head for home, or he would be caught in the downpour. *And in a little while the heavens grew black with clouds and wind, and there was a great rain.* God opened up the heavens, and it poured! **God rules** over clouds and rain. Surely, *now* Ahab would believe. What did Ahab do instead? *Ahab told Jezebel all that Elijah had done, and how he had killed all the prophets with the sword.* Jezebel was furious. She threatened to kill Elijah. Just like Ahab, her evil heart would not and could not repent.

Elijah fled into the wilderness. He was so discouraged that he prayed he would die. Instead, God sent an angel who brought him food and drink. Elijah wandered in the desert for forty days and forty nights. He came to Mount Horeb and found a cave in which to stay. He felt like he was all alone against the forces of evil. *He said, "I have been very jealous for the LORD, the God of hosts. For the people of Israel have forsaken your covenant, thrown down your altars, and killed your prophets with the sword, and I, even I only, am left, and they seek my life, to take it away."* He *felt* alone . . . but he wasn't alone. God was with him. God would use others to finish the work of destroying those who worshiped Baal. But God would spare seven thousand in Israel, *"all the knees that have not bowed to Baal, and every mouth that has not kissed him."* God would pass Elijah's role as prophet on to Elisha.

So Elijah returned and found Elisha plowing a field. Elijah passed by Elisha and threw his cloak over him. This was a sign that a person should leave home and become a prophet. God would pass Elijah's power and authority on to Elisha. Elisha would become God's courageous prophet to the people now. So Elisha left his plow and his home and followed Elijah.

Elijah was a faithful prophet. He courageously called the people to commit themselves fully to the one true God. Today, we don't usually bow down to idols made of gold, silver, or wood. But we can still have idols—things we treasure more than we treasure God, things that fill our hearts and push out the LORD.

Just like the Israelites, you cannot "limp between two different opinions." *Whom will you serve? Are you fully committed to follow the LORD? Can you, like the psalmist, say,*

> Whom have I in heaven but you? And there is nothing on earth that I desire besides you. My flesh and my heart may fail, but God is the strength of my heart and my portion forever. (Psalm 73:25-26)

MAKING YOU WISE FOR SALVATION

What does this chapter tell us about God? Talk about and apply the **biblical truths** in **bold** text.

Salvation Thread: God alone is worthy to be praised. He is the one true God and Ruler.

Why did Moses, Joshua, and Elijah all need to give Israel the same message? What does this tell you about the natural condition of man's heart?

Talk About: *Whom have I in heaven but you? And there is nothing on earth that I desire besides you. My flesh and my heart may fail, but God is the strength of my heart and my portion forever. (Psalm 73:25-26)*

What does it mean to be fully committed to the LORD? How can you tell if you have an idol in your heart–something you treasure more than God?

Pray: Thank God for being God Almighty and for answering when His people call on Him. Ask Him to give you a heart that desires Him more than it desires anything else.

Think About: *Is there anything I treasure more than I treasure God?*

CHAPTER 62

VERY DIFFERENT ENDS FOR VERY DIFFERENT PEOPLE

Ahab, Jezebel, and Elijah Come to the End of their Lives on Earth—1 Kings 20-2 Kings 2

A good name is better than precious ointment, and the day of death than the day of birth. It is better to go to the house of mourning than to go to the house of feasting, for this is the end of all mankind, and the living will lay it to heart. (Ecclesiastes 7:1-2)

When you take a test in class, you either pass or fail. Usually, you do not have a chance to take the test again. But **God is patient and gracious.** He gives man many chances to repent and turn to Him. This is what God did for Ahab. The miracle on Mount Carmel was a mighty demonstration of the power and existence of Yahweh, that **God is real and living**. Yet Ahab did not repent when he saw the power of the living God.

However, God gave Ahab another chance. The king of Syria came with a "great multitude" of thirty-two kings, horses and chariots, and soldiers to conquer Samaria. God could have let Syria defeat Israel and Ahab. Instead, God sent a prophet with this word, *"Thus says the LORD, Have you seen all this great multitude? Behold, I will give it into your hand this day, and you shall know that I am the LORD."* God would show Ahab once again that He is real, living, and powerful.

The LORD gave a great victory to Israel, and the great multitude of Syrians fled away. However, the Syrians believed in many gods. So they said that Israel won because *"their gods are gods of the hills, and so they were stronger than we. But let us fight against them in the plain, and surely we shall be stronger than they."* The Syrians did not and could not understand that **Yahweh is the one true God who rules over the whole world**—over the whole universe—not just the hills and plains!

God will not let His name be mocked. He will protect His name and His reputation. Once again, God sent a prophet to Ahab to give him a message, *"Thus says the LORD, 'Because the Syrians have said, "The LORD is a god of the hills but he is not a god of the valleys," therefore I will give all this great multitude into your hand, and you shall know that I am the LORD.'"* Again, God gave Israel a mighty victory over Syria in the valley, just as He said he would do. God proved that He is the LORD. But did it change Ahab? Did he turn to God and repent from evil? Let's see.

There was a vineyard (a field of grapes) beside Ahab's palace. The vineyard belonged to a man named Naboth. Ahab really wanted that vineyard. He wanted it so badly that he "lay on his bed and turned away his face and would eat no food." So Jezebel figured out a way to get Naboth's vineyard for Ahab. She sent official letters to the leaders of the city to invite Naboth to a feast. There, two men would lie and say that Naboth cursed God and the king. Then Naboth would be stoned to death. Her evil plan worked, and Naboth was killed. After Naboth's death, Ahab stole Naboth's vineyard. Now he had what he wanted! Ahab had not changed. He still had a hard heart.

It is true that **God is patient** and gives man many chances to repent, but **God is also just**. There comes a day when God says, "Enough." And that day came for Ahab. God sent Elijah to tell Ahab of His judgment against him. Sin is a great offense to God, and to lead others into sin as Ahab did is a very serious sin.

> *"Behold, I will bring disaster upon you. I will utterly burn you up, and will cut off from Ahab every male, bond or free, in Israel. And I will make your house like the house of Jeroboam . . . for the anger to which you have provoked me, and because you have made Israel to sin." (1 Kings 21:21-22)*

Ahab treasured the vineyard more than he treasured God and His favor. He led Israel to worship false gods, which was a great evil. Ahab was a rebellious, simple, mocking, ungodly fool. He had refused to bow and truly worship God . . . and God brought judgment on Ahab, because *There was none who sold himself to do what was evil in the sight of the LORD like Ahab, whom Jezebel his wife incited [encouraged to do evil].* But God's words of judgment humbled Ahab, and God waited to bring disaster on Ahab's family until after Ahab's death.

After three years, King Jehoshaphat of Judah and Ahab joined together to fight the Syrians. Ahab knew the Syrians wanted to kill him. So he told Jehoshaphat to wear his kingly robes into battle. But Ahab disguised himself as an ordinary Israelite so the Syrians wouldn't recognize him. The Syrians chased after Jehoshaphat in his kingly robes because they thought he was Ahab, until they realized he was not Ahab. Then they stopped chasing him and turned back. *Do you know what happened to Ahab? But a certain man drew his bow at random and struck the king of Israel between the scale armor and the breastplate.*

Do you know what "at random" means? It means by chance, accidentally. The man did not aim at Ahab, the king of Israel. He just shot an arrow. Not only did it hit Ahab, but it also went right between the pieces of his metal armor. To some people, this may seem "random," but **nothing happens by chance. God governs or rules everything in this world.** God directed that arrow. He amazingly directed it right between the scales of Ahab's armor, ending Ahab's life and his reign.

The next king of Israel was Ahaziah, who was also evil. Elijah condemned him for honoring Baal instead of Yahweh. Elijah was a faithful messenger of God to Israel for many years. Now it was time for Him to go to heaven. Elijah and Elisha were walking together. Both men knew their friendship on earth would end this day. When they got to the Jordan River, Elijah rolled up his cloak. A prophet's cloak was a symbol of authority from God. Elijah hit the water with his cloak, and God miraculously opened a path for them to cross the river—just as God had done years ago when Israel entered to take the Promised Land.

> *When they had crossed, Elijah said to Elisha, "Ask what I shall do for you, before I am taken from you." And Elisha said, "Please let there be a double portion of your spirit on me." And he said, "You have asked a hard thing; yet, if you see me as I am being taken from*

you, it shall be so for you, but if you do not see me, it shall not be so." And as they still went on and talked, behold, chariots of fire and horses of fire separated the two of them. And Elijah went up by a whirlwind into heaven. And Elisha saw it and he cried, "My father, my father! The chariots of Israel and its horsemen!" And he saw him no more. (2 Kings 2:9-12a)

Elisha asked for spiritual blessing. He wanted to be a faithful prophet like Elijah had been. Elisha had seen the horses and chariots, a symbol of God's power. He had seen the lightning and thunder of the storm. God was present, just as He was at Mount Sinai, and God carried Elijah straight into His presence. Elisha would now carry on the prophetic ministry of Elijah—fighting the battle against idolatry, calling the Israelites to return to their God and keep their covenant, and speaking God's message of justice to the people. Elijah's cloak would now be his cloak. He rolled it up and struck the Jordan River. Again, God opened a path for His prophet. God's hand of blessing was on Elisha as it had been on Elijah.

But what happened to Elijah's enemy Jezebel? Just as Elijah had prophesied, she was thrown out of a window and was eaten by dogs. Her downfall was shocking! And so two mighty people had come to the end of life on earth. Jezebel was mighty in evil and unbelief. Elijah was mighty in righteousness and faith. Jezebel died a horrific death and will experience the judgment of God forever in hell. Elijah was taken up into heaven and the presence of his God. Everyone faces the end of life someday. Some people live two hours. Others live twelve, forty-eight, or ninety years. No one knows when the end of life will come. But we do know that it will come someday. Compared to eternity . . . forever and ever and ever . . . this life is very short. At the end is either judgment or reward.

Eternity is forever, and the decisions we make in this life determine where we will spend eternity. *What will you do with the life God has given you? What will your end be? What do you want written about you when you die? Do you want to be known as a person of great faith and a faithful follower of Jesus?*

The years of our life are seventy, or even by reason of strength eighty; yet their span is but toil and trouble; they are soon gone, and we fly away. Who considers the power of your anger, and your wrath according to the fear of you? So teach us to number our days that we may get a heart of wisdom . . . Satisfy us in the morning with your steadfast love, that we may rejoice and be glad all our days. (Psalm 90:10-12, 14)

MAKING YOU WISE FOR SALVATION

What does this chapter tell us about God? Talk about and apply the **biblical truths** in **bold** text.

Salvation Thread: God is patient, calling sinners to repentance and salvation. But He is also just and will condemn those who do not repent and turn to Him. Everyone will go to either heaven or hell.

Read Ecclesiastes 7:1-2. Why don't people name their children Ahab or Jezebel? Why do some people name their sons Elijah? Why is it better to "go to the house of mourning" than to "the house of feasting"?

Talk About: *So teach us to number our days that we may get a heart of wisdom. (Psalm 90:12)*

How does thinking of your end help you today? What will you do differently now?

Pray: Praise God for being both patient and just. Thank Him for giving us examples of both evil and godliness in His Word. Ask Him to give you a heart like Elijah.

Think About: *Why are the choices we make in this life so important? How can I keep the forever life most important?*

CHAPTER 63

A LIGHT THING IN THE SIGHT OF THE LORD

God Works Miracles through Elisha—2 Kings 3-5

"This is a light thing in the sight of the LORD." (2 Kings 3:18a)

Elijah had gone up in a whirlwind, and Elisha was now God's prophet to Israel. The prophets spoke the message of God. God also used them to show His mighty acts. The name Elisha means, "My God is salvation." The meaning of names was important in the Bible. How would God show His mighty saving acts through Elisha?

Some of the miracles God did through Elisha were amazing. They almost sound unbelievable. They would be impossible for a man, even a prophet. But these miracles were done through the power of Yahweh, God Almighty, the sovereign LORD of the universe, and Creator of all things. Once, when three kings needed water for their armies and animals, Elisha prayed, and God made water bubble up from the ground of a dried-up stream. God provided an abundance of water, more than enough—"the country was filled with water." And Elisha said, *"This is a light thing in the sight of the LORD."* **Nothing is hard for God. God can do anything.**

God also used Elisha to provide for the needs of a poor widow who owed money that she couldn't pay. Her two sons were going to be taken as slaves to pay her debt. What could she do? Her husband had been a prophet and feared the LORD. So she went to Elisha for help. Elisha asked her what she had . . . but all she had was a jar of oil. Elisha told her to borrow a lot of empty jars from all her neighbors. *What would God do with all those empty jars?*

Elisha told her to go inside with her two sons and start filling the neighbors' jars with her jar of oil. When one jar was full, they took another one and filled it up. They kept filling up jar after jar . . . but the widow's jar still had oil in it! They filled up more and more jars . . . but there was still oil in the widow's jar! They kept filling jars until there were no more empty jars . . . and then the oil in the widow's jar stopped flowing. God had filled all the jars with the one jar of oil! *This is a light thing in the sight of the LORD.* Elisha told her to sell the oil, pay her debts, and there would still be enough money for her and her sons.

Another time, Elisha stayed with a family who built him a small room on the roof. He stayed there every time he was in their city. Elisha wanted to know what he could do to thank them for their kindness. The woman had no son, and her husband was old. Elisha told her she would have a son the next year in the spring. At first, the woman couldn't believe it . . . but the next spring God gave her a son! *This is a light thing in the sight of the LORD.* However, when the son had grown, he became ill and died. The woman saddled her donkey and went to find Elisha. When Elisha returned with her to her house and saw the dead boy, he prayed to Yahweh, the one true God, and life came back into the boy! This was a mighty miracle. No man could do this, not even the finest doctor. *This is a light thing in the sight of the LORD.*

Nothing is too hard for God, and **no one is beyond the kindness of God**—not even a commander in the army of the king of Syria. The commander's name was Naaman, and he had leprosy. This was a serious disease that caused skin sores and damage to arms, legs, fingers, and feet. Sometimes it even caused death. Naaman was a "mighty man of valor," and God had given Syria victories through Naaman.

In one of Syria's battles with Israel, the Syrians captured a little girl from Israel. She worked as a servant to Naaman's wife. Even though she was far from her people, she was not far from God. The girl told Naaman's wife that the prophet in Samaria, Elisha, would cure Naaman of his leprosy. Naaman told this to the king of Syria, and the king of Syria wrote a letter to the king of Israel, asking him to cure Naaman.

Naaman left Syria with the king's letter, and about 750 pounds of silver, 150 pounds of gold, and 10 changes of clothing. This was a lot of wealth! *What do you think the king of Israel did when Namaan brought him the letter and all these gifts?* The king tore his own clothes. He did this because he was worried and in great distress.

What could the king do? He couldn't cure leprosy! He said, *"Am I God, to kill and make alive, that this man sends word to me to cure a man of his leprosy?"*

When Elisha heard what happened, *he sent to the king, saying, "Why have you torn your clothes? Let him come now to me, that he may know that there is a prophet in Israel."* So Naaman went to see Elisha. But when he arrived, Elisha didn't even come out to see Naaman. He sent a messenger to him with this message: *"Go wash in the Jordan seven times, and your flesh shall be restored, and you shall be clean."*

What do you think Naaman thought of this? He was insulted. After all, he was an important commander! He expected Elisha to come out and call on the name of his God, wave his hand over Naaman, and cure him. Besides, weren't the rivers of Naaman's country nicer and cleaner than the muddy Jordan River? So he turned and "went away in a rage." He was really angry! How dare the prophet treat him like this. Naaman was a proud man. He expected special treatment.

But his servants pointed out that if the prophet had told him to do something really difficult he would have done it. What the prophet Elisha told him to do was very easy. That is, it was easy to do, but it would take humility and maybe even faith to do it. The servants convinced Naaman to follow Elisha's instructions. *So he went down and dipped himself seven times in the Jordan, according to the word of the man of God, and his flesh was restored like the flesh of a little child, and he was clean.* The king couldn't heal Naaman, but God could and surely did! *This is a light thing in the sight of the LORD.* **Nothing is too hard for God.** God can heal diseases, and He can change a proud commander's heart.

Do you know what Naaman did after he was healed? He returned to Elisha and stood before him. *And he said, "Behold, I know that there is no God in all the earth but in Israel."* God gave Syria victory so they could bring a young Israelite girl to work as a servant. He gave a proud commander leprosy. He placed the girl in Naaman's house so she could tell her mistress about Elisha. God sent Naaman to Elisha for healing...so God could display His glory, His power, and His kindness...so that Naaman would know that **Yahweh is the living God**! This is amazing power! This is amazing grace! The healing of Naaman showed the nations around Israel the greatness of God's name.

Our problems can seem very big, but **nothing is big to God**. Whatever you face today, this week, or in the years to come, whatever worry or fear you have, whatever problem comes to you, remember: *This is a light thing in the sight of the LORD.* Faith is believing that God can do anything. All that God does serves a greater plan to show His glory and bless His people.

"Ah, Lord GOD! It is you who have made the heavens and the earth by your great power and by your outstretched arm! Nothing is too hard for you." (Jeremiah 32:17)

"Behold, I am the LORD, the God of all flesh. Is anything too hard for me?" (Jeremiah 32:27)

MAKING YOU WISE FOR SALVATION

What does this chapter tell us about God? Talk about and apply the **biblical truths** in **bold** text.

Salvation Thread: God is all-powerful and can do all things. He rules over all.

Why did God perform miracles through the prophets? The miracles in the Bible sometimes seem like they can't be true. Why does believing that God is almighty make all the difference in how you see these miracles?

Talk About: *"Ah, Lord GOD! It is you who have made the heavens and the earth by your great power and by your outstretched arm! Nothing is too hard for you." (Jeremiah 32:17)*

Is your family facing problems? Can you give these problems to God and trust Him to act for His glory and your good?

Pray: Praise God for His almighty acts. Ask Him to give you the faith to believe that He is almighty and can do anything.

Think About: *Do I really believe that nothing is too hard for God? How do I know that?*

CHAPTER 64

BLIND EYES AND BLIND HEARTS

God Sends Horses and Chariots of Fire and Opens the Windows of Heaven—2 Kings 6-7

..."Do not be afraid, for those who are with us are more than those who are with them." (2 Kings 6:16)

D*o you know for certain what will happen tomorrow or next week?* Only God knows that. Only **God is all-knowing.** Only **God knows the future.** But God *did* let the prophets know about some things that would happen. When those things came true, it proved that the prophets were true prophets sent by God.

Sometimes the Syrians were at war against Israel, and sometimes they were at peace. Once, when the king of Syria was at war against Israel, he tried to make surprise raids or attacks on Israel. He and his band of soldiers would move from place to place so the Israelites wouldn't know where they would strike. But each time the Israelites were ready for the Syrians. The Israelites weren't surprised at all. How did they know where the Syrians were going to attack? The king of Syria was sure that one of his men was telling the king of Israel where the Syrians would be. He was going to find out whom this traitor was! But when he questioned his men, he found that none of them was warning the Israelites. *And one of his servants said, "None, my lord, O king; but Elisha, the prophet who is in Israel, tells the words that you speak in your bedroom."* Elisha? *How could he know what the king said in private?*

What do you think the king of Syria did then? He sent "horses and chariots and a great army" at night and surrounded the city of Dothan where Elisha was. When Elisha's servant got up in the morning and went outside, *what did he see?* He saw the mighty, impressive, frightening army of Syrians all around the city. *How would you feel at that moment?* The servant ran to Elisha in great fear! But Elisha said to him, *"Do not be afraid, for those who are with us are more than those who are with them."* Those who were with Elisha and his servant were more than the Syrians? Did Elisha not understand the problem? Elisha more than understood the situation . . . and he saw it with eyes of faith.

> *Then Elisha prayed and said, "O LORD, please open his eyes that he may see." So the LORD opened the eyes of the young man, and he saw, and behold, the mountain was full of horses and chariots of fire all around Elisha. (2 Kings 6:17)*

What were those horses and chariots of fire around Elisha? That was the mighty angelic army of the living God protecting Elisha! When the Syrians came down toward him, Elisha prayed that God would strike them with blindness. God answered Elisha's prayer and protected

him. How could the soldiers find Elisha if they couldn't see?

Then Elisha told the blind Syrians to follow him. They didn't know who they were following or where they were going. Elisha led them to Samaria. Then he asked God to open their eyes. When God "opened their eyes" and they could see again . . . they found they were in Samaria, facing the king of Israel and his army! The king of Israel asked if they should strike down the Syrians. *Do you know what Elisha said?* He told the king to give them food and water, and then tell them to go home. The king followed Elisha's advice and sent the Syrians home. What wise advice! Those Syrians would not bother Israel again because of the kindness shown to them.

Elisha had proven that he was a true prophet. His messages to the king about the Syrian army proved true. He performed miracles and wonders that could only come from the LORD. The mighty acts done through Elisha showed that **Yahweh is powerful and faithful.** Yet King Joram and the people of the Northern Kingdom of Israel still did not turn back to the LORD. So God sent a greater discipline, or trouble, to turn them back to Him.

A different king of Syria laid siege to Samaria. *Do you know what it means to "lay siege"?* In Old Testament times, they built big walls around the city for protection—like Jericho had. This way, they could close the gates of the city to keep out the attacking army. But the people of the city could not go in or out either. Eventually they would run out of food, or maybe even water, and they would have to surrender. It usually took a long time to gain a victory over a walled city. Well, this king of Syria besieged the city of Samaria for such a long time that there was a great famine in the city.

The people were starving. There was so little food that whoever had food could sell it for enormously high prices. With no food and no hope, the king of Israel wanted to surrender to Syria. But Elisha told him to wait for deliverance from God. One day, a woman complained to the king of Israel about the situation. The king only became more discouraged and upset. Instead of repenting of turning away from God, the king was angry with God! Why should the king be angry with God? **God is very gracious. His commands are clear, and the consequences of disobedience are clear.** God had warned Israel years ago at the time of Moses that this kind of discipline would happen if they turned away from Him. The king also wanted to blame Elisha for the problems they were having in the siege, but it wasn't Elisha's fault. He was only the messenger of God. The real cause was Israel's rebellion against God.

By now, the king of Israel was tired of waiting for God to act. He was ready to surrender. Then Elisha announced a prophecy: The next day there would be plenty of food in Samaria. The king's most trusted captain did not believe it. How could this happen the very next day? He told Elisha, *"If the LORD himself should make windows in heaven, could this thing be?" What was wrong with the captain's understanding of who God is?*

This would be a small thing for God! **God can do anything! God is all-powerful and rules over all creation!** God proved it to Israel the next day. Four lepers were outside the city gate, starving just like the people in the city. That night, they decided to go to the Syrian's camp. The soldiers might kill them, but they were going to starve to death anyway. Maybe the Syrians would spare their lives. They had nothing to lose. But when they got to the camp, there was no one there! *What had happened?*

Almighty Yahweh had fooled the enemy and delivered His people once again! Yes, the LORD *had* opened the windows of heaven!

> *For the Lord had made the army of the Syrians hear the sound of chariots and of horses, the sound of a great army, so that they said to one another, "Behold, the king of Israel has hired against us the kings of the Hittites and the kings of Egypt to come against us." So they fled away in the twilight and abandoned their tents, their horses, and their donkeys, leaving the camp as it was, and fled for their lives. (2 Kings 7:6-7)*

So the four men ate, drank, and gathered up silver, gold, and clothing. Then they went and told the gatekeepers of the city that the Syrians were gone. The king thought it was a trap set by the Syrians. He thought that the Syrians were just waiting for them to come out of the city so they could capture the Israelites. So he sent two horsemen to check it out. *Do you know what the men found?* They found a trail of clothes and equipment that the Syrians had thrown away as they fled in fear! When the messengers came back with the news, the people raced to the camp and took all they could.

What happened to the captain who did not believe that God could do such a miracle? Elisha had told him, *"You shall see it with your own eyes, but you shall not eat of it."* Once again, Elisha's words proved to be true, showing that he was a true prophet from the LORD. The king of Israel had put the captain in charge of the city gate. The people were so eager to get to the camp that they trampled the captain to death. He fell down in the crowd of people, and they walked over him.

God is a mighty and faithful God! He protects His people with angel armies. **He works wonders for His people**, even when they are faithless. The Israelites had seen God's power and miracles so many times, yet they did not respond to the warnings of the prophets. They did not trust God or obey His commands. Just as Elisha's servant was blind to God's great army, Israel was blind to God's greatness, goodness, and faithfulness. Only God Himself could heal their spiritual blindness. Their biggest battle was not against the Syrians. Their biggest battle was to believe who God is.

You, too, are in a spiritual battle—a battle to believe in God, to trust Him—and a battle to obey Him. *Are you fighting this battle well? Can you fight this battle in your own strength? Do you want God to give you a heart of faith?*

The LORD sets the prisoners free; the LORD opens the eyes of the blind. The LORD lifts up those who are bowed down; the LORD loves the righteous. (Psalm 146:7b-8)

MAKING YOU WISE FOR SALVATION

What does this chapter tell us about God? Talk about and apply the **biblical truths** in **bold** text.

Salvation Thread: Only God can heal spiritual blindness.

We are often blind to the real battles we face. What are some of the battles that attack your soul? What can you do to fight those battles?

Talk About: *The LORD sets the prisoners free; the LORD opens the eyes of the blind. The LORD lifts up those who are bowed down; the LORD loves the righteous. (Psalm 146:7b-8)*

How do you know if something is true, that what you are told or taught is the truth?

Pray: Ask God to open your eyes to see who He is and give you a heart of faith.

Think About: Unlike Elisha, God does not give us knowledge of the future. How can you have confidence about what might happen to you and your family?

CHAPTER 65

SALVATION BELONGS TO THE LORD!

God Has Mercy on Nineveh—Jonah

"Salvation belongs to the LORD!" (Jonah 2:9b)

Do you know what "opposite" means? Opposite means "completely different in some way." For example, *what is completely different from "up"? What is completely different from "cold"?*

The story of the book of Jonah is a true story of opposites. The country of Assyria was an enemy of Israel and Judah. Many times, Assyria fought against God's people and won. There was a very important city in Assyria called Nineveh, and the people of Nineveh were very wicked. They did not honor God but disobeyed His commands. God knew about the wicked people of Nineveh. So the LORD said to the prophet Jonah, *"Arise, go to Nineveh, that great city, and call out against it, for their evil has come up before me." Why would God be right to send Jonah to Nineveh and "call out against it"?*

But Jonah didn't want to preach to the people of Nineveh. *What might God's purpose be in giving the people this warning?* The Ninevites deserved to be destroyed. But what if God wanted to do just the *opposite*? Jonah knew that **God is a merciful God**. What if God wanted to *save* the people of Nineveh? If Jonah delivered God's warning, the Ninevites might repent and escape destruction.

Jonah was angry! He did not want the people of Nineveh to repent. He wanted God to punish them! So Jonah did just the *opposite* of what God told him to do. He ran away. Instead of obeying God, Jonah disobeyed. He got on a boat going the wrong way—*away from* Nineveh, not *to* Nineveh.

But **God will do what He plans,** even when His people are disobedient. **No one can stop the purposes of God.** Jonah thought he could run away from God on that boat going the wrong way, but **God is everywhere all the time**. God sent a big storm on the sea—such a ferocious storm that it looked like the boat would break apart! All the sailors who worked on the boat were crying out to their false gods, who could not help them. But Jonah, the prophet who knew the one true God who could help them, was not crying out to the God of Israel. Jonah was asleep!

The captain woke Jonah and told him to "call out to your god." The sailors found out from Jonah that the storm would only stop if they threw Jonah into the sea. They did not want

to do that, even though they knew Jonah was trying to run away from God. So they rowed even harder to get back to the land. But the storm got even worse! Finally, the sailors threw Jonah into the sea, and God suddenly stopped the storm. Then the sailors knew that **the God of Israel is the one true God**.

But what would happen to Jonah? Would he drown? God knew about Jonah in the water. And God had mercy on sinful Jonah. He "appointed" a big fish to swallow Jonah. *Appointed* means that God chose a fish do what He wanted. He gave the fish a job. His job was to save Jonah. God sent the fish to just the right spot and made that fish swallow Jonah. God kept Jonah alive in the belly of that big fish for three days and three nights—long enough that Jonah would repent of his sin and ask God to forgive him for doing the opposite of what God told him to do. God helped Jonah to understand that, *Salvation belongs to the LORD!* **God is in charge.** He can save whomever He wants. God is the One who would decide if the people of Nineveh would be saved, not Jonah. God would show mercy to whomever He wanted—maybe even to the wicked Assyrians. *What does this tell you about God?*

Then God spoke to the fish, and the fish spit Jonah out—not in the middle of the sea, but right onto the land. God gave Jonah another chance to obey His word. He again told Jonah to go to Nineveh to tell the people to turn away from their sin and to turn to the one true God. This time, Jonah did not do the opposite. He went to Nineveh just as God told him.

Jonah preached in Nineveh. His message was very simple: In forty days, Nineveh will be destroyed. *And the people of Nineveh believed God.* The king gave an order to his people to give up eating, to "call out mightily" to God, and to turn away from their wickedness. When God saw that the people turned away from their sin and their evil ways, God did not destroy Nineveh. God sent Jonah to Nineveh to warn the people because God is merciful. God does the opposite of what man does—He loves His enemies and offers to save them. *Salvation belongs to the LORD!* God saves whomever He wants.

Do you think Jonah was happy that God saved the people of Nineveh instead of destroying them? Jonah should have been happy that God is merciful, but He was just the opposite. He wasn't happy. He was sad. And he was mad! He said to God, "I knew this would happen! That is why I ran away. I knew You would save the people of Nineveh:

> *". . . for I knew that you are a gracious God and merciful, slow to anger and abounding in steadfast love, and relenting from disaster." (Jonah 4:2b)*

"It is better for me to die than to live. I am so upset that I want you to make me die!" Jonah was very angry, "exceedingly" angry.

Was it a good thing for Jonah to be angry? Not at all, but it was a very good thing for Jonah that **God is kind, merciful, slow to anger, and loves faithfully**. God was patient with Jonah, just as He was patient with the people of Nineveh. God did something to help Jonah to understand His mercy to undeserving sinners—like the people of Nineveh, and like Jonah.

Maybe Jonah thought his anger would make God change His mind about showing mercy to Nineveh. Maybe God would destroy Nineveh after all. He sat outside the city in the hot sun to watch what would happen to Nineveh. God was merciful to Jonah, and He appointed a plant to do a job.

God appointed a plant to grow up next to Jonah to give him some shade from the hot sun. Jonah was very glad about that plant.

But the next day, God appointed a worm. God gave the worm the job to chew on the plant to make it weak and fall over. But that wasn't all that God did. He appointed a very hot wind to blow on Jonah. The hot sun and hot wind made Jonah feel very dizzy and sick. Why did God do this? Jonah thought he and his plant deserved God's mercy. Again, Jonah was angry and said that it was better for him to die than to live.

God wanted to teach Jonah His ways. God wanted to show *mercy* to Nineveh. But Jonah thought the *opposite*. Jonah wanted God to *destroy* the people of Nineveh. Jonah didn't make the plant. It wasn't even his plant, and still he felt sorry about the plant. Jonah cared more about the plant than about the people of Nineveh. But God had made every single person in Nineveh. God had compassion, or kindness, toward the people He had made. He showed mercy to a whole city of *many people.* **No one deserves God's mercy**—not Jonah, not the people of Nineveh, and not us. God saved the Ninevites because He is *a gracious God and merciful, slow to anger and abounding in steadfast love, and relenting from disaster.*

Do you truly understand that you do not deserve God's mercy? Do you love that God is merciful? How can you show mercy to others?

"...you are a gracious God and merciful, slow to anger and abounding in steadfast love, and relenting from disaster." (Jonah 4:2b)

MAKING YOU WISE FOR SALVATION

What does this chapter tell us about God? Talk about and apply the **biblical truths** in **bold** text.

Salvation Thread: God is merciful to undeserving sinners. Salvation belongs to the LORD—God has the right to choose whom He will save.

Share with your child a time when God showed you mercy.

Talk About: *"...you are a gracious God and merciful, slow to anger and abounding in steadfast love, and relenting from disaster." (Jonah 4:2b)*

What are some ways that God shows mercy today?

Pray: Thank God for being merciful. Ask Him to be merciful to you. Pray that unbelievers you know would come to God in salvation.

Think About: *Jonah was not thankful for the mercy God gave him, so he could not be happy when someone else got mercy. Are you happy when God or someone else shows mercy to someone?*

C H A P T E R 6 6

TORN DOWN THAT HE MAY HEAL

The Destruction of the Northern Kingdom —2 Kings 17, Hosea, Amos

"Come, let us return to the LORD; for he has torn us, that he may heal us; he has struck us down, and he will bind us up." (Hosea 6:1)

For about two hundred years, the people of the Northern Kingdom of Israel rebelled against God and broke their covenant with Yahweh. In that time, they were ruled by nineteen different kings. *Do you know how many of those kings followed the LORD?* None! Not one of them followed the one true God. These kings "did what was evil in the sight of the LORD," and they led the people to follow in their evil ways.

Yet Yahweh, the covenant-keeping God, did not forget His people. With great love and mercy, God sent prophets to warn His rebellious, covenant-breaking people. In the beginning, He sent the prophets to speak face to face with the king, who had the power to make changes. But the kings did not listen. So God sent the prophets to the people themselves. Would they listen? The message that the prophets brought was not a new message. They were only reminding the people about the covenant they had made with Yahweh, Yahweh's good commands, and the consequences of breaking God's commands. This is the same message they had heard from Moses, Joshua, David, and Solomon.

The prophets had two kinds of messages. One kind of message pointed out the evil of the people and pleaded with them to repent and turn back to Yahweh. *What were some of these sins?*

Idolatry—*Do you remember the first commandment?* The first commandment is "You shall have no other gods before me." The Israelites broke this first commandment, and that caused them to break all the other commandments. They worshiped the gods of the other nations. They made idols and bowed down to them. They didn't trust in Yahweh. *Do you remember some of the ways Yahweh delivered them in battle?* Now, instead of trusting in Yahweh, they trusted in their horses, chariots, armies, and the protection of other kings they befriended.

Insincere Worship—Israel still made sacrifices to Yahweh and gave offerings, but in their hearts, they did not honor God. They went through the actions of their religious duties, but they were rebellious and wicked.

Injustice—Yahweh's commands were good and righteous because **Yahweh is good and righteous. God is loving, merciful, forgiving, generous, just, compassionate, slow to anger, patient, and kind**. But the gods of the other nations were not like Yahweh. They were cruel and evil. When the people of Israel followed these false gods, they became cruel and evil also. They robbed people of their land, made slaves of people who couldn't pay their debts, did not take care of the poor or widows and orphans, cheated people, lied, coveted, dishonored their parents and God, murdered, and committed adultery. They broke all of Yahweh's good laws. Israel was supposed to be a blessing to the nations, but instead Israel followed in the sinful ways of other nations.

Besides using words, God sometimes gave His message through the prophets with pictures or illustrations. The prophet Hosea's life was a living picture of Israel's unfaithfulness and God's faithfulness. In obedience to God, Hosea married a woman who was not a good woman. She did not deserve to be his wife. They had three children whose names warned of judgment—Jezreel (God Scatters), Lo-ruhama (No Mercy), and Lo-ammi (Not My People). *Do these names sound strange? What message was God giving the people through these names?* Hosea's wife was unfaithful and left him for other men. But her life was full of difficulty from her bad choices. Eventually, she was sold as a slave. *Do you know what Hosea did?* Hosea bought her back, not to be a slave but to be his wife again! *How is this picture like Israel and God? What does it tell you about God's heart and the hearts of His people?*

The second kind of message the prophets brought were words about the future, to tell what was going to happen before it happened. Sometimes these messages were about the coming Messiah, the Savior. Sometimes these messages were about coming judgment—what was going to happen because of the sin of God's people. This was not new either. God had already told the Israelites the consequences of breaking their covenant in the Mosaic law. Amos gave them hope that if they hated evil and loved good, if they restored justice, maybe God would be gracious. Hosea urged the people, *"Come, let us return to the LORD; for he has torn us, that he may heal us; he has struck us down, and he will bind us up."* ***How did the Israelites respond to the prophets?*** Sadly, the Israelites refused to listen.

> *. . . the LORD warned Israel and Judah by every prophet and every seer, saying, "Turn from your evil ways and keep my commandments and my statutes, in accordance with all the Law that I commanded your fathers, and that I sent to you by my servants the prophets." But they would not listen, but were stubborn, as their fathers had been, who did not believe in the LORD their God. (2 Kings 17:13-14)*

The prophets Amos and Hosea prophesied to Israel that a powerful nation would conquer Israel, destroy their cities, and take the people away into exile (take them from their own land to a different place). Amos reminded the people that, tragically, God's goodness to them had not brought repentance, and neither had God's punishments. The Israelites refused to repent. So the day of great judgment was surely coming.

Still, God would not abandon His people. **God never abandons His people. He is always faithful.** God's purpose in judging His people was to turn their hearts back to Him. Along with the warnings of judgment, the prophets always brought words of hope. God would restore them someday. He would honor His covenant with Israel even though they had been unfaithful. Amos also brought this message of promised restoration:

> *"In that day I will raise up the booth of David that is fallen and repair its breaches, and raise up its ruins and rebuild it as in the days of old . . . I will restore the fortunes of my people Israel, and they shall rebuild the ruined cities and inhabit them . . . they shall make gardens and eat their fruit. I will plant them on their land, and they shall never again be uprooted out of the land that I have given them," says the LORD your God. (Amos 9:11, 14-15)*

God is patient and slow to anger. But the time had come when God said, "Enough." Forty years after Amos predicted that disaster would come, the Assyrians invaded the Northern Kingdom. The Assyrians took most of the people of Israel into exile as servants. They even captured the walled city of Samaria, though it took them three years to do it. And this was the end of the Northern Kingdom of Israel.

The Assyrians scattered the Israelites throughout the Assyrian Empire—far and wide—in many different places. Assyria did not settle the people of Israel together in one place. Because they were not with other Israelites, they began to forget what it meant to be an Israelite. After a while, they became like the other people around them. They lost their religion and dropped their Hebrew ways.

The Assyrians also sent many people from other nations they had conquered to live in Samaria. These people brought their gods and their religion to Samaria. Before long, they added Yahweh as one of their gods. Little by little, these Samaritans dropped their idol worship. After a few hundred years, the Samaritans worshiped only Yahweh, doing what Israel had failed to do.

How **it grieves the heart of God to discipline His people.** Yet because He is just, there must be consequences for sin. Because He is faithful and loving, He disciplines to cause repentance—a turning away from sin and to God. God "tears down that He might heal." But God is not patient forever, and His judgment is real.

The destruction of the Northern Kingdom after so many warnings is God's warning to us, too. If you only go to church because your family does, but you don't really have faith in God, love His Word, or obey His commands, you are not worshiping God. You are not a true follower of the LORD. But you can turn to Him today. *What is your relationship with God?*

> "...if my people who are called by my name humble themselves, and pray and seek my face and turn from their wicked ways, then I will hear from heaven and will forgive their sin and heal their land." (2 Chronicles 7:14)

MAKING YOU WISE FOR SALVATION

What does this chapter tell us about God? Talk about and apply the **biblical truths** in **bold** text.

Salvation Thread: God disciplines to bring repentance. God's judgment is sure to those who do not repent and turn to Him.

Read Amos 5:21-24. What is the difference between "being religious" and having faith in God? What does it mean to seek for God? What is true worship? Ask your mother or father how you can have a relationship with God through Jesus.

Talk About: "*...if my people who are called by my name humble themselves, and pray and seek my face and turn from their wicked ways, then I will hear from heaven and will forgive their sin and heal their land." (2 Chronicles 7:12-14)*

Where do you see injustice in the world or in your town? What can you do about it? (You don't have to be important, smart, or wealthy for God to use you. Amos grew figs, yet God used him.)

Pray: Thank God for His patience and His warnings. Ask Him to show you what you love and trust. Ask Him for a heart of faith.

Think About: *Am I a pretender, or do I have true faith in God?*

GOD'S HEART FOR HIS PEOPLE[1]

1 *When Israel was a child, I loved him, and out of Egypt I called my son.*

2 *The more they were called, the more they went away; they kept sacrificing to the Baals and burning offerings to idols.*

3 *Yet it was I who taught Ephraim to walk; I took them up by their arms, but they did not know that I healed them.*

4 *I led them with cords of kindness, with the bands of love, and I became to them as one who eases the yoke on their jaws, and I bent down to them and fed them.*

5 *They shall not return to the land of Egypt, but Assyria shall be their king, because they have refused to return to me.*

6 *The sword shall rage against their cities, consume the bars of their gates, and devour them because of their own counsels.*

7 *My people are bent on turning away from me, and though they call out to the Most High, he shall not raise them up at all.*

8 *How can I give you up, O Ephraim? How can I hand you over, O Israel? How can I make you like Admah? How can I treat you like Zeboiim? My heart recoils within me; my compassion grows warm and tender.*

9 *I will not execute my burning anger; I will not again destroy Ephraim; for I am God and not a man, the Holy One in your midst, and I will not come in wrath.*

10 *They shall go after the LORD; he will roar like a lion; when he roars, his children shall come trembling from the west;*

11 *they shall come trembling like birds from Egypt, and like doves from the land of Assyria, and I will return them to their homes, declares the LORD.*

(Hosea 11:1-11)

1. Ephraim was another name for the Northern Kingdom. Admah and Zeboiim were cities that were destroyed along with Sodom and Gomorrah.

CHAPTER 67

OUR EYES ARE ON YOU

Judah Looks to the LORD for Help, and God Fights the Battle—2 Chronicles 19-20

"...For we are powerless against this great horde that is coming against us. We do not know what to do, but our eyes are on you." (2 Chronicles 20:12b)

What was happening in the Southern Kingdom of Judah, the royal line of David, during all this time? After the kingdom was divided, were the people of Judah keeping their covenant with Yahweh? Were they faithful to God, worshiping Him alone? Were they living rightly according to God's good commands?

One way to describe the kings of Judah is to say that they were a "mixed bag." *Do you know what that expression means?* It means an assortment of different kinds. If you get a mixed bag of candy, you might get some sour balls, some chocolates, and some peppermints. The kings of Judah were a "mixed bag"—they weren't all the same. Sadly, in this "mixed bag" of kings, most were bad, some were okay, and a few were good. But no king was a king "after God's own heart" like King David was.

Under the rule of its evil kings, the Bible tells us, *And Judah did what was evil in the sight of the LORD, and they provoked him to jealousy with their sins that they committed, more than all that their fathers had done.* Their evil was actually even greater than the evil done by the people in the Northern Kingdom of Israel. Their evil was so great that they even sacrificed their children to the false gods!

But there were some bright spots in the history of Judah. One was King Jehoshaphat, the fourth king of Judah. The Bible tells us: *His heart was courageous in the ways of the LORD. Wouldn't you like people to say that about you?* Jehoshaphat destroyed Judah's Asherah idols. He encouraged the people to trust in the LORD and sent men throughout the kingdom to teach God's law.

One day some men came to Jehoshaphat to tell him that "a great multitude" was coming to battle against Judah. *Can you imagine how frightening that must have been?* Well, King Jehoshaphat was certainly frightened when he heard that news. *So, what do you think he did?* He *set his face to seek the LORD, and proclaimed a fast throughout all Judah.* He prayed! In his fear, he turned to **God**, the One who **is fearless and almighty**.

He called all Judah to seek help from God, and he prayed in the temple court before the people, *"O LORD, God of our fathers, are you not God in heaven?* ***You rule over all the kingdoms*** *of the nations.* ***In your hand are power and might****, so that* ***none is able to withstand you****."*

He reminded the LORD of His promise to deliver them if they cried out to Him in His temple. Then Jehoshaphat ended his prayer with these words about his enemies and Judah's weakness, *"O our God, will you not execute judgment on them? For we are powerless against this great horde that is coming against us. We do not know what to do, but our eyes are on you."*

Jehoshaphat was looking for help in the right place. He did not turn to kings and armies of other nations to help him as the kings of the Northern Kingdom did. He turned to the King of kings, the Sovereign, Almighty Ruler of the Universe! And he led his people to do the same thing.

While Judah was praying, the Spirit of God came upon one of the Levites, and he said,

> *"Thus says the LORD to you, 'Do not be afraid and do not be dismayed at this great horde, for the battle is not yours but God's . . . You will not need to fight in this battle. Stand firm, hold your position, and see the salvation of the LORD on your behalf, O Judah and Jerusalem.' Do not be afraid and do not be dismayed. Tomorrow go out against them, and the LORD will be with you." (2 Chronicles 20:15b, 17)*

Then Jehoshaphat "bowed his head with his face to the ground," and all the people of Judah followed his example and worshiped Yahweh. Some of the Levites then stood up and praised the LORD with loud voices.

The next morning, King Jehoshaphat encouraged his people to trust God—***"Believe in the LORD your God, and you will be established****; believe his prophets and you will succeed."* Then he brought out Judah's mighty weapon—praise! He appointed men to sing to the LORD, praise Him, and lead the army to the battle! The words of their praise were the same words used when David brought the Ark to Jerusalem and when Solomon had the Ark placed in the

temple: *"Give thanks to the LORD, for **his steadfast love endures forever**."* The unchanging God who had been with David and Solomon was still with His people!

> *And when they began to sing and praise, the LORD set an ambush against the men of Ammon, Moab, and Mount Seir, who had come against Judah, so that they were routed. (2 Chronicles 20:22)*

At the praises of His people, God confused the armies of their enemies . . . and they turned and fought each other! The Ammonites and Moabites fought the men of Mount Seir. Then, when they had killed all the men of Mount Seir, the Ammonites and Moabites fought each other. When Jehoshaphat and Judah got to the battlefield, all of their enemies were already dead! They were lying on the ground and "none had escaped." The people of Judah did not fight the battle. They just stood firm in faith in God, and Yahweh defeated their enemies with confusion! All Judah had to do was pick up the great amount of "goods, clothing, and precious things" lying all around. There was so much that they couldn't carry it all. It actually took them three days to gather it all up. *Isn't this an amazing story of the power and grace of God?*

On the fourth day, the people of Judah blessed the LORD at the battlefield. Then they returned joyfully to Jerusalem to praise God in the temple with harps, lyres, and trumpets. A few days earlier, they had asked for God's help in the temple, and now they were thanking and praising Him for His faithfulness and steadfast love. What a glorious day of praise that was!

And the fear of God came on all the kingdoms of the countries when they heard that the LORD had fought against the enemies of Israel. (2 Chronicles 20:29)

God's mighty act caused so much fear among the nations that the rest of Jehoshaphat's reign was peaceful. Though Jehoshaphat also made some bad choices, he reigned for twenty-five years, and the Bible tells us that he "did not turn aside from . . . doing what was right in the sight of the LORD." What a great story of faith in God. What a great display of God's power and commitment to His promise. **God loves the praise of His people.**

What do you do when you are afraid? Do you look for courage within yourself, or do you turn to God and say, "My eyes are on you." Do you trust in the unchanging, almighty, ever-present, faithful God? Do you praise Him for who He is?

When I am afraid, I put my trust in you. In God, whose word I praise, in God I trust; I shall not be afraid. What can flesh do to me? (Psalm 56:3-4)

MAKING YOU WISE FOR SALVATION

What does this chapter tell us about God? Talk about and apply the **biblical truths** in **bold** text.

Salvation Thread: God hears the cries of His people and rescues them.

It is easy to take things into your own hands and try to solve problems without first looking to the LORD. Think through some situations from your life this past week. How did you respond? Could you have responded in a better way? Very practically, what can you do to "train yourself" to look to the LORD first?

Talk About: *When I am afraid, I put my trust in you. In God, whose word I praise, in God I trust; I shall not be afraid. What can flesh do to me? (Psalm 56:3-4)*

What are some of the "battles" or problems facing your family or someone you know? How can you be an encourager?

Pray: Praise God for His power and His faithfulness. Thank Him for answering His people when they call on Him. Confess your fears to Him and ask for His help.

Think About: *In what do I put my trust? Do I trust God and look to Him?*

CHAPTER 68

THE LAMP OF THE WICKED AND THE PROMISE OF GOD

The Kings of Judah Walk in Darkness—2 Chronicles 21-26

Fret not yourself because of evildoers, and be not envious of the wicked, for the evil man has no future; the lamp of the wicked will be put out. (Proverbs 24:19-20)

Most often, the role of king is passed from father to son. Jehoshaphat had seven sons, and one of them would be king. Before he died, he gave each of them "gifts of silver, gold, and valuable possessions, together with fortified cities in Judah, but he gave the kingdom to Jehoram because he was the firstborn."

The first thing Jehoram did when he became king was to kill all his brothers and some of the princes of Israel. He wanted to make sure no one took his throne. What horrific evil this man did! *And he walked in the way of the kings of Israel, as the house of Ahab had done, for the daughter of Ahab was his wife. And he did what was evil in the sight of the LORD. Do you remember who Ahab was?* He was the evil king who worshiped Baal and hated Elijah. This evil king's daughter, Athaliah, was married to Jehoram and encouraged him in doing evil.

The Bible says that *the heart is deceitful above all things, and desperately sick.* Without God's help, man will do dreadfully wicked things. Under the rule of Jehoram and some of the other kings, Judah turned further and further away from God and continued to accept the evil gods of other nations. Over time, Judah's sin grew greater and greater.

Yet the LORD was not willing to destroy the house of David, because of the covenant that he had made with David. Even though David's descendant Jehoram was evil and did not honor God, God would be faithful to continue David's kingly line. **God never breaks His promises.** But God would not allow Jehoram to continue leading

His people into evil. So the prophet Elijah sent a letter to Jehoram announcing God's judgment on him saying, *"Because you have not walked in the ways of Jehoshaphat . . . but have walked in the way of the kings of Israel and have enticed Judah and the inhabitants of Jerusalem* to turn away from God to go after other gods . . . *and also you have killed your brothers . . . who were better than yourself, behold, the LORD will bring a great plague on your people, your children, your wives, and all your possessions, and you yourself will have a severe sickness."* God was not ignorant of Jehoram's evil. **God sees all sin,** and He is serious about protecting and rescuing His world from man's evil.

The LORD "stirred up" the Philistines and Arabians to invade Judah, and they took all that belonged to Jehoram—even his sons and his wives—everyone except his youngest son. Then the LORD "struck" Jehoram with an incurable disease, and at the end of two years, he died. **Every word of God proves true.**

Jehoram's youngest son, Ahaziah, became king. But remember that his mother was Athaliah, the daughter of Ahab. *He also walked in the ways of the house of Ahab, for his mother was his counselor in doing wickedly.* One man—Ahab—had done so much wickedness not only in his own kingdom of Israel but also in Judah through his evil daughter. Ahaziah ruled only one year, and then he was killed. *Now when Athaliah the mother of Ahaziah saw that her son was dead, she arose and destroyed all the royal family of the house of Judah.* How wicked this woman was! She killed her own family—even her *grandsons*—so that she could be the queen! Surely, a great rescue was needed to deliver man from such sin. *The heart is deceitful above all things, and desperately sick; who can understand it?*

Athaliah was now the queen. She had gotten away with her evil deed . . . or so she thought. But **no one ever gets away with evil.** Not only did she bring on herself the fierce anger of God, but also her plan failed. God had protected Ahaziah's youngest son, a baby whose name was Joash. The baby's aunt had rescued baby Joash and hid him for six years in the temple, where her husband Jehoiada served as priest. This is how God had saved the royal line of David.

When Joash was seven years old, Jehoiada courageously decided it was time to put Joash on his father's throne. The Levites and army captains agreed to help Jehoiada protect Joash. They armed themselves with weapons and surrounded Joash as Jehoiada brought Joash out of hiding. Jehoiada placed the crown on the boy's head. He gave Joash a copy of the law of Moses and anointed Joash as king. The priests cried, "Long live the king," and the people of Judah praised the king in a great celebration. When

Athaliah heard the celebrating, the singing, trumpets, and other instruments, she wanted to know what was going on. She went to the temple and when she saw the king, she tore her clothes in anger. She accused the people of doing wrong in this. But instead of agreeing with her, the captains of the army put her to death. She had been replaced by the real king.

The seven-year-old king was guided by the godly priest Jehoiada. He collected money and hired workers to repair the temple. Burnt offerings were made regularly again all the days of Jehoiada. But then Jehoiada died and his godly influence was gone. The princes of Judah no longer wanted to worship Yahweh. Sadly, Joash agreed with them. *And they abandoned the house of the LORD, the God of their fathers, and served the Asherim and the idols. And wrath came upon Judah and Jerusalem for this guilt of theirs. Yet he sent prophets among them to bring them back to the LORD. These testified against them, but they would not pay attention.*

The nation of Judah was living in spiritual darkness. Their darkened hearts continually turned away from God to what was sinful. Once again, God brought judgment upon His rebellious people. The Syrians came to battle against Judah. *Though the army of the Syrians had come with few men, the LORD delivered into their hand a very great army, because Judah had forsaken the LORD, the God of their fathers. Thus they executed judgment on Joash.*

Joash's son Amaziah then became king. *And he did what was right in the eyes of the LORD, yet not with a whole heart.* After defeating the men of Seir in battle, he brought back the false gods to Judah and made offerings to them. How foolish this was. How powerful were their gods? The LORD was angry with Amaziah and sent a prophet to him who said, *"Why have you sought the gods of a people who did not deliver their own people from your hand?"* Amaziah had foolishly and sinfully traded the worship of the one true God, who is all-powerful, for useless false gods. Sure enough, he was defeated in his next battle, and eventually he was put to death.

Amaziah's son, Uzziah became king at sixteen years old. Jehoiada's son, Zechariah, was also a priest, and he guided Uzziah in what is right. Uzziah *set himself to seek God in the days of Zechariah, who instructed him in the fear of God, and as long as he sought the LORD, God made him prosper.* He won many battles, defeating Judah's enemies. He built fortress towers in Jerusalem and towers in the wilderness. He dug out many cisterns (water tanks) in the wilderness to water his large herds. His army was well equipped with shields, spears, helmets, coats of mail, and stones for slinging. He invented weapons to shoot arrows and big stones from his towers. *And his fame spread far for he was marvelously helped, till he was strong.*

All seemed to be going well for Uzziah—yet his sin nature was at work. Was he depending on the LORD, or on his weapons and army? Was power and wealth a trap for him? Things seemed to be going well. *But when he was strong, he grew proud, to his destruction. For he was unfaithful to the LORD his God and entered the temple of the LORD to burn incense on the altar of incense.*

Why was it wrong for him to burn incense on the altar? God had specifically said that only the priests could do this. But, in his pride, Uzziah broke God's command and dishonored the LORD. The priests told him to leave, and he became angry. At that moment, leprosy broke out on his forehead! **It is a serious sin to dishonor God.** Because of his sin, Uzziah was a leper until he died.

The kings of Judah weren't the only ones who turned from God, dishonored Him, and lived sinfully. Many of the people followed their bad example. They were sinners who deserved God's punishment. They would never be able to keep God's law. They were continual covenant-breakers. They were in desperate need of a sin-bearer, a perfect law-keeper, a greater King who would not only take away their sin, but also give them new hearts. They needed rescue.

You, too, are a son of Adam, born with a sin nature and in need of salvation. You cannot change your heart. Only God can give you divine rescue. Will you call on Him today?

Behold, the LORD's hand is not shortened, that it cannot save, or his ear dull, that it cannot hear; but your iniquities have made a separation between you and your God, and your sins have hidden his face from you so that he does not hear. (Isaiah 59:1-2)

MAKING YOU WISE FOR SALVATION

What does this chapter tell us about God? Talk about and apply the **biblical truths** in **bold** text.

Salvation Thread: Man is unable to keep God's law and needs a perfect law-keeper and sin-bearer.

Has man's sin nature changed since Bible times? What evidence do you see of this in the world today?

Talk About: *Behold, the LORD's hand is not shortened, that it cannot save, or his ear dull, that it cannot hear; but your iniquities have made a separation between you and your God, and your sins have hidden his face from you so that he does not hear. (Isaiah 59:1-2)*

Why did some kings start out "good" and then turn out "bad"?

Pray: Thank God that He protects the world from much of man's evil.

Think About: Why doesn't God stop all evil?

C H A P T E R 6 9

A HOLY GOD GIVES HOPE TO AN UNHOLY PEOPLE

Isaiah's Vision and Message —Isaiah 6-7; 2 Kings 16; 2 Chronicles 27-28

...I saw the Lord sitting upon a throne, high and lifted up; and the train of his robe filled the temple. (Isaiah 6:1b)

Have you heard these words before? In the year that King Uzziah died I saw the Lord sitting upon a throne, high and lifted up; and the train of his robe filled the temple.

This is the first sentence of a beautiful passage from the Bible. It describes the vision the prophet Isaiah saw of God, the King of all kings, the Ruler of the Whole Universe sitting on His throne.

> *Above him stood the seraphim. Each had six wings: with two he covered his face, and with two he covered his feet, and with two he flew. And one called to another and said: "Holy, holy, holy is the LORD of hosts; the whole earth is full of his glory!" And the foundations of the thresholds shook at the voice of him who called, and the house was filled with smoke. (Isaiah 6:2-4)*

Can you imagine what this vision must have been like? Isaiah had a vision of the glorious splendor of God, who is utterly different and set apart from anything else. The angels above Him hid their faces and feet in awe of His greatness and glory. How could Isaiah respond to such a vision of the holiness and majesty of God? Would he run away in fear? Hide his face in shame? Bow in honor?

> *"Woe is me! For I am lost; for I am a man of unclean lips, and I dwell in the midst of a people of unclean lips; for my eyes have seen the King, the LORD of hosts!" (Isaiah 6:5)*

"Woe is me" showed Isaiah's deep despair and his great dread or fear at the sight of the holiness of

God. The sight of God's purity, majesty, and holiness made Isaiah realize his deep sinfulness. He saw the dreadful sinfulness of Judah and the pure goodness and righteousness of God. There was absolutely nothing Isaiah could do to cover his sin or the sin of the people.

Then came this amazing scene: *Then one of the seraphim flew to me, having in his hand a burning coal that he had taken with tongs from the altar. And he touched my mouth and said: "Behold, this has touched your lips; your guilt is taken away, and your sin atoned for."* The Holy God of Israel, Yahweh Himself, took away the guilt of Isaiah's sin! Isaiah was a condemned man—guilty of sin, worthy of hell, eternal punishment, and suffering, but the King of all Creation, the Holy God, removed his sin from him! **God overflows with mercy! Only God, the Supreme Ruler and Holy God, can pardon sin.**

Not only did God show His kindness to Isaiah, but He also wanted to show His kindness to undeserving Judah. So in the vision, God called Isaiah to be His prophet to Judah, to plead with His people to turn back to Him, and to warn them of the consequences of continuing in their rebellion against Him. *And I heard the voice of the Lord saying, "Whom shall I send, and who will go for us?" Then I said, "Here am I! Send me."*

Isaiah was eager to warn the people and tell them of God's mercy—God's kindness to undeserving sinners. Though they were sinners, the people of Judah could receive the same kindness as Isaiah received, if they would just repent. God told Isaiah to bring His message to the people of Judah, but God warned Isaiah that they would not listen to him. Even though they would not repent, Isaiah was to tell the people anyway. *Why would Isaiah continue to bring a message that Judah would not listen to or follow?*

He would do this in submission to the Lord, the Ruler and Master of all things. Isaiah understood that **God is the Creator and Owner of the whole world. He rules over all**. Isaiah humbly bowed to God's rule. He understood that God was the Master, and he was the servant. He would serve God in whatever God asked him to do.

Isaiah faithfully announced God's message to Judah during the reign of kings Jotham, Ahaz, and Hezekiah. Jotham was a good king who tried to please God, but the people were wicked. God also sent the prophet Micah to plead with His people to turn from their wickedness and be faithful to their covenant. He reminded the people of God's good laws and what God expected of them—*He has told you, O man, what is good; and what does the LORD require of you but to do justice, and to love kindness, and to walk humbly with your God?* Isaiah and Micah warned them of God's coming judgment if they did not repent. An enemy nation would conquer them and take them to a distant country. The land of Judah would be lonely and empty, covered with thorns and prickly weeds. Their cities would be deserted, and the temple would be destroyed. After many years of living as captives and servants far from home, the Lord would raise up a great king named Cyrus. Cyrus would allow some of them—a remnant or a portion—to return to Jerusalem and rebuild the city and the temple again. It was God's desire to bring His people back.

But the people of Judah ignored the prophets' warnings. They were stubborn and would not repent. So God took away their good king and gave them an evil king. After Jotham died, his son Ahaz became king. Ahaz *did not do what was right in the eyes of the LORD . . . He even burned his son as an offering, according to the despicable practices of the nations whom the LORD drove out before the people of Israel.* Ahaz and the people of Judah had become like the Canaanites in doing evil.

When the king of Syria and the king of Israel went to war against Judah to capture Jerusalem, Ahaz didn't ask God Almighty for help. Instead, he asked Assyria for help. *Why would an enemy help Judah?* Assyria did it for money. Ahaz bought Assyria's help with the silver and gold from the temple and the king's house. But the king of Assyria wasn't much help.

Ahaz asked a priest to make an altar like the altars used to worship false gods. Ahaz himself made offerings on his new altar and threw the blood of his offerings on the altar. *Why was this so wrong?* Ahaz was not a priest. And he was not honoring Yahweh but false gods. *And Ahaz gathered together the vessels of the house of God and cut in pieces the vessels of the house of God, and he shut up the doors of the house of the LORD, and he made himself altars in every corner of Jerusalem. In every city of Judah he made high places to make offerings to other gods, provoking to anger the LORD, the God of his fathers.* Ahaz had such disrespect for the temple and Yahweh!

Not all the people were wicked in these days. Some still followed Yahweh. But most had turned away from God. Was there any hope for Judah? The people had become so wicked. Their darkened hearts had pushed them away from Yahweh and His good ways. They broke their covenant with Yahweh again and again and again. They had become just like the evil nations around them.

There was nothing sinful man could do to help himself. There was no hope that "their guilt would be taken away and their sin atoned for"—unless God Himself saved them. But why should God give any hope to such an evil, rebellious, unfaithful people? **God is merciful to undeserving sinners.** In the Garden of Eden, God had promised a Savior to crush the head of the serpent...and this promise was still true. God gave Isaiah this message of hope and promise in these very dark days of Judah's history:

> *Therefore the Lord himself will give you a sign. Behold, the virgin shall conceive and bear a son, and shall call his name Immanuel. (Isaiah 7:14)*
>
> *For to us a child is born, to us a son is given; and the government shall be upon his shoulder, and his name shall be called Wonderful Counselor, Mighty God, Everlasting Father, Prince of Peace. Of the increase of his government and of peace there will be no end, on the throne of David and over his kingdom, to establish it and to uphold it with justice and with righteousness from this time forth and forevermore. The zeal of the LORD of hosts will do this. (Isaiah 9:6-7)*
>
> *There shall come forth a shoot from the stump of Jesse, and a branch from his roots shall bear fruit. And the Spirit of the LORD shall rest upon him, the Spirit of wisdom and understanding, the Spirit of counsel and might, the Spirit of knowledge and the fear of the LORD. (Isaiah 11:1-2)*

Immanuel means "God with us." God would not abandon His people. He would keep His promise to raise up a righteous King from the royal line of David whose Kingdom of goodness, peace, justice, and righteousness would last forever!

Just like the people of Judah, you and I cannot change our hearts. We can't make ourselves want to draw near to God. We can't give ourselves a spiritual heart, or the desire to read the Bible, or to love goodness. Just like Judah, we need rescue, too. *Do you truly see that you are a sinner—"a man of unclean lips"? Do you feel the ugliness of your sin? Are you grateful that God is merciful and has made a way for sinful man to be forgiven?*

Who is a God like you, pardoning iniquity and passing over transgression for the remnant of his inheritance? He does not retain his anger forever, because he delights in steadfast love. He will again have compassion on us; he will tread our iniquities underfoot. You will cast all our sins into the depths of the sea. (Micah 7:18-19)

MAKING YOU WISE FOR SALVATION

What does this chapter tell us about God? Talk about and apply the **biblical truths** in **bold** text.

Salvation Thread: Only God can pardon sin. God promised to send a Savior who would bring everlasting peace and righteousness.

Isaiah saw his sinfulness when he saw the pure goodness and holiness of God. You can think you are pretty good when you compare yourself to others. But what are you like compared to God?

Talk About: *Who is a God like you, pardoning iniquity and passing over transgression for the remnant of his inheritance? He does not retain his anger forever, because he delights in steadfast love. (Micah 7:18)*

Why would God send Isaiah to warn the people of Judah if they weren't going to listen anyway?

Pray: Thank God for His faithful love and desire to forgive. Ask Him to show you any stubbornness in your heart. Repent of breaking God's laws and of any rebellion in your heart.

Think About: *How can a just God "cast all our sins into the depths of the sea"?*

C H A P T E R 7 0

REFORM AND RIDICULE

Hezekiah's Reforms and Assyria's Ridicule —2 Kings 18-19; 2 Chronicles 28-32

"For the LORD your God is gracious and merciful and will not turn away his face from you, if you return to him." (2 Chronicles 30:9b)

When things are going from bad to worse, it is time for a change. That's what was happening in Judah. How could they stop this darkening evil from growing? Isaiah and Micah had prophesied that judgment was coming. Only God could rescue them. But God had given them so many chances. Why should He give them another chance or help them? They didn't deserve it.

But **God is merciful; He is kind to undeserving sinners.** In mercy and faithfulness, God gave Judah another good king, King Hezekiah. Hezekiah means, "God is my strength." This is what the Bible tells us about him: *He trusted in the LORD, the God of Israel, so that there was none like him among all the kings of Judah after him, nor among those who were before him. For he held fast to the LORD. He did not depart from following him, but kept the commandments that the LORD commanded Moses.*

Hezekiah set to work and started changing things. He destroyed the high places of idol worship and tore down the altars and temples of the false gods. He also broke into pieces the bronze serpent Moses made. Does this seem strange? *Why would Hezekiah do this?* The people of Judah were making offerings to the bronze serpent! Moses made the bronze serpent to encourage the Israelites to trust in Yahweh, but now the people were treating it as an idol! Hezekiah could not allow this great offense to God. He also reopened the temple his father, Ahaz, had closed. He gathered the priests his father had sent away and

asked them to clean the temple—to throw away all the unclean things—"to carry out the filth from the Holy Place," and put back everything that belonged in the temple so the people could worship God there again. When the priests finished the work, they made sacrifices, and the Levites praised the LORD with cymbals, harps, lyres, and trumpets. *And the king and all who were present with him . . . sang praises with gladness, and they bowed down and worshiped.* That must have been a very joyful day!

For many years, Israel and Judah had not kept God's command to keep the Passover feast. So Hezekiah sent messengers with letters inviting them to the Passover and urging them to return to Yahweh:

> *"Do not be like your fathers and your brothers, who were faithless to the LORD God of their fathers, so that he made them a desolation, as you see. Do not now be stiff-necked as your fathers were, but yield yourselves to the LORD and come to his sanctuary, which he has consecrated forever, and serve the LORD your God, that his fierce anger may turn away from you. For if you return to the LORD, your brothers and your children will find compassion with their captors and return to this land. For the LORD your God is gracious and merciful and will not turn away his face from you, if you return to him." (2 Chronicles 30:7-9)*

The messengers went throughout the land of Israel and Judah. Sadly, most of the people left in the Northern Kingdom of Israel just laughed and mocked them. Only a few came. But *the hand of God was also on Judah to give them one heart* to obey the command. How wonderful it was that the people of Judah came to Jerusalem to celebrate the Passover! But first, they destroyed all the idol altars in Jerusalem. *Do you remember what they celebrated during the Passover?* The Passover celebrated God's rescue of the Hebrews from Egypt. The angel of death had passed over the houses of the Hebrews because they had the blood of the Passover lamb on their doorposts. Hezekiah and the people celebrated the Passover for seven days. They praised God with music, the priests taught the law, and they made sacrifices. After seven days, they decided to celebrate for seven more days! Then they went throughout Judah and destroyed the idols and the altars where people had worshiped idols. This was a very good time in Judah!

This happened after some of the people of Israel had been taken captive by Assyria, and while Assyria was laying siege to the walled city of Samaria. Remember that it took three years for Assyria to conquer Samaria. Samaria was finally conquered because the people of Israel *did not obey the voice of the LORD their God but transgressed his covenant . . . They neither listened nor obeyed.* And that was the terrible end of the Northern Kingdom of Israel. God had given the Israelites so much. He had made them a nation. He had given them the Promised Land, freedom from slavery, His protection and favor—everything they needed. And the people of the Northern Kingdom lost it all because of their stubborn rebellion against God. Can there be any greater sadness than this?

After conquering Samaria, Assyria attacked the fortified cities of Judah and took them. So Hezekiah prepared to defend Jerusalem by repairing the walls and building towers. He made an "abundance" of weapons and shields. He even cut a tunnel under the Jerusalem wall for the water from the spring to flow into the city. Most importantly, he told the people, *"Be strong and courageous. Do not be afraid or dismayed before the king of Assyria and all the horde that is with him, for there are more with us than with him. With him is an arm of flesh, but with us is the LORD our God, to help us and to fight our battles." And the people took confidence from the words of Hezekiah king of Judah.* Hezekiah was right. The Assyrians only had their own strength, but the people of Judah had the LORD God Almighty to help them fight the battle!

Then Hezekiah stripped the gold from the doors and doorposts of the temple, emptied the temple and the king's house of all the silver, and sent 22,500 pounds of silver and 2,250 pounds of gold to Sennacherib, the king of Assyria. He hoped this gift would cause Assyria to leave Judah alone. The king of Assyria did leave for a while . . . but later he and his army came back. Sennacherib sent his officers ahead to Jerusalem to tell the people that he was coming to destroy Jerusalem. Their message mocked Yahweh, the Almighty, Sovereign God: *"Thus says the king: 'Do not let Hezekiah deceive you, for he will not be able to deliver you out of my hand. Do not let Hezekiah make you trust in the LORD by saying, The LORD will surely deliver us, and this city will not be given into the hand of the king of Assyria . . . do not listen to Hezekiah when he misleads you by saying, "The LORD will deliver us." Has any of the gods of the nations ever delivered his land out of the hand of the king of Assyria?'"*

What do you think of this message? Can anyone defy the living God and win? Oh, the pride and defiance of the Assyrians! How dare they think their army and their false gods were stronger than the all-powerful King of the Universe, the one true God! **How despicably sinful it is to mock God!**

Hezekiah commanded the people of Jerusalem not to answer the Assyrians, and they did not even answer one word to such a disrespectful, mocking message. What would Hezekiah do now? What would Yahweh do? Hezekiah "tore his clothes and covered himself with sackcloth." Sackcloth was what you wore when you were mourning, or really sad. Hezekiah was deeply troubled. He sent a message to the prophet Isaiah saying, *"This is a day of distress, of rebuke, and of disgrace . . . "* He told Isaiah that the messenger of the king of Assyria had mocked the living God and asked Isaiah to pray. What would happen? Would God rescue

Jerusalem and Judah? Would Yahweh defend His great name?

We can hardly believe that the king of Assyria would think that he was greater than Yahweh. But we, too, sometimes show the same kind of pride. When we doubt God's Word, when we think God should do something different from what He is doing in the world, when God doesn't answer prayer the way we think He should, or when we get upset because He doesn't give us what we want or do what we ask, we are showing the same kind of pride. Though our words may not be mocking words, we are mocking God's wisdom and goodness in our hearts. *Is there any way in which you are questioning God's goodness or wisdom? Do you truly believe that God is greater than anyone or anything else?*

To whom then will you compare me, that I should be like him? says the Holy One. (Isaiah 40:25)

MAKING YOU WISE FOR SALVATION

What does this chapter tell us about God? Talk about and apply the **biblical truths** in **bold** text.

Salvation Thread: God is eager to forgive, but He will not be mocked. He will defend His name and His fame. He will honor those who honor Him and bring judgment upon those who dishonor Him.

Read 2 Kings 18:28-35. What is so wrong and so offensive about these words and the heart attitude behind them?

Talk About: *To whom then will you compare me, that I should be like him? says the Holy One. (Isaiah 40:25)*

Why is God not to blame for Israel's downfall? How was God merciful to both Israel and Judah?

Pray: Thank God for His mercy and for not turning away anyone who repents and comes to Him. Confess any way in which you have questioned God's goodness or wisdom. Ask God to give you a strong faith in Him.

Think About: *How can I be like Hezekiah and encourage others to trust in God?*

C H A P T E R 7 1

RESCUE, REBUKE, AND FUTURE REDEMPTION

God Rescues Jerusalem and Promises Redemption for His People—2 Kings 19-20; 2 Chronicles 32

"So now, O LORD our God, save us, please, from his hand, that all the kingdoms of the earth may know that you, O LORD, are God alone." (2 Kings 19:19)

Jerusalem was surrounded by the massive Assyrian army. Surely, Sennacherib, the king of Assyria, thought his army would conquer God's people by the power of his army. The LORD encouraged King Hezekiah, however, with these words given through the prophet Isaiah: *"Thus says the LORD: Do not be afraid because of the words that you have heard, with which the servants of the king of Assyria have reviled me. Behold, I will put a spirit in him, so that he shall hear a rumor and return to his own land, and I will make him fall by the sword in his own land."*

Just think of the sovereign power of God—He can cause a rumor to go around, He can cause the king of Assyria to hear it, and He can cause the king to go back home! **All things are under God's control.** The king of Assyria could not mock the living God without severe consequences. He would die for his great offense against God's name. **God always defends His name.**

Proud king Sennacherib sent another messenger to Hezekiah with a letter mocking God again. He pridefully stated that God could not deliver Jerusalem! His words were an insult to the name of the LORD! When Hezekiah read Sennacherib's letter, he went to the temple. He "spread the letter before the LORD."

> *And Hezekiah prayed before the LORD and said: "O LORD, the God of Israel . . . you are the God, you alone, of all the kingdoms of the earth; you have made heaven and earth. Incline your*

ear, O LORD, and hear; open your eyes, O LORD, and see; and hear the words of Sennacherib, which he has sent to mock the living God. Truly, O LORD, the kings of Assyria have laid waste the nations and their lands and have cast their gods into the fire, for they were not gods, but the work of men's hands, wood and stone. Therefore they were destroyed. So now, O LORD our God, save us, please, from his hand, that all the kingdoms of the earth may know that you, O LORD, are God alone." (2 Kings 19:15-19)

Hezekiah had great confidence in God, the maker of heaven and earth. God would not allow the evil nation of Assyria to mock Him. The living God gave the prophet Isaiah a word of encouragement and victory for Hezekiah:

"Therefore thus says the LORD concerning the king of Assyria: He shall not come into this city or shoot an arrow there, or come before it with a shield or cast up a siege mount against it. By the way that he came, by the same he shall return, and he shall not come into this city, declares the LORD. For I will defend this city to save it, for my own sake and for the sake of my servant David." (2 Kings 19:32-34)

What a wonderful word from the LORD! Hezekiah prayed to the LORD, and God spoke words of great promise to the prophet, Isaiah. Sennacherib's victories were not because of his great might, but because God had planned all that had happened. Since the king of Assyria had mocked God, God would judge him. God would defend Jerusalem to show the greatness of His name and to honor His promise to David. He would also provide food for His people and cause their crops to grow.

So, what happened? Did Isaiah's prophecy come true? *And that night the angel of the LORD went out and struck down 185,000 in the camp of the Assyrians. And when people arose early in the morning, behold, these were all dead bodies. Then Sennacherib king of Assyria departed and went home and lived at Nineveh. And as he was worshiping in the house of Nisroch his god . . . his sons*

struck him down with the sword. Sennacherib pridefully boasted that he would conquer Jerusalem but when he heard that his army had been struck down, he returned home in shame. There his own sons killed him. **The word of the LORD is always true**. Sennacherib was not greater than Yahweh—and neither was his god greater than Yahweh. **God will defend His name** and prove that **He is the one true God.**

After this, Hezekiah became very ill and was near death. Though he had become proud, he humbled himself and prayed to the LORD. God heard his prayer and promised him fifteen more years of life. God also promised Hezekiah and Jerusalem safety from the king of Assyria. All the days of Hezekiah, Jerusalem was safe, and Assyria never conquered Jerusalem. The Assyrians conquered the entire area surrounding Jerusalem, but they could not conquer Jerusalem.

The king of Babylon had heard that Hezekiah had been sick, so he sent messengers with letters and a present to Hezekiah. Hezekiah welcomed them and showed them all his treasures: his silver, gold, spices, precious oil, his armory (weapons and shields), and "all that was in his storehouses." He showed them everything he had. But when Isaiah heard what Hezekiah did, he had a word of prophecy from God. *"Hear the word of the LORD: Behold, the days are coming, when all that is in your house, and that which your fathers have stored up till this day, shall be carried to Babylon. Nothing shall be left, says the LORD. And some of your own sons, who shall be born to you, shall be taken away . . ."*

Isaiah prophesied that someday Babylon would conquer Jerusalem. But there was peace and safety in Judah the rest of Hezekiah's days. Hezekiah was a godly king, and he encouraged the people to destroy their idols and turn to the LORD. But Hezekiah could not deliver God's people from their sinful hearts. Judah would return to idol worship again and turn away from God. The day was coming when God's judgment would come upon Judah, as Micah and Isaiah had warned. Instead of being a light and a blessing to the other nations, Israel and Judah had become like them. God would also judge the other nations for their evil.

But God always gives His people hope. Along with their message of judgment, Micah and Isaiah also gave a message of hope. They told about the coming Messiah and gave many clues, or prophesies, about Him. These clues would help people recognize the Savior when He came. Micah prophesied that from Bethlehem would come *one who is to be ruler in Israel, whose coming forth is from old, from ancient days.* Isaiah promised that God would comfort His people and would send a Deliverer: *Behold, the virgin shall conceive and bear a son, and shall call his name Immanuel.* **The only hope for God's people for salvation is from God alone.** This Deliverer has an eternal Kingdom, yet he would come as a **suffering servant.** He would bring peace and healing. He would not come to rule as king, but to be hated, beaten, and killed. *Why would He do this? Could this be true?*

> *For he grew up before him like a young plant, and like a root out of dry ground; he had no form or majesty that we should look at him, and no beauty that we should desire him. He was despised and rejected by men; a man of sorrows, and acquainted with grief; and as one from whom men hide their faces he was despised, and we esteemed him not. Surely he has borne our griefs and carried our sorrows; yet we esteemed him stricken, smitten by God, and*

afflicted. But ***he was pierced for our transgressions; he was crushed for our iniquities; upon him was the chastisement that brought us peace, and with his wounds we are healed. All we like sheep have gone astray****; we have turned—every one—to his own way; and the LORD has laid on him the iniquity of us all. He was oppressed, and he was afflicted, yet he opened not his mouth; like a lamb that is led to the slaughter, and like a sheep that before its shearers is silent, so he opened not his mouth. (Isaiah 53:2-7)*

Isaiah was a true prophet of God. Every word of his prophesies about the King of Assyria came true. Someday his prophecies about the coming Messiah also would come true. Until then, God's people had to wait and hope. Would they recognize the Messiah when He came?

The only hope for our sinful hearts, the only hope of salvation for us is, in God's Deliverer, God's Sin-Bearer. *Are you trusting in your own goodness or righteousness, or are you trusting in God's Deliverer? Are you trying to be good enough to be acceptable to God and trying to do what is right? Or do you recognize that your sin nature cannot be broken, and you need God's salvation?*

All we like sheep have gone astray; we have turned—every one—to his own way; and the LORD has laid on him the iniquity of us all. (Isaiah 53:6)

MAKING YOU WISE FOR SALVATION

What does this chapter tell us about God? Talk about and apply the **biblical truths** in **bold** text.

Salvation Thread: Salvation is only possible through God's Deliverer.

What can you learn about prayer from Hezekiah's prayer? What does this story show you about God's zeal (enthusiasm, passion) for His name?

Talk About: *But he was pierced for our transgressions; he was crushed for our iniquities; upon him was the chastisement that brought us peace, and with his wounds we are healed. All we like sheep have gone astray; we have turned—every one—to his own way; and the LORD has laid on him the iniquity of us all. (Isaiah 53:5-6)*

Discuss Isaiah 53:1-7. What does it tell you about the Deliverer? What kind of peace and healing did Isaiah mean?

Why did Israel and Judah keep turning from God? What does this tell you about the human heart?

Pray: Praise God for His promise of deliverance. Thank Him for His salvation. Ask Him to turn your heart to Him.

Think About: *Why do I need a Savior?*

THE NEW HEAVENS AND NEW EARTH

Although Isaiah preached about judgment to the people of Israel, he also brought a message of great hope. This message of great hope was about the coming Deliverer, the Messiah, the Savior who would come. But it was also about the Kingdom He would someday create—a new Kingdom of joy, love, and peace where He would rule. *How different is this Kingdom from our world now? How can this be an encouragement to God's people in all times?*

"For behold, I create new heavens and a new earth, and the former things
shall not be remembered or come into mind.

18 *But be glad and rejoice forever in that which I create; for behold, I create*
Jerusalem to be a joy, and her people to be a gladness. 19 *I will rejoice in*
Jerusalem and be glad in my people; no more shall be heard in it the sound
of weeping and the cry of distress.

20 *No more shall there be in it an infant who lives but a few days, or an old*
man who does not fill out his days, for the young man shall die a hundred
years old, and the sinner a hundred years old shall be accursed.

21 *They shall build houses and inhabit them; they shall plant vineyards and*
eat their fruit. 22 *They shall not build and another inhabit; they shall not plant*
and another eat; for like the days of a tree shall the days of my people be, and
my chosen shall long enjoy the work of their hands.

23 *They shall not labor in vain or bear children for calamity, for they shall be*
the offspring of the blessed of the LORD, and their descendants with them.
24 *Before they call I will answer; while they are yet speaking I will hear.*

25 *The wolf and the lamb shall graze together; the lion shall eat straw like the*
ox, and dust shall be the serpent's food. They shall not hurt or destroy in all
my holy mountain," says the LORD. (Isaiah 65:17-25)

C H A P T E R 7 2

TRUE REPENTANCE AND TRUE FAITH

Manasseh Sins and Repents; Josiah Follows Yahweh and Finds the Lost Book of the Law—2 Chronicles 33-35

Blessed are those whose way is blameless, who walk in the law of the LORD! Blessed are those who keep his testimonies, who seek him with their whole heart, (Psalm 119:1-2)

H*ave you ever played or watched a game of tennis?* The ball goes back and forth from side to side until someone misses the ball. And then it starts again. The people of Judah were like that tennis ball. First, they were on the side of worshiping Yahweh, then they were bouncing to idols, then back to Yahweh, and then bouncing over to idols. A lot of the time, the Israelites were just mixing them all together—adding Yahweh to all the idols they were worshiping.

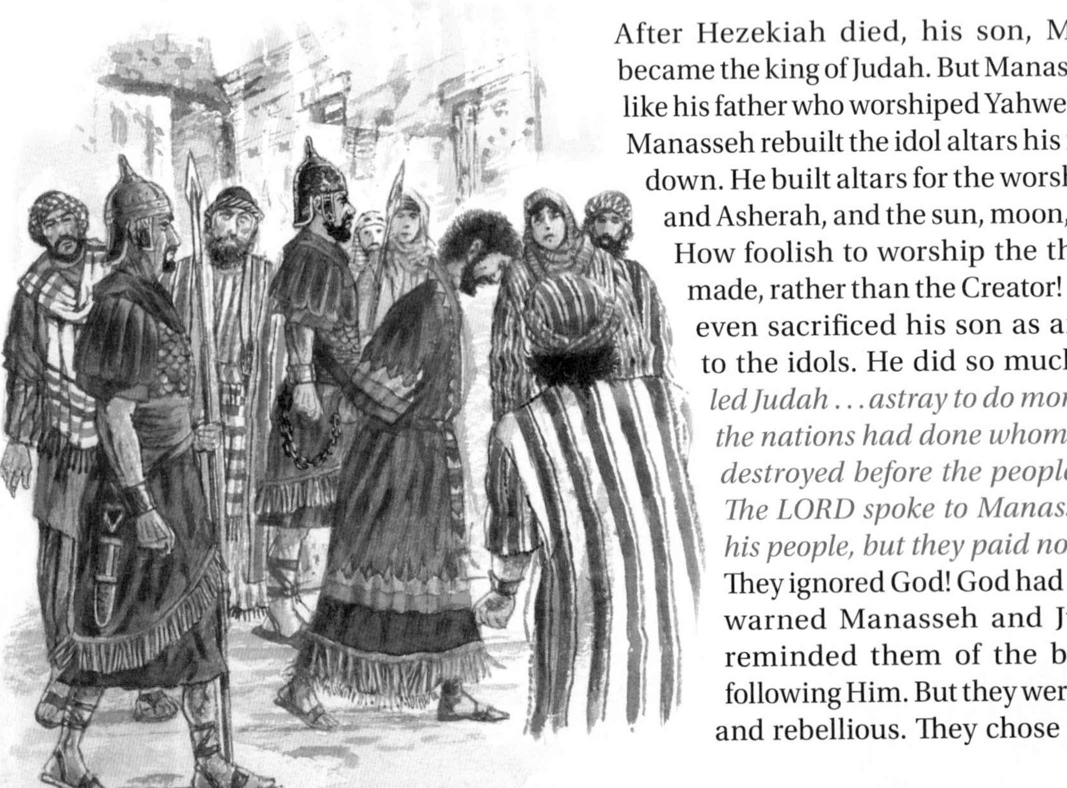

After Hezekiah died, his son, Manasseh, became the king of Judah. But Manasseh wasn't like his father who worshiped Yahweh. Instead, Manasseh rebuilt the idol altars his father tore down. He built altars for the worship of Baal and Asherah, and the sun, moon, and stars. How foolish to worship the things God made, rather than the Creator! Manasseh even sacrificed his son as an offering to the idols. He did so much evil and *led Judah . . . astray to do more evil than the nations had done whom the LORD destroyed before the people of Israel. The LORD spoke to Manasseh and to his people, but they paid no attention.* They ignored God! God had mercifully warned Manasseh and Judah and reminded them of the blessing of following Him. But they were stubborn and rebellious. They chose manmade idols instead of the living God. The gods of the nations were not like Yahweh. The people were afraid of those false gods. They brought sacrifices to keep the gods from being angry. Then they brought more sacrifices so that the gods would give them sunshine, rain, and a good harvest. But **Yahweh is a faithful God who loves His people with steadfast, everlasting love—a God who protects, provides, and works for His people**. Even so, Judah turned away from Yahweh.

So God "brought upon them" the commanders of the Assyrian army, and they captured Manasseh and brought him to Babylon. *And when he was in distress, he entreated [begged] the favor of the LORD his God and humbled himself greatly before the God of his fathers. He prayed to him, and God was moved by his entreaty and heard his plea and brought him again to Jerusalem into his kingdom. Then Manasseh knew that the LORD was God.* God could have ignored Manasseh's prayers, but **God is eager to forgive those who repent.** God's heart toward His people is very tender. He is so eager to bless them. Yahweh, the God of amazing grace, forgave this evil king who deserved God's fierce anger. God disciplines His people to turn them back to Him, and when they repent, He gives them His kindness instead of His wrath.

> *"Behold, blessed is the one whom God reproves; therefore despise not the discipline of the Almighty. For he wounds, but he binds up; he shatters, but his hands heal." (Job 5:17-18)*

When Manasseh returned, he took away the foreign gods and "commanded Judah to serve the LORD, the God of Israel." "He restored the altar of the LORD" and made offerings of thanksgiving and peace to Yahweh. He had truly repented and wanted to serve the LORD. This is a glorious example of God's redeeming grace!

But after Manasseh died, his son Amon ruled Judah. He worshiped idols and served them. *And he did not humble himself before the LORD, as Manasseh had humbled himself, but this Amon incurred guilt more and more.* Finally, his servants plotted against him and put him to death.

The people of Judah then made Josiah, Amon's son, the king. Josiah was only eight years old, yet *he did what was right in the eyes of the LORD, and walked in the ways of David his father; and he did not turn aside to the right hand or to the left . . . In the eighth year of his reign, while he was yet a boy, he began to seek the God of David . . . and in the twelfth year he began to purge Judah and Jerusalem of the high places, the Asherim, and the carved and metal*

images. And they chopped down the altars of the Baals in his presence, and he cut down the incense altars that stood above them. Even at a young age, a person can truly follow God and encourage others to do the same!

Josiah also ordered the repair of the broken, crumbling temple. He had money collected from all around to hire carpenters and builders, and the work began. While they were repairing the temple, they found something very precious. *Do you know what that was?* The priest found the Book of the Law of the LORD. When Josiah heard the words of the Book of the Law, he was so deeply troubled that he tore his clothes. He knew God's fierce anger was upon Judah because the people had not kept the word of the LORD but had disobeyed Him. **God's Word is powerful and accomplishes His purpose.** When Josiah heard God's Word, he wanted to obey God with his whole heart and keep His law. God's Word was the good guide that Josiah needed to lead his people to worship Yahweh and live rightly. God was faithful to Josiah to give him a heart for His Word and the strength to lead His people.

King Josiah called all the elders of Judah and Jerusalem and went to the temple with all those who lived in Jerusalem "and the priests and the Levites, all the people both great and small." He read all the words of the Book of the Covenant to them. Josiah was serious about obeying God and leading his people! Then, Josiah made a promise or covenant to keep God's law "with all his heart and soul." He also asked the people to make the same promise.

Josiah was faithful to keep his promise to God. He kept the Passover and appointed priests to serve the LORD. The celebration was done exactly according to the law that God had given. They kept the Passover and the Feast of Unleavened Bread seven days. *None of the kings of Israel had kept such a Passover as was kept by Josiah* and his people.

Josiah's heart was committed to the LORD, and he had true faith in God. But most of the people were still like that tennis ball, bouncing back and forth. After Josiah died in a battle against Egypt, the rest of the kings of Judah were evil, and the people followed in their evil ways. They were just like the people of Israel, whom Elijah challenged, *"How long will you go limping between two different opinions? If the LORD is God, follow him; but if Baal, then follow him."*

You, too, can be like the people of Judah and Israel—limping between two different opinions. *Will you love this world and the things of this world, or will you love God, His ways, and His Word? Is God's Word hidden away on a shelf or hidden in your heart?*

The law of the LORD is perfect, reviving the soul; the testimony of the LORD is sure, making wise the simple; the precepts of the LORD are right, rejoicing the heart; the commandment of the LORD is pure, enlightening the eyes; the fear of the LORD is clean, enduring forever; the rules of the LORD are true, and righteous altogether. More to be desired are they than gold, even much fine gold; sweeter also than honey and drippings of the honeycomb. Moreover, by them is your servant warned; in keeping them there is great reward. (Psalm 19:7-11)

MAKING YOU WISE FOR SALVATION

What does this chapter tell us about God? Talk about and apply the **biblical truths** in **bold** text.

Salvation Thread: True repentance brings a heart change and obedience to God.

Why is back-and-forth "tennis ball-like" faith not true faith? What is true faith? What are the evidences of true saving faith?

Talk About: *Blessed are those whose way is blameless, who walk in the law of the LORD! Blessed are those who keep his testimonies, who seek him with their whole heart, (Psalm 119:1-2)*

How can your family encourage others to trust the Word of God?

Pray: Praise God for being a forgiving God. Thank Him for His steadfast love and faithfulness. Thank Him for His Word, and ask Him to give you a desire to read and obey His Word.

Think About: *Where do I stand with the LORD? Do I have true faith?*

Memorize: Choose a verse from Psalm 119 to memorize.

C H A P T E R 7 3

A QUESTION AND AN UNEXPECTED ANSWER

Habakkuk Questions God and Determines to Trust Him—Habakkuk

Though the fig tree should not blossom, nor fruit be on the vines, the produce of the olive fail and the fields yield no food, the flock be cut off from the fold and there be no herd in the stalls, yet I will rejoice in the LORD; I will take joy in the God of my salvation. (Habakkuk 3:17-18)

After the death of Josiah, the people of Judah turned away from God again! They truly were like tennis balls bouncing back and forth, "limping between two opinions." In their rebellion, they became more and more evil. Just as God had sent Elijah, Elisha, Hosea, and other prophets to warn Israel, God sent many prophets to warn Judah. The prophets had the worst of news . . . and the best of news. They told the bad news that judgment was coming—news about destruction and captivity. This news did not make the people of

Israel or Judah very happy. In fact, it made them mad! Even though the prophets also told the best of news—news of the coming Savior and King and His glorious Kingdom—the bad news that they had to announce made them very unpopular. *What do you think life was like for the prophets?* They gave warning after warning, but most people did not listen to them. People often hated them for the bad news they brought. They were mistreated—ignored, mocked, hunted down, driven away into the wilderness, threatened with death, thrown in jail, thrown down a well. They lived through times of suffering and much evil. *Do you think it was easy for these men to be God's messengers? Do you think they always understood what God was doing and why He was doing it? How do you think they could have felt?*

One man who shows us how difficult it was to be a prophet was Habakkuk. Habakkuk lived through the good reforms, or changes, King Josiah made in Judah. But then he saw the evil that followed the reign of Josiah. Habakkuk knew judgment was coming. He knew that the people of Judah could not continue in their evil ways, and he called out to God.

> *O LORD, how long shall I cry for help, and you will not hear? Or cry to you "Violence!" and you will not save? Why do you make me see iniquity [wickedness], and why do you idly look at wrong? (Habakkuk 1:2-3a)*

Habakkuk could not understand why God didn't *do* something. Why was God letting evil continue? But God *was* doing something. He was working out His plan for His people and the nations. God answered Habakkuk, but the answer God gave Habakkuk didn't make sense to Habakkuk. Judah needed to be punished, but God would use a nation *even more evil* than Judah to do it! God was sending the Babylonians to conquer Judah. Babylon deserved punishment even more than Judah did! Habakkuk couldn't understand the ways of God. Why would God use the horribly evil nation of Babylon to stop the evil in Judah? **God is sovereign—He rules over all, and all His judgments are always right.** Habakkuk knew he had to trust God—even if he didn't understand what God was doing.

Habakkuk only saw a little part of God's bigger plan. It is like looking at one piece of a puzzle. One piece alone doesn't look like much. It might even look a bit strange. But the piece is part of a bigger picture, and the maker of the puzzle knows what the picture looks like when all the pieces are put together. God had a bigger plan than the "right now" puzzle piece. He had a big picture plan for the future—a plan that would be for a later time, a time when *the earth will be filled with the knowledge of the glory of the LORD as the waters cover the sea.*

God would send judgment on Judah through evil Babylon. But God would "preserve a remnant"—He would save a group of His people. And God would also remember the wickedness of Babylon. Babylon's turn would come. God would punish Babylon for its evil and completely wipe it out. There would be no remnant. Their own evil and pride would cause their complete destruction. But this would not happen soon. It would take years to see this happen—but God would not forget. **God is always just.**

Habakkuk realized that he needed to think beyond "right now." He needed to trust that, in God's time, God would do what is right and bring justice. God would surely punish Babylon and the other evil nations. Habakkuk just needed to wait and be patient, trusting that God knew what to do and when to do it. **God is trustworthy—He can be trusted.**

Habakkuk knew that the coming judgment on Judah would be severe. That was a fearful thing to him: *I hear, and my body trembles; my lips quiver at the sound; rottenness enters into my bones; my legs tremble beneath me.* But he would not be angry with God or complain about God's plan: *Yet I will quietly wait for the day of trouble to come upon people who invade us.* He trusted that **God's justice is sure and right**. So Habakkuk made a decision, or a commitment. He would not complain about what was going to happen. He would trust God's wisdom, justice, and goodness. Not only would he trust God, but he would also *praise* God!

> *Though the fig tree should not blossom, nor fruit be on the vines, the produce of the olive fail and the fields yield no food, the flock be cut off from the fold and there be no herd in the stalls, yet I will rejoice in the LORD;* ***I will take joy in the God of my salvation. GOD, the Lord, is my strength;*** *he makes my feet like the deer's; he makes me tread on my high places. (Habakkuk 3:17-19a)*

No matter what the situation—even if none of the crops would grow, all the sheep and cattle were lost, and there was great famine—Habakkuk would trust God. He would rejoice in **Yahweh, the self-sufficient, sovereign, almighty, eternal, unchanging God**. He would take joy in **Adonai,** his **Lord and Master**. He would find his strength in trusting God. He would not only trust God, but he would be joyful in God's good, big-picture plan. God would make him spiritually strong—like the feet of a deer, which could safely leap up to high places.

Like Habakkuk, there are times when we don't understand why things are the way they are. We are looking at a little puzzle piece of our life, and it doesn't look quite right. But we are only seeing a tiny piece, not the big picture. We don't see how all the pieces fit together to make a beautiful picture. We don't see that the dark pieces are necessary and belong in the picture. But God sees the whole picture and is placing each piece very carefully and wisely.

Right now, something difficult might be happening in your life. Perhaps someone you love is sick, or you did poorly on a test, or your parents won't let you have a pet, or your dad doesn't have a job. You might think that the piece of life you have right now is strange looking or has the wrong shape. Maybe it doesn't seem like it fits in the puzzle. Or maybe it looks like it belongs to a different puzzle. It just looks wrong. But when God puts the whole puzzle together, that piece will be just right and will fit perfectly into the bigger picture. You can't see that big picture right now. But you do know that **God is Yahweh, the self-sufficient, sovereign, almighty, eternal, unchanging God,** and **He can be trusted.** You do know that **God is Adonai**, your **Lord and Master**. *Will you trust Him with today's puzzle piece? Do you trust that God is in control and is working out His good purposes the right way and in the right time? Will you be happy in God in the good times and in the hard times? Will you bow to Adonai and say, "Whatever you do is right and good. I will obey and trust you"?*

"...the righteous shall live by his faith." (Habakkuk 2:4b)

MAKING YOU WISE FOR SALVATION

What does this chapter tell us about God? Talk about and apply the **biblical truths** in **bold** text.

Salvation Thread: God is just and can be trusted to judge evil in His right way and timing. God will surely restore His people. God has all things under His control.

Ask Mom and Dad about a hard time in their lives. How can they see now that God had everything under control, and that His plan was good and right? Why can God always be trusted?

Talk About: *"...the righteous shall live by his faith." (Habakkuk 2:4b)*

What injustices do you see in this world? *How does Habakkuk help you to trust God with these situations?*

Pray: Thank God that He is a God of justice. Thank Him that He can always be trusted. Ask Him to give you the faith to trust Him no matter what the circumstances. Pray about any difficulty your family or someone you know is going through. Pray for faith to trust God.

Think About: Sometimes it is a battle to trust God. How can you prepare to fight that battle?

CHAPTER 74

WARNINGS AND WORDS OF HOPE

Jeremiah Preaches, but the People Refuse to Repent—2 Kings 24; Jeremiah 36

O LORD, do not your eyes look for truth? You have struck them down, but they felt no anguish; you have consumed them, but they refused to take correction. They have made their faces harder than rock; they have refused to repent. (Jeremiah 5:3)

The kingdom of Judah was coming to an end. God had sent prophet after prophet to warn His people that judgment was coming if they did not repent. But the people of Judah ignored God's warning. All of the last four kings of Judah were evil. Jehoahaz, Josiah's son, only reigned three months. Then Pharaoh came from Egypt and took him away in chains. Pharaoh appointed Jehoiakim, Jehoahaz's brother, as king, and forced Judah to pay him large amounts of silver and gold.

None of this was a surprise to God. **God is never surprised. He knows all things and controls all things.** God had been warning Judah since the time of Josiah through a priest and prophet named Jeremiah. When God called Jeremiah to bring His message to His people, He told Jeremiah, *"Before I formed you in the womb I knew you, and before you were born I consecrated [set apart] you; I appointed you a prophet to the nations."* God had chosen Jeremiah to warn His rebellious people. God's people had broken their covenant with God. But **God is faithful to His covenant and loves His people with an everlasting love**. So He gave the prophets messages of hope and promises of future blessing.

God told Jeremiah about the punishment He was sending to the people of Judah. Jeremiah spoke God's words, and a man named Baruch wrote them on a scroll. Judgment was coming because of sin. The people of Judah were not kind and did not protect the rights of the poor. They did not judge fairly. They were not honest in buying and selling things. They were greedy and cheated people. They did not respect God's Word and were not sorry for their sin. Instead, they were stubborn and rebellious. They would steal, murder, commit adultery, worship false gods . . . and then pretend to worship God in the temple.

If they would turn away from their sin, God would show them mercy. But if they didn't repent, God would send Babylon to punish them. They would be taken away from their own country to live in exile for seventy years. Jerusalem would be a "heap of ruins." The cities of Judah would be deserted (empty), and crops would not grow on the land. But after seventy years, God would bring them back to their land. *Do you think hearing these punishments would cause the people to turn away from their sin?*

Jeremiah wanted the people to repent and escape punishment. So Jeremiah told Baruch to read the scroll in the temple for *"It may be that their plea for mercy will come before the LORD, and that every one will turn from his evil way, for great is the anger and wrath that the LORD has pronounced against this people."* When Baruch read the LORD's words from Jeremiah's scroll to the king's officials they became very afraid. The officials told Baruch and Jeremiah to hide while they brought the scroll to Jehoiakim. While they read the scroll to the king, he was warming himself by the fire. After every few sections of the scroll were read, the king cut them off and threw them in the fire! He was burning God's Word! How could he show *such disrespect* for God and His warning? He ignored his advisors when they warned him not to burn the scroll. Instead, he burned the whole scroll! Then he sent men to find Baruch and Jeremiah, "but the LORD hid them."

Jehoiakim and the people of Judah had heard the Word of God and had rejected it. But God did not give up on them. He continued to call His people to repentance, and to warn them of the terrible things to come. God told Jeremiah to take another scroll and write down the words again. Once again, Jeremiah spoke, and Baruch wrote down the words. This time the scroll included something new—the judgment God would bring on Jehoiakim and his offspring.

But the people of Judah ignored all of God's warnings. So God sent Nebuchadnezzar, the king of Babylon to defeat Pharaoh. Then Nebuchadnezzar attacked Jerusalem, and Jehoiakim surrendered. Now instead of paying silver and gold to Pharaoh, Jehoiakim had to pay silver and gold to Nebuchadnezzar. Nebuchadnezzar also took some of the smartest young men from each city in Judah as captives and brought them to Babylon.[1]

Eventually, Jehoiakim grew tired of paying money to Babylon. He wasn't going to do it anymore! *What do you think Nebuchadnezzar thought of that?* Nebuchadnezzar sent groups of soldiers against Judah. They stole what they could find. They even took some of the gold and silver objects from the temple and brought them to Babylon. Nebuchadnezzar took these holy things from the temple of Yahweh and put them in the temple of his false god! How awful! Then Babylon laid siege to Jerusalem.

After Jehoiakim died, his son Jehoiachin[2] became king. Jehoiachin only ruled for three months. Then Nebuchadnezzar defeated him. The king of Babylon "carried off all the treasures of the house of the LORD and the treasures of the king's house." Then he gathered all the people who were royalty, wealthy, educated, or skilled—the king and his family, the leaders, builders, blacksmiths, carpenters, and soldiers—and took them to Babylon. *None remained except the poorest people of the land.* Truly, this was a day of great sadness. God's people had refused to repent, ignored His warnings, and mocked His prophets. And now they were being taken away from their land.

But the Babylonians did not spread the people out around their kingdom like the Assyrians did to the people of the Northern Kingdom. They sent all the captured people of Judah, the "Judeans" or "Jews," to Babylon. Because the Jews stayed together in one place, they kept their religion, their Jewish traditions, and their Jewish identity. Jeremiah wrote letters to the people of Judah who were in exile in Babylon. He encouraged them to repent and gave them words of instruction and hope.

> *"Thus says the LORD of hosts, the God of Israel, to all the exiles whom I have sent into exile from Jerusalem to Babylon: Build houses and live in them; plant gardens and eat their produce. Take wives and have sons and daughters; take wives for your sons, and give your daughters in marriage, that they may bear sons and daughters; multiply there, and do not*

decrease. But seek the welfare of the city where I have sent you into exile, and pray to the LORD on its behalf, for in its welfare you will find your welfare . . . For thus says the LORD: When seventy years are completed for Babylon, I will visit you, and I will fulfill to you my promise and bring you back to this place. For I know the plans I have for you, declares the LORD, plans for welfare [good] and not for evil, to give you a future and a hope. Then you will call upon me and come and pray to me, and I will hear you. (Jeremiah 29:4-7, 10-12)

After seventy years in exile, God would bring his people back to their land. He would forgive their sin and send them a Deliverer. He would *raise up for David a righteous Branch, and he shall reign as king and deal wisely, and shall execute justice and righteousness in the land.* **God is gracious and merciful. He is faithful to His covenant and His people.**

Jeremiah's message to return to the LORD, obey His good commands, and delight in God is a message that everyone needs to hear. *Thus says the LORD: "Stand by the roads, and look, and ask for the ancient paths, where the good way is; and walk in it, and find rest for your souls."*

There are two ways you can respond to this good teaching. You can respond like Judah, who said, *"We will not walk in it,"* and bring great sorrow on yourself and destruction to your soul. Or you can seek God—you can open your heart to His Word, pray that He will give you a heart to know Him and follow Him, and put Him first in your life. *How will you respond to Jeremiah's message and God's call to know Him?*

"... you will call upon me and come and pray to me, and I will hear you. You will seek me and find me when you seek me with all your heart." (Jeremiah 29:12–13)

MAKING YOU WISE FOR SALVATION

What does this chapter tell us about God? Talk about and apply the **biblical truths** in **bold** text.

Salvation Thread: God gives many warnings before He brings punishment. There is always hope of restoration with God.

How can you seek after God with your whole heart?

Talk About: *"... you will call upon me and come and pray to me, and I will hear you. You will seek me and find me when you seek me with all your heart." (Jeremiah 29:12–13)*

As you are able, look at the blessings for obedience and the curses for disobedience in the covenant between God and Israel (Deuteronomy 28). Did Israel keep the covenant? Did God keep the covenant? Was God's judgment right?

Why would God love such a rebellious people?

Pray: Thank God for His tender love and forgiveness. Ask Him to give you a heart to seek after Him with all your might.

Think About: *Is God number one in my life, or do other things crowd Him out?*

1. Included among the captives were Daniel, Hananiah (Shadrach), Mishael (Meshach), and Azariah (Abednego).
2. He was also known as Jeconiah.

CHAPTER 75

TOTAL DESTRUCTION, YET HOPE REMAINS

The Destruction of Jerusalem and the Promise of God —2 Kings 25; Jeremiah 37-39

The LORD, the God of their fathers, sent persistently to them by his messengers, because he had compassion on his people and on his dwelling place. But they kept mocking the messengers of God, despising his words and scoffing at his prophets, until the wrath of the LORD rose against his people, until there was no remedy. (2 Chronicles 36:15-16)

H*ave you ever heard the saying, "A picture is worth a thousand words"?* It means that it is sometimes easier to understand something when you see a picture of it than if you just hear about it. Jeremiah spoke thousands of words to the people of Judah, but Jeremiah and other prophets also gave the people many pictures to understand God's message. These pictures were given to them by God, who gave His people every chance to understand the coming judgment and to repent.

Jeremiah took a new cloth and hid it in a pile of rocks by the river. Later, he dug out the cloth, and it was ruined. God warned the people that, *"This evil people, who refuse to hear my words, who stubbornly follow their own heart and have gone after other gods to serve them and worship them, shall be like this loincloth, which is good for nothing."* Another time, Jeremiah took a flask, or bottle. He showed it to the leaders and priests and said, *"Thus says the LORD of hosts, the God of Israel: Behold, I am bringing such disaster upon this place that the ears of everyone who hears of it will tingle. Because the people have forsaken me . . ."* Then Jeremiah broke the bottle and continued, *"So I will break this people and this city, as one breaks a potter's vessel, so that it can never be mended."* Jeremiah gave many other pictures, too—but the people still refused to repent.

After Nebuchadnezzar defeated Jerusalem and took the captives, he needed someone to rule Jerusalem and the poorest Jews. So he made Jehoichin's uncle the king in Jerusalem and changed his name to Zedekiah. Zedekiah thought that, with the help of Egypt, he could defeat Babylon and get rid of Nebuchadnezzar's rule. But Jeremiah warned Zedekiah that he was fooling himself. His plot would fail. God had said that the Babylonians would not go away but would someday burn Jerusalem. The important leaders or officials were so angry with Jeremiah that they beat him and threw him in jail. Zedekiah and his leaders refused to accept Jeremiah's warning, and they rebelled against the king of Babylon.

Zedekiah questioned Jeremiah again, and once again Jeremiah told him, *"You shall be delivered into the hand of the king of Babylon."* Jeremiah warned the people that they would die *"by the sword, by famine, and by pestilence"* (disease) if they fought the Babylonians. This sounded horrible! But there was another choice—a better choice. If they surrendered, they would live. Oh, this made the leaders mad! They did not like Jeremiah's message—but the message was a warning from God. They were not really rejecting Jeremiah; they were rejecting Yahweh. They were so mad at Jeremiah that they threw Jeremiah into a deep muddy well. They thought that they had gotten rid of Jeremiah and his bad news. They thought there was no way for Jeremiah to escape. But a friend rescued Jeremiah.

So Jeremiah was back. And once again, Zedekiah asked Jeremiah what would happen. *Did he think the answer would change?* God had spoken His warning. *What two choices did Zedekiah have?* Jeremiah told him the same thing *again* starting with. *"Thus says the LORD, the God of hosts, the God of Israel . . ."* These were not Jeremiah's words. The warning was from God—the LORD, the God of hosts, the God of Israel. Jeremiah could not have been more clear that God was telling them to give up without a fight! **Only God knows what will happen in the future. Only God can control the future.** He was warning His people, but they would not listen.

Then the king of Babylon marched against Jerusalem and laid siege to the city. Just as God had said, the Babylonians conquered Jerusalem in eighteen months. Nebuchadnezzar killed Zedekiah's sons in front of him. Then he *"put out the eyes of Zedekiah and bound him in chains to take him to Babylon."* The Babylonians burned the king's house, the other houses, and the temple. They broke down the walls of Jerusalem. Then they took most of the people left in the city away into exile to Babylon. Nebuchadnezzar left only some of the very poorest people in Judah.

The land was now deserted. Judgment had come. Everything happened exactly as God had said it would. **God's Word is always true**. Tragically, the Southern Kingdom of Judah had come to a bitter end. It was such a long and terrible fall from the greatness of God's people under King David to an exiled people, leaving broken walls and ashes. Judah lasted more than a hundred years longer than the Northern Kingdom of Israel, but Judah's wickedness was even greater. **Sin is a great offense to God. God is a God of justice, and His judgments are sure and severe. God is holy**—both utterly different from anything or anyone and unique in all ways, and perfect in purity and righteousness.

But God protected Jeremiah, just as He had promised him. Jeremiah was a faithful prophet preaching to a people who would not listen, would not turn from evil, and would not turn back to God. Jeremiah is called "the weeping prophet." *Why do you think he is called the weeping prophet?* Jeremiah predicted many sorrows and saw much disaster and suffering. He saw the people reject God and stubbornly refuse to repent. Jeremiah wept over the sinfulness of Judah and the destruction of the temple and Jerusalem.

But Jeremiah also had great hope, for **God is faithful, merciful, and gracious. He is a covenant-keeping God who loves His people with an everlasting love and will never abandon His people.** Someday, God would raise up from the line of David a Fountain of Living Waters, a Great Physician, a Good Shepherd, a Righteous Branch, a Redeemer, the LORD is Our Righteousness. He would make a new covenant with His people and bring them back to their land.

> *"Behold, the days are coming, declares the LORD, when I will make a new covenant with the house of Israel and the house of Judah, not like the covenant that I made with their fathers on the day when I took them by the hand to bring them out of the land of Egypt, my covenant that they broke, though I was their husband, declares the LORD. For this is the covenant that I will make with the house of Israel after those days, declares the LORD: I will put my law within them, and I will write it on their hearts. And I will be their God, and they shall be my people. And no longer shall each one teach his neighbor and each his brother, saying, 'Know the LORD,' for they shall all know me, from the least of them to the greatest, declares the LORD. For I will forgive their iniquity, and I will remember their sin no more." (Jeremiah 31:31-34)*
>
> *"Behold, I will gather them from all the countries to which I drove them in my anger and my wrath and in great indignation. I will bring them back to this place, and I will make them dwell in safety. And they shall be my people, and I will be their God. I will*

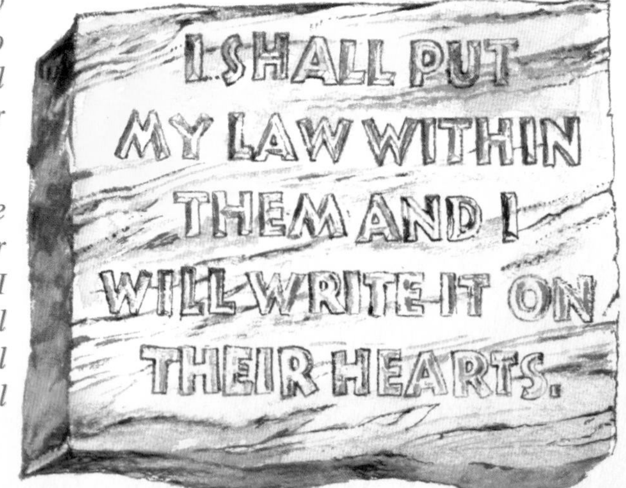

give them one heart and one way, that they may fear me forever, for their own good and the good of their children after them. I will make with them an everlasting covenant, that I will not turn away from doing good to them. And I will put the fear of me in their hearts, that they may not turn from me. I will rejoice in doing them good, and I will plant them in this land in faithfulness, with all my heart and all my soul." (Jeremiah 32:37-41)

God would someday judge Babylon and the other nations for their wickedness, but He would restore His people. He would give them a new heart and write His law on their hearts. He would give them a love for His Word and His ways! What a wonderful promise to undeserving people! *Why is there hope for undeserving sinners?*

But this I call to mind, and therefore I have hope: The steadfast love of the LORD never ceases; his mercies never come to an end; they are new every morning; great is your faithfulness. "The LORD is my portion," says my soul, "therefore I will hope in him." (Lamentations 3:21-24)

MAKING YOU WISE FOR SALVATION

What does this chapter tell us about God? Talk about and apply the **biblical truths** in **bold** text.

Salvation Thread: Sinners need a new heart that only God can give. God promised to make a new covenant to replace the old covenant.

Why did God's people need "new" hearts? What was the problem with their "old" hearts?

Discuss Jeremiah 31:31-34. Why would God call Himself Israel's husband? What is the new covenant God is talking about? How is it different from the old covenant? Why is this good news?

Talk About: *But this I call to mind, and therefore I have hope: The steadfast love of the LORD never ceases; his mercies never come to an end; they are new every morning; great is your faithfulness. "The LORD is my portion," says my soul, "therefore I will hope in him." (Lamentations 3:21-24)*

Continue to look at the blessings for obedience and the curses for disobedience in the covenant between God and Israel (Deuteronomy 28). Did Israel keep the covenant? Did God keep the covenant? Was God's judgment right and necessary? Why?

Pray: Praise God for His heart for His people and His everlasting love. Confess your sin to Him and ask for His forgiveness.

Think About: *Why is there always a reason for Christians to have hope?*

CHAPTER 76

GOD SCATTERS HIS PEOPLE, BUT WILL GATHER THEM BACK

Ezekiel Gives His Prophetic Message to the Exiles—Ezekiel

How lonely sits the city that was full of people! How like a widow has she become, she who was great among the nations! She who was a princess among the provinces has become a slave. (Lamentations 1:1)

Do you remember how many times Babylon took captives from Judah into exile? There were three times when different groups of people were taken away from Judah to Babylon. When Jehoiakim decided not to make payments to Babylon, Nebuchadnezzar took the smartest young men from different cities in Judah and brought them to Babylon—smart young men like Daniel, Hananiah, Mishael, and Azariah. After Nebuchadnezzar defeated Jehoiachin and carried off many of the treasures from the temple and the king's palace, he took the "upper class"—the people who were royalty, wealthy, educated, or skilled—including a priest named Ezekiel. So Ezekiel left Judah before Jerusalem was destroyed—before the houses, palace, and temple were burned and the walls broken down. The third time Nebuchadnezzar took captives was after the city was destroyed.

It was not a mistake that Ezekiel was taken in the second group of exiles. It was God's sovereign plan, and His kindness to the people in exile. The "Judeans" or "Jews" in Babylon needed a priest and a prophet. Their God had not abandoned or left them—He gave them a messenger of truth, even in Babylon. Ezekiel was only twenty-five years old when he was taken captive. He lived in a community of ten thousand Judean exiles in Babylon. Sadly, even after being taken captive, most of the Jews did not return to the LORD but continued to worship idols.

After being in Babylon five years, God gave Ezekiel a vision. It was a strange vision of a storm cloud with four strange living creatures in it. Above the living creatures was a throne with brightness all around it. The Bible tells us that it was *"the appearance of the likeness of the glory of the LORD."* When Ezekiel saw it, he fell on his face. Then he heard the voice of God, *"Son of man, I send you to the people of Israel, to nations of rebels, who have rebelled against me."* God was calling Ezekiel to be a prophet to His people in exile. Ezekiel reminded the Jews that they had broken their covenant with Yahweh. They were captives in Babylon because of their sin. Before they could have any hope of returning home, they must turn back to God.

Seven days later, God spoke to Ezekiel again, *"Son of man, I have made you a watchman for the house of Israel. Whenever you hear a word from my mouth, you shall give them warning from me."* Ezekiel's job was to warn the people to turn from their sin in order to save their lives. God called Ezekiel to be faithful in speaking His word, but it was not Ezekiel's fault if the people did not listen to him.

God gave Ezekiel His words to speak to the exiles. But He also gave Ezekiel messages to act out. *Why would God use other ways of giving His message?* Ezekiel made a model of Jerusalem under siege. The model had a ramp built against the wall of the city so the enemy could attack it. Ezekiel was giving the Jews a picture of what would happen to Jerusalem. Nebuchadnezzar would lay siege to the city. God would not listen to their cries for deliverance because of their sin. He was warning the Jews of the total destruction of Jerusalem, the city they loved. Ezekiel gave the people all kinds of strange signs, acting out God's judgment. These things were sad and frightening to hear! **Sin is destructive and brings great sadness.** Ezekiel even moved his stuff out of his house to show that more of the Jews would be taken captive after the destruction of Jerusalem. They would leave their home and live in exile, as refugees, in Babylon.

God gave Ezekiel another vision—a vision of His glory leaving the temple and going toward Babylon. Judah's sin and hard-hearted rebellion had caused God to leave the temple. The temple would be destroyed. But God was with His people, even in Babylon. **God is faithful and will not abandon or forget His people.** God sent His people into exile because of their sin, but He also made a wonderful promise to them:

"Therefore say, 'Thus says the Lord GOD: I will gather you from the peoples and assemble you out of the countries where you have been scattered, and I will give you the land of Israel.' And when they come there, they will remove from it all its detestable things and all its abominations. And I will give them one heart, and a new spirit I will put within them. I will remove the heart of stone from their flesh and give them a heart of flesh, that they may walk in my statutes and keep my rules and obey them. And they shall be my people, and I will be their God." (Ezekiel 11:17-20)

What a wonderful promise of God's mercy to His undeserving people! Judah was compared to a burned useless vine, a rebellious bride, and a dangerous lion taken captive. God would bring total destruction to Judah. After that, He would bring judgment on the nations around Israel. But God would not abandon His people.

Judgment would be followed by hope for God's people. God would restore Israel: *"Behold, I, I myself will search for my sheep . . . As a shepherd seeks out his flock . . . that have been scattered, so I will seek out my sheep, and I will rescue them from all the places where they have been scattered . . . . And [I will] bring them into their own land . . . I will feed them with good pasture . . . I myself will be the shepherd of my sheep . . . I will make with them a covenant of peace . . . and I will send down the showers in their season; they shall be showers of blessing . . . And they shall know that I am the LORD their God . . . It is not for your sake, O house of Israel, that I am about to act, but for the sake of my holy name, which you have profaned among the nations . . . And I will vindicate the holiness of my great name . . . And the nations will know that I am the LORD."* **What tender love God has for His people, and what great jealousy He has for His name. God will protect His name and His reputation.**

God gave Ezekiel still another strange vision of what He would do. In this vision, God brought Ezekiel to a valley of dry, dead bones. *Do you know what He asked Ezekiel?* He asked Ezekiel if the bones could live again. Then God gave Ezekiel a prophecy that the dry bones would live again, and skin would cover them, and breath would come into the bodies! *What did this vision mean?*

> *Then he said to me, "Son of man, these bones are the whole house of Israel. Behold, they say, 'Our bones are dried up, and our hope is lost; we are indeed cut off.' Therefore prophesy, and say to them, Thus says the Lord GOD: Behold, I will open your graves and raise you from your graves, O my people. And I will bring you into the land of Israel. And you shall know that I am the LORD, when I open your graves, and raise you from your graves, O my people. And I will put my Spirit within you, and you shall live, and I will place you in your own land. Then you shall know that I am the LORD; I have spoken, and I will do it, declares the LORD." (Ezekiel 37:11-14)*

God would raise up a new David, a future King who would change His people. He would **give them a new heart and put His Spirit in them**. There would be hope, not just for Israel but also for all nations. Once and for all, God would destroy evil. There will be a new temple and a new city in a new world. God will one day restore all creation, and God Himself will dwell with man again! **God's glorious promise of a future restored Kingdom is sure!**

Do you look forward to God's coming Kingdom—where there is no evil, and love and peace reign? Do you look forward to being in God's presence? Do you pray for that day when all things will be made new and all evil will be destroyed?

"My dwelling place shall be with them, and I will be their God, and they shall be my people." (Ezekiel 37:27)

MAKING YOU WISE FOR SALVATION

What does this chapter tell us about God? Talk about and apply the **biblical truths** in **bold** text.

Salvation Thread: God promised to raise up a future King who would change the hearts of man. He will restore all creation and dwell with man again in a new world.

Are you amazed at God's faithfulness to His people? Why would God show such faithfulness to His people?

Talk About: *"And I will give them one heart, and a new spirit I will put within them. I will remove the heart of stone from their flesh and give them a heart of flesh, that they may walk in my statutes and keep my rules and obey them. And they shall be my people, and I will be their God." (Ezekiel 11:19-20)*

What will a world without sin look like?

Pray: Praise God for the greatness of His name! Thank Him for His promise to make all things new someday. Confess any hard-heartedness or stubbornness to God.

Think About: *Do I have a heart of flesh, or a heart of stone? How do I know this?*

CHAPTER 77

STANDING STRONG, EVEN IN BABYLON

Daniel Determines to Honor God—Daniel 1-2

..."Blessed be the name of God forever and ever, to whom belong wisdom and might." (Daniel 2:20b)

W*as Babylon a city or a country?* If you said both, you are right. Babylon was the name of a powerful but evil kingdom. And Babylon was also the name of a city within the kingdom of Babylon. The city had palaces, temples, walls, bridges, and gardens. It was a beautiful city, but it was full of idol worship and much wickedness.

When Nebuchadnezzar brought his first captives to Babylon, he commanded Ashpenaz his servant *to bring some of the people of Israel, both of the royal family and of the nobility, youths without blemish, of good appearance and skillful in all wisdom, endowed with knowledge, understanding learning, and competent to stand in the king's palace, and to teach them the literature and language of the Chaldeans [Babylonians].* For three years, the Babylonians would teach them in the city of Babylon. They would give the captives the same food and wine as the king. Then they would bring the captives to the king to serve him.

One of these captives was Daniel, a young man from the royal line of David. He was only sixteen when he was captured, along with his friends Hananiah, Mishael, and Azariah. When they were brought to his palace, King Nebuchadnezzar changed their names. *Why do you think he did this?*

Nebuchadnezzar wanted these young men to forget their God and their Israelite culture. He wanted them to be like the Babylonians. All four of these young men worshiped Yahweh, and their names honored God. Daniel means, "**God is my Judge**." Hananiah means, "**Yahweh is gracious**." Mishael means, "**who is what God is?**" showing that **there is no person or no god like the one true God**. And Azariah means, "**Yahweh has helped**."[1] But now, they were given Babylonian names—Belteshazzar, Shadrach, Meshach, and Abednego. These new names were meant to honor the gods of the Babylonians. Babylon would wipe out any memory of Yahweh, or so Nebuchadnezzar thought.

But Daniel resolved that he would not defile himself with the king's food, or with the wine that he drank. Do you know what "resolved" means? It means he was determined. He was strong in his decision. He would not change his mind. Daniel did not want to eat or drink the king's food and wine because some of the food was forbidden or not allowed in the law of Moses—it would be "unclean." Daniel did not want to do anything that would displease His God or disobey His laws. He was determined to be faithful to Yahweh.

God honors those who honor Him, and *God gave Daniel favor and compassion in the sight of [Ashpenaz].* But Ashpenaz, Nebuchadnezzar's servant, was a little worried. What if the health of Daniel and his friends became worse than the health of the others who did eat the king's food? The king would be angry with him. So Daniel suggested they do a trial or test. For ten days, they would eat vegetables and drink water. After ten days, Daniel and his friends were healthier than the other young men were! So the servant continued to give them vegetables and water. Daniel, Hananiah, Mishael, and Azariah honored God, and God blessed them.

> *As for these four youths, God gave them learning and skill in all literature and wisdom, and Daniel had understanding in all visions and dreams. At the end of the time, when the king had commanded that they should be brought in . . . the king spoke with them, and among all of them none was found like Daniel, Hananiah, Mishael, and Azariah. Therefore they stood before the king. And in every matter of wisdom and understanding about which the king inquired of them, he found them ten times better than all the magicians and enchanters that were in all his kingdom. (Daniel 1:17-20)*

One night, Nebuchadnezzar had a very troubling dream. The Babylonians believed dreams were messages from their gods. So this dream was important to Nebuchadnezzar. He called his magicians, enchanters, sorcerers—his "wise men"—who were priests of the false gods. These men said they knew the future. Nebuchadnezzar asked them to tell him his dream and what it meant. If they couldn't do it, they would be killed. If they could do it, they would receive great rewards and honor. His "wise men" didn't think this was fair! If Nebuchadnezzar told them the dream, they would tell him what it meant. But they couldn't tell him *what* he dreamed. No one could do what the king asked! They said that only the gods would know this! Nebuchadnezzar was so angry that he commanded that *"all the wise men of Babylon be destroyed."*

When Daniel found out what happened, he asked to meet with the king. He would explain or interpret the dream for the king. Then Daniel asked Hananiah, Mishael, and Azariah to *seek mercy from the God of heaven concerning this mystery.* The king's dream and its meaning was a mystery—a mystery known only to the one true God. Daniel couldn't possibly know the dream and its meaning. But God did—**nothing is hidden from God**. And Daniel asked God to be merciful and show him what no man can know on his own. Yahweh was faithful to Daniel. He showed Daniel the mystery in a dream or vision. *What do you think Daniel did then?* The Bible tells us that Daniel praised the God of heaven.

> *..."Blessed be the name of God forever and ever,* ***to whom belong wisdom and might. He changes times and seasons; he removes kings and sets up kings****; he*

gives wisdom to the wise and knowledge to those who have understanding; he reveals deep and hidden things; he knows what is in the darkness, and the ***light dwells with him****. To you, O God of my fathers, I give thanks and praise, for you have given me wisdom and might, and have now made known to me what we asked of you, for you have made known to us the king's matter." (Daniel 2:20-23)*

Though Daniel was just a young man, he was very strong in faith. He determined to honor God, even though he was far from home in a place where God was not honored. God was pleased with Daniel's faith and trust in Him. Even though Nebuchadnezzar had changed Daniel's name, he could not change Daniel's faith in his God.

God loves it when we depend on Him. *Do you want to have a faith like Daniel? Do you want to stand firm, trusting God's Word even when those around you think it is foolish? Will you honor God no matter what may happen to you?*

In the way of your testimonies I delight as much as in all riches. I will meditate on your precepts and fix my eyes on your ways. I will delight in your statutes; I will not forget your word. (Psalm 119:14-16)

MAKING YOU WISE FOR SALVATION

What does this chapter tell us about God? Talk about and apply the **biblical truths** in **bold** text.

Salvation Thread: God is wise and powerful. He knows all things and is sovereign over all things. He honors those who have faith in Him.

Why couldn't Daniel just eat the king's food? (Make sure your child understands the danger of compromising, and how one step of disobedience and faithlessness can lead to another.)

Talk About: *In the way of your testimonies I delight as much as in all riches. I will meditate on your precepts and fix my eyes on your ways. I will delight in your statutes; I will not forget your word. (Psalm 119:14-16)*

What does dependence on God look like? What does dependence on yourself look like?

Pray: Praise God for His sovereign control over all things. Praise Him for being all-knowing. Thank Him for hearing the prayers of His people.

Think About: "*... those who honor me I will honor, and those who despise me shall be lightly esteemed." (1 Samuel 2:30b)*

1. S. R. Miller. *Vol. 18: Daniel. The New American Commentary (64).* (Nashville, Tenn.: Broadman & Holman Publishers, 1994).

CHAPTER 78

THERE IS A GOD IN HEAVEN

God Reveals the Future to Daniel through Nebuchadnezzar's Dream—Daniel 2

..."Truly, your God is God of gods and Lord of kings, and a revealer of mysteries, for you have been able to reveal this mystery." (Daniel 2:47)

D*o you know what will happen next year—what you will do on your next birthday, what the biggest news story will be?* No one knows the future. No one but God. **God knows everything that will happen because He is sovereign—He rules over all things.** Nebuchadnezzar's dream was about what would happen in the future—the future only God knew, and only God could make happen. To prove He is God, God showed Daniel Nebuchadnezzar's dream and its meaning.

> *Daniel answered the king and said, "No wise men, enchanters, magicians, or astrologers can show to the king the mystery that the king has asked, but there is a God in heaven who reveals mysteries, and he has made known to King Nebuchadnezzar what will be in the latter days." (Daniel 2:27-28a)*

Then Daniel told Nebuchadnezzar what he saw in his dream. The dream was about an enormous statue made from four kinds of metal. It was frightening because of its great size and its brightness. The head was made of gold. Its chest and arms were silver. Its middle and thighs (upper legs) were bronze. Its lower legs were iron, and its feet were a mixture of iron and clay. Then a stone was cut out—but not by a human person's hand. This stone smashed into the feet of the statue, making the whole statue shatter into pieces. The iron, clay, bronze, silver, and gold broke into pieces that the wind blew away. The wind blew them so far away that no piece could be found. But then the stone became a "great mountain and filled the whole earth."

This certainly was a strange dream! But it was also an extraordinary dream sent by God for Daniel to explain to Nebuchadnezzar. The dream was a serious warning, and yet it was also an amazing promise. Babylon was a great nation, and Nebuchadnezzar was a powerful king. Daniel explained that part of the dream:

> *"You, O king, the king of kings, to whom the God of heaven has given the kingdom, the power, and the might, and the glory, and into whose hand he has given, wherever they dwell, the children of man, the beasts of the field, and the birds of the heavens, making you rule over them all—you are the head of gold." (Daniel 2:37-38)*

God gave Nebuchadnezzar his kingdom and power. **God rules over all the nations of the world.** *He removes kings and sets up kings.* Each part of the statue was a different kingdom. The day was coming when Babylon would be conquered by another nation—the nation shown by the chest and arms of silver. Later in a vision, God would show Daniel that the arms were the kingdom of the Medes and Persians. They would join together and defeat Babylon. The ruler of this kingdom would be a man named Cyrus.

Persia would in turn be defeated by the kingdom of bronze. Years later, God showed Daniel in a vision that the kingdom of bronze that would defeat Persia was the Greek Empire. We know from history that Alexander the Great was the conqueror of the Persian Empire and the ruler who made the Greek Empire great. But we know from the Bible that God put all these rulers in power and caused their kingdoms to become great and to fall. *He removes kings and sets up kings.*

Do you know what kingdom would come into power next? The legs of iron were a symbol of the Roman Empire. The Romans would conquer the Greeks. Rome was a very strong empire—just as iron is stronger than gold, silver, or bronze. But the iron empire of Rome would become weaker and weaker—like iron mixed with clay. Finally, it would split into many little nations—like the toes on a foot. All these kingdoms would be destroyed by *"a stone cut out by no human hand."*

The dream of the rise and fall of these kingdoms was given hundreds of years before some of these things happened. How could this be? God foretold the future in this dream. God controls all of history—all the events of this world. He knows everything that will happen. **Nothing happens apart from His control. He is sovereign—He rules over all things.**

But this was not the end of Nebuchadnezzar's dream. *The stone that struck the image became a great mountain and filled the whole earth.* Daniel told Nebuchadnezzar that *the God of heaven will set up a kingdom that shall never be destroyed. Whose Kingdom is this?* Even though Daniel did not fully understand it, he was foretelling the coming of the Messiah and His coming Kingdom. Jesus would establish the Kingdom that God promised to David. It would be an everlasting Kingdom and would put an end to all the sinful kingdoms of man. **Jesus' Kingdom will "stand forever."** It will be a Kingdom of peace and justice that will never end.

Do you know what Nebuchadnezzar did when he heard the meaning of his dream? You might think he got mad about his kingdom ending. But instead, he "fell on his face" before Daniel to show honor and respect to Daniel. *Why would Nebuchadnezzar do this?* Nebuchadnezzar was an idol worshiper. He worshiped many false gods. In those days, the people even believed that kings were gods. So Nebuchadnezzar just added another god to his list of gods to worship. He not only bowed down to Daniel but to Daniel's God, saying that Daniel's God was greater than the gods of Babylon were. *The king answered and said to Daniel, "Truly, your God is God of gods and Lord of kings, and a revealer of mysteries, for you have been able to reveal this mystery."* But Nebuchadnezzar did not believe that Daniel's God is the one true God—the only God worthy to be worshiped.

King Nebuchadnezzar gave gifts to Daniel and made him the ruler of the city of Babylon. Nebuchadnezzar also put Daniel in charge of his "wise men." God had put Daniel in a place of honor and power in the land of his exile. Daniel asked the king to give Shadrach (Hananiah), Meshach (Mishael), and Abednego (Azariah) important jobs in ruling Babylon also. Nebuchadnezzar agreed, so all four of these faithful young men obeyed Jeremiah's instructions to *seek the welfare of the city where I have sent you into exile, and pray to the LORD on its behalf, for in its welfare you will find your welfare.*

Just as God *removes kings and sets up kings*, so He rules all things. He was the One who showed Daniel the dream and its meaning. He was the One who put Daniel and his friends in high positions of power. And He is the one true God whom Daniel, Shadrach, Meshach, and Abednego worshiped.

God is still ruling all things—every king, every nation, and even you. Just as God had a plan for Daniel, so He has a plan for you. He has planned every day of your life. *Do you trust Him, His wisdom and His love? Do you truly believe that all His ways are good and right?*

...“Blessed be the name of God forever and ever, to whom belong wisdom and might. He changes times and seasons; he removes kings and sets up kings; he gives wisdom to the wise and knowledge to those who have understanding.” (Daniel 2:20-21)

MAKING YOU WISE FOR SALVATION

What does this chapter tell us about God? Talk about and apply the **biblical truths** in **bold** text.

Salvation Thread: God is sovereign over all things and will establish the Messiah’s everlasting Kingdom of peace and righteousness.

How could the meaning of Nebuchadnezzar’s dream have come true so many hundreds of years later?

Talk About: ...*“Blessed be the name of God forever and ever, to whom belong wisdom and might. He changes times and seasons; he removes kings and sets up kings; he gives wisdom to the wise and knowledge to those who have understanding.” (Daniel 2:20-21)*

Read Psalm 139:1-18. *How can God know each person so personally? What does this tell you about Him? How can these verses help you to trust God?*

Pray: Praise God for His sovereign rule over the world. Thank Him for knowing you and planning each day of your life. Ask Him to give you the faith to trust His sovereign rule.

Think About: *If nothing happens by chance, but all is under God’s control, do I need to worry?*

C H A P T E R 7 9

THE GOD WHO IS ABLE TO RESCUE

God Rescues Shadrach, Meshach, and Abednego—Daniel 3

"... our God whom we serve is able to deliver us ... But if not, be it known to you ... that we will not serve your gods or worship the golden image that you have set up." (Daniel 3:17a-18b)

D*o you remember what the head of the statue in Nebuchadnezzar's dream was made of?* It was made of gold. It represented, or was a symbol of, Nebuchadnezzar and Babylon. Now Nebuchadnezzar wanted to build a real statue—a statue or "image" of gold. It would be a really tall statue, an enormous statue—about the size of an eight-story building! When it was finished, Nebuchadnezzar gathered all the important people in Babylon at the statue—the rulers, governors, military commanders, counselors, judges, and government officials. Then Nebuchadnezzar made a law. He commanded all the people to fall down and worship the golden image whenever any kind of music was played. Whoever did not fall down and worship the statue would be thrown into a "burning fiery furnace." *What do you think of that law?*

Do you remember the first commandment? God's first commandment is, ***"You shall have no other gods before me."*** *What is the second commandment?* The second commandment is, ***You shall not make for yourself a carved image*** *. . .* ***You shall not bow down to them or serve them, for I the LORD your God am a jealous God."*** Nebuchadnezzar's law would be a big problem for anyone who worshiped Yahweh—like Daniel, Shadrach, Meshach, and Abednego.

The Babylonians knew this, and some of them really did not like "certain Jews" who had been given important jobs by Nebuchadnezzar. They were jealous of these captives. They should be servants, not leaders! They told King Nebuchadnezzar that Shadrach, Meshach, and Abednego disobeyed his law. Their words were, *"These men, O king, pay no attention to you; they do not serve your gods or worship the golden image that you have set up."* The Bible tells us that when Nebuchadnezzar heard these words, he went into a furious rage. This means he was VERY angry! He ordered Shadrach, Meshach, and Abednego to be brought to him.

When the three Jews came, Nebuchadnezzar gave them a second chance. If they would bow down and worship the image, everything would be fine. But if they wouldn't, they would immediately be thrown into a burning fiery furnace. Then he said something very foolish. Nebuchadnezzar said, *"And who is the god who will deliver you out of my hands?" Why was this such a foolish question?*

God will protect His name and His fame! No one, not even a king like Nebuchadnezzar can mock the living God! Shadrach, Meshach, and Abednego were true worshipers of the one true God. They boldly answered the king:

> *. . . "O Nebuchadnezzar, we have no need to answer you in this matter. If this be so,* ***our God whom we serve is able to deliver us*** *from the burning fiery furnace, and he will deliver us out of your hand, O king. But if not, be it known to you, O king, that we will not serve your gods or worship the golden image that you have set up." (Daniel 3:16b-18)*

Shadrach, Meshach, and Abednego would rather be put to death—burned in a fiery furnace—than betray or dishonor the God they worshiped. They would obey God no matter what happened! *What do you think Nebuchadnezzar thought of their reply?*

Nebuchadnezzar was "filled with fury"! He was VERY, VERY angry! He "ordered the furnace heated seven times more than it was usually heated." He wanted the furnace, really, really, really hot! He ordered some soldiers to tie up Shadrach, Meshach, and Abednego and throw them into the blazing furnace. When the soldiers opened the furnace to throw in Shadrach, Meshach, and Abednego, the flame from the furnace killed the soldiers, and Shadrach, Meshach, and Abednego fell into the hot, fiery furnace.

But something very surprising—and amazing—and miraculous happened!

> *Then King Nebuchadnezzar was astonished and rose up in haste. He declared to his counselors, "Did we not cast three men bound into the fire?" They answered and said to the king, "True, O king." He answered and said, "But I see four men unbound, walking in the midst of the fire, and they are not hurt; and the appearance of the fourth is like a son of the gods." (Daniel 3:24-25)*

How could there be four men—unbound (not tied up)—walking around in the fire? **God**, who cannot be mocked, was proving that He **is able to deliver His people**. Nebuchadnezzar yelled out to Shadrach, Meshach, and Abednego, *"Servants of the Most High God, come out, and come here!"* And so they did. Then the rulers, governors, military commanders, and counselors gathered around them to check them out. What they saw was amazing! They saw that the fire had not hurt the three men in any way! The men were fine! Their hair was not burned. Their clothing was fine. They didn't even smell like fire!

> *Nebuchadnezzar answered and said, "Blessed be the God of Shadrach, Meshach, and Abednego, who has sent his angel and delivered his servants, who trusted in him, and set aside the king's command, and yielded up their bodies rather than serve and worship any god except their own God. Therefore I make a decree: Any people, nation, or language that speaks anything against the God of Shadrach, Meshach, and Abednego shall be torn limb from limb, and their houses laid in ruins, for there is no other god who is able to rescue in this way." (Daniel 3:28-29)*

Then the three men, who had just been thrown into the fire, were given even more important jobs in Babylon. But more important than their new jobs was their faithfulness to God and His pleasure in their trust in Him. **God honors those who trust Him.**

The day may come when some ruler demands that you worship him or something other than the one true God. Even now, there may be times when you have the choice to stand up for what the Bible says is right and true, or to refuse to do something that God says is wrong. Will you trust God no matter what the consequences may be? *Do you now have the courage to stand up to those who mock God, say untrue things, or want you to disobey the Bible?*

...fear not, for I am with you; be not dismayed, for I am your God; I will strengthen you, I will help you, I will uphold you with my righteous right hand. (Isaiah 41:10)

MAKING YOU WISE FOR SALVATION

What does this chapter tell us about God? Talk about and apply the **biblical truths** in **bold** text.

Salvation Thread: God is the one true God and is able to deliver His people.

Why did Shadrach, Meshach, and Abednego have the courage to stand up to the king? What can you learn from them?

Talk About: ...*fear not, for I am with you; be not dismayed, for I am your God; I will strengthen you, I will help you, I will uphold you with my righteous right hand. (Isaiah 41:10)*

Do you speak the truth and stand up for what is right even when it is hard to do so? Give an example. Ask your mother or father for an example. *What can you do that will help you do this?*

Pray: Praise God for His power. Thank Him for being a rescuing God. Ask God to give you the faith to stand strong, even if you must stand alone.

Think About: *Do I trust God even when I am afraid?*

CHAPTER 80

THE MOST HIGH RULES THE KINGDOM OF MEN

God Humbles Nebuchadnezzar and Shows His Sovereign Will—Daniel 4

How great are his signs, how mighty his wonders! His kingdom is an everlasting kingdom, and his dominion endures from generation to generation. (Daniel 4:3)

Once again, Nebuchadnezzar had a dream. Once again, his "wise men" could not tell him the meaning of the dream. And once again, Daniel went to the king to interpret the dream. The dream was simple. Nebuchadnezzar saw a tree that "grew and became strong, and its top reached to the heaven." The whole earth could see it. It had beautiful leaves and a lot of fruit. Animals rested in its shade, birds lived in the branches, and it gave food to all. Then "a watcher, a holy one," or a messenger, came down from heaven and ordered that the tree be chopped down, its branches and leaves cut off, and the fruit scattered around. But the stump and roots would be left in the ground. Then the dream went on like this, *"Let his mind be changed from a man's, and let a beast's mind be given to him; and let seven periods of time pass over him. This sentence is . . . to the end that the living may know that the Most High rules the kingdom of men and gives it to whomever he will."*

Once again, God gave Daniel the meaning of the dream. The tree in the dream was about a real person. *Do you know whom the dream was about?* The tree was Nebuchadnezzar, a king whose greatness and power reached very far. He was also a very proud and ungrateful king. So God would cause him to "be driven from among men" to live with animals. He would eat grass like an ox for seven years until he understood that *the Most High rules the kingdom of men and gives it to whom he will.* But after he understood this, God would give his kingdom back to him. The dream was a warning to Nebuchadnezzar.

Then Daniel gave the king some very good advice. *What would be good advice for Daniel to tell Nebuchadnezzar?* Daniel told Nebuchadnezzar to turn away from his sins and do what is right. He should show mercy to those who were mistreated. Maybe then, God's judgment would be delayed, or put off until later.

But Nebuchadnezzar didn't take Daniel's advice. Instead, he became prouder and more ungrateful to God. A year after his dream, the king was walking on the roof of his palace looking around at the great city of Babylon. It was a beautiful city with fancy palaces, large temples, walls, bridges, and amazing gardens. King Nebuchadnezzar said, *"Is not this great Babylon, which I have built by my mighty power as a royal residence and for the glory of my majesty?" What was wrong with what Nebuchadnezzar said?* Nebuchadnezzar thought it was by his mighty power that he had built the city. He thought the city showed off his glory—his greatness. He did not understand that God had put him in a place of power, that God had given him the idea of how to make a great city, that everything he had came from God. He did not thank God or give glory to God for what God had done through him. He wanted all the glory, praise, and honor to go to himself.

While the proud, boasting words were still in Nebuchadnezzar's mouth, a voice came from heaven,

> *..."O King Nebuchadnezzar, to you it is spoken: The kingdom has departed from you, and you shall be driven from among men, and your dwelling shall be with the beasts of the field. And you shall be made to eat grass like an ox, and seven periods of time shall pass over you, until you know that the Most High rules the kingdom of men and gives it to whom he will." (Daniel 4:31b-32)*

Immediately—right away—these words came to pass. His dream came true. Nebuchadnezzar became mentally ill—sick in his mind. He was "driven from among men" and ate grass like an ox. He thought he was an animal, and he acted like one. His hair grew wild, and his nails became long like bird's claws.

God had given Nebuchadnezzar a whole year to listen to Daniel's warning, a year to decide to follow Daniel's advice, a year to repent—to turn away from his sin. But Nebuchadnezzar was proud and stubborn. He refused to honor God. So for seven years, Nebuchadnezzar behaved like an animal. At the end of the seven years, however, he lifted his eyes to heaven, and God healed his mind. His heart was changed and he praised God. This is what Nebuchadnezzar said:

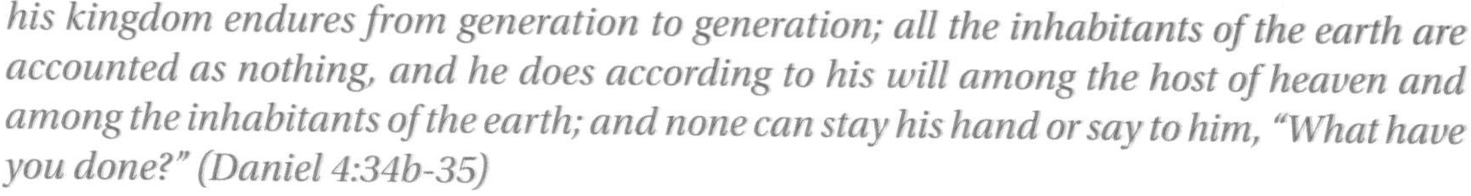

> *...I blessed the Most High, and praised and honored him who lives forever, for his dominion is an everlasting dominion, and his kingdom endures from generation to generation; all the inhabitants of the earth are accounted as nothing, and he does according to his will among the host of heaven and among the inhabitants of the earth; and none can stay his hand or say to him, "What have you done?" (Daniel 4:34b-35)*

What did Nebuchadnezzar now understand about God? He understood that **God is sovereign—He rules over all things, and His rule is forever. God's will cannot be resisted**—no one has the power to stop Him. God does whatever He pleases. God does not answer to anyone—no one can question God or tell him what to do. **God is the greatest authority.**

When Nebuchadnezzar's mind was healed, his counselors and officials put him back on the throne, and his kingdom grew even greater. But Nebuchadnezzar now praised the King of heaven, and his boasting was very different. Now he boasted in the greatness of God.

> *Now I, Nebuchadnezzar, praise and extol and honor the King of heaven, for **all his works are right and his ways are just**; and those who walk in pride he is able to humble. (Daniel 4:37)*

Nebuchadnezzar had refused to repent, and because of that, God had brought judgment on Him. It would have been so much better if Nebuchadnezzar had just listened to Daniel's advice. Instead, he learned the hard way—through consequences. **God is patient,** giving man time to repent, **but His patience isn't forever.** God has graciously given us His Word to show us who He is and what He expects of us. It is so much better to turn from sin before God must bring punishment to teach us to obey Him.

Like Nebuchadnezzar, you can boast in yourself. Or you can see that God has given you everything you have. **Everything good comes from God**—musical talent, athletic ability, artistic skill, a good mind, a strong body, and every good character quality such as kindness, generosity, thoughtfulness, joy, patience, faithfulness—everything good about you is because of God's grace to you. *Do you thank God for what He has given you? When someone praises you, do you recognize that the praise belongs to God for working in you and through you? Do you praise God for who He is and what He has done?*

I will bless the LORD at all times; his praise shall continually be in my mouth. My soul makes its boast in the LORD; let the humble hear and be glad. (Psalm 34:1-2)

But this is the one to whom I will look: he who is humble and contrite in spirit and trembles at my word. (Isaiah 66:2b)

MAKING YOU WISE FOR SALVATION

What does this chapter tell us about God? Talk about and apply the **biblical truths** in **bold** text.

Salvation Thread: God is patient and gives man time to repent.

Give some examples of what pride looks like in everyday life. What does humility look like? In what ways do we fail to give God the praise He deserves?

Talk About: *But this is the one to whom I will look: he who is humble and contrite in spirit and trembles at my word. (Isaiah 66:2b)*

What sin must you repent of? Is there any way in which you are offending God?

Pray: Praise God for being sovereign, righteous, and powerful. Thank Him for the abilities and good gifts He has given you. Ask God to show you the sin in your heart and confess your sin to Him. Ask Him to give you a humble heart and a heart that hates sin.

Think About: *How can I bring glory to God's name? How can I tell the greatness of the LORD?*

C H A P T E R 8 1

WEIGHED IN THE BALANCES AND FOUND WANTING

God Writes on a Wall and Judges Babylon—Daniel 5

"...you have been weighed in the balances and found wanting;" (Daniel 5:27)

Did you have a stuffed animal or something when you were little that was very special to you? Even if you don't use it anymore, is it still special and important? How would you feel if someone took that stuffed animal and smeared dirt all over it? Would that person be showing respect to you?

Nebuchadnezzar died and, in time, his grandson, Belshazzar, became the king of Babylon. He gave a great feast with much wine for thousands of his leaders. During the feast, Belshazzar sent for the sacred vessels (containers) of gold and silver that Nebuchadnezzar had taken from the temple of the Lord. The vessels were filled with wine. Then the leaders, Belshazzar, and his many wives drank wine "and praised the gods of gold, silver, bronze, iron, wood, and stone." *How is this like smearing dirt all over something precious to you?* They had dishonored the name of God. They had treated the sacred, special vessels with disrespect. Instead of praising the God who made the whole universe, they praised the idols that they had made.

"Immediately the fingers of a human hand appeared and wrote" on the wall! *How scary would that be?* Belshazzar saw this very strange and frightening thing, and "the king's color changed, and his thoughts alarmed him; his limbs gave way, and his knees knocked together." He was terrified! The laughing and partying suddenly turned to stunned fear. *What would you think if suddenly you saw a floating hand that was writing on your wall?*

The king called loudly for his advisors. Belshazzar offered a reward of royal purple clothing, a gold chain, and the third highest position in the kingdom to the person could read the writing. But none of the "wise men" of Babylon could read it. Now Belshazzar was really, really upset! The queen heard the loud noise from the banquet hall and rushed to the king. She told him not to be upset—there was a man with understanding and wisdom who had interpreted dreams, explained riddles, and solved problems for Nebuchadnezzar. This was Daniel.

So Daniel was brought before the king. Belshazzar asked him to read the writing and tell him the meaning of the words. If Daniel could do this, he would give Daniel the rewards he had promised the "wise men." Daniel didn't want the rewards, but he would read the writing and explain the meaning of the words. But first, Daniel reminded Belshazzar what Nebuchadnezzar had learned.

"O king, the Most High God gave Nebuchadnezzar your father kingship and greatness and glory and majesty...But when his heart was lifted up and his spirit was hardened so that he dealt proudly, he was brought down from his kingly throne, and his glory was taken from him. He was driven from among the children of mankind, and his mind was made like that of a beast, and his dwelling was with the wild donkeys. He was fed grass like an ox, and his body was wet with the dew of heaven, until he knew that the Most High God rules the kingdom of mankind and sets over it whom he will. And you his son, Belshazzar, have not humbled

your heart, though you knew all this, but you have lifted up yourself against the Lord of heaven." (Daniel 5:18, 20-23a)

Belshazzar had seen what had happened to Nebuchadnezzar, but his heart was hardened and proud. Instead of honoring God, he used the vessels from God's house as common drinking goblets. He praised false gods of silver, gold, bronze, iron, wood, and stone—gods that could not see, hear, or know anything. But the God of all creation, the God who gave Belshazzar life and kept him breathing, the God who deserves to be honored, Belshazzar did not honor. So God Himself sent the hand to write His words on the wall.

The words on the wall were MENE, MENE, TEKEL, and PARSIN. *What do you think these words mean?*

"This is the interpretation of the matter: MENE, God has numbered the days of your kingdom and brought it to an end; TEKEL, you have been weighed in the balances and found wanting; PERES,[1] your kingdom is divided and given to the Medes and Persians." (Daniel 5:26-28)

God was ending Belshazzar's kingdom because he was an unrighteous ruler. He had proudly opposed God. He mocked the Most High God by treating the gold vessels from God's temple as ordinary. **God will not allow His name to be mocked**. So God was breaking up Belshazzar's kingdom and giving it to the Medes and the Persians—the silver chest and arms of the statue in Nebuchadnezzar's dream. Nebuchadnezzar's dream was becoming real life. **Everything God says comes true.** That very night Belshazzar was killed and Darius the Mede took his place. The Babylonian empire came to an end, and the empire of the Medes and Persians was raised up next. The great and mighty Babylon was no more. The prophecy of Habakkuk had come true—God did punish the evil nation of Babylon, just as He had told Habakkuk he would. God used the evil nation of Babylon to discipline Judah. But Babylon could not escape God's judgment. **Every one of God's purposes happens as He has planned.**

The LORD of hosts has sworn: "As I have planned, so shall it be, and as I have purposed, so shall it stand," (Isaiah 14:24)

Judgment will come on all who reject God—all who do not honor Yahweh as the one true God. **God gives man many chances to repent, but God is not patient forever. God is just, and He must judge evil.** Someday, just like Belshazzar, you will also "be weighed in the balances"—God will look at your heart and see if you are trusting in Him and His provision of righteousness. If your heart is hard and stubborn and rebellious, you will "be found wanting," and judgment will come. Only God can give you a repentant heart. Only God can "remove the heart of stone" and give you "a new heart of flesh." *What does it mean to be stubborn toward God? Will you turn to Him in faith, or will you resist Him?*

I will instruct you and teach you in the way you should go; I will counsel you with my eye upon you. Be not like a horse or a mule, without understanding, which must be curbed with bit and bridle, or it will not stay near you. (Psalm 32:8-9)

MAKING YOU WISE FOR SALVATION

What does this chapter tell us about God? Talk about and apply the **biblical truths** in **bold** text.

Salvation Thread: Judgment will come on all who reject God. God always brings about, or accomplishes, His purposes.

What does this story show you about Belshazzar's heart? What does "weighed in the balances and found wanting" mean? How had God given Belshazzar the opportunity to know the truth about who He is? (See Daniel 5:18-23.)

Talk About: *I will instruct you and teach you in the way you should go; I will counsel you with my eye upon you. Be not like a horse or a mule, without understanding, which must be curbed with bit and bridle, or it will not stay near you. (Psalm 32:8-9)*

How is it that God always accomplishes His purposes?

Pray: Thank God for His patience. Ask Him to give you a "heart of flesh."

Think About: *Am I stubborn before God? Do I have a teachable heart?*

1. "Peres" is the singular form of "Parsin"

CHAPTER 82

THE LIVING GOD IS A STRONG DELIVERER

God Delivers Daniel from the Mouths of Lions—Daniel 6

"May your God, whom you serve continually, deliver you!" (Daniel 6:16b)

When Cyrus, the king of Persia, conquered Babylon, he placed Darius the Mede as ruler over Babylon. King Darius set up 120 governors throughout his kingdom and three rulers to be in charge of these governors. Daniel had served Nebuchadnezzar and Belshazzar, "seeking the welfare of the city" where he had been sent into exile. Now Darius made Daniel one of these three rulers. Daniel became very good at his job—better than all the rest—"because an excellent spirit was in him." So King Darius decided to put Daniel in charge of the whole kingdom. *What do you think the other governors and rulers thought of this?*

They were jealous, and they plotted against Daniel. After all, he was an exiled Jew. Why should he have such a high position? But they had a problem. They couldn't find any fault or anything wrong with Daniel or his service to the king. The only thing they could do was to set a trap for Daniel by attacking his devotion, or dedication, to God. So they came up with a cunning plan. They told King Darius that all the rulers, military commanders, governors, and counselors thought the king should make a new law. The law commanded that any person who prayed to any god or man except King Darius for the next thirty days should be thrown into the den of lions. They asked Darius to put the law in writing and sign it so it could not be changed. *What do you think Darius did?* Darius signed the law, and it could not be changed by anyone, not even King Darius.

When Daniel heard that the king had signed the new law, he went home. He courageously went to his upper room right in front of the windows facing Jerusalem where he could be seen. Not once, not twice, but three times a day, he got down on his knees and thanked God—just as he had been doing. He didn't hide or pray in secret. *Why did he do this? Do you remember what the name Daniel means?* Daniel means, "God is my judge." Darius was not his judge. The other governors and presidents were not his judge. He would answer to God, not to any man. No law would stop him from praying to his God! He would not pray to any man, human king, or false god. He would thank Yahweh, the one true God. He would be faithful to his God.

These evil men agreed to spy on Daniel and find him praying, and that is just what they did. They quickly went to the king and reminded him of the law. Can you imagine them saying, *"O king! Did you not sign an injunction, that anyone who makes petition to any god or man within thirty days except to you, O king, shall be cast into the den of lions?" What do you think was in their hearts when they said this?* When the king agreed that he had signed the law and it could not be changed, they said, *"Daniel, who is one of the exiles from Judah, pays no attention to you, O king, or the injunction you have signed, but makes his petition three times a day."* Now they had caught Daniel. The king would have to throw him in the lions' den. Their evil scheme had worked.

The king was very upset when he heard their report about Daniel. He tried to figure out a way to save Daniel. But there was no way to change the law, and the other officials came to remind him of this. They definitely wanted to get rid of Daniel! The king must follow the law. *Then the king commanded, and Daniel was brought and cast into the den of lions.* But Darius said something quite interesting. *The king declared to Daniel, "May your God, whom you serve continually, deliver you!"* It was as if the king wanted Daniel's God to save him. Would God save Daniel, or would the lions attack him?

Then they covered the opening of the lions' den with a stone, and the king sealed it with his own royal seal and the seal of his lords. A royal seal was the mark or stamp of a ring in clay. This clay seal was placed over the crack where the stone covered the opening. That way no one could move the stone without breaking the seal and being discovered. No one was going to move that stone and free Daniel.

Do you know what the king did then? He went to his palace. He was so troubled and upset that he didn't eat, and he couldn't even sleep. As soon as morning came, the king eagerly rushed to the lions' den. The Bible tells us that when he got there, "he cried out in a tone of anguish." *The king declared to Daniel, "O Daniel, servant of the living God, has your God, whom you serve continually, been able to deliver you from the lions?"* Darius certainly was concerned about Daniel, and he certainly was determined to find out if God had rescued Daniel.

What happened then? Was Daniel unable to answer because the lions had eaten him for dinner? Or did God rescue him? *Then Daniel said to the king, "O king, live forever! My God sent his angel and shut the lions' mouths, and they have not harmed me, because I was found blameless before him; and also before you, O king, I have done no harm"... So Daniel was taken up out of the den, and no kind of harm was found on him, because he had trusted in his God.* God rules over even ferocious lions. **Nothing is too hard for God!** God had been faithful and honored Daniel's trust in Him. He saves His people. He shuts the mouths of hungry lions. And He shows the ungodly that He is the God of heaven. **God is a refuge in time of trouble.**

Then the king was exceedingly angry with the evil men who had plotted against Daniel. As punishment, the king commanded that these men and their families be thrown into the den of lions. Before they even reached the bottom of the den, the lions viciously pounced on them and broke all their bones in pieces. The living God did not save them as He had saved Daniel who trusted in Him.

> *Then King Darius wrote to all the peoples, nations, and languages that dwell in all the earth: "Peace be multiplied to you. I make a decree, that in all my royal dominion people are to tremble and fear before the God of Daniel, for* ***he is the living God****, enduring forever;* ***his kingdom shall never be destroyed****, and his dominion shall be to the end.* ***He delivers and rescues; he works signs and wonders*** *in heaven and on earth, he who has saved Daniel from the power of the lions." (Daniel 6:25-27)*

God is a mighty God. He delivers His people. He is a place of safety for all those who trust in Him. You do not have to be afraid of what might happen to you if you take a bold stand for the Lord. *Who is your judge—God or other people? Whom do you want to please? Will you take a bold stand of faith trusting in God?*

The LORD is my rock and my fortress and my deliverer, my God, my rock,
in whom I take refuge, my shield, and the horn of my salvation,
my stronghold. (Psalm 18:2)

God is our refuge and strength, a very present help in trouble. (Psalm 46:1)

MAKING YOU WISE FOR SALVATION

What does this chapter tell us about God? Talk about and apply the **biblical truths** in **bold** text.

Salvation Thread: The living God is a refuge. He rescues those who trust in Him.

Think about the life of Daniel. How did he show that God was first in his life?

Talk About: *God is our refuge and strength, a very present help in trouble. (Psalm 46:1)*

What situations are you in where you can take a bold stand for God?

Pray: Thank God for being a refuge, a rock, a fortress, and a deliverer. Pray that God will give you a bold heart, and that you will make Him first in your life.

Think About: *When I have problems, do I turn to the LORD?*

Memorize: Psalm 46:1

CHAPTER 83

STRANGE VISIONS AND GREAT HOPE

God Gives Daniel Visions of the Future, and Daniel Prays for His People—Daniel 7-9

And to him was given dominion and glory and a kingdom, that all peoples, nations, and languages should serve him; his dominion is an everlasting dominion, which shall not pass away, and his kingdom one that shall not be destroyed. (Daniel 7:14)

Do you ever skip ahead in a story or book to see how it ends? God gave Daniel a look at the end of history on this earth. *How did God do this?* God gave Daniel several visions. Those visions showed Daniel that kings come into power, and they fall from power; empires become strong, and then they are defeated and fade away. All the kingdoms of this world are temporary—they last for a little while. But when rulers and people become proud and rebellious, their own wickedness brings destruction on them.

History shows us that Nebuchadnezzar's dream and Daniel's visions came true. Babylon rose up, and then was destroyed. Then Persia rose, and fell. Next, the Greek Empire became powerful, and then was defeated. Then came the Roman Empire, but it didn't last. All the kingdoms of this world are only powerful for a time. But then they become powerless because they reject God and follow wickedness. *God removes kings and sets up kings.* **God is in control of all of history. He is the unchanging true King.**

Daniel saw in his vision that there will also be a powerful ruler who will come at the end of history. This ruler will say untrue things about God and rule with great cruelty. He will "cause fearful destruction" and make "war with the saints." His wicked rule will bring much suffering, pain, and trouble on those who trust in God. But like all other human rulers, he will only rule for a time. He, too, will be overthrown but by a different kind of King—One who will rule over a very different Kingdom from all the rest—a Kingdom that will last forever where God is the King; a Kingdom of peace, love, justice, and goodness.

Daniel tells us about this glorious Kingdom and how it will be set up by God Himself, who is called the Ancient of Days:

> *"As I looked, thrones were placed, and the Ancient of Days took his seat; his clothing was white as snow, and the hair of his head like pure wool; his throne was fiery flames; its*

wheels were burning fire. A stream of fire issued and came out from before him; a thousand thousands served him, and ten thousand times ten thousand stood before him; the court sat in judgment, and the books were opened. I looked then because of the sound of the great words that the horn was speaking. And as I looked, the beast was killed, and its body destroyed and given over to be burned with fire." (Daniel 7:9-11)

"I saw in the night visions, and behold, with the clouds of heaven there came one like a son of man, and he came to the Ancient of Days and was presented before him. And to him was given dominion and glory and a kingdom, that all peoples, nations, and languages should serve him; his dominion is an everlasting dominion, which shall not pass away, and his kingdom one that shall not be destroyed." (Daniel 7:13-14)

Daniel saw that one day God will redeem and restore His creation—the world and His people. He will destroy Satan and evil forever. God will set up His Kingdom. **God's Kingdom will be an everlasting Kingdom** that will never fall. God will be the King—the greatest King of all, the King of kings. The Son of Man, the Messiah, will bring in this Kingdom. **All peoples, nations, and people of all languages will bow before the Son of Man**. God's people, the true remnant, will bow in worship. Others will bow in fear before the great and mighty Savior they have rejected.

How do you think Daniel responded to this vision God gave him of the future? He prayed for his people. But he didn't just pray. He prayed *earnestly*—with heartfelt passion, determination, and seriousness. First, he called God the Lord, or Master, *the great and awesome God, who keeps covenant and steadfast love with those who love him and keep his commandments.* He recognized who God is and what He is like. He also understood that God's covenant keeping and steadfast love is not toward everyone, but toward those who are truly His people. Daniel knew his people did not love God and keep His commandments. They were sinful and rebellious. This was so troubling to Daniel that he confessed the sin of his people:

> *". . .we have sinned and done wrong and acted wickedly and rebelled, turning aside from your commandments and rules. We have not listened to your servants the prophets, who spoke in your name to our kings, our princes, and our fathers, and to all the people of the land. To you, O Lord, belongs righteousness, but to us open shame. . ." (Daniel 9:5-7a)*

Daniel admitted that the troubles the Israelites had were their own fault. Moses had warned them about what would happen if they rebelled, so had Joshua, and the prophets. The Israelites deserved their punishment. Even through suffering in Jerusalem and captivity in Babylon, the people of Judah had not repented. But Daniel asked God to have mercy on them. How could Daniel ask for mercy? The Israelites didn't deserve any mercy or kindness from God! They were a stubborn and rebellious people. Yet Daniel prayed:

> *"O my God, incline your ear and hear... For we do not present our pleas before you because of our righteousness, but because of your great mercy. O Lord, hear; O Lord, forgive. O Lord, pay attention and act. Delay not, for your own sake, O my God, because your city and your people are called by your name." (Daniel 9:18-19)*

Mercy is never deserved. **Mercy is undeserved kindness.** Daniel could pray for mercy, *not* because his people were righteous, but because **God is merciful**. He could pray for the Israelites because they were God's people, called by His name. Daniel knew that **God protects His name and His reputation**—what people think about who He is. He would be merciful because His great name deserved to be honored. What would people think of the God of Israel if God did not show mercy to His people?

In many ways, the book of Daniel is a book of hope. We know the end of the story for the people of God. For those who trust in God, we will live forever with Him in His Kingdom. Even though there is a time of great suffering coming for the people of God, we know that there will be a time when **God will put an end to all wickedness and evil.** The stories of Shadrach, Meshach, and Abednego in the fiery furnace and Daniel in the lions' den are stories of deliverance. They are stories that give us hope because **God delivers His people.** God has given us these stories so we will see that He is a God who is faithful, a God who rescues His people, a God who is always with His people—even in exile. We can stay strong by remembering who God is and what He has done.

Just as Daniel, Shadrach, Meshach, and Abednego were in a strange land that was not their own, we are exiles, too. For the children of God, this world is not our real home. We are strangers here, and heaven is our real home. **Those who have true faith in God can look forward to a glorious future Kingdom.** Whatever suffering we find here on earth is for a time—but heaven is forever. Just like Daniel, Shadrach, Meshach, and Abednego, we must stand strong in our faith in

God in a world that is evil. The people of God must trust God and do what is right—even if it means that we are treated badly. In the end, **God will deliver His people. God always wins.**

Are you a child of God? Do you have true faith in God's power, wisdom, love, and justice? Will you remember the glorious deeds of God and the wonders He has done, and trust Him? You may feel small and weak, but "God is the strength of His people." Will you trust that God will give you the strength to stand strong? If you are not a child of God, know that God is merciful to those who repent and seek Him.

For you, O Lord, are good and forgiving, abounding in steadfast love to all who call upon you. (Psalm 86:5)

I will remember the deeds of the LORD; yes, I will remember your wonders of old. I will ponder all your work, and meditate on your mighty deeds. Your way, O God, is holy. What god is great like our God? (Psalm 77:11-13)

MAKING YOU WISE FOR SALVATION

What does this chapter tell us about God? Talk about and apply the **biblical truths** in **bold** text.

Salvation Thread: God will redeem His people. Those who have true faith in God can look forward to a glorious future Kingdom.

Talk with Mom or Dad about your faith in God. Do you know if you are a Christian or not? Explain.

Talk About: *For you, O Lord, are good and forgiving, abounding in steadfast love to all who call upon you. (Psalm 86:5)*

I will remember the deeds of the LORD; yes, I will remember your wonders of old. I will ponder all your work, and meditate on your mighty deeds. Your way, O God, is holy. What god is great like our God? (Psalm 77:11-13)

How can remembering God's past mighty deeds, His "wonders of old," give hope and strengthen the faith of His children?

Pray: Praise God for being the King of kings. Thank Him for His mercy and the hope of eternal life. Confess your sin to God.

Think About: *Where will I be when the Ancient of Days judges all men?*

CHAPTER 84

THE PROMISED RETURN

God Keeps His Promise to the Exiles—Ezra 1-4

"...Return to me, says the LORD of hosts, and I will return to you, says the LORD of hosts." (Zechariah 1:3)

Daniel's visions happened during his time in exile in Babylon and Persia. *Do you remember Jeremiah's prophecy about the people in exile?* God would bring His people back to their home after seventy years in exile. **God always does what He says He will do. God's promises never fail.** The book of Ezra starts by showing the fulfillment of God's sure promise:

> *In the first year of Cyrus king of Persia, that the word of the LORD by the mouth of Jeremiah might be fulfilled, the LORD stirred up the spirit of Cyrus king of Persia, so that he made a proclamation throughout all his kingdom and also put it in writing: "Thus says Cyrus king of Persia: The LORD, the God of heaven, has given me all the kingdoms of the earth, and he has charged me to build him a house at Jerusalem, which is in Judah. Whoever is among you of all his people, may his God be with him, and let him go up to Jerusalem, which is in Judah, and rebuild the house of the LORD, the God of Israel—he is the God who is in Jerusalem." (Ezra 1:1-3)*

Why did Cyrus decide to let the Jews go home and rebuild the temple? God "stirred up the spirit of Cyrus." God put it in his heart. **God is sovereign over the hearts of men.** God was working out His great purposes and plan for His people. This was prophesied years earlier by Isaiah, Jeremiah, and Ezekiel. In fact, the prophet Isaiah had foretold the coming of Cyrus more than a hundred years before Cyrus was even born, saying: *"I say about Cyrus, 'He is my shepherd. He will accomplish everything I want him to. He will say about Jerusalem, "Let it be rebuilt." And he will say about the temple, "Let its foundations be laid."'"* **God is sovereign over all history.**

Not only did King Cyrus let the people return, but he also gave them silver, gold, "goods and costly wares," animals, and even whatever offerings the people gave. He also returned the vessels, or containers, from the temple that Nebuchadnezzar had taken.

Not all the Jews returned. Only those "whose spirit God had stirred to go up to rebuild the house of the LORD" went. The Jews had built houses and planted vineyards in Babylon, so some of them wanted to stay. Some were too old to make the almost nine hundred-mile trip back to Jerusalem. But those who wanted to return and worship Yahweh in the temple were ready to return home. So about fifty thousand Jews returned to Jerusalem and Judah under the leadership of Zerubbabel and Jeshua, the High Priest. Zerubbabel was the son

of Jehoiachin. *Do you remember who Jehoiachin was?* He was the king of Judah who only ruled for three months before Nebuchadnezzar invaded Jerusalem and took him and other important leaders captive. So Zerubbabel was from the royal line of David and the head of the tribe of Judah.

Before building the temple, Zerubbabel and Jeshua and others built the altar. *Why did they build the altar first?* The altar and sacrifices were the center of their worship. This was how they showed their faith in God and their understanding that their sins needed to be covered with the blood of a sacrifice. As soon as the altar was built, they made burnt offerings to the LORD in the morning and evening—just as the law of Moses commanded them.

The Jews hired masons (men who built with stone) and carpenters to start the work on the temple. They traded with other nations to get the great cedar trees needed for building. The Levites who had returned to Jerusalem from Babylon were in charge of rebuilding the temple. When they had built the foundation (lower part) of the temple, they had a big celebration to praise God. They blew trumpets and crashed cymbals together, and sang and thanked the LORD—*"For he is good, for* ***his steadfast love endures forever*** *toward Israel."* There was great excitement and shouting because the foundation had been laid. *But many of the...old men...wept with a loud voice. Why do you think they wept?* Perhaps they remembered how glorious Solomon's temple was, and they wept when they thought of how small and simple

this temple would be. Perhaps they wept because of all the suffering sin had brought on their people and all that they had lost because of their disobedience. The weeping of the old men was mixed with shouts of joy from others, and together it made such a loud sound that it could be heard far away.

But there were people living in Judah who heard that the Jews had returned from exile and were rebuilding the temple. They came with a suggestion, *"Let us build with you, for we worship your God as you do, and we have been sacrificing to him ever since the days [the] king of Assyria. . .brought us here." Do you know who these people were?* They were the people the Assyrians had conquered and brought to live in Samaria when Assyria conquered Israel. These people brought their false gods and their religion to Samaria. In time, they added Yahweh to the gods they worshiped. *What is wrong with this?*

Yahweh is the "jealous God" who will not share His glory. He is the one true God, so there are no other real gods. His command is to worship Him alone—*"You shall have no other gods before me."* So these Samaritans were trying to do what Israel had done—to worship God and worship idols, too.[1]

But Zerubbabel, Jeshua, and the other leaders would not allow them to help because they were not true worshipers of Yahweh. Then these people tried to discourage the Jews and make them afraid. They made it very difficult to rebuild the temple. So the Jews stopped working on the temple for many years and built their own houses instead. What would happen now? Would the people ever again worship God according to His covenant laws? Would God turn away from the Jews?

Yahweh is the faithful, covenant-keeping God. He loves His people with steadfast love. In His kindness to His people, He sent them two prophets—Haggai and Zechariah. These two prophets spoke God's words to the exiles who had returned to Judah and Jerusalem. They spoke both words of reprimand, or scolding, and words of hope. Haggai told the people of

Judah that they were poor and didn't have enough food because they cared more about building houses for themselves than about building God's temple.

> *"Thus says the LORD of hosts: These people say the time has not yet come to rebuild the house of the LORD"..."Is it a time for you yourselves to dwell in your paneled houses, while this house lies in ruins? Now, therefore, thus says the LORD of hosts: Consider your ways. You have sown much, and harvested little. You eat, but you never have enough...Consider your ways. Go up to the hills and bring wood and build the house, that I may take pleasure in it and that I may be glorified, says the LORD. You looked for much, and behold, it came to little. And when you brought it home, I blew it away. Why? declares the LORD of hosts. Because of my house that lies in ruins, while each of you busies himself with his own house." (Haggai 1:2, 4-6a, 7-9)*

Zechariah urged the people to turn back to God. *"Thus declares the LORD of hosts: Return to me, says the LORD of hosts, and I will return to you, says the LORD of hosts."* Would the Jews listen to the prophets? Would they rebuild the temple and return to the LORD? God had kept His promise to return the Jews to their own land. Would the Jews now keep their covenant with God?

Just like the Jews, we can start serving the LORD with great energy and excitement. But when things get difficult, it is tempting to become discouraged and give up. We need God's help to persevere. We need God's help to believe in him, to do what is right, and to do good to others. *Do you ask God for His help? Do you ask Him for strength each day?*

The LORD is my strength and my shield; in him my heart trusts, and I am helped; my heart exults, and with my song I give thanks to him. (Psalm 28:7)

MAKING YOU WISE FOR SALVATION

What does this chapter tell us about God? Talk about and apply the **biblical truths** in **bold** text.

Salvation Thread: Yahweh is a faithful, covenant-keeping God who always keeps His promises. Just as the exiles returned to Judah, so God would turn rebellious people back to Him.

What does Zechariah 1:3 tell you about God? How does this story show you the steadfast love of God for His people?

Talk About: *The LORD is my strength and my shield; in him my heart trusts, and I am helped; my heart exults, and with my song I give thanks to him. (Psalm 28:7)*

Is it right for God to be a jealous God? Why? Why is it good that God is a jealous God?

Pray: Praise God for His steadfast love. Thank Him for being a promise-keeping God. Ask Him to give you a heart that trusts Him and depends on Him daily for strength.

Think About: *Why do we need God's strength every day?*

1. Later, the Samaritans worshiped God alone, but at this time, their idol worship was mixed with the worship of God.

CHAPTER 85

THE PRESENCE OF THE LORD STRENGTHENS HIS PEOPLE

The Temple is Finished, and the People are Taught—Ezra 5-9

Therefore, thus says the LORD, I have returned to Jerusalem with mercy; my house shall be built in it, declares the LORD of hosts...(Zechariah 1:16a)

Have you ever run a long race? When you get near the end of a long race, it can be hard to keep going. *What helps a runner to keep running when he is tired?* One thing that helps is encouragement. *What kinds of words would you say to a tired runner to encourage him?*

Haggai and Zechariah were encouragers, too. They gave many messages of hope to Zerubbabel and the Jews. Some of the messages gave hope for their time. Others were messages of hope for the distant future. These messages were about a coming eternal Kingdom of God and a new Jerusalem. The temple would be an important part of this new Kingdom. God gave Haggai and Zechariah these messages of hope to encourage the people to continue building the temple and to worship Him:

> *Work, for I am with you, declares the LORD of hosts, according to the covenant that I made with you when you came out of Egypt. My Spirit remains in your midst. Fear not. (Haggai 2:4b-5)*
>
> *Therefore, thus says the LORD, I have returned to Jerusalem with mercy; my house shall be built in it, declares the LORD of hosts...(Zechariah 1:16a)*
>
> *"I will strengthen the house of Judah, and I will save the house of Joseph. I will bring them back because I have compassion on them, and they shall be as though I had not rejected them, for I am the LORD their God and I will answer them." (Zechariah 10:6)*
>
> *Behold, a day is coming for the LORD...On that day living waters shall flow out from Jerusalem...And the LORD will be king over all the earth. (Zechariah 14:1a, 8a, 9a)*

God used Haggai and Zechariah's words to encourage Zerubbabel, Jeshua, and the people.

> *Then Haggai, the messenger of the LORD, spoke to the people with the LORD's message, "I am with you, declares the LORD." And the LORD stirred up the spirit of Zerubbabel...and the spirit of Joshua [Jeshua]... the high priest, and the spirit of all the remnant of the people. And they came and worked on the house of the LORD of hosts, their God, (Haggai 1:13-14)*

So the people started to build the temple again. But then they ran into another problem. The Persian governor of the land wanted to know more about what the Jews were doing. Who gave them permission to rebuild the temple? Who was in charge of the building project? "But the eye of their God was on the elders of the Jews," and the governor let them keep working while he checked things out. Darius the Great was now the king of Persia, so the governor sent a letter to Darius. He explained that the Jews were rebuilding the temple. The Jews had told the governor that King Cyrus had given them permission to do this. Was this true?

When King Darius got the letter, he ordered a search of the records to find out if the report was true. Sure enough, Cyrus had given the Jews permission to rebuild the temple. Then, not only did Darius tell the governor to let the Jews keep building, but he even told him to provide the materials they needed with money from the royal treasury! The governor should give the Jews whatever they needed—even animals for the daily sacrifices. If anyone tried to change Darius's order, that person should be severely punished. Not only had God protected the building project of the Jews, He even gave them the money and protection to keep building! **Yahweh is an all-powerful God who works for His people!**

The governor was very careful to do everything Darius ordered. With the encouragement of Haggai and Zechariah, the Jews worked very hard and finished the temple. It had taken them twenty years to rebuild the temple. Imagine the joy they must have felt when it was finished! They dedicated the temple and offered one hundred bulls, two hundred rams, four hundred lambs, and twelve male goats as a sin offering for all Israel. The priests began to serve in the temple again. Once again, the people of God celebrated the Passover and other feasts. After more than seventy years, God's people finally had a temple again!

Almost sixty years later, a priest named Ezra brought another group of Jews back to Jerusalem. Ezra was a descendant of Moses' brother, Aaron, the High Priest. *He came to Jerusalem, for the good hand of his God was on him. For Ezra had set his heart to study the Law of the LORD and to do it and to teach his statutes and rules in Israel.* The king of Persia had given Ezra permission to bring back this new group of Jews and gave him gold and silver to bring with him. The king sent this money to make the temple beautiful. He also gave Ezra a job to do:

> *And you, Ezra, according to the wisdom of your God that is in your hand, appoint magistrates and judges who may judge all the people in the province Beyond the River, all such as know the laws of your God. And those who do not know them, you shall teach. (Ezra 7:25)*

Ezra prayed that God would forgive His people for their great sin. He followed the king's command to make biblical laws in the land of Judah. He set up judges who would judge the people according to God's good law.

Zerubbabel, Jeshua, Haggai, Zechariah, and Ezra could lead others in doing what is right, not because they were mighty men, or because they were smart or had good personalities. They encouraged the people to do good because the Spirit of God was with them. They did not depend on themselves, but on God. **God's Spirit strengthens His people and gives them success.**

You, too, can encourage others to be wise and good if you trust the LORD. In your own strength you are just one little person—but **God is a great and mighty God**. If you depend on Him, you can be strong in standing for what is right and good. *Will you depend on yourself, or ask God to put His Spirit in you? Will you take a bold step of faith and depend on God to work in you and through you?*

"Not by might, nor by power, but by my Spirit, says the LORD of hosts." (Zechariah 4:6b)

MAKING YOU WISE FOR SALVATION

What does this chapter tell us about God? Talk about and apply the **biblical truths** in **bold** text.

Salvation Thread: God's Spirit strengthens His people.

How has God worked for your family? Thank Him for His faithfulness.

Talk About: *"Not by might, nor by power, but by my Spirit, says the LORD of hosts." (Zechariah 4:6b)*

How can you encourage someone to trust in God or to persevere when things are hard?

Pray: Thank God for working in and through His people. Ask God to help you to depend on His Spirit.

Think About: *Do I try to do things in my own strength?*

CHAPTER 86

ROYAL ORDERS...AND GOD'S SOVEREIGN PLAN

God Gives Esther Favor and Places Her in the Palace—Esther 1-4

"For if you keep silent at this time, relief and deliverance will rise for the Jews from another place, but you and your father's house will perish. And who knows whether you have not come to the kingdom for such a time as this?" (Esther 4:14)

Back in Persia...a big feast was taking place. Who was giving this great feast? After Cyrus and Darius ruled Persia, Ahasuerus[1] ruled. The Persian kingdom was very large by now, and King Ahasuerus was giving a great feast for all his officials. *How long do you think the feast lasted?* Five hours? All day? It lasted 180 days! The king wanted to show the riches and splendor of his greatness: his marble pillars, couches of gold and silver, floors of marble and precious stones, and gold drinking goblets.

When the feast was over, guess what Ahasuerus did? He had another feast! This one was for "all the people...both great and small" in the capital city of Susa. But this was only a seven-day feast. On the last day, "when the heart of the king was merry with wine," he called for Queen Vashti to come and show off her beauty to the men at his feast. But Queen Vashti refused to come, which made the king furious! How would he punish Vashti, who had dared to refuse his order? He decided that Queen Vashti could never come before the king again, and he would choose another woman to be his queen.

Who would be the next queen? There were so many beautiful young women in the kingdom of Persia. The king must have the best. The king's officers gathered women from all over the kingdom—including a young woman named Esther. They took these women to the palace to prepare them to be presented to the king. But Esther had a secret. *Do you know what her secret was?*

Esther had another name. It was Hadassah. *Why would she have this other name?* Esther was a Jew, and Hadassah was her Hebrew name. Esther was her Persian name. Esther's parents had died, so she was raised by her older cousin, Mordecai, who treated her like his own daughter. Not all the Jews in exile returned to Judah with Zerubbabel. Some stayed in Persia, including Mordecai and Esther. When Esther was taken to the palace, Mordecai told her not to tell anyone that she was a Jew, and Esther obeyed him. *Why do you think Mordecai told Esther this?*

Mordecai was protecting Esther, because many of the Persian people did not like the Jews. But God gave Esther favor with the man in charge of all the young women, and he gave her a high position among the women. Every day Mordecai faithfully checked to see how Esther was doing. *Now Esther was winning favor in the eyes of all who saw her. And when Esther was taken to the King Ahasuerus...the king loved Esther more than all the women, and she won grace and favor in his sight more than all...so that he set the royal crown on her head and made her queen.* Imagine, out of all the thousands of beautiful, young women in the Persian kingdom, the king chose Esther to be queen. Without knowing it, he picked a Jew, one of God's chosen people. Why would God give Esther favor and put her in such an important position?

One day, while Mordecai was sitting at the king's gate, he found out that two of the guards were angry with the king. They wanted to kill the king! *How was it that Mordecai just happened to be there to find out about the evil plot?* **God is sovereign over all things.** God put Mordecai at just the right place at just the right time. Mordecai quickly told Queen Esther about the plot. Esther warned the king, telling him what Mordecai said. Was this report true? The king had the report investigated—and sure enough, it was true. The king would put an end to this plot. He had both men "hanged on the gallows" and killed.[2] This would be a warning to anyone else who plotted against the king. Then it was recorded in the official book of the king, "the book of the chronicles," that Mordecai saved the king's life.

After this, King Ahasuerus appointed someone to be above all the officials—to be the next highest person after the king. *Who do you think that was? Was it Mordecai?* No, it wasn't Mordecai, the man who had saved the king's life, it was a man named Haman. The king made a law that everyone should bow down to Haman and give him respect and honor. But Mordecai wouldn't do this. Day after day, he refused. *What do you think Haman thought of this?*

Haman was a proud man, and he was "filled with fury." That means he was extremely angry! He was so angry that he didn't want to kill only Mordecai. He wanted to destroy *all* the Jews! So proud, angry Haman asked the king to make a law that on a certain day all the Jews would be killed—"young and old, women and children"—and their belongings stolen. If the king would make this law, Haman would give the king 10,000 talents of silver (750,000 pounds)—an enormous amount of money. So the king made a royal order, or decree, and sealed it with his ring. Then it was sent to every province in Persia. Every Jew in the whole Persian Empire was to be killed.

When Mordecai heard about the order, he was so upset that he "tore his clothes, and put on sackcloth and ashes, and went out into the midst of the city, and he cried out with a loud and bitter cry." In every province, there was "great mourning among the Jews, with fasting and weeping and lamenting, and many of them lay in sackcloth and ashes." They were extremely troubled and terribly frightened.

Esther heard about Mordecai. What was wrong? She sent a messenger to find out why Mordecai was so troubled. Mordecai sent back a copy of the king's decree to kill the Jews. He asked the messenger to beg Esther to plead with the king to save the Jews. What could Esther do? A person who went to see the king without an invitation could be put to death! The king had not asked for Esther for thirty days. She couldn't just go in and talk with him. Esther sent this message to Mordecai.

But Mordecai sent an answer back to Esther:

> *"Do not think to yourself that in the king's palace you will escape any more than all the other Jews. For if you keep silent at this time, relief and deliverance will rise for the Jews from another place, but you and your father's house will perish. And who knows whether you have not come to the kingdom for such a time as this?" (Esther 4:13-14)*

How do you think Esther answered this message? How would you answer? It is easy to say that we would be brave and do the right thing. But when we are in a difficult situation, we sometimes give in to fear and find that doing the right thing becomes very hard. Until we are in that difficult spot, we don't really know what we will do. That is why it is important to remember that each of the stories you read in the Bible are MORE THAN A STORY. Each story reminds us of great, important truths about God—truths like **God works for His people, God works through His people**, and **God is with His people all the time**—even in the hard times.

In the day of my trouble I call upon you, for you answer me. (Psalm 86:7)

MAKING YOU WISE FOR SALVATION

What does this chapter tell us about God? Talk about and apply the **biblical truths** in **bold** text.

Salvation Thread: God sovereignly watches over His people and is always at work in all circumstances.

What does Esther 4:13-14 show you about Mordecai's faith in God?

Talk About: *In the day of my trouble I call upon you, for you answer me. (Psalm 86:7)*

Why did Esther gain favor with the king? Read Proverbs 21:1.

Pray: Praise God for being sovereign over all things. Thank Him for paying attention to every detail of your life.

Think About: *Can I trust God to control the circumstances of my life?*

1. He was also called Xerxes.

2. This probably means that they were stabbed or caused to fall upon a sharpened spear or stick, and then hung on a sharp pole, or gallows, for all to see them.

C H A P T E R 8 7

THE GOD OF GREAT REVERSES

God Delivers the Jews—Esther 5-10

...on the very day when the enemies of the Jews hoped to gain the mastery over them, the reverse occurred: the Jews gained mastery over those who hated them. (Esther 9:1b)

Did God put Esther in the king's palace for a reason? **God does everything He does for a reason. Nothing is by chance. He is always fulfilling His purposes in all that happens.** Mordecai had sent the message to Esther, *"And who knows whether you have not come to the kingdom for such a time as this?" Do you know how Esther responded to Mordecai's question?*

Esther's response was to send a message to Mordecai to gather all the Jews in the city of Susa. She asked them to fast—to not eat or drink—for three days and nights. Esther and her servants would also fast. After that, she said, *"Then I will go to the king, though it is against the law, and if I perish, I perish."* So even if it meant death to her, she would try to save the lives of the Jews.

On the third day, Esther stood in the court in sight of the king. When the king saw Queen Esther, "she won favor in his sight." The king not only welcomed Esther, but he also said, *"What is it Queen Esther? What is your request? It shall be given you, even to the half of my kingdom." Why did the king respond like this? The king's heart is a stream of water in the hand of the LORD; he turns it wherever he will. Can you change the direction of the water coming out of your faucet? How?* By putting your hand under the water, you can make it go sideways. Just as you can change the direction of water, God can change hearts—even the hearts of kings. It is a small thing for Him to do, and God Almighty, the God of Israel, turned the heart of the king toward Esther.

But Esther didn't ask the king to save the lives of the Jews. Instead, she invited the king and wicked Haman to dinner. At the feast, the king asked Esther what she wanted. He would give it to her—even up to half of his kingdom. But Esther still did not ask for protection for the Jews. God had given her a strategy. Again, Esther invited the king and Haman to a feast the next evening; she would tell the king her wish then.

It was a great honor to be invited to a feast by the queen. So Haman left the feast "joyful and glad of heart"...until he saw Mordecai at the king's gate. Mordecai did not bow to him again and wasn't even afraid of angering Haman. This "filled [Haman] with wrath against Mordecai." When Haman got home, he bragged about his high position, his riches, and the great honor of being invited to dinner with the king and queen again. He alone had been given this special invitation! But his pride was hurt—*"Yet all this is nothing to me, so long as I see Mordecai the Jew sitting at the king's gate."*

Haman's wife and friends had a solution for the Mordecai problem. They told Haman to build gallows seventy-five feet high. In the morning, Haman could ask the king to have Mordecai hanged on it. Then he could go to the feast joyfully. Evil Haman liked the idea, so he had the gallows made.

However, *it just happened* that on that particular night the king couldn't sleep. So he asked for "the book of memorable deeds, the chronicles" to be brought to him. *Do you know what he learned?* The king heard about Mordecai's warning regarding the plot to kill him. He asked his servants what had been done to honor and thank Mordecai for saving his life. Nothing had been done! Haman *just happened* to arrive at the court then. He was going to talk to the king about having Mordecai hanged. The king called for Haman, but before Haman could ask his question, the king had one of his own—"What should be done to the man whom the king delights to honor?" *What do you think Haman thought?*

He thought there would be no one the king would delight to honor more than him! Certainly, no one was more deserving than he was. Haman had a grand suggestion. The king's servants should dress "the man" in the king's royal robes and crown, set him on the king's horse, and parade him through the city square, loudly shouting that this man was being honored by the king. Imagine Haman's surprise, and horror, when the king told Haman to hurry and do all this for *Mordecai!* Haman had no choice but to parade Mordecai through the streets as the one the king wanted to honor. This was a great "reverse," or the opposite of what Haman thought would happen.

That night, the king and Haman went to Queen Esther's feast. Again, the king asked Esther what she wanted. This was the moment that God had set up to give Esther success—and Esther took it. She asked the king to spare her life and the lives of her Jewish people who were to be killed. The king asked what man would dare do this. *And Esther said, "A foe and enemy! This wicked Haman!"*

The king was furious! He ordered Haman to be hanged. Haman had built the gallows to hang Mordecai, but instead, wicked Haman was hung on them for all to see. Esther was given Haman's house. When she told the king that Mordecai was her cousin, the king took

the official ring he had given Haman and gave it to Mordecai. Then Esther begged the king to change the decree that the Jews be killed. However, the law of the Medes and Persians could not be changed. But there was still something that could be done. The king gave Esther and Mordecai permission to write whatever law they wanted in his name and seal it with his ring. So they wrote a law that allowed the Jews to defend themselves against anyone who would attack them.

The king gave Mordecai Haman's job, which was the second highest position in the kingdom. Mordecai wore royal robes and a golden crown. *And the city of Susa shouted and rejoiced. The Jews had...gladness and joy and honor.* The Jews had great feasts, and fear of the Jews came on many of the people of Persia. *On the very day when the enemies of the Jews hoped to gain the mastery over them, the reverse occurred; the Jews gained mastery over those who hated them...no one could stand against [the Jews], for the fear of them had fallen on all peoples.* The "reverse" or the opposite happened! The king's officials, military commanders, and governors actually helped the Jews instead of killing them! They were afraid to kill the Jews *for the fear of Mordecai had fallen on them. For Mordecai was great in the king's house, and his fame spread throughout all the provinces, for the man Mordecai grew more and more powerful.*

The Jews defeated their enemies, and Mordecai sent a letter to all the Jews creating a new two-day feast each year. This feast was to celebrate that "sorrow" had been turned into "gladness" and "mourning into a holiday." The Feast of Purim was to be kept every year to remember what God had done.

God is a God of great "reverses." Haman thought he would be honored. Instead, Mordecai was honored. Haman wanted to hang Mordecai. Instead, Haman was hanged. The Jews were going to be killed. Instead, the Jews were helped! Only God can bring such great changes!

God had made Esther the queen of Persia. God had given the king a sleepless night so he would learn about Mordecai's loyalty. God had given Esther favor with the king, so she was able to help the Jews. None of these things *just happened.* **God is in control of all things. He is sovereign over everything. He works all things according to His plan and purposes.**

Just as the Jews were told to remember the goodness of God, so we should remember His "mighty acts and the wonders he has done." *Do you worship God as the Sovereign Ruler of the world? Do you trust Him to direct your life? Do you thank Him for His mercies that are new every morning?*

The LORD has done great things for us; we are glad. (Psalm 126:3)

"Let not the wise man boast in his wisdom, let not the mighty man boast in his might, let not the rich man boast in his riches, but let him who boasts boast in this, that he understands and knows me, that I am the LORD who practices steadfast love, justice, and righteousness in the earth. For in these things I delight, declares the LORD." (Jeremiah 9:23-24)

MAKING YOU WISE FOR SALVATION

What does this chapter tell us about God? Talk about and apply the **biblical truths** in **bold** text.

Salvation Thread: God is sovereign over all things and is faithful to rescue His people. Someday, He would send an even greater rescue.

What is God's sovereignty? Where do you see God's hand at work in this story? God is at work in your life, too ... even if you can't see His purposes right now.

Talk About: *"Let not the wise man boast in his wisdom, let not the mighty man boast in his might, let not the rich man boast in his riches, but let him who boasts boast in this, that he understands and knows me, that I am the LORD who practices steadfast love, justice, and righteousness in the earth. For in these things I delight, declares the LORD." (Jeremiah 9:23-24)*

Why should this story give you confidence in God? Is there anything in your life that seems difficult? Can you trust God to be at work and do what is best?

Pray: Praise God for His sovereignty. Praise Him for accomplishing His purposes and for caring for His people. Thank Him for watching over your life. Confess any doubts you have about God. Ask Him to give you a heart of faith.

Think About: *Am I proud or humble? Do I boast in what I can do, or do I boast in what God does?*

CHAPTER 88

REBUILDING THE WALLS THROUGH PRAYER

God Gives Nehemiah Favor in Rebuilding the Walls of Jerusalem—Nehemiah 1-4, 6

. . . "Do not be afraid of them. Remember the Lord, who is great and awesome, and fight for your brothers, your sons, your daughters, your wives, and your homes." (Nehemiah 4:14b)

Have you ever gotten bad news? Nehemiah was a Jew living in Susa who got some bad news. After King Ahasuerus died, Artaxerxes became king. Sadly, after becoming king, Artaxerxes had stopped the rebuilding in Jerusalem. One day, Nehemiah's brother and some other men had come from Judah. They told Nehemiah that the exiles who returned to Judah were in great trouble. The Jerusalem wall was broken down, and the gates still lay torn down and burned. This made Nehemiah so sad that he wept and mourned for days. He also prayed:

> *. . . "O LORD God of heaven,* ***the great and awesome God who keeps covenant and steadfast love with those who love him and keep his commandments****, let your ear be attentive and your eyes open, to hear the prayer of your servant that I now pray before you day and night for the people of Israel your servants, confessing the sins of the people of Israel, which we have sinned against you . . ." (Nehemiah 1:5-6a)*

Nehemiah asked God to give him favor with the king. God had put Nehemiah in a good position close to the king as the king's cupbearer. *Do you know what a cupbearer is?* There were people who wanted to kill the king and take his throne. So the king needed a cupbearer, someone he could trust to make sure there wasn't poison in his drink. Sometimes the cupbearer even had to take the first swallow. Nehemiah's job was to protect the king and, because of that, he was very important to the king.

One day, when he brought the king's cup to him, Nehemiah looked very sad. Artaxerxes knew something was wrong and asked about Nehemiah's "sadness of heart." Nehemiah told the king he was grieved because the city of Jerusalem was in ruins. So the king asked Nehemiah what he wanted him to do. *Do you know what Nehemiah did then?* He "prayed to the God of heaven." He knew only God could make the king agree to help. Then he asked the king to send him to Jerusalem to rebuild it...and to give him wood to fix the gates and walls. This was a big favor, but the king gave Nehemiah everything he asked for. *Why did Artaxerxes do this, even though he was the one who had stopped the rebuilding?* Nehemiah tells us in the Bible that it was because "the good hand of my God was upon me." God had changed the king's heart! The king even sent army officers and horsemen with Nehemiah.

When Nehemiah got to Jerusalem, he inspected the gates and wall. They were in terrible shape. They were broken down and burned. Nehemiah called the Jews in Jerusalem together and encouraged them to rebuild the wall. He told the Jews that God was with them and that the king had promised his help. So the people decided to get to work. Some enemies of the Jews—Sanballat, Tobiah, and Geshem—heard about their plan. They made fun of the Jews and accused them of rebelling against the king. But this would not stop Nehemiah. He told these evil men, *"The God of heaven will make us prosper, and we his servants will arise and build, but you have no portion or right or claim in Jerusalem."*

Each family took a part of the wall to rebuild. Once again, their enemies tried to stop them. Sanballat was "enraged," and he made mean, mocking comments to the Jews. *"What are these feeble Jews doing? . . . Will they revive the stones out of the heaps of rubbish?"* Tobiah joined in, *"Yes, what they are building—if a fox goes up on it he will break down their stone wall!"* But Nehemiah didn't talk to them. He talked to God instead and prayed that God would defeat their enemies—and he kept building the wall. The families joined their parts of the wall together and built it to half its height, "for the people had a mind to work."

What do you think their enemies thought about this? They gathered their peoples and plotted to fight against Jerusalem and the Jews from all sides. Once again, Nehemiah prayed to God—and set up guards day and night. But the Jews started to become discouraged, saying the job was too hard and there were too many stones and ruins in the way. Besides, they were afraid that their enemies might kill them.

What would happen? Would the people give up? Would Nehemiah go back to Persia? Nehemiah grouped the people by families behind the lowest parts of the wall with swords, spears, and bows. But then he told them about their greatest weapon, *"Do not be afraid of them. Remember the Lord, who is great and awesome, and fight for your brothers, your sons, your daughters, your wives, and your homes."* **God was stronger than all their enemies were**. He was their greatest weapon! When their enemies heard that the Jews knew about their plot, they did not attack the Jews. *God had frustrated their plan.* **God is great and awesome and works for His people!**

After this, half of the people worked on the wall, and the other half stood guard with their weapons. Those who hauled the building materials had a weapon in one hand and materials in the other. The builders had their swords strapped to their sides while they worked. As Nehemiah inspected the work, a guard followed him with a trumpet. Nehemiah told the people, *"The work is great and widely spread, and we are separated on the wall, far from one another. In the place where you hear the sound of the trumpet, rally to us there.* ***Our God will fight for us.****"* They stayed within the walls of Jerusalem and even slept with their clothes on. They were ready to work and ready to fight.

Still, their enemies did not give up. They sent a message asking Nehemiah to meet them on the plain outside the city. But Nehemiah knew they wanted to harm him. He sent messengers with his answer, *"I am doing a great work and I cannot come down. Why should the work stop while I leave it and come down to you?"* Even though Sanballat, Tobiah, Geshem, and the rest of the Jews' enemies sent for Nehemiah four times, Nehemiah did not give in. Then, his enemies sent a messenger with a letter to Nehemiah. The letter stated that the Jews were planning to rebel against the king and choose their own king. They threatened to tell the king of Persia these things unless Nehemiah met with them. Still, Nehemiah refused to be afraid and stop the work. He sent a message back to his enemies, saying that their words were not true—they were made up, they were lies—and he prayed, *"But now O God, strengthen my hands."*

Do you think their enemies finally gave up? No, they hired a man to pretend to be a prophet. This man told Nehemiah to hide in the temple because his enemies were coming to kill him. But Nehemiah refused to hide. He realized that the man had been sent, not by God but by Sanballat and Tobiah. Nehemiah would not be afraid but would continue to build the wall. He would not give up!

Finally, the wall was finished! It took fifty-two days to build. When the enemies of the Jews heard about it, all the nations around Judah were afraid because they knew that "the work had been accomplished with the help of. . .God."

Why could Nehemiah continue with such confidence? Nehemiah's job was to get the wall built, but he was not a builder first of all. He was, first of all, a man of faith and prayer. Nehemiah trusted God and prayed to Him for strength. He knew God was with him. Instead of focusing on his enemies and how big the job was, Nehemiah kept looking at how "great and awesome" God is! You, too, can focus on the problems around you, or you can focus on God. *Will you trust God and keep your eyes on Him?*

> "Blessed is the man who trusts in the LORD, whose trust is the LORD. He is like a tree planted by water, that sends out its roots by the stream, and does not fear when heat comes, for its leaves remain green, and is not anxious in the year of drought, for it does not cease to bear fruit." (Jeremiah 17:7-8)

MAKING YOU WISE FOR SALVATION

What does this chapter tell us about God? Talk about and apply the **biblical truths** in **bold** text.

Salvation Thread: God is great and awesome and fights for His people. Just as the Jews rebuilt the wall, so God would rebuild and restore His people someday.

How can your family members first be people of faith and prayer? How would you do your everyday tasks if prayer and faith were your focus?

Talk About: *"Blessed is the man who trusts in the LORD, whose trust is the LORD. He is like a tree planted by water, that sends out its roots by the stream, and does not fear when heat comes, for its leaves remain green, and is not anxious in the year of drought, for it does not cease to bear fruit." (Jeremiah 17:7-8)*

How can you encourage someone who is weary and needs to be reminded that God will fight for him?

Pray: Praise God for being a great and awesome God. Ask Him to make you a person who looks to Him and prays.

Think About: *Do I trust God when I face problems in my life?*

CHAPTER 89

MANY REFORMS BUT THE SAME PROBLEM

Nehemiah's Reforms and the Jews' Stubborn Hearts—Nehemiah 5, 8-12

"Yet you have been righteous in all that has come upon us, for you have dealt faithfully and we have acted wickedly." (Nehemiah 9:33)

Nehemiah wasn't just interested in rebuilding the wall of Jerusalem. He was more interested in rebuilding the Jews' faith in God and obedience to His law. Nehemiah was governor of Judah for twelve years. In that time, he worked very hard to encourage the people to follow God. He brought many reforms, or changes, among the people, encouraging them to obey God's law.

The law of Moses did not allow the Jews to charge interest (extra money) when other Jews borrowed money from them. But Nehemiah found out that the rich Jews were disobeying God's law. They were charging interest to the poor Jews, who had to borrow money for food or to pay their taxes. When the poor Jews couldn't pay the money, sometimes the rich Jews took their land or vineyards from them. Nehemiah was angry that some people were suffering because others were selfish and greedy. He told them this was not the way God had told them to treat their own people. He told the rich people to return what they had taken from the poor and to obey God's good laws. The people listened to Nehemiah and agreed to return what they had wrongly taken. But this was not the only way Nehemiah followed God's desire to help the poor. Nehemiah did not tax his people as other governors had done. Instead, he freely fed many people with his own money.

Ezra had been teaching the people God's Word. After the wall was finished, the people gathered together at one of the gates while

Ezra read the Book of the law of Moses. *And the ears of all the people were attentive to the Book of the Law. . .And Ezra blessed the LORD, the great God, and all the people answered, "Amen, Amen," lifting up their hands. And they bowed their heads and worshiped the LORD with their faces to the ground.* They heard about the Feast of Booths that Moses commanded the people to keep. So the people brought branches to make booths, or shelters, and lived in them for seven days. This was to remind themselves of the days when the Israelites wandered in the wilderness.

When the people heard the law, they confessed their sin to God for hours with much mourning. They "cried with a loud voice to the LORD." The Levites reminded them of their history—of who God is and what He had done for them.

> ***"You are the LORD, you alone****. You have made heaven, the heaven of heavens, with all their host, the earth and all that is on it, the seas and all that is in them; and you preserve all of them; and the host of heaven worships you." (Nehemiah 9:6)*

They told the people about God choosing Abraham and the covenant God made with him. God had kept all His wonderful promises. He had rescued His people from slavery in Egypt with amazing signs and wonders, and miraculously opened the Red Sea. He spoke to them from Mount Sinai with thunder and lightning. He gave them "right rules and true laws, good statutes and commandments." God gave them bread from heaven and water in the dry wilderness. God had done all these amazing miracles for His people. But the people of Israel had been stubborn and rebellious and had not obeyed God's commandments. Even though Israel had rebelled, God was ***ready to forgive, gracious and merciful, slow to anger and abounding in steadfast love, and did not forsake them****.* He did not forsake them, even when they made a disgraceful golden calf. He gave them kingdoms and cities, rich land, vineyards, and fruit trees in their own land. But the Israelites still disobeyed and rebelled, and killed the prophets "who had warned them" to turn back to God. They deserved the punishment they received. God had acted righteously and faithfully.

After hearing all this, the people made a written covenant to obey God. They agreed that their sons and daughters would not marry people from the other nations. They would live as a separate people—different and apart from the other nations. They would keep the Sabbath by not working, buying, or selling on the Sabbath. They would give money to care for the temple and the Levites, and make the offerings for their sin.

Nehemiah asked the Levites from all over Judah to come to Jerusalem to celebrate the dedication of the wall. They came with musical instruments to praise God and thank Him. Nehemiah formed two large choirs to sing their thanks to God while walking joyfully along the top of walls—the walls that their enemy said would not even hold a fox! *And they offered great sacrifices that day and rejoiced, for God had made them rejoice with great joy; the women and children also rejoiced. And the joy of Jerusalem was heard far away.*

After this, Nehemiah returned to Persia to serve Artaxerxes again. "After some time," he asked the king if he could return to Jerusalem. But when Nehemiah returned to Jerusalem, he was greatly saddened to see that the people were not keeping the Mosaic law. They were not giving money to care for the temple and the Levites. The Levites were not taking care of the temple but were working in their fields. The Jews were working, buying, and selling on the Sabbath. Sadly, many of the men had disobeyed the law of Moses and had married Philistine, Ammonite, and Moabite women. The children from these marriages did not even speak Hebrew (the language of Judah). How extremely disappointing this must have been for Nehemiah! Faithful Nehemiah tried to correct things and rebuked, or scolded, the people for their covenant breaking.

The Jews were back in their land with their temple—but they still had the same hearts. Nehemiah could make many reforms, or changes, but in the end, he could not change the hearts of the people. **Only God can take out stubborn hearts of stone and replace them with new hearts**. They needed new hearts of flesh—hearts that were soft toward God, obedient, and full of goodness.

Nehemiah was right to call people to repentance and obedience. He faithfully obeyed God and tried to help his people. He was responsible to be a faithful witness. But he was not responsible for the response of the people. Most of the Jews did not learn from the mistakes of the past. *You have the benefit of learning from the history of Israel. You can be faithful like Nehemiah or turn away from God. Will you learn from God's Word? Will you trust the Lord?*

You, too, can be a faithful witness, telling of the greatness of God and the goodness of His ways. Many people may not listen, but some may. Only God can remove their hearts of stone and give them hearts of flesh. Will you be a faithful witness? Will you encourage others to trust in the Lord and follow Him? Will you pray for the hearts of those who do not follow God?

"The hand of our God is for good on all who seek him, and the power of his wrath is against all who forsake him." (Ezra 8:22b)

For whatever was written in former days was written for our instruction, that through endurance and through the encouragement of the Scriptures we might have hope. (Romans 15:4)

MAKING YOU WISE FOR SALVATION

What does this chapter tell us about God? Talk about and apply the **biblical truths** in **bold** text.

Salvation Thread: Only God can take out stubborn hearts of stone and replace them with new hearts.

Talk with your parents about the difference between doing what is right because there is pressure on you to do the right thing, and doing what is right because your heart is right. (What is obedience from the heart? What is true repentance and faith?)

Talk About: *"The hand of our God is for good on all who seek him, and the power of his wrath is against all who forsake him." (Ezra 8:22b)*

Why is it important to read and act on God's Word?

Pray: Praise God for being a righteous God. Ask Him to give you a heart that loves righteousness.

Think About: *Do I truly love what is right? Am I seeking God? Why do I need to watch over my heart diligently?*

CHAPTER 90

COLD HEARTS AND FAITHFUL LOVE

God Sends His Messenger to Argue His Case Against Judah—Malachi

"From the days of your fathers you have turned aside from my statutes and have not kept them. Return to me, and I will return to you, says the LORD of hosts." (Malachi 3:7a)

Suppose you ask your parents if your family could take a special camping trip and visit the national parks. You are very excited about this idea. Your parents decide that your family can't do this now, but it will be your present when you graduate. You are so excited, because you will graduate from sixth grade in just three months. Sixth grade graduation comes, and your family does celebrate—by having a picnic at a small city park—and you are very disappointed. But your parents didn't break their promise. Their promise was for your *high school graduation*. You just didn't understand that.

This is similar to what the Jews experienced when they returned after the exile. They had been given God's promises through Isaiah, Jeremiah, Daniel, Haggai, and Zechariah of a glorious new Kingdom—a Kingdom of peace, justice, and righteousness that would never end. Their Messiah-King from the royal line of David would come into Jerusalem and rule in His forever Kingdom. All the wonderful promises of the prophets would be fulfilled. And the LORD would be King over all the earth! But it wasn't happening. Instead, they were facing drought and famine. They were poor and powerless. There was still injustice and evil. Judah was a struggling nation, and they didn't have a king. The people were disappointed, fearful, and had little hope. They questioned God's love and faithfulness. They were no different from their ancestors who lived before the exile. But just because the promised Kingdom had not come yet didn't mean it wasn't coming. It just wasn't coming *then*. It wasn't "high school graduation" yet. Judah just didn't understand this.

What would God do with Judah? Was He giving up on the Jews? God never gives up on His people. **God is always faithful. . .even when His people are unfaithful.** So God sent another prophet to them—Malachi. Malachi means, "my messenger," and Malachi had a message for God's people. Malachi gave the Jews example after example of God's goodness—and Judah's unfaithfulness. He called the people to repent and turn back to the LORD.

Instead of agreeing with God's message given through Malachi, the people argued with God! *Can you even imagine arguing with the almighty and all-knowing God?* God had chosen the Jews to be His people. He had forgiven them time and time again. He had been faithful to His covenant with them. He had brought His disobedient, dishonoring people back to their own land. Yet Judah doubted God's love. They accused God of not loving them. This is utterly unbelievable! *How had God shown His special love for His special people for hundreds of years?*

Malachi told the Jews that they had not honored God. Again, the people disagreed. So God had to show them through Malachi that they had "despised [His] name" by bringing blind, lame, and sick animals as sacrifices. Even the priests had dishonored God by accepting these animals. *What was wrong with the Jews' attitude toward God?* Their sacrifices to God were not made from a heart of true worship, honor, and devotion. **God is holy, righteous, just, pure, loving, and good. He is worthy of the best** the people had, not the worst.

Malachi brought messages pointing out their sin of marrying people from the nations who worshiped false gods. Then the Jews followed these false gods, too. The Jews were divorcing their wives and not keeping their marriage promises. They were being unfaithful to one another and to God. God had given His people steadfast love and taken care of their needs. Yet the Jews were selfish. They did not give their money to care for His temple or bring offerings to thank God. But, if they would be generous toward God, He would *open the windows of heaven. . .and pour down. . .blessing until there is no more need.* **God is very generous.**

God was tired of the Jews' disrespect toward Him. But the Jews thought they were judging God fairly. They refused to admit they were guilty of any wrongdoing. They were angry and accused God of not correcting evil. It seemed to them that God did nothing to stop injustice. But **God is a God of justice. He can be trusted to keep His word and to do what He says He will do.** But God will do it in His own timing. Malachi gave the people a terrifying warning about the Day of the LORD, when God will come to judge the world.

> *"But who can endure the day of his coming, and who can stand when he appears? For he is like a refiner's fire and like fullers' soap. He will sit as a refiner and purifier of silver, and he will purify the sons of Levi and refine them like gold and silver, and they will bring offerings in righteousness to the LORD." (Malachi 3:2-3)*

God would first send a messenger to prepare the way for His coming. God will come suddenly and like a blazing fire. He will burn away injustice, idolatry, and other evils. Only those who are faithful to God will be spared. They will be made pure and beautiful like gold and silver. But they must wait patiently for that day. Those who do not honor or fear God will be condemned. **God's just punishment will be severe, certain, and final.**

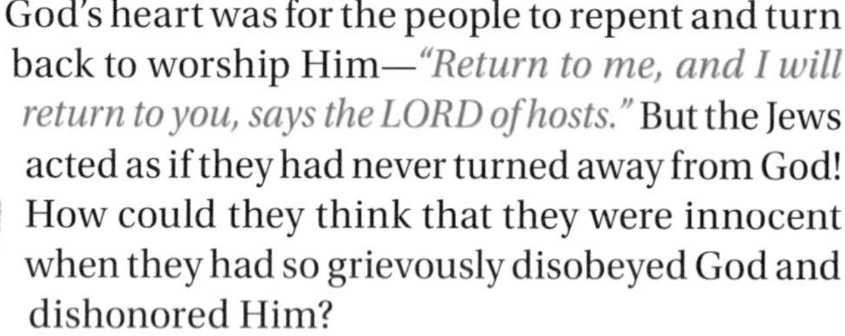

God's heart was for the people to repent and turn back to worship Him—*"Return to me, and I will return to you, says the LORD of hosts."* But the Jews acted as if they had never turned away from God! How could they think that they were innocent when they had so grievously disobeyed God and dishonored Him?

The people of Judah said it was not worth it to follow God—it was useless. After all, they thought, the wicked succeed, and God did nothing to stop them. So why should they follow God? But Malachi reminded them of the "book of remembrance," which had been "written of those who feared the LORD and esteemed his name." The Jews knew what a book of remembrance was. The kings of Persia, where they had been exiled, had these books. They recorded the deeds or acts of service of those who had been faithful to the king. Later, sometimes much later, the king would reward these people—like Mordecai who was rewarded for his warning about the plot to kill the king. **Someday those who have been faithful to the King of kings will be rewarded**, too. But in the meantime, **God calls His people to be faithful**.

For every message Malachi brought from God, the people had an argument. Instead of agreeing with God and repenting, they denied their sin. The Jews' love for God had grown cold; it was very weak. They doubted His love, accused Him of injustice, disobeyed His commands, treated Him disrespectfully, and acted sinfully.

But God would not abandon His people. So Malachi told them again about God's horrifying warning and glorious promise: The "day of the LORD" has been set. It will be a great and terrible day. God will destroy the wicked. But for those who honor and fear Him, it will not be a terrifying day but a wonderful day, a day of healing, life, and great joy! Before that day comes, Malachi said God was giving His people a promise:

> *"Behold, I will send you Elijah the prophet before the great and awesome day of the LORD comes. And he will turn the hearts of fathers to their children and the hearts of children to their fathers, lest I come and strike the land with a decree of utter destruction." (Malachi 4:5-6)*

God would send His people a prophet like Elijah to heal their hard hearts and bring them back to Him. What a glorious day that will be! What a wonderful promise for God's people! **God will restore His people and destroy evil forever!**

God's Word, the Bible, shows us who God is, what He is like, and what He has done. It is the faithful record of the gracious God of Israel and all the promises He has made to His people. It tells of God's unchanging love for His people. All the good He has done for His people in the past can give us hope that His grace will be there in the future for all who honor Him. When you are tempted to think God has forgotten to be kind or to punish evil, remember that God is the same God who shows unfailing faithfulness and has said, ***"For I the LORD do not change."*** The fearful and wonderful "day of the LORD" is coming! *Will you be among those who rejoice in that day?*

As a deer pants for flowing streams, so pants my soul for you, O God. My soul thirsts for God, for the living God. (Psalm 42:1-2a)

One thing have I asked of the LORD, that will I seek after: that I may dwell in the house of the LORD all the days of my life, to gaze upon the beauty of the LORD and to inquire in his temple. (Psalm 27:4)

MAKING YOU WISE FOR SALVATION

What does this chapter tell us about God? Talk about and apply the **biblical truths** in **bold** text.

Salvation Thread: The day of the LORD is coming when God will judge evil and purify His people. Before that day, a prophet like Elijah would prepare the way for the Lord.

Did Judah win their argument with God? Why not?

Talk About: *As a deer pants for flowing streams, so pants my soul for you, O God. My soul thirsts for God, for the living God. (Psalm 42:1-2a)*

How do you treat God? What is your attitude toward Him? God is working, even when you cannot see what He is doing. *Do you have the faith to trust Him to do what is right?*

Pray: Praise God for being worthy of our praise. Confess any way in which you have dishonored Him. Ask Him to give you a heart of passionate love toward Him.

Think About: *Do I fear the day of the LORD, or do I look forward to it with excitement and joy?*

FOUR

HUNDRED

YEARS

OF SILENCE

400 YEARS OF SILENCE . . .

Silent . . . But Not Inactive (The Intertestamental Period)

The counsel of the LORD stands forever, the plans of his heart to all generations. (Psalm 33:11)

Where was God? Had He forgotten His people? For four hundred years, God was not directly speaking to the Jews. There were no prophets or visions, no communication from God. There was just silence.

But God was still at work. He was at work bringing about His grand purposes. He was fulfilling prophecy. He was "changing times and seasons." He was "removing kings and setting up kings." Do you remember Nebuchadnezzar's dream of the enormous statue made of gold, silver, bronze, iron, and clay? Each part of the statue was a different kingdom. *What kingdom was the head of gold?* The head of gold was the Babylonian kingdom, which defeated Judah and took the Israelites into captivity. Babylon was conquered by the Medes and Persians—the statue's chest and arms of silver. The prophecy was right. **God's Word is always true.**

The Persian kings Cyrus, Darius, and Artaxerxes allowed the Jews to return to Jerusalem and rebuild the temple and the wall of Jerusalem. Then came the four hundred years of silence. The Bible does not record what happened during the four hundred years of silence, but history does—and it follows Daniel's interpretation of Nebuchadnezzar's dream exactly. The Persian kingdom was conquered by the Greeks, led by Alexander the Great. This was the kingdom of bronze—the statue's middle and upper legs. Alexander the Great conquered many nations, which made up a large part of the world of that day, including Israel. As he conquered, he spread Greek culture and language. In time, the Greek language became the common language used throughout his entire kingdom. This was just the opposite of what happened at Babel.

But the Greeks were very worldly and ungodly. They did not believe in the one true God, but in many gods. Just as God raised up the Greek kingdom, He also brought it down. The Greeks were conquered by the "legs of iron and feet of iron and clay"—the Roman Empire. Pompey conquered Israel, and it came under Roman control. The Romans built many roads to connect all parts of their empire. They also brought Roman laws and peace to their conquered nations, making travel safer and easier. Emperors ruled over the Roman Empire with increasing power and authority.

Now, Israel was a mixture of Hebrew, Greek, and Roman culture. The name "Judah" became "Judea," and the Jews once more grew in number. Many lived in Judea, but others were scattered throughout the Roman Empire. Before, the temple had been the place of worship. But during the Babylonian captivity, the Jews could not worship in the temple, so they began to build synagogues (like churches). In time, there were synagogues throughout the Roman Empire wherever there were Jews.

Other things changed, too. Instead of just the priests being the religious leaders, two other groups appeared and became important—the Pharisees and the Sadducees. The Pharisees were very strict in their devotion to God's law. They did not accept any king unless he was from the line of David. The Pharisees added laws to the law of Moses—not laws that God gave them, but laws that they made up. The Pharisees thought God would accept them if they followed all their strict laws.

The Sadducees were from the wealthy and noble people (upper class). They rejected all the books of the Old Testament except the Mosaic books: Genesis, Exodus, Leviticus, Numbers, and Deuteronomy.

The Roman emperor made Herod the king of Judea. Under Roman rule, the Jews were taxed and tightly controlled. So again, they were a conquered people with little hope of being their own nation again. But they held on to one hope—that the Messiah would come, conquer those who ruled over them, free them again, and return their country to them. They had the prophecy of Daniel that God would destroy the kingdoms of man:

> *". . . a stone was cut out by no human hand, and it struck the image on its feet of iron and clay, and broke them in pieces. Then the iron, the clay, the bronze, the silver, and the gold, all together were broken in pieces, and became like the chaff of the summer threshing floors; and the wind carried them away, so that not a trace of them could be found. But the stone that struck the image became a great mountain and filled the whole earth." (Daniel 2:34-35)*

But they did not understand what kind of Kingdom the Messiah would establish. They thought it was an earthly kingdom, a time of peace from their enemies, and restored wealth and lands. They didn't understand Jeremiah's prophecy about a new covenant or the prophecies about God's eternal Kingdom.

> *"Behold, the days are coming, declares the LORD, when I will make a new covenant with the house of Israel and the house of Judah," (Jeremiah 31:31)*

> *"And in the days of those kings the God of heaven will set up a kingdom that shall never be destroyed, nor shall the kingdom be left to another people. It shall break in pieces all these kingdoms and bring them to an end, and it shall stand forever," (Daniel 2:44)*

Though the Jews had God's promises, they were not looking for spiritual blessing. They were not looking for a restored relationship with God. They wanted comfort and wealth in this life. And they thought the Messiah would give it to them.

What was God doing during these silent years? He was not standing by just waiting. He was not asleep or inattentive. **God is always at work in the world.** In these four hundred years of history, God was preparing the world for the coming of the messenger, a prophet like Elijah:

> *A voice cries: "In the wilderness prepare the way of the LORD; make straight in the desert a highway for our God . . . Behold, I send my messenger, and he will prepare the way before me . . . Behold, I will send you Elijah the prophet before the great and awesome day of the LORD comes." (Isaiah 40:3; Malachi 3:1a, 4:5)*

Not only did the Jews have little faith in their religion, but the Romans and the Greeks were losing faith in their many gods as well. The Hebrew Scripture had been translated into Greek, which meant that others besides the Jews could read about God's mighty works, His law given to Moses, and His Word spoken through the prophets. *Why was this so important? What eternal plan was God bringing about? Do you trust God to be at work in the world, working out His eternal purposes at all times? Do you trust that when He is quiet, He is still active?*

O LORD, you are my God; I will exalt you; I will praise your name, for you have done wonderful things, plans formed of old, faithful and sure. (Isaiah 25:1)

IN TIMES OF SILENCE

How do you fight for faith when God is silent?

Pray: Read Psalm 69:1-2, 13. Wait patiently as you pray to God. Ask Him to give you faith as you wait for His deliverance.

Remember: Read Psalm 77:7-14. Remember God's mighty deeds and His past faithfulness. Remember who God is and how He works for His people.

Speak Truth to Your Soul: Read Psalm 42:11. The psalmist is discouraged. He is at first "listening to his feelings." But then, he speaks truth to himself, reminding himself of who God is. He tells himself not to be upset, but to hope in God. Speaking truth defeats the lies of Satan. Fight the fight of faith by rehearsing or repeating the promises of God.

Watch over Your Heart: Read Proverbs 4:23-27. Reject any wrong thinking about God. Guard your heart from turning away from God. Confess your unbelief and ask God to strengthen your faith.

Praise and Thank God: Read Psalm 103:1-2 and Psalm 34:1. Praise God for who He is and thank Him for His faithfulness, goodness, wisdom, and power—even when you don't feel like it. Offering praise when it is hard to do so is a sacrifice that is pleasing to God.

Memorize: Choose some promises from the book of Psalms to memorize.

NEW TESTAMENT
SALLY MICHAEL
ILLUSTRATED BY FRED APPS
MORE
THAN A
STORY
EXPLORING THE MESSAGE OF THE
BIBLE WITH CHILDREN